"This is such a beautifu  1
Spirit to rise fully and overc 1
abuses that many of us have 2
who has gone through so much more than most, and had to deal with
targeting and surviving things that only a powerful spirit, leader and
pioneer could get through. This book is a treasure and a huge piece
towards our healing and transformation on Earth. This amazing
woman is doing so much to inspire us and help us through and find
our sovereignty. She will help you release yourselves from spiritual
bondage and step into your divinity."

Laura Magdalene Eisenhower

~~~

"Love always wins in the end darling daughter. Bless this beautiful
book."

Holy Mother Ammachi

~~~

"This book is a 'must-read' for anyone with chronic illness and a
history of trauma. Salini's heart-felt words and sharing of her long
and difficult journey gives us all hope and truth that we can all heal
from trauma, no matter how severe, with the inclusion of positive
thought and knowledge of higher forces leading us on truly spiritual
paths."

Daniel Beilin, O.M.D., L. Ac. Aptos, California, Doctor of
Integrative Medicine, Lecturer in Regulation Thermography.

Emerging
From the
Matrix

Healing Human Trauma and
Ending Global Enslavement

S A L I N I

BALBOA.
PRESS

A DIVISION OF HAY HOUSE

Balboa Press books may be ordered through booksellers or by contacting:

Balboa Press
A Division of Hay House
1663 Liberty Drive
Bloomington, IN 47403
www.balboapress.com
1 (877) 407-4847

Because of the dynamic nature of the Internet, any web addresses or links contained in this book may have changed since publication and may no longer be valid. The views expressed in this work are solely those of the author and do not necessarily reflect the views of the publisher, and the publisher hereby disclaims any responsibility for them.

The author of this book does not dispense medical advice or prescribe the use of any technique as a form of treatment for physical, emotional, or medical problems without the advice of a physician, either directly or indirectly. The intent of the author is only to offer information of a general nature to help you in your quest for emotional and spiritual well-being. In the event you use any of the information in this book for yourself, which is your constitutional right, the author and the publisher assume no responsibility for your actions.

Any people depicted in stock imagery provided by Thinkstock are models, and such images are being used for illustrative purposes only.
Certain stock imagery © Thinkstock.

Print information available on the last page.

ISBN: 978-1-5043-3490-7 (sc)
ISBN: 978-1-5043-3492-1 (hc)
ISBN: 978-1-5043-3491-4 (e)

Library of Congress Control Number: 2015909364

Balboa Press rev. date: 9/17/2015

I've looked upon your horrors and am no longer afraid.
Maya, you have no more power over us...we are free.

~ Salini

Dedication

This book is dedicated to my beloved Mother, Eulalia Mae, whose love, spiritual teachings, introductions to Great Masters, and devotion to me saved my life and preserved my spirit through the long years of darkness. She believed in me utterly and in my spiritual power seeing in me a great light when I could not see it in myself. It is further dedicated to my sweet precious sister whose motherly contributions, nurturing and protection saved my life during the course of profound, sustained child abuse. It is dedicated in honor of the sacrifice they should never have had to make living in the dangerous world of ruthless patriarchal power and privilege, where women, children and the poor die silently, desperately and anonymously by the millions.

This book is further dedicated to my darling daughters, Erin and Rani, whose presence on Earth sustained my heart and reminded me that all hope is never lost because the cycle of life, love, death, healing and rebirth are ever eternal. Thank you for your patience and love during my healing. I return it to you in the form of my unconditional love for you a thousand fold eternally.

It is additionally dedicated to the Holy Mother Mata Amritanandayi, a stupendous incarnation of the Divine Mother, whose mother love and immense spiritual power healed my heart and soul. She awakened and activated the spirit of the Divine Mother within me, a sacred path of divine unconditional love towards everyone I now walk. I am so grateful.

I also dedicate this book to our beloved Jesus of Nazareth, whose domain and protection we dwell within, who stood silently and steadfastly beside me, whether I realized it or not, and loved, protected, supported and healed me in ways I'll never fully know. Thank you Jesus.

I further dedicate this book to Reiki Grandmaster Hawayo Takata, who, after my Mother, was my first and foremost mentor, teacher, healer and guide. Sensei Takata saved my life by giving me healing treatments, love, attunements and her spiritual teachings throughout my childhood and early adulthood. She initiated me into my spiritual power, mentored me into my gifts and stood as a sane, spiritual mentor in the midst of my dark journey. I am humbled by her greatness.

And finally it is dedicated to all those still struggling to survive the trauma of the patriarchy and its related abuse, ravages and violence while searching for their shattered souls. There is a way out. I offer it here in this book. Let me heal your hearts and be the door to your awakening.

Om Namah Shivaya

Acknowledgements

I acknowledge those in the background who contributed to keeping me on this planet and aiding in my healing over the years. I see clearly now how God puts the stepping stones in place to make life happen. You just have to have the courage to step on those stones.

I acknowledge my former husband's family, who gave me a family when I had none to speak of. Their love for me made it possible for me to see and feel what a family looks like and started me on the path to healing. I thank all of you from the bottom of my heart. I will always love you.

I thank all the healers who worked on me and contributed to saving my life.

I acknowledge my dearest friends who stood by me and helped me. First and forever, Donna, who has been my closest friend since we met on the first day of kindergarten. She is like a tall, burnt-brown Redwood tree in the forest of my life. Her arms are wide branches. I am always sheltered there. Greg, who stood by me in hard times, gently reading me spiritual verse and reminding me of my strengths and believing in me, love you forever brother. Robert #1, who counseled me wisely in all things legal and personal in life. He showed me I had a legal path to walk on when the patriarchs blocked my path. And especially Robert the Magical for the incredible and deep human being he is, with a heart of pure golden love and the wisdom to match. He saved my life with his healing gifts; he nurtured my sister in her last days and brought peace to every gathering. He performed miracles of magic every day and taught me the power of love and belief. Deep in my heart you are, Robert, my magical Wizard friend. Laurie, thank you for the joy you brought into my life. And Sharon and Josie, my Soul Sisters, who walk the path of the Heroine's Journey with me. Nadine and Adrienne, my beloved cousins, who shared the truth with me and some good times too. Blessed Gordon, my forever grumpy Scottish friend and hero who showed me the respect of the sacred feminine from a man, healing my heart in the process. Love you always Mr. Grump. And Gerald for the healing you triggered. Trish for her beautiful illustrations, love, friendship and bringing happiness back into my life. And Madukwe for being so precious to me. My prayer partner Michael, one of God's giant Angels on Earth, for keeping me in faith while I wrote this book. To Peggi for loving, inspiring and supporting me. To Valentine, my powerful Maui Guardian Angel always looking out for me. To precious Rafe, who lived the truth and the pain alone and in secret, and paid the ultimate price.

And especially beloved Gus, my global Guardian Angel who brought so much love to my heart.

And Marianne, whose wisdom, love and faith guided my path for many years and awakened my soul time and time again. She stood by me in hard times, showing up with sacred prayers to bring me ever closer to God. She kept me on the path of righteousness and sacredness. She is a saint among women, a renunciate of the highest order, blessed by God wherever she walks. I surrender to her wisdom, faith and strength.

Thank you all....Om Namah Shivaya

Dedicated to all those seeking to reclaim their souls and their power

For those born into oppression and without opportunity, whose soul gifts were left to wither on the vine, your time has come...

For those who fear there is no path out of suffering........or no forgiveness left for them,

For those who have had to sacrifice their energies, bodies, spirits and childhoods for the twisted gratification of a perpetrator,

For those who have been orphaned by their families since telling the truth about their sexual abuse........and left for dead by those who raped them,

And for those who have had to split into multiple personalities to maintain the wholeness of their soul,

For those who compassionately bore the pain and anger of the ignored wounded among us,

For those who experienced soul theft and displacement and wander lost,

For those who have had to hide behind food, alcohol, drugs or other addictions to avoid the devastating reality of their trauma,

For those whose bodies are ill, twisted and exhausted from carrying the toxic energy of their abusers and the lie that it never happened,

For those who had to carry the shame, blame and denial of their offenders as well as their own scars...and have been bullied, denied and scapegoated ever since,

For those who are missing soul parts that search for the nest of their lost soul base,

For those whose health was stolen from them first by trauma, then by an uncaring, profit-driven health system and haven't the strength to fight back,

For those who have been in abusive relationships, or who have sold their adult bodies and souls and believe they are worthy of such treatment,

For those who suffer from post-traumatic stress disorders, depression or ADHD from enduring unrelenting trauma and having the strength to survive it,

For the end of the denial of those in power who know, but by neglecting the issues of cultural, physical, psychological and sexual trauma, support a continuing cycle that serves them,

For the wounded children and adults who walk among us today ignored, untreated and unloved,

For those who through trauma forgot…and through trauma re-membered again….that unconditional love is your birthright, wholeness your natural state and forgiveness yours forever…

YOUR TIME HAS COME, THE
TRANSFORMATION HAS BEGUN!

May the promise of transformation spark,
The flame of hope to continue to burn,
So all souls may one day return,
To wholeness,
And live in their turn….
In peace, love and harmony…eternally.

~ Salini

About The Author

Salini was born and raised in California where she was trained and initiated by several Master spiritual teachers throughout her childhood. She continued her spiritual training and initiation for the rest of her life, culminating in advanced spiritual and healing gifts. Salini uses these gifts to guide and heal all those sent to her by the Holy Spirit.

Today, Salini has a spiritual practice dedicated to healing, restoring and awakening humanity through the path of the Divine Mother. She is available to teach, heal or awaken anyone interested in the path of spiritual awakening through the heart of Divine Mother love. She is the Divine Body Electrician and can rewire and restore your body's energy grid in preparation for ascension.

Salini is a ReikiMaster and shaman. Her work includes chronic illness, trauma recovery, mental and emotional illness, addiction recovery, chronic pain, shamanic healing, and any other conditions brought to her. Salini works at the level of the soul issues and addresses all aspects of body, mind & spirit when working with clients.

Additionally, Salini trains individuals in the healing of the split of duality within the human mind to bring individuals, collectives and cultures to wholeness.

Contents

1   The Silence. 1

2   The Beginning. 21

3   The Wound ~ Sex Slavery 41

4   Walking Dead ~ The Separation 77

5   Initiations 107

6   The Sacrifice 133

7   The Secret Holocaust 151

8   Exiting the Matrix 181

9   The Rape and Resurrection of The Divine Mother 195

10 Energetic & Emotional Anatomy. 233

11 The Trauma Codes. 271

12 Trauma as Transformation 311

13 Sacred Alchemy, Reiki & The Truth About Healing 343

14 Soul Transformation & Reiki Healing Miracles. 371

15 The Great Awakening 449

16 Glossary of Terms. 473

Notes

Throughout the book you will see words or phrases that are bolded and italicized with an asterisk next to them. These bolded terms are from my **Glossary of Terms** that I created specifically for this book. They represent a new vocabulary of terms designed to help explain the concepts I am presenting in this book.

Examples of this would be – *Chakras** or *Kundalini** or *The Split**.

Whenever you see these terms, flip to the back of the book and you will find the **Glossary of Terms** that define and explain them there. All terms are alphabetized for easier browsing. Once we fully understand these concepts, we are no longer easy prey for deception, mind-control and enslavement. My hope is that people come to fully understand and embrace these concepts and that they become part of the lexicon of our times.

THE TRUTH WILL SET US ALL FREE

Every person in this story is sacred and every person played the role they were intended to play, even the perpetrators, as we are all part of the whole of creation and its human drama, destined for divine awakening. All names used in this book have been changed to protect the identities and lives of those whose stories I've included. I wish to respect their right to continue their respective healing journeys anonymously.

Introduction

This book was birthed from the crucible of intense suffering, the kind of suffering that brings death and destruction…..or transformation and rebirth.

This is not an autobiography, although some of my life story is there. Nor is it a story about abuse, although there is abuse included. No, this is your story, and everyone's story…..a story of shedding the lie to discover the truth. And it's a story that hasn't really been told, and carries a fresh and much deeper perspective to an age-old problem. It's a story of awakening to divinity, and how everything is possible.

I had to make a monumental choice few adults are capable of making. And I had to make this choice when I was only 4 years old and living in terrible danger. Then I had to keep making it work for a lifetime, even though I had no idea how to do that, or what that might entail. How could I know? I was just a child.

So I did it, with all the power a pure, innocent little girl is born with. I could never have imagined how harrowing it would be…

One tiny day at a time, I stepped precariously out into a terrifying world of dark, stealthy lords, brutal behaviors and power brokering – all in the name of the smiley-faced American dream - never knowing what the outcome would be, only that this is where God placed me and I had to venture forth. I stepped out with nothing but the faith instilled in me by my deeply spiritual Mother and my loving, gentle sister, alongside the spiritual strength and wisdom that was, and is, my birthright as a woman of power and knowledge - an ancient sha-maness returned to complete a vitally important task. I didn't know it then, but soon I discovered that this journey was a life or death battle fought not just for my own life, but the lives of so many others who died for the ruthless addiction to patriarchal profit and pleasure of those in power, including my mother and sister.

I took the Shaman's journey - the Heroine's journey- deep into the murky mystical heart of the human soul, where breathtaking mysteries and veiled enigmas abound, to unearth the secrets of hu-man suffering and return with the Holy Grail of Healing, for all to benefit from.

What follows is a true chronicle of timely lessons learned at the hands of dark power and cruelty, tempered by the forces of light. On one side, a daughter of Nazis from a legacy of hatred, and on the other side, a child of powerful female shamans and healers hailing from a long lineage of love & light - forced to reconcile the two together to prevail, and in doing so bringing forth a great healing power to alleviate humanity's suffering.

I came to realize I had the power of choice in the life or death of this body, though few believed I could do it. Against all odds and the death march of the traumatized human soul, while facing near death from cancer, viral meningitis, fibromyalgia and pneumonia, I chose transformation and rebirth over death. Getting there is what this book is all about.

On her deathbed at a youthful 51, my sister said to me, "You were right about the healing path you've been trying to tell me about. I just wouldn't listen, and I see now that it would have saved my life. Please tell everyone what you've learned and what you tried to show me. I see that it saved your life. Make my death worth something. Go save as many lives as you can. Do it for me!" And then I lost her, and soon my mother too - the Great Matriarchs of the Heart that had silently and selflessly sustained me throughout my life. And trauma's death toll kept on rising with so many other women I loved, and countless others worldwide since then passing tragically on without solutions or hope…..at the hands of the Patriarchs of Death.

It took me a long time to recover from the void of Mother Energy created by the deaths of all the women I loved so much. I learned staggering lessons in the process, and regained lost portions of myself I never knew existed. It was as though all these beloveds died in front of me one by one so I would document and bring the lost knowledge of resurrection forth. So, I set forth to document the process of reclaiming ones' body and soul from the soul stealers of death and profit.

It would be a crime against the memory of their sacrifice, the energy of the Divine Mother, and her still-suffering Earth children, to waste the power of this knowledge. These are the lessons we urgently need to embrace as a civilization, if you can call us that, as we stand at the brink of man-made global annihilation. These are the critical lessons unknown and still unlearned we must master today if we are to survive the burgeoning crises facing everyone on Earth. So I offer it now to you. And I will walk you through it because I walked it for decades before now…

This is what my eyes beheld within the fiery inferno of the dark side of the patriarchy, these are the lessons learned as a sex slave. This is who I've become in dying and resurrecting myself. And this is the healing I bring for those still in bondage…

For those who lost the battle, or who are still fighting for the power and faith to overcome the trauma of life on Earth as it is today….it is to all of you that I dedicate this hard-won wisdom.

With the deepest love, reverence and respect for your journey…
~ Salini

Chapter 1

The Silence

And no one dare disturb the sound of silence….
~ Simon and Garfunkel

I was slumped over my desk again. My neck and back ached. I must have fallen asleep writing.

"Damn, not again. Why do I always fall asleep when I get to this point?" I said to myself out loud.

I got up and walked around. I stretched my arms down to my toes. Then I sat down and did some yoga until I felt the muscles release. Soon I was gripping the soles of my feet. The blood began to flow. I went into the child pose and stayed that way a while. I did my breathing exercises and soon I felt a peace enter in. I walked outside to the lawn where the weeping willow was. I sat under it and started meditating. Eventually, I felt the serenity flow through me. I chanted my mantra 108 times with my mala beads in hand. Again, peace flowed through me. I was ready to write again. So, I went back inside and sat at my computer.

So what was it? What was it that kept happening?

It was *the silence* and it was back again…the nameless, invisible, everywhere choking void…. so elusive and all-pervasive. It just snuck up on me…like a foggy morning camping at the seashore……on you before you even woke up. I never saw it coming and didn't understand what I was feeling….not then anyway. All I knew was that every time I sat down to write this book, there it was - threatening me, holding its dark hand of terror to my face, as though it were about to cover my mouth. It was so close that sometimes I thought I could see it. Something was warning me to stay silent….*or else*.

But what was the *or else*? That was the inexorable crux of the problem. Like an ever-present, unseen Facebook friend with an anime icon, it refused to tell me its real name… but continued to threaten me every time I tried to express the truth. I felt totally thwarted, frozen in time and place, unable to speak or change the reality of the situation. And I stayed that way for a long time.

I'm not certain when the silence began, but I'm sure it was very early, because I can never remember not feeling the terror. The terror of…*you must never, ever tell…**anyone!*** But the irony was I knew I wasn't supposed to tell, but I couldn't remember what I wasn't supposed to tell. At least not at first. Why was everything so murky, dark, and creepy? I had questions a small child cannot answer for herself. And when you live with adults who themselves cannot or will not answer them, and who also live in terror, there is nowhere to go with this reality but deeply inward.

So, that's where I went back then. Deeply inward to another, safer self than the one who had to live outside in the terror. I traveled to a place where there was light, beauty, peace and a sense of oneness with something greater… more benevolent. But I didn't know what that was either then. How could I? I was just a little girl. I just knew I always wanted to be there instead of where I was living every pain-filled day of my young life.

I found it for a while in the tree behind the house. I still don't know what kind of tree it was, but it sure was big. This sprawling tree with its thick, twisted fingers of strong branches grew behind the hidden woodshed in the back yard of the house on Davis Street. It was only accessible by walking the edge of the high fence behind the house, or by making your way into the fenced-off jungly foliage behind my bedroom where no one ever went. It was far too scary to venture into that jungle. Seeing what was in there was impossible. It lent itself to my imagining frightening scenarios going on in there, like prehistoric monsters or magical forest creatures I had read about in books.

Either way, no one dared to follow me or look for me there, so I frequently stole back to the tree and climbed it. No one could see me once I got into the tree. The branches and leaves were just too thick. They made a billowy canopy that felt like a cool blanket lightly draped over me. I imagined myself to be a camouflaged bird, unseen and unheard, safe from predators. So the tree became one of my safe havens. Sometimes I brought lunch up there and sat there for hours, munching apples or potato chips. After eating, I would lie on a branch and meditate amongst the leaves.

And if I felt extra adventurous, I would walk onto one of the branches straight onto the roof because the bigger branches straddled the bedroom roof. I could just stroll right out onto the rooftop. I did that when I felt bolder and wanted to see Mom and Dad come out looking for me. I would walk over to the chimney and lean against it. Someone would come out and call my name. I would sit down so they couldn't see me and watch for them to reach the grassy yard and come into view. I could see them but they couldn't see me. It made me feel just a little bit powerful for once. Their voices called out, but I never answered. The roof and the tree were my sanctuaries, the places where they couldn't find me. They couldn't hurt me there. So I went there whenever possible and found the place of light inside myself.

There were other sanctuaries along the way, other hiding places to run from the monsters. But in the tree, at the church nearby and inside my soul, these were the most treasured sanctuaries to this small girl....little Mighty McGinty as they often called me. Nicknamed me after an old Irish priest of all things. And what a magical leprechaun of a guy he was. I guess I lived up to the nickname because my adventures just kept on coming.

Yep, I came to this place called Earth on a quest, the heroine's journey. But what little girl knows that? Even if she is named the Mighty McGinty.

That was when my soul transformation began. I had been gravely wounded then, but I was already seeking relief from the pain in God. I just didn't know it yet. I thought this was how all little girls lived – afraid, alone and in pain every single day.

So, I slipped on my SuperGirl cape, strapped on what weapons I had gathered in life so far, and ventured forth into the frightening jungle called life. Mighty McGinty was born.

But I never, ever broke the silence. Not until today…

~~~~

It was dinnertime, or the tail end of dinner I should say. Another gourmet meal from Mom. Wieners and sauerkraut, sliced white bread and milk. That was it. We were allotted one serving of each at dinners usually. Rarely was anything left over, there was so little to eat most nights. Except on wieners and sauerkraut night. No one wanted to eat much those nights. It was slim pickings when it came to food at our house. Mom and Dad were Depression-era parents and they never got over it. You had to eat every bite, or else, whether it was any good or not. And it could be cold leftovers, something out of a can, or just a disgusting slab of liver. There was always a hard piece of wood or a belt nearby to remind you just in case you resisted. But, I always knew how to get around that. Hell, that's what napkins were for, and glasses of milk…and dogs. Saved me a few beatings, those sweet dogs did. They suffered alongside me stoically and loyally. We knew what was in store for us if we disobeyed, so they never betrayed me. Partners in crime we were.

"Pass the wienies and sauerkraut please." Dad barked loudly. I jumped a mile. He had his napkin stuck in his collar and it was hanging down in the shape of a triangle protecting his chest from a possible waterfall of sauerkraut juice. A strong possibility the way he ate. A fork and a knife were in each hand held upright like weapons. There was even a string of sauerkraut stuck to his cheek. It seemed like we were all seated at a medieval round table, waiting for the King to speak. I stared at his cheek. The sauerkraut there bothered me.

Mom specialized in weird, quickie dishes like this. I was used to it, but this one was my least favorite meal. This, and liver and onions night. Tonight it was canned sauerkraut that she boiled into limp, lifeless ribbons with chopped up coins of spongy wienies floating on top, soft and colorless…just water, no spices. A foggy, void soup of a meal. So, yeah, there was definitely some leftover. Other nights we were treated with defrosted, pre-packaged chicken pot pies. At least those had some sauce and flavor. Sometimes there was Spam. Dad hated it when she served Spam. That's all he had to eat during the war so he didn't much like it. I think that's why Mom served it. All she knew how to do to get back at Dad when he was mean, which was pretty much all the time, was passive-aggressive stuff like that. He was too scary to confront directly. You took your life in your hands if you challenged him.

My favorite meal was salad, rice and teriyaki beef sandwiches. They made that meal special for my birthdays. Dad loved to barbecue, so he would barbecue it himself for me. Those were the good nights. And at least once in a while, we had a good meal…and a night of peace.

Looks like Dad was going for it. He took the sauerkraut bowl from Mom.

"Don't you want some McGinty?" Dad taunted me.

I shook my head. "No. I don't like sauerkraut, you know that Dad." He laughed and scooped the rest into his plate and began to chomp it down. He took a few swigs of whatever he was drinking. Probably some scotch or gin. I had seen the liquor bottles out so I knew he was drinking. Mom probably was too, always vodka for her. They both drank most every night but I never realized how much back then.

Everyone finished up eating, mostly in silence. Dinner could be touchy. We never knew when Dad would get upset again. So most of the time we didn't talk a lot, or we talked about school. I listened to my siblings talk about their school experiences. I had finished my meal. I waited until I thought enough time had passed.

"May I be excused?" I asked looking around cautiously.

"Sure honey." Mom said. She smiled at me.

"But start cleaning up," Dad snorted, "We have guests coming over soon."

I took my plate into the kitchen and washed it and my utensils, putting them into the drain board. I came back and cleared some empty serving bowls and washed those too. I had done my part. My siblings would have to do the rest. Then I went to my room and closed the door. That was where I could be alone, safe and quiet. I could think things over; I could play with my dolls and make happy family scenarios. After a while there was a knock on my door.

"Come on out McGinty!" Dad was at the door.

"What do you want?" I answered.

"It's the Coopers. I told them about you and what you could do. Come out and show them sweetie."

"Oh, not again, really?" I opened the door. He was grinning. He probably had enough gin to make him happy. Maybe it will be a good night tonight, I thought.

When he was nice, sometimes he was okay. I smiled at him.

"Okay, Daddy. Give me a minute to get ready. Tell everyone to be ready." I knew what I wanted to be when I grew up. An actress for sure. I never enjoyed anything as much as performing. Mom and

Dad seemed to really like it, so every so often they would ask me to perform for their friends. Looks like tonight was going to be one of those nights.

I got out my special costume and put it on. I had some lipstick I borrowed from Mama so I got it out and put that on too. I even had her long costume diamond earrings. I put them on, then caught a glance in the mirror. A smile spread across my face. I was ready.

"Won't they be surprised?" I whispered to myself. And then I slipped out of my bedroom door, into the hall and burst out into the living room.

Everyone was in the living room waiting for me. I went into my Mae West routine. I hunched up my shoulders, put my hands on my hips and swiveled them around. Then I tossed my hair back with one hand and strutted across the room.

"Hey there big boys!! Why dontcha come up and see me sometime?"

Everyone burst out laughing. I had my long satin dress on, the one I found at the neighbor's garage sale. It was purple and had sparkles on it. So pretty and shiny. Definitely a show dress. Mama had some pretty long gloves, black ones with beads on them. I was wearing those too. I started singing Mae's big hit……and danced around the room.

Frankie and Johnny were lovers
Swore to be true to each other
But there sat her lover man Johnny, makin' love to Nellie Bly
Yeah he was her man, but he was doin' her wrong

When the song ended, the whole room was in an uproar of laughter and cheering. I closed it out by sashaying over to Mr. Cooper and winking and repeating Mae's line, "Why don't you come up and see me sometime?"

They gave me a standing ovation. I looked over to Mama and Daddy. They were smiling at me. I had pleased everyone tonight. I could rest peacefully this time.

"Good girl. Now go to bed honey." Mom said.

I kissed her goodnight, waved goodbye to everyone and went back to my room. Got my jammies on, brushed my teeth and got in bed. I got out a book and read awhile. After some time, the noise quieted down. I fell asleep.

Then, I felt something next to me. I don't know how long I had been asleep or how much time had passed but the house was quiet. My sister wasn't home. Someone was shaking me awake. And then I felt his sweaty hands…and his hot, alcoholic breath on my neck.

"Daddy, no!" I gasped in terror. "I was a good girl wasn't I? I tried so hard; didn't I do a good job?"

"Yes, but it doesn't matter," he growled deep into my ear. "You'll always be my bad girl. And no one will ever, ever love you, not like I do, not like this. Just remember that always."

I started to cry and shallow breathe. I thought I might vomit. I felt his hand come quickly over my mouth to silence me. "Shut up if you know what's good for you." He whispered threateningly and tightened his grip on my face until my cheekbones hurt. I sucked in a sharp, scared breath and held it in. And it began, just like it had so many nights before, for as long as I could remember…..until I couldn't bear to remember anymore….and he taught me how to forget.

And so it continued throughout my childhood, and in different ways into my adulthood. He was my own personal lifetime stalker. He never left me alone, always appearing and threatening me in some way. I stopped remembering somewhere in there out of sheer survival instinct. The situation was so hostile and dangerous that even as a small child I knew my life was in danger. I suppressed it when I was very small. I didn't remember then. Not until much later.

But during that period I also experienced the first of my mystical encounters. I was too small to understand what was going on and usually too scared to look. But every night when I was in bed crying and trying to sleep, I saw a man sitting in the corner of my room looking at me. He often came out of the closet as soon as I returned from an abuse episode and walked towards me. I was terrified of him. I would cry and tell him to stop and go away. He would obey and stop and just watch from a distance. I saw him nearly every night for years. One night, when I was about 3 years old, I was crying hard and chewing on my hand after an abuse episode. I was too distraught to realize he was coming towards me until it was too late. Suddenly he reached me. I was scared and took a deep in-breath. He leaned down gently over me and held my hand, softly pulling it from my mouth. He sat near me for a moment and said, "You don't need this anymore. I'm here to protect you now and always." I stared at him and realized he wasn't going to hurt me. Later I realized he was a guardian angel there to comfort me after the abuse. Or perhaps Jesus himself. I allowed him to be near me after that but at some point he disappeared. Or I couldn't see him anymore. I was receiving so much abuse that after a while my perception was dulled. I prayed for him, he may have been there. But I couldn't see him. But now I knew there was someone looking out for me.

Life went on. And they devised so many special ways to silence me. As a result, I learned to hold in my feelings very deeply and tried to control my responses unnaturally. I was being conditioned into suppression. And so I learned to be silent, and I learned to forget, escaping into a world of creativity, writing newspapers, music, plays, stories, movies and home melodramas that I wrote, staged and acted out myself or with my best friend.

Part of the abuse included the family ridiculing my feelings. Compassion or comfort for me was forbidden. Of course, they were always at risk as well. Forgetfulness, denial and then unconscious behavior set in for everyone. When the abuse began, they fogged out. That's the only way a disempowered person can live in such an environment. The blame had to rest elsewhere....and I was chosen. They had their scapegoat.

Dad was a professional con man and embezzler. He so enjoyed the art of conning people out of their money, their security and their joy. He embezzled so many people that he was always in one lawsuit after another from unsuspecting clients who had trusted him. He even embezzled his own family members out of their life savings, me included, until I finally woke up. Once he told my beloved uncle and his own brother, that he had a job for him in Los Angeles running a business. Dad told him to sell their home in San Jose and he would pick them up and drive them to Los Angeles to their new home and job. He never showed up and left them standing on a street corner with their three children with nowhere to turn. It nearly destroyed them. That was dear old Dad, destroying people one way or another every day. He had a straight job too. And some of it was legit because it came from the good side of his being. He was talented at design-ing shopping malls and even cities. He was a real estate and land appraiser and even designed the entire layout and establishment of a city in California. Dad had dark *and* light in him, like everyone did. I saw his light self especially at Christmas and when I performed at school in one of my activities. He couldn't hide his pride in me then. And I saw it especially when I gave him healing which he loved. But he was ***fallen*****. His dark self had overtaken his light self long ago. It appeared from time to time, but Dad simply wouldn't or couldn't sustain his higher self.

It was my mother who supported the family. She worked a full-time job she hated for 35 years, paying all our bills, cooking, cleaning, buying our clothes and taking care of us children alone without Dad's help. Despite wanting desperately to be a full-time author, musician and columnist, Mom sacrificed her dreams and carried the load of everything. But she was always sad because of it. This kept her drinking, to endure the emptiness of jobs beneath her caliber of brilliance. I never saw her happy except when we went together to spiritual retreats. She belonged in a concert hall, at the head of a newspaper, designing engineering projects or leading a spiritual retreat. Dad was spending his money on himself; we were never allowed to share in his bounty and neither was Mom. If she bought anything for herself, he made her return it. She learned to live on nothing; we all did. When he passed, I found that he had stolen my identity and put it on all sorts of documents, properties and businesses that I had never seen or heard of. I don't know what happened to those properties; some other criminal in his life got them.

He went on to befriend others who had stolen from me or betrayed me and would gang up on me with them as well. Those who sided with Dad were rewarded financially. They enjoyed investments, opportunities, and good ole boy support to fatten their wallets and portfolios. Scratching each other's backs, ripping off those without sophisticated lawyers and accountants, bankrupting the innocent and trusting, committing white collar crimes, rubbing shoulders with banksters, dirty hedge fund managers, Wall St. fraudsters, people on the inside who look good and scrub up clean after they rape you dry, and other petty criminals who wear suits but commit crimes and launder their dirty money through fake corporations and businesses, then strut around like peacocks in their polished white bread world which smells of death and is rotting secretly on the inside. Those who stood up to him and told the truth, which was me alone, were isolated, financially punished, lied about, ridiculed, abused and exiled from the family, time and time again.

Eventually, others I loved joined in the sadism. It broke my heart. The lengthy cycle of persecution was excruciating and left me despairing and feeling suicidal more than once. Only God's love kept me going, and my faith that God needed my service in saving lives.

Then, on rare occasions, Dad would do something to help me, and show me a shred of ragged, bloody love from his tortured dark soul. It always made me sad because those moments were so few and far between. I wanted it to last forever, but I knew he could strike out at me again at any moment.

But never did anyone think Dad did anything wrong. On the outside, he appeared to be the respectable businessman. Men like him always do. And there are so many of them around in today's diseased culture. He had his insider people to cover for him and keep him squeaky clean. He got out of everything, even when he was charged with tax evasion, securities fraud and embezzlement. So he had to find someone to blame his crimes on. It's usually the least powerful person in the life of a sociopath. Especially if it's a woman. That's how I became the scapegoat….the receptacle of all their pain, pent-up destructive emotions, for life. No one dared to confront Dad on his behavior. So, if Dad was mad about something, he would turn it onto me, blaming me for whatever angered him, and I received a beating. Sometimes Dad would instruct Mom to write it in a letter and have the whole family sign it. And I learned to accept this position, silently, partly because of the abuse, and partly because I loved them all so much and would rather it be me than them.

Eventually, the brainwashing set in to shift the burden of painful emotions to me because it was part of the programming in the abusive family system - the power structure of unequal, unshared power in a violent, patriarchal, misogynistic, alcoholic household. And so I became the family exile. Ridiculed, denied opportunity and forever unloved. And I learned to stay evermore silent…. I had long ago forgotten how it all started because I was too young to remember…an infant in a dangerous world. It was now a solid part of my self-image, self-belief and lack of self-esteem, fused into my energy matrix, unconsciously driving my life and my beliefs. So, I became silent, and craved their love, and tried to please them, in a fruitless attempt to become a full-fledged family member. I accepted this, except for the times my warrior spirit kicked in. And that was the beginning of both the crushing of my spirit and the emergence of my spiritual warriorship. I had entered the crucible of transformation. I was being both destroyed and reformed, melted down and re-forged, killed and resurrected into something yet to be revealed…an alchemically transformed person whose over-abundance of lead experiences turned her into a chalice of pure gold…. Yet to emerge.

But these were the easy memories. The ones that weren't forbidden. They were out in the open, for all the family to see. This was normal family interaction. Food shoved down my throat until I vomited. My arm twisted behind my back while I'm being choked. My toys burned and thrown into the trash. The sodomy out by the woodshed. My pets killed or given away. Regular fun times at our household. Just a sampling of good old-fashioned American values.

Deeper and deeper I buried my pain. Soon I tried to hate him, but somehow never fully could the way I thought he deserved. There

was just too much love in my heart, and I could never close that down. It was stronger than all the beatings and all the terror. It would save me more than once, and carry me through many years of suffering. But for now, I was silent. I didn't even remember the molestation then. My surface personality was completely formed, strong and functional. I had buried and hidden my pain thoroughly. For now, as I grew into a lovely teen-age girl, I escaped into school, activities and boys. I was an Honor student, Student Body President, Cheerleader and many other things. I did very well in school and looked forward to college. And for a while, that worked.

But that was only one half of my childhood, the shadow half.

There was another half, and it was filled with the initiations into light, healing, love and forgiveness. Despite the insanity and violence of my father, my mother managed to mentor me into her spiritual path. Mom was a great spiritual soul. She was one of the most gifted people I have ever met. She was a concert pianist who was given a full scholarship to Juilliard. She was also a math and engineering genius and was the #1 math student in the nation. She was also offered an engineering scholarship. She was the top student and only woman in the engineering department at the University of Wyoming. Mom was even a co-winner of the Pulitzer Prize in journalism. That doesn't even count her skills as a painter, especially Japanese Brush painting. She was a true Renaissance woman, a female Leonardo DaVinci, a genius. She was also spiritually gifted, was psychic, was a practicing Zen Buddhist, and could heal from my earliest memories. She was healing people and animals long before she became a ReikiMaster. She practiced automatic writing and handwriting analysis and frequently went into trances and channeled amazing information through her automatic writing. She prophesied many things that have come true.

Mom didn't know what Dad was doing on those dark nights. She used alcohol to numb herself to the pain of marriage to a violent, schizophrenic, sociopathic alcoholic. Back then, it wasn't so easy to leave with three children. She had lived through the Depression and World War 2. So Mom just escaped into her two worlds – drinking and spirituality. I was the beneficiary of that. Fortunately, it was the one thing Dad approved of and never interfered with, the beautiful enfoldment of my spiritual training. In fact, he believed in it and enjoyed it. His mother was a devout Christian and he had been raised to believe in God. Watching us seeking was somehow soothing to him. I observed that and took note. Any time I spoke of God with him, he would calm down. I learned to soothe the demons and the insanity in people by working on my Dad. He allowed me to give him Reiki and other healing treatments even when I was a child. It seemed he began to experience some healing. In many ways, working on Dad was an urgent piece of training for my future healing work. It was my scientific observations of the split psyche within Dad as Dr. Jekyll and Mr. Hyde informing, teaching and driving the split in my awareness of life and the people in it.

By the time I was five years old, I was healing and meditating. Mom taught me that my hands held powerful energy that could heal things. We began with animals. I remember taking my sick turtle into my hands. He seemed to get better. Or the day we found our fish floating sideways on the top of the water. We both put our hands around the bowl; she recovered and began to swim again. Soon, I began to believe powerfully in my ability to heal, to restore and to bathe everything in God's love and light. I worked on trees, bugs, plants and strangers coming to the house, anyone and anything I could get my hands on. I had a special affinity for bone-cracking. All the neighborhood kids allowed me to adjust their necks and spines throughout my childhood. And I really loved doing it. I could feel when their bones were out of place very easily and seemed to know exactly how to put them back in. Perhaps in another life I was a chiropractor. As I practiced these things, I learned to soothe my own pain and suffering. I became my own first patient in what would become a lifetime healing career.

Mom was a practicing Zen Buddhist. She taught me to meditate and still my mind. I was five and I was on the roof meditating like that. I was seven and I sat in the highest point in the trees that I could reach and I would meditate like that. My sister gave me Bible instruction. We read the Bible every night in our shared room and she would explain who Jesus was, and what was going on back then. I was fascinated by all things spiritual. I wanted to know how Jesus performed miracles and healed people. After all, he was in a human body. If he could do these things, why couldn't we? Didn't Jesus tell us that we shall do greater things than he did? These are the questions

I pondered with my sister then. She and Mom taught me to pray and I created the most beautiful prayers imaginable. Since we lived next door to a Greek Orthodox Church, I would often hide there and take refuge from my father, praying to God to relieve me of the suffering and to heal our family.

But the greatest thing Mom brought into my life was **Reiki Grandmaster Hawayo Takata***. Even though Dad's dark behavior was always lurking in the background, nothing deterred my mother from seeking God and exploring metaphysical teachings. There she stood in her power and overrode any objection he may have had and just held classes, brought in healers and shamans, and in general created a mystical atmosphere at home. It was her saving grace and the pathway she gave us children out of Hell. But I was the only one to seize it.

She was especially drawn to healing. At some point early in my childhood, my mother met Hawayo Takata, the great Reiki GrandMaster, who was carrying on the tradition of **Reiki*** as was rediscovered by **Dr. Mikao Usui***. Starting around age 9, my mother brought Mrs. Takata to California and she began teaching Reiki from our home. She taught several classes a year from our home in San Jose, California. Yes, right there where dear old Dad was. Amazingly enough, Dad was very supportive of all her classes, even attending a **First Degree Reiki Class***. Whenever Mrs. Takata was there, Dad would calm down. And over the years, I noticed that Reiki had a profound healing effect on Dad. Later in life he would often ask me for a Reiki treatment. By the time Mrs. Takata started teaching from our home, the worst of the ritual abuse was over. Having the steady presence of healers definitely smoothed things over, but not all of it. Whenever Dad drank, the demons came out again.

Hawayo Takata became my mentor then. She began to teach me everything about healing, energy, enlightenment, living sacredly and honestly and evolving into a person of merit. Only she wasn't there all the time. I yearned for the times when she would visit and I could speak to her, receive healing treatments and listen in on Reiki classes. Whenever she taught at our home, I was the patient on the table every day of class. Mrs. Takata gave me untold dozens of treatments throughout the last half of my childhood and attuned me to Reiki. I'm certain those treatments and attunements into Reiki mitigated the abuse and saved my life. I received the benefit of full mentoring from Reiki Grandmaster Hawayo Takata for 20 years. She saved my life, I hold her in the highest esteem. I began to entertain the possibility of a healing career.

But the story of my development isn't complete without mentioning the arrival of my surrogate family into my life. On my 15th birthday, my first boyfriend entered my life. He brought with him his large Hispanic family. This family became my family and I treasured them with all my heart. Through spending time at their house and joining in family celebrations, I learned what it really meant to be a family, to care about each other, to celebrate each other's lives, to enjoy holidays and life together and to love each other. Christmas was a huge event at their house. Tamales were prepared for a month in advance. I'll never forget the tantalizing smell of the tamale sauce cooking and watching Mom (she's Mom to me) prepare the fillings for hundreds of tamales. Fragrant Spanish rice simmered on the stove daily. Ornate desserts and cakes were baked every day leading up to Christmas, the smells wafting through the house for weeks before the big day culminating in joyous decorating sessions. Paper decorations were strung around the ceiling and dishes of candy could be discovered everywhere in the house. When the big day arrived, presents were piled to the ceiling and relatives stopped by in the dozens. Shouts and hugs of welcome were abundant, and laughter was non-stop. It was a many days long celebration. Every birthday, graduation, Mother's Day and so on was the same. It was music to my soul. I loved the Mexican culture so much that I eventually moved to Mexico to live for a while. It's embedded in my soul now.

There was far more love and bonding than I had ever seen before. My boyfriend eventually became my husband and his family became my family. Their love carried me through years of abuse and helped me to know that I could be loved despite what my family had told me. Although the marriage didn't survive, they will always be my family and I will always love them. The influence of their love on my life will never be erased or forgotten.

And one other special teacher came along just as I arrived at college. I took a job as secretary to a local eccentric Yogi. He taught Kundalini yoga. I was responsible for all his paperwork, correspondence, bills and phone calls as he prepared to build his yoga retreat in the mountains above Santa Barbara. I became his closest sidekick. He taught me Kundalini yoga until I was good enough to be his protégé. Soon we were traveling and teaching yoga and I was his demonstrator of Kundalini yoga technique. He became a father figure and mentor to me and was very nurturing and kind, taking the place of the father I never had. I experienced the beginnings of my life work there as I practiced Kundalini yoga, meditation and **mudras***. He also took me on a spiritual journey to meet some famous Master teachers. I was fortunate to meet Swami Satchinanda and Yogi Bhajan while they were still in the body. Thank you beloved Yogi Haeckel for your sweet, divine nature. You set my feet upon the path of yoga and began my return to health. It was another stage of my divine awakening.

Aside from my childhood teachings with sages, psychologists, yogis, mystics and healers, another vital early stage of my healing was in 12-step programs. I had an eating disorder. I was **bulimarexic***. When I found out I was pregnant, I knew it was vital to eat properly. So, I went to Overeater's Anonymous to relearn to eat and unlearn what Dad had done to me. I learned to eat what we called **grey sheet abstinence*** back then. It was very sparse, no carbs or sugars. Just meat and veggies and an occasional fruit. And I had to call in my food every day to my sponsor. I stayed religiously abstinent for 7 years and worked the 12 steps daily. Turning my life and my will over to a higher power every day to conquer my food addictions taught me how to surrender to God and create a deeper connection with Spirit. During the course of my 30 years of regular attendance at various 12 step meetings, I began to be relieved of some deep-seated neuroses. Just as is promised, things were being lifted off of me through devout prayer and 12-step work.

I was unable to control my *bulimia** on my own; it had become automatic. One day, after a particularly bad episode and the veins around my eyes had all burst open, I got down on my knees and prayed to God, "I don't need this behavior anymore God. I am abstinent now for many years, I am no longer addicted to food. The daily vomiting is ruining my eyes. I lay it at your feet and ask you to lift it please forever." And that was the last day I was bulimic after more than 20 years of it.

After making my way through first Overeater's Anonymous, then Al-Anon, then Adult Children of Alcoholics, then Codependency Anonymous and Incest Survivors Anonymous, I had the program down. I then took it out into the world and used it in every area of my life. If I hurt someone, I made amends. If I found something I was powerless over, I turned it over to God. And a roadmap was laid before me that worked to heal my life. Eventually I would save hundreds of lives of addicts, alcoholics, prostitutes and street kids with this program and Reiki, God, prayer and a lot of unconditional love.

It was these people and these teachings, prayers and meditations which I practiced throughout my childhood that made it possible for me to survive 18 years of child abuse. And I continue to practice them to this day. As bad it as it sounds, it was my initiation into how life wounds us and where the healing is. I received the wound of Chiron, in preparation for a life as a wounded healer. It was a very special kind of training by God in healing and alchemy, practices I would utilize to save many lives later in my life.

These are the lessons of my story. It's not a story of pain or survival. On the contrary, it's a story of resurrection, redemption, mystery, magic, miracles, and our ever-present power to restore ourselves given us by God. I offer these lessons now to you.

Until a new day dawned, the sounds of silence ruled my world then…

She lived in pregnant darkness see,
Verdant rich with choking possibilities,
Little girl, of spirit bright,
Walking solo in the night,
Into darkness, pain and fright
Still she held to springtime dreams,
Sparkling visions sprinkled round,
Till her heart was heard to pound,
So violent and tender upon her ears,
A prayer of promise, faintly told,
To stir her heart, for one day bold…..
You will, My Child, you will, you'll see…..
One day, My Love,
You will be free.
~ Salini

And so I continued on year after year, in trust and faith and love, that God had a plan for me. Something better than this. And it turns out God did.

~~~~~~~~

Chapter 2

The Beginning

Someday…there will be a story you want to tell for no better reason than because it matters to you more than any other. You'll stop looking over your shoulder to make sure you're keeping everybody happy and you'll simply write what's real and true; that's when you'll finally produce the work you're capable of.

~J.D. Salinger

Mighty McGinty eventually became grown-up Teri. A lot happened in-between, but fast forward many years and I'm separated living with my two children. I told myself things were going along fine. It was how I coped; it was part of my personal denial system. Even though I was going through a divorce and there were problems, I thought I would eventually be alright. I was preparing for the future, for myself and my children. Changes were happening, but they seemed to be normal life changes. Little did I know what was on the horizon for me.

It all started that day Danny and I went out to dinner. It was an East Coast kind of chilly night, with some swirling winds that kept licking at my ears. I hate it when the wind goes into my ears. They get so cold and achy and it puts a damper on things. This isn't New York I grumbled inwardly. So I was dealing with that and bundling up. I think we went to that sweet Mexican restaurant uptown but I can't be sure now. It was a nice place with plenty of ambience. We'd been there before and I knew the food was good and it was warm. That's all I cared about for the moment. I was starved.

Danny was Irish and about as feisty as an Irishman could be. That included a strong thirst for rich, throaty beer. We sat at a plain square table with a perky blue-checked tablecloth. The waitress brought some sticky menus and Danny ordered two Dos Equis just for himself. I got a hot tea to warm my soul. We were debating what to order when Danny started in. Whenever he got into "that mood", I knew things were going to get rocky. He started complaining about one of his clients who owed him money. I listened a bit then said I was going to get a certain dish to try to steer the conversation towards a milder topic. He kept getting more and more riled up and after each sentence he would take another swig of beer.

"And then that bastard said he didn't like the roofing material. That was AFTER we had already installed it. He said he wasn't going to pay me. He was going to look it over later. Asshole."

I tried to listen but he was getting steamed and started to point his finger with short, choppy jabs at me. That was never a good sign. The waitress came by to take our order. We both got enchiladas and rice. As soon as she left, he kept going. I just listened and tried to be supportive.

It didn't take long for Danny to direct his rage towards me. Before I knew it, somehow I was the one who caused the problem. Scapegoated again, now it was me he was mad at. He was mumbling grumpily but looking at me with narrowed eye slits. I wasn't going to meet those eyes because I knew it would trigger the explosion. Soon, our dinner arrived and I began to eat in silence. But Danny was just getting warmed up.

"You know you always ruin everything don't you?" he said intensely to me. I kept looking down and eating.

"Are you listening to me? Do you realize if we didn't have to go to dinner I could have stayed longer at the job and maybe got my money? That's your fault you know because you just had to see me. Why do I put up with you anyway." He's glaring at me now.

"Danny, please, this isn't about me. I didn't do anything. I didn't even know about your job today. I understand you are upset about your money. Just calm down and eat dinner please." I calmly asked him.

"Don't tell me what to do. I have a right to be angry and I'm going to be." I tried to just keep eating but even that made him mad.

"So you aren't going to say anything?" His voice was rising. "You're just going to sit there and disrespect me?"

I looked up at him. "No one is disrespecting you. I'm sorry you went through that today. There's nothing you can do about it tonight. Try to relax and eat your dinner."

"I'm too pissed to eat." He grumbled. "Dammit! You pay attention to me!" He was getting ready to blow.

Suddenly, Danny is up out of his seat screaming at me an inch from my face. I don't even remember what he said after that. Something about why was he wasting his time with me.

I'm now beginning to curl into a protective stance. The waitress comes over and asks if she can help. He tells her to leave and knocks his beer off the table where it shatters on the floor. The evening is over and I am now frozen and scared. Danny is yelling at me at the top of his lungs in the restaurant but I feel like I am far away in another time and place. I'm starting to get a terrible feeling deep inside.

"It's time to go Danny. Please take me home." I get up and he leaves some money and follows me, yelling all the way. The waitress looked concerned but I kept going.

We get in his truck and he drives me home while glaring at me the whole way. I retreat inward and say nothing. He hurls a few more choice insults my way but I don't answer. I've closed off and shut him out for safety.

Danny dropped me off at my house and as I walked up the walkway I could still hear him yelling at me.

"I'm not done telling you what I think! Are you listening?"

"I'm going inside and going to bed Danny. Good night." I said calmly. And that was the end of our conversation…for good.

"I'll call you later….or maybe I won't." Danny threatened. The projection and power struggle were on bigtime.

I turned my back to Danny and went to my door. I opened it, went inside and locked it. I went up into my bedroom where I curled up into a ball on my bed. Finally, I got into my pajamas but couldn't sleep. I just grasped myself and prayed all night. I didn't feel good at all.

I had no idea what was coming for me in the following days. It was the beginning and the end all rolled into one.

When dawn broke, I was still curled into a ball, rocking myself. I hadn't slept and now I was feeling strange. I managed to get through the day but felt funny. That night there was going to be a **Codependency Anonymous*** meeting. I needed to shake off Danny's behavior from the before. So, I got myself cleaned up and headed out to the meeting.

It was a speaker meeting and the speaker was a woman. I sat in the back and tried to get comfortable but I was still feeling weird. She began to tell her story. These meetings are about relationships and how to take care of oneself in a healthier way within them. She took off in another direction entirely. As I sat there she began to describe some sexual abuse experiences. She went into great detail and I began to get extremely nauseous.

After about half an hour of her story, I didn't feel I could handle anymore. I was feeling queasy and dizzy. I got up to leave and found it difficult to even walk to my car. I sat in my car awhile until I felt better, and then drove home.

After I got inside my place, things didn't improve much. I had very frightening feelings and felt out of sorts. I was now two days without sleep. I managed to fall asleep for a while that night. But when I woke up, the feelings of dizziness returned. As I walked around my house, I began to feel extremely fearful. This feeling persisted throughout the day and began to peak in the afternoon. I did not feel safe inside my own house and I became afraid. The feeling intensified until I just knew I could not stay there that night. I packed a bag and decided to go to a motel. I felt a strong feeling of something dangerous around but did not know what that could be. I couldn't see anything unusual. But I didn't want to be in the house anymore. There was a sense of extreme foreboding.

I loaded up the car and went for gas. I had brought some books from the **CODA*** meetings, pictures of loved ones, spiritual books and a picture of Jesus. When I paid for the gas, I found it hard to hear the attendant speaking. I couldn't figure out what was going on. I proceeded on to the grocery store and purchased a few items for the trip. When I reached the counter to pay for my items, I felt as though I were in another dimension, very far from the store and the clerk. I could see and hear her, but it seemed there was an invisible wall between us that prevented me from hearing her well. I wondered if she could hear me. Everything was in slow motion and I wasn't sure if I seemed odd to her or if it was me seeing the oddness in everyone else. I thought maybe I was just tired and it would end as soon as I got to the motel. As I was driving north on Highway 101 in California towards a motel I reserved for the night, I began to feel extremely nauseous. The dizziness began accelerating and I wasn't sure I could drive properly. I decided to pull off the road and rest a bit.

Soon I was retching out of the open car door on the roadside and my body began to feel as though it was going to burst open. What was wrong? Did I have the flu? I wasn't feverish, but felt achy and weird. I needed to get to a bathroom, I needed to find the motel but I wasn't sure how much farther I had to go. I began to pray. Then I remembered one of the books I was reading and had brought along. It was on the seat next to me. I reached for it, <u>The Courage To Heal</u>, the bible for sexual abuse survivors. I hadn't gotten to the end of it yet, but there was a chapter called "In Case of Emergency". I opened that and began to read.

A ways down it read, "If you are experiencing any of these symptoms, stop whatever you are doing and find a safe place to be." Then there was a list of symptoms, some of which were: dizziness, nausea, urge to urinate, vomiting, feeling disconnected or spacy, can't hear properly, and on and on. A good number of those symptoms I was experiencing at that moment. Further down it read, "If you find yourself in a car driving while having these symptoms, pull over. Do not drive; you are having memories of sexual abuse and could lose consciousness or have an accident.

Boom! It hit me like a ton of bricks. That was it! I knew I had been molested and I was certain it was Dad, but it felt like much more than that. I was in the middle of having memories of sexual abuse! Danny, who always reminded me of Dad, had triggered them by his rage-filled outburst, something Dad did to me regularly. Now what?

Once I read that, I actually felt a sense of relief that at least what was happening to me had a name. After catching my breath, drinking some water and breathing deeply for a few minutes, I felt better. I decided it was ok to drive on to the motel. Turns out I wasn't far from the motel and it was a quick drive to get there. I checked in, brought my stuff in, went inside the room and closed the door. I turned the lock and heard the click of the deadbolt going into the shaft. As soon as I heard that, I suddenly felt safe. And I could relax.

Unpacking, I took out the family photos and the picture of Jesus and set them up on the motel table. I went over to the bed and settled in. I had some snacks and got them out, laying them on the bed. I turned the TV on and started watching something. After a while, I knew I had to call my mother. She would be worried. I didn't want anyone to know where I was, but I wanted her to know I was ok. And frankly, I needed my Mom.

So, I settled in comfortably, heaved a big sigh and dialed her number on the hotel phone. She picked up.

"Mom? Is that you?" I asked.

"Yes honey, what's going on? I've been trying to reach you. Are you ok?" Mom answered.

"Oh, thank God you're there. I'm ok." I replied.

"Where are you?"

"I'm at a motel. Don't worry, I'm fine."

"Why are you in a motel instead of your house?" Mom asked.

"Because I was too scared to stay home Mom." I replied.

"Why would you be afraid to be home at your own house?"

"Because I think I'm having memories of being sexually abused." There, I said it.

There was a long dead silence.

Finally Mom spoke. "I always thought you were sexually abused."

And with a sudden and shuddering explosion, a strange and unknown energy swept over me. It hit my face, my head and then rushed down and around my body. I felt synapses in my brain connecting and neurotransmitters firing. I heard an inner crackle and fire, like electrical circuits firing up and coming to life, and I began to tremble and shiver all over. Nausea swept through me. Then quite abruptly and simultaneously, I smelled something awful and tasted something worse. I don't know exactly how long this went on.

Mom spoke urgently. "What's happening right now? Talk to me."

I kept smelling and tasting something disgusting. Then I felt tremendous pressure on my chest. I was having what is known as body memories. Smell, taste, touch but no pictures.

"Teri, are you there?" Mom asked breathily. "Why aren't you talking? What's happening?"

And then the lights went on to my movie. My personal drive-in movie....My Life and Times as a Sexually Abused Child. The download began. I had just retrieved a **reclaimed fragment*** of memory and soul record, or **Akashic Record***.

Lights, camera, action, the screen began to roll out a film I had never seen before, never realized was there, but at some level, felt deep down in my gut. Before my eyes, I was seeing everything from the past as though it was happening today, right there in that room. The suppressed memories came forward like a movie reel. I was the spectator in a darkened theater watching a personal horror movie of my own life. A movie I never knew I starred in, never knew existed, but there it was, plain as day, in living Technicolor. It happened a long time ago, but here it was...a clear, vibrant visual memory of the experience in real time.

This movie was the story of my life. It was playing out like I was in a movie theater watching someone else's life, but it was me up there on the screen. It reminded me of the scene in Star Wars where Princess Leia is a hologram projected out of R2D2's memory bank into the air. Except that it was me projected out into the air and it was coming from my memory bank and I was watching it. I was dumbstruck.

Once I saw what had happened to me, a huge wave of relief washed over me. I finally knew what the gnawing anxiety was I carried all my life. A ton of emotions flooded out, along with much of the fear, and I began to move through the memories.

It was the first of hundreds and hundreds of memories that began downloading that night that went on a long time. I had the bulk of them in that first month. Hearing my mother's voice, the only person in the world I felt safe with and fully trusted, liberated the rest of the memories. Danny's rage had triggered them, Mom made it safe to have them. The life-long trapped energy was finally free.

I was crying now. "Mom, I'm having memories as you are talking. Just keep talking to me. I see it all now."

"Oh God honey, I am so sorry." Mom cried back.

So, Mom and I talked a long time that night. During most of the conversation I was seeing my movie. I saw various scenarios of molestation, different times and places, different ages, and finally different men. Much older men, often in their sixties. Most of them included violence. Often extreme and frightening. I stayed at the motel for 3 days, until the worst of the memories were over…for a while anyway. Then I went home and a whole new life began…

But before I could do that, I had to process the new memories and the impact they had on my body, mind and spirit. They had been suppressed and separated from my conscious mind a lifetime; now they were making their way back into my memory, my spirit and my cells. I returned home after this adventure hoping to settle back into some semblance of normalcy. Now I knew what had been nagging me in the back of my mind and heart for so long. Always looking over my shoulder, feeling sick to my stomach, chronic vomiting and migraines. My eating disorder. The stress of some internal threat that I could not identify, but felt to the core of my being. I thought perhaps these feelings would simply dissipate. They did not. On the contrary, everything suddenly intensified. Something was about to happen.

I was ok for maybe, two days, then I started to feel very sick. At first I thought it was the flu. But soon it worsened. I began to drip with hot, sticky sweat even though it was still winter. I had sent my children to stay with someone so they didn't have to witness this. I wasn't sure if I would have more memories and I knew I couldn't be there for them. There was a premonition of death I couldn't bear to face but wondered if it would occur. I didn't want them to see it all go down. If I was going to die, I didn't want them there to see it. Once they were somewhere safe, I let myself move into the next phase. But

I always made sure their picture was nearby to give me strength and the will to live.

Soon the sweating turned to fever, a hot burning fever. I could still make my way to the bathroom and kitchen, so I made sure I had water and got a thermometer. My fever was rising and read around 101 degrees at that point. I could feel myself getting weaker. I began to pray and chant. I called on the Angels and the healing masters to help me. Two days turned into three days, three into four. Things began to deteriorate. My fever was now 103 degrees and I was alone. I knew no one was coming by to help me. I had to go through another crisis alone in my room, like so many before.

Even though I was sweating buckets, I had to pee. I tried to rise to go to the bathroom. I could barely lift myself off the bed. With great effort, I dragged myself to the toilet. Afterwards, I rinsed my face off and climbed slowly back in bed. Little did I know that would be my last time up. It didn't take long for my condition to worsen even more after that. I felt weaker and weaker with each passing hour. I decided to take my temperature to see what was happening. As I tried to move my arm, I found it difficult to even reach the nightstand. Finally I grabbed the thermometer and put it in my mouth. After a few minutes, I checked it. 105 degrees. Wow. Now I'm getting worried.

I laid there and began to give myself long distance Reiki. I also prayed to God to get me through this. I don't know how long I lay there like that but I decided I needed to call someone to come over. 105 was just too high a number. I could seize at that temperature. So, I tried to stretch over to where the phone was on the other nightstand. Suddenly I realized I was immobile, paralyzed, and unable to move my upper body at all. I could move my feet and legs some, but otherwise, nothing at all. I could still blink, but even my speech was impaired. Now it was too late to call for help. I couldn't move myself over to the phone, I couldn't hold the water cup to drink the water, I couldn't move period. But my fever raged on unabated. Sweat poured from me, soaking my nightgown and bedcovers through. I looked up at the clock and heard a distant slow ticking….tick…..tock….tick…. tock. Time stood still as though I was in another dimension.

I wasn't even able to fall asleep, my body ached too much and the heat was searing. Strange, I couldn't move my body but I could feel it. I could feel what seemed like ancient pain, long ago suffering, and the muted voices and cries of people from somewhere else, as though they were trapped in a dark pit and crying out to me. It was as though I carried the pain for thousands of others suffering helplessly somewhere. I sensed them asking me to heal it for them because they didn't know how. They seemed to think I could do this for them. I was the bearer of the pain of many, their hopes resting on my ability to transform it for them. I felt ripples of excruciating pain that I had to endure motionless. I felt the full wrath of Dante's inferno, as though the Devil himself had brought his minions and they were watching the show gleefully. I felt their scorn and laughter from some unseen place. But I always knew God was watching over me. When would this stop God? What was going to happen to me?

I could still see the calendar from the bed. I began to count the days I lay there like that. It must have been at least a week and a half now. Throughout I prayed to God to heal me. I glanced at the picture of my children, and prayed I would live to see them grow up. Nothing was more precious to me than my beautiful girls. I focused on their picture and meditated. I visualized Angels coming down over the three of us, healing us, loving us. A measure of peace settled over me briefly. I had had no food for a week, but had managed to tip the water glass with lid and straw over with my shoulder and got a little water here and there.

Somewhere in the third week, I moved into total paralysis. I was unable to move most anything except maybe my eyes, feet and lower legs. I was totally weakened, I could hardly feel my body. Slowly, I felt the energy leaving my body, like air leaving a flattened balloon.

My consciousness never changed. I was always aware of my surroundings, the clock, the room, the bed, the window. But now, quite suddenly it seemed, I was rising above my body. I couldn't figure it out at first. I thought, am I floating? Am I in the air? What's happening to me? After a few minutes of this, I realized I was high up on the ceiling. I was at the highest point of the ceiling! How was this possible? My mind was the same, my thoughts were the same. Was I soul travelling?

I was enjoying the sensation of floating free and high and looking around when I looked down. There below me was my body, motionless, eyes closed. I was barely breathing at all. And it hit me. I was my consciousness, but below me was my body, and we were now separating. But how could this be? In shock and horror, I realized I was dying. I could not make my body move no matter how hard I tried or how much I willed it. It was a separate entity. It was down there, a person, not this awareness I was experiencing, but a still piece of flesh lying peacefully below. And I was up here, thinking like I always think. I did not know if I was still connected in any way to the body below. I did not know if it was too late to return to my body.

But I wasn't afraid. I felt peaceful, free of suffering for the first time in my life. I could just go home to God I thought. After all, it had been a painful life, filled with betrayal, abandonment, abuse and ridicule by all those I loved the most. I was going through a crushing divorce. What was there to return for? I was suspended in a timeless zone where choice is offered. Stay or go, but I wasn't clear on how to do that or what to decide.

Existential issues leaped to my awareness. What was my purpose? Had I accomplished what I came for? Was there more for me to do? Why was this happening God? What about my healing career? What about school? What about the journey I had begun? It wasn't over.

And then this consciousness that is me, looked over, from high above my motionless, dying body, at my girl's pictures. I looked into their beautiful eyes, their bright spirits and their innocent faces. I thought about what life would be like for them without me. No one would care for them like I did. I was the one who fought for them; I was the one who brought the healing to their lives.

Then my consciousness went even deeper, I felt my heart start to beat, yet I wasn't even in my body. Where was this heart? Was it my heart….or a Universal Heart? How was I feeling this without a body? I felt the vast love I feel for my girls coursing through my soul, the spirit that was now floating above my body. The love I felt for them superseded any and all other decisions. I was their mother. My job was not completed. I needed to finish raising them and do as much as I could for them. I needed to share it all with them. And I was just be-ginning to get to the point where I had something to share, wisdom to offer, abundance of my own to give them. The power of the Universal Divine Mother kicked in. Love was more important than pain, than death, than the self. Loving them had awakened my universal heart and given me meaning again. I wasn't done loving them, or loving humanity. I had so much more to give them, and to the world. I was only just beginning to heal, and somehow I knew there was much more love down the road. Love I wanted to share with the world. The love I felt for my girls gave me the will to live. I managed to pull up more will and determination; I was determined to live.

And so I turned to God and prayed. I could feel the omniscient presence of something huge and vastly graceful, an enveloping pres-ence of love and warmth. God was THERE! AROUND ME! I was held, loved and cared about, even if only in the Spirit world. I could feel God with me in this moment, reassuring me silently. I am a **ReikiMaster*** and know that healing is always possible. Surely my situation was no different than thousands of other souls God has saved, miraculous healings, and other evidence of God's work in our lives. I didn't know how much time I had, how long my spirit could hover in the room. So I began a dialogue with my Creator.

"Holy Spirit, I learned throughout my healing studies that Jesus healed any and all conditions upon asking for your help, even at the brink of death, even after death. I learned that sincere prayer brought your grace and your miracles of love and healing. I ask that you let me be one of those miracles tonight. My children need me. I'm not done raising them, there is much work to do and many healings they still have to experience. Please let me stay and finish raising them. I humbly ask this of you now, in full knowledge that you have the power to heal any and all conditions. Further, I have just begun my healing practice. I want to give to my students and patients the kind of healing you are capable of. I promise you that if you restore my body to wholeness, and show me how you did it, I will heal all you send my way. I promise I will give you credit for these miracles and teach others how to turn to you for healing. Please share the truth about healing with me that I might share it with others."

I received a message from somewhere deep inside my soul, "It won't be easy. There will be pain and suffering, and more work to do."

I heard this and responded, "I know I'm not done healing. But I'm ready to keep going; I am ready to dedicate my life to you." After saying this out loud in my mind to God, I began to pray deeply for the chance to live again, to heal again and to be with my daughters again. I prayed for a short period of time and then, when I said as loud as my spirit could say to God, "I believe you can heal anything and that if I ask this of you now, you will grant me my life again"; And with a sudden bolt of lightning, I suddenly dropped down from the ceiling back into my body. It was like a sudden parachute drop. I could feel everything again sharply, the pain of this illness, the suffering of this world, the paralysis this body was still experiencing. And I felt a showering of Divine Energy drop down upon me. God was blessing me with healing grace.

I felt pain suddenly, but I felt my consciousness awaken brightly and look around. I was seeing from my body's eyes again. I was inside

Teri's body, the body I took for this lifetime! Because of my prayer and my faith, I was given another chance. I began to breathe deeply; it felt so good to feel the breath coming in and out of my body again. And then I cried…hard. I still had enough juice in my tear ducts to have a good cry. And I mumbled prayers of thanks to my Creator for the miracle of resurrection. I lay there for a while, not aware of how much time passed, not able to discern time at all. And then the miracle began.

Quite suddenly, above me in the air inside a bubble within a cloud, there appeared healing information, sacred information, in a vision. I saw a series of sacred texts with very clear writing in English describing truths about healing. They appeared within the context of the vision. Clear, distinct and outlined by a bubble cloud. These texts stayed above me until I mastered them, memorized them, then they moved to the next page. The information presented to me was staggering and deep. It explained the true nature of illness, the causes, elements and cures. The entire program was laid out before me. I was dumbfounded.

And then a realization dawned on me. I was thunderstruck. This is what happened to Dr. Mikao Usui, the first Reiki GrandMaster, when he went up on the mountain to ask for the truth about healing! This is what he experienced after meditating for 21 days! All his questions were answered. And now it was happening to me. I was humbled and cried hard that I was having such a profound experience. And it was so clear, so bright and so deep. It stayed until I mastered it, then it would disappear and the next page would appear. And so it went, until all the information was presented. And then I further realized, it was the 21st day after I had the memories of sexual abuse had first surfaced in the motel! 21 days since this event began, and I was being given the secrets of healing the human mind, body and spirit. Just like Dr. Usui.

After the vision ended, my fever began to die down. A calm

settled over me and soft energy began to filter in, relaxing and healing me. Within a day, I could move my upper body some. I was beginning to come out of it. As soon as I could move enough to get up, I got water. But I was shocked to realize I wasn't hungry, or didn't feel the need for food. I hadn't needed to use the restroom for two weeks! I hadn't eaten for that same period of time. My body had been altered somehow. Again, just like Dr. Usui, I was experiencing an initiation of some kind. Energy had been transferred to me like a Reiki attunement. I was different energetically. I was living on the energy of Divine Grace just given me by the Holy Spirit.

I rested for a day or so, then when I felt strong enough, I took myself to see a doctor to find out what was going on with my body. I told him that I had been very ill with a high fever for over two weeks. I told him that I had been paralyzed in my neck and upper body for most of that time and that I didn't eat, drink or use the bathroom during that period. He was dumbfounded and decided to take a blood test on the spot. He had a lab in his office and could test it there. He drew my blood and bandaged my arm. I lay back on the table and waited for the test results. After about 20 minutes, he came rushing back into the examination room and his face was white as a sheet.

He shouted at me, "There are absolutely zero red blood cells in your bloodstream, only dead white blood cells! You have the blood of a dead person. I've never seen blood like this except in a corpse in medical school. You can't live without red blood cells. How are you walking around? Your body needs red blood cells, yet you are standing!! I can see your body has obviously been fighting a terrible infection. We need to hospitalize you immediately, you could pass today! Let me drive you over there."

"No," I replied calmly. "The crisis has passed. I already died and left my body."

"What do you mean? What happened? You should be dead."

"But I'm not. I asked the Holy Spirit to heal me and I was healed, just like that. My spirit left my body and was rising up. I prayed to God to spare me and heal me. And that is exactly what happened. I saw the healing take place. I returned to my body after saying the healing prayer for God's grace. God healed me when I asked reverently."

"I don't know what to say. That's amazing." The doctor said concerned. "But I still think you should go into a hospital."

"If I were going to die, it would have happened that day. I've been steadily improving since that day. I have faith God is healing me as we speak. I wish to allow that to take place fully."

"I don't understand how you are still standing without red blood cells. Your brain would be starved for nutrition without red blood cells. It defies science."

"God is capable of anything, especially beyond the limited understanding of what we know in science. There are more worlds to conquer there still. I asked for God's healing grace. It was granted."

"What do you want me to do then?"

"Just tell me for sure what I have. And is there anything else I can do?"

"You have viral meningitis! It's nothing to minimize. Depending on the type and severity, it can be fatal. And there isn't much I can do since it's viral and not bacterial. Go home and rest. Fluids, chicken soup and the like. And call me and tell me how you are. If you get a fever back, come into the hospital. It's incredible you're ok."

"Nothing is incredible with God. Ok, I will let you know. Thank you."

So, I went home and finished healing myself. God was always there with me. My girls came home, life went on. I didn't tell them what happened. I didn't share much of my spiritual transformation at that stage of the journey. I didn't understand it all yet and there was more work to do…as the deep voice had told me. I knew it wasn't over. Intuitively I knew this was the beginning of my healing, not the end, and that the biggest part was still to come.

To be so honored to be in the presence of the Holy Spirit, ask for my life, and have it be granted, is something I will never get over. I know there will be some who don't believe it ever happened to me. Yet it did. I know there will be many who don't believe it possible to completely heal from serious illness. But I know it is possible, because that isn't the only near-death experience I've had. I went through many more such initiations, as all healers and shamans do to become the healers they eventually become. And it is this very faith in God's ability to heal anything that has made me such a strong healer. It is my faith that healed me that incredible day when I looked down on my limp body, a body that had carried me through so much pain, and loved it and asked God to give me another chance to walk inside it.

For now, I had had my first real memories, verifying the pain and suffering I had been carrying a lifetime, but had been suppressed deeply within my body and tissues. Something had broken loose that had been carefully hidden from me. A huge onion layer had been peeled back, exposing a raw, dripping core never before seen, never exposed to the light of day. New feelings and new awareness came along with that raw core. It stung badly for a while, just like a juicy cut-up onion will. And the tears flowed freely. But soon, that new layer began to dry up. It granted me a peek at even deeper cores below. As the layer dried, I could almost feel them coming. But I wasn't quite ready. I needed a breather from transformation for a time. And an even more exciting life was beginning.

It didn't take long for God to call me on my promise. Soon, my office was filled with clients, students and addicts, since I was also an addictions counselor. My healing and counseling practice took off. Every Wednesday I had a Reiki healing circle, every month at least one Reiki class. Some of them had cancer, some had other serious illnesses, some were addicts and some just needed counseling. All of them left healed. God had given me the gift of full healing abilities. It worked on everyone who was sincerely ready to heal. But it was always God who accomplished the task. My classes were always full, I was in high demand. I felt confident.

I went on to found two charitable healing projects. First, the **_The Reiki Recovery Project_**©*, where I took in street alcoholics and addicts who were chronically addicted and nightly arrested, only to return to the streets. Judges began sending addicts to me where I turned their lives around. The courts couldn't deal with the influx of street alcoholics, so they were sent to me. And I worked on them for free, since they had nothing. It was a success. The second charity I founded was the **_SAFELOVE Foundation_***, an acronym for **_The Salini Foundation for Empowerment and Love_***. **SAFELOVE** was for healing and assisting victims of sexual abuse, trafficking or slavery. I found that many addicts were once sexually traumatized so the two charitable projects went hand in hand. A sexual abuse victim often became an addict; an addict healed was often a sexual abuse victim. Today, I have combined these two projects under the umbrella of my **Salini Foundation**. **The Salini Foundation** will help all those traumatized victims and more. It assists with homeless teenagers, child sex slavery, counseling, domestic violence and more.

As I healed, I found that each person who crossed my path brought a gift of awakening. All of them sacred in their own way. Each of them had light and dark within. And all of them gave me things I needed to awaken. Some of them were beautiful. Some of those gifts were painful. But sometimes that's what it takes. I bless them all for the lessons held therein. I love them and forgive them all. They remain in my heart forever.

My practice was jammed to the gills for five straight years. I was the hot healer in town then, even went on national TV. I had started this book and worked on an Oscar-nominated screenplay. I was moving right along, handling my business so well that thought I was headed for fame and fortune. Maybe I was the next big thing.

Until that day I got the thudding news, as though someone had clapped me behind my head with a heavy rubber object, blunt and hard it came. My beloved sister, Elizabeth, who was like a mother to me, was in the hospital with seizures. Her husband had called me. It was serious. I was being summoned to come immediately. The next chapter of my life was about to commence, and fame and fortune were definitely not on the menu. No, on the contrary, that's when my whole world came crashing down.

My soul was in crisis; everything I had grown accustomed to was falling away. I was transforming into someone or something else. Inside a mysterious crucible I lay in agony and confusion while a fiery mold constantly tested, burnt, fired and reformed me... the metals of sacred alchemy were purifying my being from an abused child, into a healer doing God's work.

And this was where I began to see and understand the transformation. So much more to come, so many more miracles, so much of God's love to absorb still.

Yes, this was the beginning. And what a journey it's been.

Chapter 3

The Wound ~ Sex Slavery

We live in a culture that lacks common power, truth and accountability. We've grown accustomed to bullying. So we blame the powerless victim who cries out the truth of our world in pain from the violence and injustice done to her ... and then we gang up on her again. Until we make sure she is forever silent.

~ Salini

It was the deepest of wounds. The kind that others can't see but is felt in every act, in every waking moment, and in the tiniest molecule of your body. It's a forever wound, one that sticks on you like sweat on a hot summer day. You won't be shaking it off anytime soon. It's the kind of wound that finds its way back. If it doesn't find its way back to the perpetrator, it will find its way back to society, in crimes of violence, rape or injustice that pass on the original blow to new victims. The energy just keeps circling around the planet with new cries of revenge, new eyes filled with hate and new graves dug.

And all the while it eats a hole in your gut, your brain and your heart every day. That was what I was carrying. And as big as it was, it had been a secret to me. Of secret origins, but not of secret pain. I always knew I was in pain, just not why. A secret kept from the person holding the wound was quite a secret indeed.

How that could be was something that would take me a long time to understand. But it was in the understanding I eventually arrived at that an even bigger secret emerged. A secret affecting millions of people globally today. It's the single largest unacknowledged and untreated condition around the world; a little understood phenomenon. And it became my personal matrix of Hell for a long time. But it also burned through a doorway to awakening, and opened my eyes and heart to a deep truth. A truth that must be shared to help so many others suffering today as I once was. So, for this reason I lay out the steps of how my consciousness was violated, damaged, and eventually healed.

The earliest formative episodes began at home. The conditioning wasn't subtle there, but it started so early that it seemed normal to me then. I don't remember ever not being abused.

"You know that no one will ever love you, don't you? I have to beat you to prove it." Dad would whisper in my ear just before the first blow of a good, long whupping. His board would leave thick, red square indentations in my back for days. Sometimes he used his belt buckle all over my body. I wasn't allowed to cry.

I was too little to understand then why I needed to be beaten to prove I was or wasn't loved. But looking back now, I realize that I understood quite well that it didn't make any sense at all. I understood enough that I began questioning this line of thought from about 3 years old on.

My mother confirmed it when she said years later, "You were always so brave. You were only 3 years old, but you stood up to Dad and asked him why it was necessary to beat us all. Everyone was shocked when you would stand up and ask those questions, but often it stopped him in his tracks. And you never stopped challenging him."

The conditioning went on slowly and steadily like this throughout my childhood. I would try to assert myself. I would try to get away. I would try to talk people out of hurting me. If I cried, I was held to the ground and silenced, or isolated in my room. If I made a mistake or disobeyed, the punishment was doubled. If I wanted to achieve something, my father would try to sabotage it. So, all efforts on my part to be a full-fledged, respected family member were totally thwarted. As time wore on and I grew to be a teenager, I came to realize that something very dark was running the show with Dad, possibly not even his own personality or soul. I observed him closely to try to understand what was going on. He seemed to be possessed.

But this all took place when Dad was in his dark self. Since he was schizophrenic, at times he could be ok and would be fun-loving. This stark opposition of life at home was characterized by Dad's good moods and times when Mom was sober. If he was in his good-Daddy-schizoid-split side, he would come home all slap-happy and wanting to play. We jumped to those moments because it was then we could be normal and just enjoy life, grab a little joy here and there. And there were a number of those good moments to remember that kept me going during those dark years. That was the beginning of my observation and understanding of the split between good and evil, dark and light that exists within every human on Earth. And what a priceless piece of education it turned out to be.

So on went the creation of the split in my consciousness. Was I a good girl or a bad girl? Was today a day we would go to the fair and get an ice cream, or was it a day when I would be beaten and raped? I never knew; I had to be on guard 24 hours a day, every day, to ward off potential attacks. These were no longer conscious thoughts but a deeply buried survival mechanism that ruled my daily life. It had developed that way over many years of steady threats and violent moods. Safety was unavailable…a raw, bloody feeling of being split open and laid bare permeated daily life. I couldn't find protection anywhere but searched for it everywhere. No one came to my aid, no one protected me, no policeman showed up at the door to rescue me. These thoughts were pondered at an unconscious level, in the deepest levels of brain function that rules survival in a dangerous situation.

This was how my emotional development was shaped and molded, in a crucible of fear and danger. I was like a tiny soldier in a daily battlefield and the enemy was always there looming over you, at home with you, sitting across from you at the dinner table. I could never, ever relax. The only safe retreat was into your mind. There you could take refuge and create a world that was impenetrable. There you could be whoever you wished - strong, vibrant, beautiful and most importantly, safe. So, it was there I retreated often. It was there I created a life, characters, and people who cared about one another in the hopes that one day I might meet people like that. I was shaping an ego persona to survive in the world as I was experiencing it, a very unsafe place. My mask of civility was forming for the world I would have to enter and survive in. But behind it was buried pain and terror.

Although still a small child, I increasingly began to show signs of anxiety, stress and fear. I began having rashes constantly. The

doctors then called them hives. But now I understand they were a reaction to the constant stress of never knowing when the axe would fall and I would again be getting a whipping or be raped, the precursor to lifelong PTSD. I became hyper-vigilant, always watching for when he would show up and learned to monitor his moods. I watched Mom's drinking and his anger very closely. I learned to ignore my own feelings and focused entirely on theirs to make sure I was always doing the right thing, doing what they wanted, never making a mistake since mistakes were not allowed in our household. This of course was impossible. Soon I developed an eating disorder - bulimarexia, and was secretly vomiting or binging in my room when no one could hear me. It was my private addiction, one that assuaged all my emotional pain. First the food comforted me, then the guilt rose up from the binge, then I had to punish myself by vomiting. Round and round the circle of pain. It was the cycle of my addiction, a metaphor for the cycle of abuse.

But since I was told I was unwanted, unloved and that anything I needed in life was not going to be forthcoming I began to suppress my true self, my needs and my life expectations. An internal struggle was beginning to take shape. One part of me was beaten down, in pain and devastated… another part was powerful, intelligent, successful and rebellious. These two parts of me took over the battle long after the worst of the abuse was over. I had internalized their message. I was unworthy and unlovable, hopeless and laughable. At least my ego self believed that. My higher self knew better and watched impassively. And that divine self soon began to fight back to reclaim my soul, mind, and heart from those who wished to take me down. The spiritual battle for my life and spirit was underway.

And to think that was the easy part of my wound. The hardest part would take years to uncover, more years to heal, and a lifetime of discipline and spiritual practice to fully overcome. But it was worth every blow and every tear….because it was with those I earned my entry into the sacred temple from where all God's blessings flow. From there I embarked on the sacred alchemical journey that turns lead to gold, and leads you directly to…….the Holy Grail.

Those were the first memories to surface in the early days of my soul transformation. They were the first painful **traumatic shocks*** to jar me awake from my slumber and push me onto the rollercoaster ride of transformation and awakening. After integrating those memories, I moved through years of healing myself and others. It included more near death experiences and many more memories filled with pain and heartbreak. But there are far too many stories to tell for this book, and the healing is really where I want to go. So, I'll skip forward to the most important set of memories. These are the nameless, faceless memories that held me hostage for so long. Terror ruled the day then. Yet I didn't even realize I was terrified. My ego mask was ever so solid and impenetrable then.

Following the near death experience where I saw the secrets of healing, I enjoyed years of a successful healing practice. My practice was continuously busy and I was building on my career by appearing on television. In the middle of this phase, my older sister Elizabeth fell ill. She had been more of a mother to me than a sister. As a child, I looked to her for guidance and protection. She was so calm and wise. We shared a bedroom throughout our childhood. Then one day she married, she was barely 19. It was so painful to me to lose her then. She was my surrogate mother, my nurturer through the pain, my rock of Gibraltar. Seeing her leave with her husband was the saddest day of my life then. I cried myself to sleep for a week and never stopped missing her. Until that day 32 years later her husband called me to come and save her life.

"Elizabeth's in the hospital. We need you to come at once." He said to me urgently.

"Why? What's wrong with her?"

"She's having seizures. She wants natural healing. She wants you. We need you to save her life."

"I don't know that I can save her life. What are the doctors saying? Why do they think she's having seizures?"

"They don't know. Please come as soon as possible. They don't know if they can save her."

"Oh dear God. Ok, I'll get there as soon as I can. But all I can do is try."

Elizabeth's Story – *Elizabeth was living her life when suddenly she began having seizures. She had to be hospitalized due to the severity of the seizures. After medical tests were performed, it was discovered* *that she had a malignant brain tumor in her brain stem. The doctors told her it was inoperable and recommended chemotherapy and irradiating her entire brain, which would have given her an 80% chance of being a vegetable for life, if she lived, and those odds were even less. She rejected this option. She had lived a holistic life and didn't want that to change now. But it wasn't always like that. Elizabeth had a series of health issues leading up to this event. She had broken her foot and it wouldn't heal after 1 and ½ years in a cast. She wasn't sleeping well. She had become a workaholic, was very stressed out and was working herself to exhaustion. By the time she got to the hospital, she was partially paralyzed on one side of her body. Elizabeth also exhibited a very flat emotional affect and rarely expressed emotions or got close to anyone. After a time in the hospital, Elizabeth shared with us her history of abuse that she had kept secret from everyone.*

Elizabeth had come to visit me a year earlier although I was not working with her or her healing program. She was a healer herself so I thought she was taking care of herself. When I saw her, the closer I approached to her, the more pain I felt in my body. As I reached her, the pain was nearly unbearable. I stepped back several times to test what I was feeling in my energy field. Every time I came closer to her, I felt pain entering my own energy field first, then into my body. Something was clearly wrong with Elizabeth, but she herself was not yet aware of it and had suppressed the pain completely. I told her back then that I felt something was wrong and made some recommendations, especially emotional healing because I knew in general she lived a healthy life. She said she would follow through on it. Later, when we talked, she said she would work on it. Next thing I knew, she was hospitalized with seizures. Apparently things were getting worse, but she wasn't telling me.

Even though Elizabeth ignored warning signs leading up to the seizures, she decided to undertake a holistic program of treatment at the last stage of her illness. The doctors had given her a slim chance of recovery. We worked out a program that included herbs, vitamins, stretching and Reiki among other things. A special Native American herbal combination for brain cancer that included black walnut was made up for her to take as well. There were other brain cancer patients who had survived on this regimen including the holistic practitioner who brought it to us. But Elizabeth was well into the last stages of what turned out to be a malignant brain tumor, a glioblastoma, with a very low prognosis of recovery. Realistically, this was not one of the cases with a rosy outlook no matter what form of treatment she undertook. Nevertheless, Elizabeth wanted to see what she could accomplish holistically anyway since that was the lifestyle she had chosen to live.

Elizabeth was a masseuse and bodyworker. She had been a vegan for some time, exercised regularly, never drank or smoked and was a very positive, active, upbeat person. She had a special water system that filtered out impurities installed in her house as well as in her bathroom appliances. She grew her own vegetables and took care to eat only organic foods. She was involved in bicycling, tennis, walking, and yoga and was a green activist. With all that, Elizabeth should have been the picture of health. But she overlooked something. She had taken care to handle her physical health and was beginning a spiritual program, but Elizabeth had not addressed the other two quadrants of health - mental and emotional. She never once looked at her shadow self.

*After I gave Elizabeth a series of deep **Reiki Soul Treatments***, which utilize divine energy to access Akashic memory and process stuck emotions healthfully; she began to release ancient pent-up emotions. She went into long crying jags, and became very angry. She shared many episodes of abuse. On the 7th day of working through the surface layers of emotions, Elizabeth hit the Mother lode of stored toxic emotional memory so deeply held and forgotten that she was shocked to realize they had occurred.*

These emotions turned out to be the most painful and pointed to a toxic family secret. Elizabeth had also been sexually abused in early childhood. She hadn't allowed herself to remember because these memories were so frightening and occurred when she was very young. Her unconscious mind had protected her conscious mind from dealing with the traumatic memories. They were literally "frozen in place" in her tissues, stored there and compartmentalized for safety until a time when she could handle them. However, that did not stop them from becoming a host for disease. This type of trauma interferes with the body's natural energy flow through the mental, physical and emotional bodies thereby disrupting the natural healthy development of the abused child. It becomes a stream of toxic energy that flowed in and took root there, eating away at her *tissue. Her energy field was blocked from childhood on and had become diseased. These **frozen memories*** were stored in her brain stem.*

*As Elizabeth began to move through her back-logged emotional database, a free-flow of energy began to occur, a rapid download if you will. She stated she felt "energy" or "liquid" moving down the back of her neck. As this continued for several days, Elizabeth's body loosened up and she began to have a return of movement to her limbs and neck. Soon she was walking around the hospital room again and talking normally and happily. The memories continued on until she re-covered a large **reclaimed fragment*** of her early life with rich detail and recall. She was able to remember an eight year period of her childhood she had forgot-ten. With each memory she said she felt her body come back to life. But much long-term damage had already been done.*

The doctors estimated the tumor had been there at least two years and had done significant damage to her brain stem. Yet Elizabeth was able to recover large portions of her early life and called for a family intervention to reveal the truth. She stated this was the most important thing she had ever done and even if she didn't survive, she wanted to tell her story.

After much improvement, Elizabeth was able to go home. She was able to express her long-held pain-ful feelings about everything that had occurred. She was greatly relieved to finally get the truth out and ex-pressed this continuously to me throughout her period of improvement. After realizing nothing was going to change in the family, Elizabeth became depressed and began to decline again. Eventually she was hospitalized again and remained there until her passing. Elizabeth's tragic case is a prime example of how trauma can create disease and kill when left suppressed, denied and unexpressed. If she had addressed the emotional wound held in her shadow self earlier, she could have intervened on the tumor in time. The neurosurgeon told me if she had done something a year earlier, her life may have been saved. It was the emotional and mental work of healing her memories that she overlooked. The revelations came too late. Her shadow self claimed her life.

Elizabeth's death was devastating to everyone who knew her. She was a bright light of love and joy wherever she went. I was especially devastated. Suddenly the family secret was out. The problem was, Elizabeth wasn't here to talk about it with everyone, to help us get through it or to validate my memories anymore. As soon as she was gone, the scapegoating began anew. Somehow, this was my fault. When in reality, Elizabeth had died of a lifetime of abuse that had built up and that she held in until she just couldn't take anymore. Her tissues just couldn't hold any more mental or emotional toxins. And one day, the stored trauma within her cells just burst open and exposed the damage it had done.

Not long before Elizabeth died, I had begun to have new memories. I didn't understand them at first. They seemed like dreams, even visions. Many of them recurring dreams telling me something I wasn't able to fully grasp. They turned out to be the first memories of outside groups being involved in our sexual abuse. I never shared my memories with Elizabeth earlier as she never wanted to talk about what happened in our family before her illness. But during her period of **Akashic Recovery***, she began to describe similar events. More than one man, a group setting. She went on to describe what she saw happen to me. Since she was 7 or 8 years old at the time and I was 1 and 2 years old, her recall was much clearer. She watched my abuse unfold.

"It was unbearable to me to watch you be abused. I blocked it all out. It was just too terrifying. He threatened our lives…he threatened Mom's life…he threatened the lives of our future children. I couldn't let myself remember it….not until now." Elizabeth had told me. "I want to apologize to you for how you were treated by the family. You always told the truth and no one listened. No one believed you. You were ignored and scapegoated. It's been my greatest sorrow, that not one person stepped forward to protect you. We were all just too scared. I'm so sorry."

The impact Elizabeth's memories and apology would have on me was astronomical. It would reverberate within me for the rest of my life. It was the first time anyone verified what I remembered. It was the first time I had heard details of my abuse by someone who witnessed it. It validated years of pain I had carried about all the scorn I had endured. I had been *gaslighted**. The ultimate denial of the truth. It left me in profound personal doubt. I couldn't even trust myself, much less anyone else for so long. Now everything I had ever remembered was validated, verified and certified true. She was my witness to the truth. She backed up everything that happened to me. And then, poof, just like that, I lost her. And I was alone again.

Elizabeth's passing was the turning point in my life. I was never the same after that. I was deeply depressed and saddened. My motivation changed dramatically. Elizabeth's revelations marked the onset of a new download of information about our childhood. A new layer of the onion had been ripped back suddenly. And this one went much deeper. It exposed what felt like organ tissue – heart, lungs and gut. I began to grieve very, very deeply for the loss of my sister, the life I had lost and the life I thought I was living. I became incapable of functioning. The grief was overwhelming, the information coming through was shocking. I needed to process. So, I moved to Mexico to heal myself. And a new life chapter began.

In Mexico I started writing furiously, meditating and researching spirituality. I had many major spiritual awakenings, some of the most incredible shamanic experiences of my life and witnessed the miracle of nature. The primal state of the tropical Mexican desert in Baja California was incredible. Overnight, I was a tribal warrior in a jungle fighting for my life. Stalked by giant rattlesnakes, bitten by centipedes, trapped in hurricanes. And that was just what I needed then. But that is another book, of pure shamanic adventures and Indiana Jones-style thrills. This is the story of the wound and how I healed it. It's too important to sidestep.

But the most important thing that happened in Mexico was the moment I discovered an Indian saint named **Ammachi***. I read about her in my studies, began meditating to her and she came to me during meditations. She saved my life there in Mexico, and again later. For now, let's lay down the matrix of how we are wounded on this planet and what it takes to heal from it.

Midway through my new job in Mexico as a spa manager and retreat organizer, I received a call. My mother was now gravely ill with cancer. She wasn't expected to live. She was missing me. She was dying of lung cancer and asked me to come be with her in the end of her life and take care of her. As hurt as I was, I knew I had to be with her. There is no greater action to take than forgiveness. For most of her life, Mom had tried to teach me everything she knew. She had tried to make an impact on me spiritually, teach me to heal and awaken. She had accomplished that. I was committed to the path of awakening. Nothing would deter me. That included compassionate actions. My mother now needed me. So, I went.

Soon I was staying with Mom and Dad again, caring for Mom. She was weakening and needed food prepared, medicine administered and in general to be watched. I did it all because I loved her so much. It was another sad time, just one year after Elizabeth's death. During that time, my best friend and cousin had also died. It was a year of death. But this was a period of healing in the family. The family rallied around Mom. Peace was temporarily restored. As Mom declined, I practiced compassion since my personal experience of it was growing rapidly. I concentrated on unconditional love, forgiveness and peace. I wanted the atmosphere of Mom's passing to be loving, peaceful and compassionate. She was moving to her next life. I wanted to help her get there in serenity.

On December 22, 1997, my mother passed peacefully in my arms. I had rocked her a long time as I saw her slipping away. She tried to speak to me, but could no longer speak. I didn't know what she was saying, but I felt it. …..I love you darling daughter….I will miss you sweetheart…..and then she was gone. The third woman I loved to die in my arms in one year. It was excruciating, and my body was beginning to feel the strain.

I stayed on awhile to help Dad with the funeral and Mom's things. I took my mother's ashes to the Land of the Medicine Buddha for a Jang Wa ceremony to purify her ashes for the next life. Hopefully she would have a happier one to come. But before long, I began to see signs of Dad's mental instability returning. I had given up my job and my life to care for my mother. Despite being a multimillionaire, Dad gave me nothing to start my life over with once again. He was becoming his old insane con man self again. I knew it was time to go back to Mexico to see what was left of my life there. I caught a plane back and upon arriving, I saw that my life there was over. I was ready to return to California. It was time to grieve once more, this time for my mother.

I returned to Santa Barbara to restart my life. I wasn't feeling well after all the caretaking I had been doing. I checked in with a doctor. My right breast was aching intensely and I had several large lumps in it. I got my diagnosis a few days later, it was breast cancer. Now it was my turn. Only this time, there was no one to take care of me. I had a part-time job and a new apartment. I still had to work, but was very sick. Suddenly, I had to go through the gauntlet of decisions, feelings and pain all cancer patients go through. Only I had to do it on my own. Because I had no health insurance or money, the doctors just shrugged and almost said, "Oh well, see you in the next life."

I contacted all my healer friends and students and told them my situation. Many of them showed up for me and showed me what true love and compassion are. I devised a healing protocol. Two dear friends in particular stayed by my side throughout….two heroes I will never forget and a couple temporary heroes along the way. One great soul, my beloved ReikiMaster friend, who could hear the plants and the animals speaking, gave me a Reiki treatment every single day for six months. He was the most powerful healer I've ever known and the humblest, most loving soul I've ever met. He had come with me to help me heal Elizabeth. Now it was me who needed healing. He told me he saw my broken heart and spirit and that my soul was deciding whether or not to live. It was the stark truth. All I felt was pain and sorrow. Losing my mother, sister, and two more women I loved and the men in the family abandoning me left me with little desire to live. The grief was like hot burning coals ripping through my breast every day. It felt like I was carrying a sack of boiling hot rocks in my breast. But it wasn't just the breast that hurt. My heart hurt too. And my lungs and deep in my soul. Rivers of sorrow flowed through my energy meridians firing up each energy junction and creating massive inflammation throughout my body. A heavy cloak of grief lay like a stone blanket over me, immovable, thick and death-like. I lay under it just feeling the pain of my life, those I had lost, the soullessness of others and the lack of support. I had no one to turn to, except of course, God. Inwardly, I was once again in a soul crisis, a transformation. Where that would lead I did not know.

I could still walk around. It's like that with breast cancer. You don't have the flu or a fever; you're just inwardly suffering all the time, agonizing about what to do, and very exhausted. Having no money, no family and no medical insurance and not being able to see any doctors, I was in a deep dilemma. I was frozen with grief and pain and unsure what to do. One day I went to lunch with a friend and she brought a friend of hers unknown to me. He turned out to be a **medical intuitive***, people who can read the body like an X-ray and see what your condition is, but I didn't know. He stared at me intently throughout the meal, perhaps waiting for the right moment to speak. We were all just talking. Suddenly he said, "The Angel of Death is standing at your shoulder, directly behind you."

I was blasted into alertness. I stared at him, "What do you mean? What do you see?"

"Just like I said. The Angel of Death is standing there. He awaits your decision. Whatever is going on with your breast and shoulder is going to kill you. Unless you make a new decision. It's solid black all the way from your breast up to the top of your shoulder."

I was shocked. "What else does he say?" I asked intensely. I thought I had seen the Angel of Death that day I rose from my body with viral meningitis, but far off in the distance. The presence of God was so much stronger.

"The Angel knows you are in the process of deciding whether or not you wish to live or die. He awaits your decision but has been sent ahead because your time is close. You don't have much time left to decide. You must make a clear decision and act on it or you will be gone soon. I say no more than 3 months if you do nothing because his image is strong and powerful at your shoulder."

Needless to say, I was thunderstruck. Here I was again, facing death from a serious illness. Why did I have to go through this again I asked God inwardly? I felt a tingling go through my body and the hairs stand straight up on the back of my neck. To think the Angel of Death was standing there was just too terrifying. I turned my head slowly to look, because I really didn't want to see, but couldn't help myself. Nothing was there that I could see, but I had learned a long time ago not to discount the gifts and visions of others. They could be very powerful. And the Universe never failed to send me direct messages, although sometimes I miss them. This time, it was crystal clear. I felt shaky after hearing that. It brought the lunch date to an abrupt halt.

"Thank you for that information. I deeply appreciate it. Looks like I have some decisions to make. You two enjoy your lunch. I don't want to spoil things for you."

"Are you okay?" My friend asked me.

"As much as I can be with breast cancer and the Angel of Death at my shoulder." I shrugged.

It didn't take long for me to decide what course to take. I still had my beloved daughters to live for. In many ways, my life was just beginning. Career, kids, happiness beginning to crack the edges of my journey. It was time to decide. I knew I still wanted to live. So, I made that great prayer again to God. I chanted and meditated deeply. I saw a clear sign I would be assisted if I stayed.

Then I plunged into the process. I devised a dietary change, meditation, yoga, walking and plenty of Reiki, every single day. And with advanced Reiki, tons and tons of emotional release. Cancer is first and foremost an emotional wound. The most important healing you should undertake with cancer is emotional release around stored emotional pain. Now it was my turn to do what I had walked so many cancer patients through. All the years of abuse, suppression and family ridicule began to surface. New memories arose triggered by Elizabeth's confirmation of my child abuse. New energy flowing in that had been trapped and suppressed. The resulting explosion might as well have been a volcano exploding from my breast. It throbbed with each new revelation, each new emotional outpouring. The energy was on the move.

Along with the emotional suffering came relief, flowing energy and released power. It was like a dam bursting. Years of blocked off feelings and experiences came rushing through the opening of my soul's willingness to heal. Once I gave the word inside, the dam came crashing down. I started crying, and hard. I cried every single day for at least two hours for two whole years. Each day I cried I opened a new space in my energy field for love to come in. Every released chunk of pain made way for restored energetic connections and a restructuring of my energy matrix. I was healing, rejuvenating, overcoming, resurrecting. It didn't take two years for me to heal from breast cancer, that took less than a year. But it took two years to get over the loss of all the great women I loved so much. My body was healing and I was bouncing back. But I missed my sister and my Mom so, so much. That never left me completely. It just became bearable.

This time though, I wasn't healing from child abuse memories as much. This time I was grieving the loss of humanity in our family…the apathy and self-interest of the men….and the sacrifices the women made with no reward or thank you's. It was expected and demanded of the women to give up their lives, their bodies and their goals, without recompense or complaint, in silence and submission, to the men of the family. Any resistance or complaint about this resulted in what I was experiencing, exile and derision. I grieved the loss of the potential of these brilliant, beautiful and talented women who were oppressed, abused and exploited for the ambitions and greed of the heartless men in their lives. And I felt this ancient problem that had plagued all women since the beginning of time continue on, to new generations of women, to me and other women I loved. I felt the breast that nurtured the men I loved so much fill with their selfishness, hatred and then…their own pain, the loss of their own sacred feminine. I felt them hurt me as they had once been hurt. I felt how the men who had fathered them had killed their sacred feminine and how they placed that murderous pain deep inside me to carry for them, to transform it for them. My heart still ached for their pain and the loss of their hearts. I was carrying their hearts inside of mine; waiting for the day they could come and reclaim them. I still loved them, because they could not love themselves enough to keep going. I did it for them. As all women do for the men they love. I felt their crushing unconsciousness and denial as they bulldozed over the feelings, hearts and lives of all the women around them. They were so entitled that they actually believed what they were doing was right. They were so heartbreakingly unconscious. And still they walked on asleep, as their women fell by the wayside and died, patriarchal robots marching to their programmed death rhythm. I cried for them too, and the loss to all of humanity when everyone is so out of balance. Then I felt the places where my breast gave milk and was feminine be disrespected. I felt the hurt deep inside my nurturing part and cried out, "This is the body that loved you, received you, bore you, nurtured you, sheltered you, yet you trample it profanely. You speak to and see this incredible gift unsacredly. The pain of this is too great to survive." And I collapsed.

And inside my soul I cried the agonizing wail from deep within my very breast, where I kept my secret self, where the Great Woman lived. And my breast spoke to me. Her life force rose up to tell me her story, the story of all women who had gone before me and lived inside my breast's cellular tissue memory, deep in my DNA. I heard her wracking sob… finally. It was an ancient sound, a roar that reverberated throughout the ages, but was forever silenced. Yet it was I who was hearing her call now. I heard all her many and varied voices…the steady drumbeat of the indigenous Native women of all corners of the Earth as they are swallowed by "progress", denied, re-programmed and crushed underfoot….the soft, lilting whispers of weeping Asian women of old…bound, silenced and worked to death, their silky skins and flowery faces melting into the landscape to create new bouquets for the next man…….then I heard the Highland pipes of Falkirk and the fairy winds of County Clare that carry the long-sleeping magic of Scots and Celts through their watery tears of sorrow…green were their auras but blood red were their hearts so often broken on the morrow…….right quick then came the rhythmic clanking and strong, gospel song of the African mothers who carry not just their babes, but all the world's babes in their arms covered with rusty iron chains, carrying the heavy burden they do, the charcoal beauties of the Earth…..….yet even more was I to hear now the pulsing, shaking of tambourines and coins on the hips and veils around kohl-lined eyes so hypnotic and enticing, lalalalala was their cry….of a pain so deep of their magnificent power long denied hidden behind veils and lies, wiping their tears dry…..but soon came the motherly howl and mourning behind dancing fiestas of the Santa Madre who carries so many babes, so many husbands, fathers, sons and sisters to graves of poverty where they live as people of the Earth, ever joyful, ever re-spectful of God with crucifixes in hand as they weep….as their cries died down I began to hear the soft moans of the women of Europe wherever they had migrated, witness to many wars, diggers of many graves, bearers of many children taken in war, their voices muted by the Patriarch's whip, their heads bowed down in sorrow awaiting the next blow…..and I heard down into the marrow of my bones the cacophony of pain, my mother bones connected to their mother bones in one great energy field of sorrow. I felt my heart surge, leap and pound as their suffering coursed through me and I struggled to process their pain, to do them justice, to honor their forgotten dreams and gifts. Give me strength Goddess to carry their pain, to bring their souls back to now and climb out of the graves of old to live out their promise anew, I prayed. …Then deep down and way off in the faintness of my DNA I heard another great sound through their cries….. I heard strength, strength to rise and mother again the babes of the world we love so much even in the face of so much pain…..I heard them ask me to rise again for them, and go forward with their hopes, wishes and love sewed into my patch-worked broken heart….I heard Eulalia and Wangaari and Deni and Veena and White Buffalo Woman and Joan and Muhktarin and Quan Yin and Adrienne and Amrita and Xchoatyl and Maria and Helga and Katsumi and Evelyn and Dagny and Josie and Queeneth and Leilani and Elizabeth all cry in unison…."Take our bones to strengthen you, we offer the memory of our soul's achievements to empower you, and use the energy of our hearts to love you through this"……and so I cried hard as I felt them all enter me.

I felt the great vastness of the wound, the same wound that all of humanity is now experiencing. The wound of the crushing of the sacred feminine within all of us, and the devastation wrought upon the Earth because of it. So much unconsciousness, so much death and torture, so many patriarchal death machines, so many sweet souls crushed underfoot. I could take no more. My body was the vessel for all women's pain and all that was divine and feminine everywhere on Earth. I slipped into the restless, silent sleep of pain and truth.

I stayed that way a long while. A foggy weakness settled over me that year as I processed all the suffering and grieved the women I loved. I needed to integrate the centuries of energy upon me. Until finally, I began to love that part of me, the nurturing part, my breast. I loved it where they could not. I had to, to recover; I refused to give up. I had to bring up my own reserves of love for myself. I called upon these women ancestors to help me rise again. Then I grieved the great heart pain that I had no one in my family in my corner helping me to become the gifted person I was, no one seeing my brilliance and helping me reach long-treasured goals. I spent many days and nights moving through these feelings while I was sick with breast cancer. Every feeling felt and released left a clear space in my breast and a little less pain, a smaller lump.

Finally, I had the big memory from college burst out. I went off to college but soon after my father came and withdrew me from school. I was in class and never saw him, but he left a letter in my room. It read, "The family is ashamed of you and wishes you had never been born. You are a financial loss to the family and we have decided to write you off the family books. We leave you now for good. We don't care what happens to you. You aren't worth the trouble. Goodbye." The note was signed by each member of the family, although I doubt they really signed it. He probably did it himself. But it didn't matter. The devastation was complete. I was stamped and branded as worthless to the family. There was nothing left to live for.

I contemplated suicide, but like an aging boxer face-down on the canvas, bloodied and semi-conscious, my fighting spirit just kept rising again. I heard the referee counting me out as I had so many times before, but I also heard the voices of Angels, of the Masters, of Jesus, of my mother telling me I could make it and the soft lilting voice of my sister telling me she loved me. I lay awhile to rest while remembering these great blows. With my face buried in the mat of cancer, I prayed for strength and guidance. Can I rise with so many foes lined up to knock me down? Foes that I loved so much? I don't know but I have to try, for all of them. To inspire them to keep going.

As the memory continued I contemplated this crushing experience. I felt and remembered fully that something in me died that day; the person I wanted to be disappeared. I don't know where she went but that **soul fragment*** disappeared completely. A huge portion of my life goals were now unattainable, but worse, I was told I was not worthy enough to ever reach those goals. The weight of this realization was greater than a ten ton block of cement. It was a burden I couldn't shake off nor could I progress far under its weight. Their love meant the world to me. …….. *I had blocked this memory because it was too crushing to my soul. But here it was. I had to process it out. I returned to it to face it down*…….Dad left me on the streets that day, penniless once more. I had to live in my car; I had no food, money or gas. My loyal dog Essence was there with me. I had to eat food thrown out by grocery stores. I lived like that until I finally found work… months later. No one in my family ever called to see what happened to me. No one lent a hand. I had been an honor student, a student leader, a beauty queen, a campus humanitarian and a scholar. More than anything on Earth I wanted a college education so I could help people. This was the deepest cut of all. I wasn't even valued enough to care about my future. I grieved this out a long time. But I have never recovered from it. It was a life-altering event. So much ended that day. Sometimes I still cry for that honor student, the gifted athlete, the thespian, the editor and writer, the student leader, the dancer, the homecoming Queen, the science president. Where did she go? Later I would find out she became someone else completely. Her death gave birth to something greater. But I still had a ways to go. I allowed the full weight of the loss to pass through me and not cling to me any-where. I prayed for release from the pain of it.

Until one summer day of my cancer journey I reached peace. I kept thinking about my girls, how gifted and beautiful they were. How much I wanted to help them. I thought about beloved Jesus and Ammachi. I imagined what it would be like to heal people of all illnesses with the knowledge God gave me. I had been given a different kind of education. A more valuable one that came directly from the Holy Spirit. I felt comforted by that. I prayed, chanted and meditated for months. And soon my breast stopped hurting. It wasn't a sack of hard rocks anymore. All the feelings were drained out of me; now I was a limp rag. I knew I was going to be ok. Just like I knew the Angel of Death was gone. I could feel a space. There was air at my back. I was going to live.

My magical healer was giving me a Reiki treatment one day. He was always very quiet, but suddenly he spoke, "So you've decided to live."

I was quiet awhile after he spoke. "Yes, I have." I said softly.

"Good, because we have a lot of people to heal. Let's get started."

From then on I recovered further, until I was back to normal, whatever that is. And once again clients began to come. I had quite a few cancer patients after that. And they did very well. Of course, they were all financially destitute because they had been to cancer doctors who stripped them of their last dollar and put them through painful, ineffectual treatments. I saw them anyway. I knew they might die if I didn't, they had run out of money and options. Doctors wouldn't see them without a fat bank account. So I would. What was important was they got well. And they did. It healed me even more.

But this was still not the end of the story of the wound. The worst chapter was still to come. I needed to be healed of all the rest to be strong enough for this one.

After a time of returning to health and working, my healing practice once again began to pick up speed. Only this time, the economy of Santa Barbara had changed dramatically. Billionaires had moved to town and purchased all the apartment complexes and businesses. Rents doubled. People could no longer afford Reiki treatments, counseling or my classes. It was the beginning of the 1% stripping the middle class of everything, and Santa Barbara was Ground Zero. I watched the poor and middle class be thrown into the streets, lose jobs and begin working two jobs to survive. Women over 50 began moving into their cars with their dogs and living in parking lots underneath the homes of billionaires looking down upon them. The rich had begun to destroy the poor, and it was happening first in my home town. A tragedy that would encompass all of America was enfolding in my home town. I was deeply saddened to watch it happen.

I couldn't make enough to even afford an apartment after having been a homeowner there for years before my divorce. One day, the stark realization hit me that without a spouse and two incomes, I could not afford to live in Santa Barbara and have my Reiki practice. This realization hit all the healers and spiritual teachers in town and there was a mass exodus of the spiritual community out of town for good. Unless you had family who owned property, you couldn't stay. That year, 3,000 healers, artists and grounded spiritual souls left Santa Barbara, taking the spiritual heart of the town with them. Soon I was on another journey, looking for my true home. Leaving there was heart-breaking, but Spirit called me to the next level of consciousness. I could not turn away. Once you begin the Hero's journey, there is no turning back. Your past falls away as though there was a great earthquake and the ground splits open swallowing it. You are severed from the world you once knew. A new path opens up before you, one that is unknown. You must conquer your fear and take it. It brings untold gifts and awarenesses.

During this journey, I experienced more amazing events and healings. I lived a while with the Hopi tribe in Arizona and was taken into ceremony and initiated there. I arrived in Santa Fe, New Mexico to quite a spiritual jolt and an attack from fallen Angels. I sojourned to Sedona, Arizona for a massive healing and awakening. And I spent some time in Las Vegas, Nevada in the desert walking through darkness. But what was most important was the onset of the release of the last stage of memories.

Those memories began filtering in then and hit me strong when I made it to Santa Cruz, California. I had made a round trip home to my old childhood stomping grounds. There I settled in to life, work and healing for years. Then one misty forest day, my father died. He was finally gone. I was safe at last for the first time in my life. More importantly, my children were safe. I could never allow myself to fully remember as long as he was living and my children were nearby. The memories were suppressed but my sister had reminded me of his threats so they were close to the surface. My consciousness held back the truth, even from myself, to protect my children. I had lived in a state of frightened limbo, broken into two halves. But now, the barrier of silence began to dissolve and the wholeness was emerging. His death caused a dam to break open and everything still unremembered, unseen and unfelt burst through. The pain of the next layer surfaced and a fresh new chunk of the onion starting peeling off. How much deeper could I go I thought? I guess as deep as the truth can take me. This time, all the way into my soul.

But still I began to feel the suppression struggle to take hold again. I fought it off. My throat choked up. I was trying to write my book, but the silence was still there. I asked the Universe for help and prayed. I had been teaching Reiki and seeing clients again. One day, one of my most gifted students came by to study with me. He was born in Mexico City and had strong shamanic talents. He understood things few of my American students could understand. He had lived amongst the **brujos*** and **curanderos*** in Mexico. He knew the powerful magic of Mexico and those trained in vast magical arts, both dark and light. He had seen many things that I had also seen while living in Mexico. Particularly he had seen the power of black magic, which is the total opposite of loving, healing Reiki. We both understood that there are those who can cast spells upon you and you may never know about it. That day he was going to practice his new Reiki skills, so he began working on me. As he reached my throat, his hands froze on my throat chakra and shoulder. He told me he was unable to move his hands at all. The heat emanating from them was tremendous. I felt a burning sensation move through my throat. I asked him what he was experiencing. He said he saw a black, jelly-like cube that had been placed inside my **throat chakra***. He said it was a black magic spell to block my speech and was placed there a long time ago. While working on me, he told me he saw an Angel tell him to stay on this spot until the cube lifted out. It took about 45 minutes on that one spot and suddenly he lifted his hands. He said the cube had risen from my throat and was now floating in the air. I couldn't see it. I asked him to surround it with Angels and send it to the light. We did that together and I felt the energy of darkness leave my body and the room. My throat began to open. After that session, I felt the memories slowly begin to surface again. I was able to speak finally.

But I was living near my old childhood home then. I couldn't have these memories so close to where I was abused. Some of these nearby locations were where Dad had taken me to be abused. My soul would not allow me to see the whole picture there. I had to move. I loved the area, but it was holding me back. I meditated for months on where to go. I had taken a vacation to Maui earlier and felt tremendously drawn there. Spirit made it clear; it was time to move to Maui. Reluctantly, I packed up. Yes, as beautiful as Maui is, I loved Santa Cruz and was happy there. But I could not progress in my healing or finish my book. I had to go where I felt safe and it wasn't Santa Cruz.

As soon as I arrived in my new Maui home, the new memories began to flood out into my conscious mind. Soon I was living the pain again every single day, but not as bad as before. It was again debilitating, but in a different way. As I was remembering these new, even more horrific memories, I injured my foot and my leg. These injuries forced me to sit still and feel the pain and look inward. As much as I wanted to run from this experience, I couldn't escape. There was nowhere to go. I had to remember clearly without distraction. And once again, Part Two of the movie of my life began to appear before me. I finally knew the whole truth. I didn't want to see it, but there it was, as plain as day. It was time to deal with it. It was time to tell my story. And it was then I began to write this book in earnest. And it coincided with global revelations of abuse and pedophilia. The time for it had arrived. I knew it would be ground-breaking for so many people today.

But this time, I didn't need to get sick to remember. By this time, I had found the Holy Mother Ammachi who had cleared years of abuse off my soul and ended all my sickness. I was free of it and moving into higher consciousness. I was praying and meditating continuously. Peace and health had begun to settle into my life. I had a safe foundation to go deeper into my healing. Dad was gone; he couldn't get to me or my children anymore. The memories were coming together powerfully, in pieces, like a puzzle. I would see a scene, feel something, or have a vivid memory. A pattern emerged. I documented what I saw.

I saw many chunks of disturbing experiences. I was removed as I observed these scenes. I was given the gift of standing back like the Ghost of Christmas Past. It afforded me some sense of safety. I didn't have to re-experience the pain after all; it was no longer traumatic. As I moved through these memories, they came together as a shocking story….a story I didn't want to know. But it was true, it had happened to me. And the time has come to tell it, because I saw that it was happening to millions of children all over the world. I was one of the lucky ones who escaped and healed myself. I needed to return and help those I could. And so I let the truth emerge.

As the puzzle took shape, I realized that I had been taken into a special program. I was very small, maybe 2 years old or less. This program was run by a secret society and was conducted in secret locations. My father was a member of this society, as was his father and grandfather. They were all powerful members of either the military, politics or the intelligence community.

The program is ancient, passed down through generations and is known as the [Secret Society] Virgin program. This program utilized only virgin girl children. But it was updated to include new techniques that my father and his cronies had probably learned in the military during World War II. The young girls must remain virgins throughout their trauma-based rituals so as to ruin their future credibility if they remember what happened to them. No one would believe a virgin was raped for years. So all sexual programming is done elsewhere on the body. She is ritually abused and sent out into the world to be a sexual robot for future secret society members. That was what had happened to me. When I finally saw and remembered it all, I cried for that sweet little child who could not escape what was being done to her…and at the same time saluted her courage and survival skills to live through the horror. And that little girl was me. What a heroine I was.

As I remembered it all and saw how people are programmed, it explained many things to me. And as I understood, my anger and pain began to lift. I prayed for all those who participated in such evil, abusers and children alike. I knew they were acting out some ancient ritual that had likely been done to them. I knew I had been allowed to experience this to be able to bring healing to others. I believe my father was also an early programmed secret society child who likely also experienced trauma-based mind control. He was split, schizophrenic and often did not remember his dark behavior. It helped me to forgive him and begin to forgive it all. Dad had been a captain in the U.S. Army in charge of supplying the troops in the Pacific. Because he was an architect and real estate specialist, he was the first officer flown into Hiroshima following the dropping of the atom bombs. He was asked to report on structures standing, soldiers and civilians living and what resistance the Allies could expect. He reported back by telegram. "No resistance expected. Nothing left standing. Massive casualties. Send food, water and medicine to save the thousands dying."

I will never forget his telling me what it was like and how horrified he was. He showed me his humane side whenever he spoke of the war and what it did to men. "They just wanted to protect their families." Dad would cry. "They were just men, who had to give up what was sacred for a stupid war. And they never got to see their families again. War destroys us all."

My father's war experiences tormented him, especially the sight of women and children in Nagasaki and Hiroshima dying of radiation sickness. There was a spark of light within him I saw then. But these experiences, and those in the Korean War where he also fought, twisted and damaged his psyche further. He brought this torment home to us years later. And somewhere in there he learned about an even more twisted program developed by none other than the Auschwitz Angel of Death himself, Nazi Dr. Josef Mengele - the CIA-sponsored **MK-Ultra program***.

Somewhere around 2 years old, I was taken into the **MK-Ultra trauma-based mind-control program*** at several gathering places somewhere in San Jose, California where I was tortured. This is what my sister was also describing bits and pieces of to me before she died. She knew I was experiencing this and witnessed some of it but she didn't have the full picture. The existence of this program was verified by many individuals from various government organizations including Astronaut Gordon Cooper, who was one of the original seven Mercury astronauts. Astronaut Cooper reported that the MK-Ultra program was administered by NASA in the 1950's and 1960's during his interview with Mike Siegel on the radio show Coast to Coast. According to Gordon Cooper, the goal was to create super-intelligent children who could communicate with aliens in the future. In many cases this included trauma-based mind-control and sexual abuse. However, in 1977 former CIA director Stansfield Turner reported that the program consisted of 149 sub-projects contracted out to 80 different agencies. According to Freedom of Information Act documentation released years later, the program was green-lighted by the CIA in 1953 by then director Allen Dulles, and most likely there were overlaps of individuals and agencies administering the experiments and training. It is estimated that 30 million people walk among us today who have been tortured and mind-controlled in these programs. And those are the ones **still living.** This is no longer a secret as many former child victims like me have grown and are now coming forward with their stories. Many of them have yet to be de-programmed and have no memory of what happened to them.

So my Dad was a sex trafficker of a special kind, an internal secret society version where I belonged to him alone and was used for experimentation within the organization. He took me to places and sold me for sex to other men in his secret society, mostly between 1-5 years old. Like ancient slave traders, he made good money at this and was supported by the patriarchal power structure. Then he took me to trauma-based mind-control sessions. I was too little to know where I was taken, only that it was a dark room somewhere, sometimes a graveyard, other times a basement. I was subjected to ritual abuse, which is an extreme and severe form of steady controlled abuse intended to destroy the spirit and separate you from love and life. Breaking your soul's connection to God is a prime objective, because if they can do that they can control your mind and your soul. As the shattering began, the very structure of my mind, body and soul was being re-arranged. It was painful, frightening and chaotic.

I was selected for **Beta programming***, or sex kitten programming, to be trained in sexual slavery and related behaviors to be used as a sex slave. I was traumatized and abused into submission. This part of the programming lasted for several early years, prior to age 7, before being taken to the next level. After that, I was taken to special classes for intellectual programming, enhancing brain power, memorization, speed-reading, etc. Their goal was to create a SuperGirl – sexually hyperactive and beautiful, like Barbarella, with extremely heightened mental skills. I was expected to remain thin, fit and beautiful at all times. I was constantly harassed about my weight and appearance. It triggered my eating disorder. The classes were sporadic, especially as I grew older, but continued until I was 16 or 17 years old. By then, I did not remember the Beta sex slave programming because terror is such a big part of the trauma-based conditioning. They will terrorize you into forgetting by whatever means necessary. Terror induces amnesia. Most of it occurred when I was small, so the terror is what I felt and what kept me in check. The greater the trauma and terror, the greater the amnesia. In fear for your life, your brain reverts to survival and experiences are split off and compartmentalized, to be held in an inaccessible block of memory cells, much like your computer hard drive. Once your will is broken and partitioned off away from your daily persona, a submissive, compliant behavior takes over so you can survive the encounter. If this happens often enough, the compliant persona becomes the dominant one. Any rebellious behavior is met with harsher and harsher punishment. Such is the programming of slavery. And that is the goal they are seeking, total compliance, total obedience.

In addition to the beta and trauma-based programming, my father added special discipline at home, including regular beatings with a thick board or whippings with his belt and belt buckle on my body where no one would know. That way no one could see the bruises at school. He often did this when we were alone so no one would believe me later. Then, when I was 12 years old, my father told me they would no longer support me and I had to support myself. I was told that I could still sleep at home, but I would have to work to survive, would be given no clothes or food for the remainder of my childhood. I was not to ask for anything or speak about it to anyone. It was the age-old power struggle with him, over even my food. So, I taught myself to sew and worked odd jobs wherever I could to be able to purchase food until I was old enough to get a real job. I worked small side jobs doing chores at neighbor's houses for a few bucks here and there. I saved it up to buy fabric so I could sew my clothes. Whenever I had a spare second, I would sew so I had clothes for school. Otherwise, I would have had nothing to wear. My first real job was at a restaurant when I turned 15, so I finally had enough food to eat. I also could eat at my boyfriend's house after we began dating. After being at my house, if we went to his house, his mother would leave out food for us because she knew I never had enough to eat at home. She always looked out for me, and I loved her so much for it. My father also gave me enormous amounts of chores to do including yard work at his many rental properties. At this point, I was his personal slave.

My life went in a cycle of trauma conditioning, school and homework, working to support myself, sewing my clothes and non-stop chores. And I almost forgot, my mother wanted me to be a concert pianist so I had 12 years of classical piano training and had to practice every single day throughout my childhood until I told her I just couldn't fit it into my schedule of work anymore. I didn't think it was unusual then because the pressure, abuse and work all started so early. And I was so programmed by then. But years later several of my classmates commented that they were always so shocked at my grueling work schedule and intense pressure my father put on me to work, make my own clothes and support myself during high school while he controlled my every move. It was years later I realized others had noticed although no one talked about it back then. None of my parent's friends ever stepped in to help me. In fact, if my mother's best friend came over, I was going to get abused after she left. Whenever they drank, some form of abuse was soon to follow. And it would always be one of the worst abuse episodes.

My father was not mentally stable enough to advance in the ranks of the secret society order. To become one of the people they choose to move into positions of power, you have to be able to behave calmly and rationally on a daily basis. Dad's mental illness made him unfit for this and turned out to be my saving grace, along with Mom's spiritual training. Dad eventually fell away from the program. The last class I took that was part of the mind-control program was a Speed Reading course during high school. I learned to read an entire book in a matter of minutes while still absorbing the material. This actually helped me excel in school. My father was always present with me guiding the programming. All the other student's fathers were there too. All the students in those classes were products of the MK-Ultra trauma-based mind-control program. And there were thousands of us across America. All innocent, beautiful, talented, trusting, brilliant sons and daughters of the collective mind controllers of our time. Our power, gifts, goals, minds and freedom were being stolen from us slowly without our knowledge. And soon...we would become the future leaders of America. The people running America today.

As awful as this sounds and was, there were more vital lessons to be gained from this experience that I would not understand for many years to come. It was here I began to change alchemically. I was too young then to make a conscious decision to go through this transformation, but my soul had made this decision long before. Long before entering into this Earth plane, long before entering this body. My soul existed in the Universe as part of the One Mind, a little chunk of God that dropped down into this body to fully awaken. I had chosen this experience and these lessons, but I had no realization of this then. I could only walk through the pain of it gripping onto my faith to get to the other side. For now, I lived within the apartheid of my soul, separated from my spiritual grace, unaware of my gifts and spiritual power, being used for the machinations of sick patriarchs. At some level, I knew I had to survive it. I had more important work to do someday. And that day has arrived.

*I am not my body but I am the
perfection that is my soul...*
~ *Salini*

By now, I'm sure you get the idea. There was sustained physical, sexual and psychological trauma throughout my childhood that broke my spirit and health temporarily. I was sustained by the spiritual teachings, love and practices of my mother and of Reiki GrandMaster Hawayo Takata, my early mentor and healing master, by Jesus, and by my continued spiritual pursuits and practices. I used those teachings to heal myself, and the hundreds of clients and students that eventually came to me. The details of my torture, abuse and trauma are less important to me than the outcome. I overcame everything that was done to me and triumphed, becoming a successful healer, counselor, teacher, author, spiritual visionary, speaker and spiritual guide for many. My experiences helped to catapult me into a position of guide to many who later came to me with the same issues from their childhoods filled with suffering, their own individual versions of torment. I came to realize that there were literally thousands of us, and eventually millions of others who went through some form of sexual trauma, abuse or mind-control. After more than 35 years of doing this kind of healing work, I realized it's time to tell the world how prevalent this is and help more people to heal from this.

But first, I had to walk the spiritual gauntlet of healing and awakening…a journey fraught with fear and obstacles. Walk with me as I take you along for a bird's eye view of the shaman's journey to spiritual awakening….the path of the wounded healer and Divine Mother.

Chapter 4

Walking Dead ~ The Separation

All strong souls first go to hell before they do the healing of the world they came here for. If we are lucky, we return to help those still trapped below....
~ *Clarissa Pinkola Estes*

And so I began my journey into the long, dark night of the soul....a journey into abject fear, total unknown, and midnight blackness. It was a place of sealed off solitude....with an invisible dimensional wall that forever separated me from everyone else. All of my actions were geared towards getting to the other side of the wall where everyone else was, and to make sure no one knew I was on the other side, but believed me to be one of them. Instead, I was sliced down the middle, with half of me living in the fiery inferno of damnation, and the other half anchored in light by Angels. I was a shamed, cast out child with a dark secret, and believed no one would ever love me. How in the world was I ever going to reconcile the two halves? How would I ever come back together as one?

And that became my heroine's journey deep into the heart of the human soul, where I walked awhile in purgatory. Programmed death and survival as they take it all away from you.......and leave you to survive with nothing but your body, wits and soul. If you still have a soul when they get through with you.

I was shattered. Utterly. Completely. Wickedly. But I was also being led somewhere. To where I couldn't yet see. I only felt destroyed then. I couldn't see the light on the path at first because they had done so much damage to me mentally, emotionally and physically. They so delighted in shattering me, those dark ones. They stood over me and laughed as they crushed me, body, mind & spirit……..I could hear the snickering as all the broken molecules of my being scattered everywhere on the wet, dirty ground. Here and there I felt a boot heel grind into my neck or a hard kick to my midsection every so often as I continued on. But the brunt of the damage was done early, before I could protect myself. Mostly I lay helpless and powerless and in pain a long, long time. I could not move, my spirit had long since fled my body in terror and my mangled self was too weak and destroyed to move forward, metaphorically. So I just remained there, frozen in place. Eventually they grew bored of their twisted game of destruction. Tired of the soul they believed they had destroyed and went seeking new horizons, new victims, fresh innocence to suck the life out of. I was tired and boring. I had stopped struggling, they had me. I didn't even know who I was anymore. I simply stayed frozen and that just wasn't fun for them anymore. They wanted to yank the confidence out of someone else.

So, they left. Left me with bloody pieces of my ravaged heart in my hands, ragged fragments of my sense of self that made no sense at all to me anymore, and my broken body to drag around. Oh, I kept walking, I kept smiling, I kept pretending……because it was the only way to stay safe, the only way to keep living. The minute you let them know you are in pain, they gather round to watch. That's when they get their greatest satisfaction, to know that you now carry their pain for them, and they can go on relieved because they did their duty.

But I had to stumble on alone searching for relief and a way to make sense of what had happened to me. And that's how I began my journey home…..walking through my time in the scorching, empty desert of life, searching for an oasis of love and nourishment....believing that I was separated from others....believing I was unloved.... believing most painfully that I was separated from God and outside God's love. The pain of that was excruciating.

Little did I know that God was with me all along....taking me through powerful transformations and reshaping my soul, heart and persona. I didn't understand that then. It was like being the lone survivor of a plane crash in a desert in a foreign land. You're injured, you're exposed, you're exhausted, you're thirsty and hungry all the time, and there is no one around for miles and miles to turn to for assistance, directions or shelter. Nothing looks familiar and you think you are the only one out there. Even though I lived in a city, I always felt alone and isolated because there was an invisible wall of separation between me and others. It's energetic, not physical, and exists within the human aura. It was placed there through the rituals I was taken through. The wall was made of shame, trauma and fear and it was so thick and invisible that I didn't even know I was inside of it. I thought it was normal, that there was something wrong with me, and that I was just inferior to other people. I was unable to see my own light and realize that I had everything I needed to survive and prosper. In fact, I was actually Divine, a fragment of God's soul in human form.

They had accomplished their task...for a time. I lived inside a partial internal darkness but with my external light still showing outward. Others could see it and would tell me so. I was still able to heal people, speak to people and help people, but I was suffering on the inside...and it was invisible to me. That was the skill and thoroughness with which they had covered my True Self. That was the spell they had placed upon me and my thinking that made me believe I was worthless and shameful to the world.

And that turned out to be the mission assigned to me by my Creator. My soul remembered it one day much later in my journey....

*I am going to drop you down inside a place of darkness, with people who have lost their way and are in terrible pain and confusion. They can't see their light or their Oneness with God. You will be their light. They will attempt to take it from you. They may hurt you. Your mission will be to protect your light and your soul. You must also take on the energy of their pain and transform it back into light. I've given you the ability to do that energetically. That is your gift in this lifetime. There will be many who bring their pain to you and many who will try to take your light. Stay the course. After you have transformed this energy, you must share this wisdom with the world. We warn you, there will be danger along the way, beings sent to stop you, obstacles almost too huge to overcome, and unexpected difficulties and interruptions. But remember always…. we will be here to assist you - Angels, Guides, Masters and Loved Ones, all of the realm of the Holy Spirit - ready at your call to come to your aid. The opposition will attempt to make you forget we are here, but I will constantly remind you. They will cast a spell of forgetfulness and confusion over you; you must bring yourself out of this. That is how your soul gains strength. Pray unceasingly, it will bring you power, faith and courage. In the accomplishing of this task you will receive great gifts. They are for you to discover along the way. It seems clear to you now, but once you descend into the realm of dense matter, the clarity of the truth will be harder to see. You will have to find it amongst the lies and deception. Know that we will be loving you always and that we are not separate from you, only in a different form. Our energy matrix intersects with yours because there is but one connected consciousness, a unified field. But for a time, you will carry a dense human body over your energy field. It is that body that will bring confusion. We give you these gifts to take with you to use on your journey…..joy, love, healing, creativity, intelligence, charisma and the power to transform everyone you meet to light. But you must remember you have them. Go now and take the journey of life……*as the memory of my soul's **dharma*** faded, I saw myself enter physical form and begin the **Dharmic*** path.

When I was among the walking dead, separate and walled off, I didn't fully remember my mission. A shroud had been cast over me. I was too overwhelmed with emotional, mental and physical pain. But it called to me from within my soul steadily. I couldn't ignore its presence or its voice. It showed up in so many places, so many ways. As I worked through my pain, I asked for that voice to guide me. And slowly it did but I often didn't realize it. I had to learn to hear the voice and recognize the guidance. That took a long time. Messages came my way that I must have missed, or I didn't understand. They were hidden in the wind, delivered by people I did not know, left for me on restaurant tables, in post office boxes and at grocery stores….they floated down babbling brooks I sat by and were mirrored everywhere in nature. My eyes were clouded and my heart was in pain so these messages could not penetrate then. But the Universe continued dropping me clues, as it does for everyone, if we only listen.

The lessons continued on seemingly endlessly for a while. Some of them were years long in resolving. The act of working them out developed soul muscles, emotional strength and courage. Each recovered piece of my soul returned to me power lost or stolen. Each part carried lost information, misplaced purpose and long forgotten Akashic memory. I was Humpty Dumpty and had fallen off the wall. There were a lot of broken pieces. Slowly I pieced these lost parts back together to remake my soul. It was long, slow process. But this was a process likely begun in earlier lifetimes. This was the lifetime I came to finish the job.

While I was healing, I lived in my small self….the person I was taught I was. I had diminished expectations, missing motivation and was always prepared for the worst. It was very hard to believe in anything. That had been systematically taken from me. Whenever I tried to believe in anything, my father would go out of his way to sabotage it. So, I slipped into my small self to escape detection, to escape punishment. I needed them to forget about me completely so I could concentrate on healing myself. Even that was a decision I didn't make consciously. My higher super-conscious, or True Self, was handling things deep on the inside while my scared ego self was coping on the outside. The separation between them meant that the ego persona that fit into the groove I was expected to live in dealt with daily issues. The fires of transformation continued on inside, often without conscious knowledge. Except when there were flare-ups of illness or extreme emotional pain.

And this is the universal model of **Programmed Survival*** within the death matrix of diminished consciousness that rules here. The traumatized person learns to live in the traumatized society, whether that is I or someone else. It's true for us all. My story may seem extreme, but as I walked through the dead zone a while, I found so many others just like me, with different twists to their trek. They were taking their own long walk through the dark night of the soul. I observed their journeys, heard their stories, worked on them, helped them, met them, became their friend, their healer or their guide. I came to fully understand what makes someone go into the dark; they were trying to bury the truth of not being loved. Eventually they get stuck there and couldn't find their way out. The enormity of the pain here was not lost on me. It drove me to find the solution to our agony. I care too much about everyone not to try.

In order to end the suffering you enter into a bargain with yourself and society. A bargain thought to keep you safe from the constant barrage of the persecution of a deceptive, violent culture. Instead of breaking free and expressing our Divine Nature, which is fluid, loving, free and limitless, we settle for **The Program***, the hemmed-in, squared-off set of values that is drummed into us from birth. The fear of confronting the culture is greater than the promise of self-realization at this stage. The gifted child as I was, was too gifted, too truthful and too threatening for the patriarchal status quo of a society steeped in fascism, sexism, racism, ageism, silence, oppression and greed. The voices of the deprived, starved and dying were ignored amongst the fanfare and worship of the rich, arrogant and bloated. We are like sticks of kindling thrown into the ovens of capitalism, fueling their dreams of death yet clinging to our visions of a new life.

> *We are like sticks of kindling thrown*
> *into the ovens of capitalism.*
> ~ *Salini*

The fertile soil of dead dreams and lost American values made a rich crucible within which my soul was incubated along the way. I was the child of the visions of our white founding fathers - fair-skinned - free to worship and live as I please. Or so they promised. But I was also the amalgam of those whose bodies and souls they walked upon to arrive here. They could deny those voices whispering in the background; but I could not. I was born here in the blood-drenched Earth of my ancestors so their blood was my blood, their memories my memories and their lineage my lineage. It mattered not that my skin was white this time because my soul was rainbow-colored. I knew I had been each one of them in other lifetimes, that time was relative and I had been with them when they fell, or were hung, shot, sacrificed or died of the fever. I felt their souls as I took each step…I heard their yelps and wails as I moved through their lands… my beautiful Native brothers and sisters galloping across the prairies on painted ponies, proud-sharp cheekbones, feathers flying behind….mitake oyasin Sitting Bull…. .Pocahontas…Crazy Horse….. Geronimo …..Chief Joseph….Sacagawea…..Red Cloud ….Black Elk and millions of other lost indigenous souls ground under the conqueror's boot…… And again in the Chinatowns of the West I smelled the rich aromas of exotic dishes and felt them penetrate my soul and enrich my spirit…..the soft, lilting sounds behind swinging red-tasseled lanterns and bright Asian lights masking the deep sorrow of an ostracized culture steeped all at once in delicate beauty, ancient tradition and grinding poverty......And then I walked through the barrios and trailers of southwestern farm workers sweaty with thick, bushy mustaches and Spanish passion dripping from their bodies and faces as they waltzed to the mariachi's song and wailed under the machete's blow. ....Then I traveled on down into the Southern ghost plantations where I could hear the ancient cries of grief of long-dead African mothers whose enslaved families were not even theirs to command, who could lose a child one day on the auction block as easily as we send a newborn male calf to slaughter without ever knowing the comfort of his mother's teat. I heard their deep, resonant voices singing the blues from the Savannahs of Georgia and South Carolina, to the cotton fields of Alabama and the graveyards of Mississippi and on to the gin joints of New Orleans. .....yes, their agony was mine. I felt my bones shake and shiver in an earthquake of their pain rattling up my spine. And all the melting pot of nations and cultures who arrived here to start again and became one soupy stew called the American Dream, the Land of the Free and Home of the Brave....and I ate this stew and drank this soup and became one with the entirety of the American Soul.....yes, this land was my land. Yet I looked around and I saw people of every color, race, culture and tradition and realized we were living in a steamy, vibrant casserole of diverse souls, the new world where we become one. When I heard and felt these things, I felt a deep energetic roar rise up from my soul. It was a flash of connection, a moan of recognition of their pain, and a rhythm in time with the pulse beat of their soul. I felt the Universal cosmic rhythm go down....fa so la ti do... ... solfeggio...... 528 kHz ....and knew we were one and the same...our souls were one.....we marched to the beat of the same drum.

And it was then their souls became my soul, it was then their pain became my pain and it was then their memories became my memories. What was done to them was done to me. It was then a healer was made, it was then a shaman was born out of the mud and mulch of a dying world once called America. And it was then the voices of those gone before me…..who left me their legacy of pain, truth and suffering….asked me to speak for them. I saw them in my quiet time, I heard them in my meditation and they told me their stories. And their story was my story, even though I was a white child, I was still a woman and we know their pain. Yes, we women know what pain is. And in a severely patriarchal society like America, a woman is less than any man of any color. In the world I grew up in, a woman was even less than that. Our deaths meant nothing to men whose greed and ambition exceeded their compassion. We were fodder for their empires. They had lost their way and hurt the world, and in doing so were killing their own hearts alongside of ours. I know because they brought those hearts to me to heal. And they gave me their pain. But they still didn't see. Even they were my children. And I the Mother to them all. And I welcomed them into my heart.

And so I was qualified to speak for all my ancestors - red, brown, black, yellow and white, male or female. All their oppression and suffering had culminated in where we stand today, with entitled capitalistic males continuing to rape the land's resources and leave the bodies in their wake, to be buried by the lowest among us, burying their own brothers and sisters. And so an American shaman was born, but I was a shaman for everyone. Because now the blood, bones and voices of our ancestors had all merged together as one here in this time and place called America. The indigenous prepared the way by caretaking the very land they died on, the Africans built the country upon their enslaved backs where they suffered to give birth to America, the Chinese built the West and the railroads to connect us to one another while they disappeared in the background, the Mexicans tilled the land to grow our food and feed us only to be relegated to the barrios and fields for the life of a peasant, and then the Irish, the Slavs and the Italians came to labor and start businesses to bring culture and commerce to our empty lands only to lose it to gangster bank-sters, and soon the Jewish people came to bring their brilliance and vision to further develop this place only to be sacrificed in the name of greed, and all the other beautiful cultures who came to taste the land of milk and honey….the Japanese, Koreans and Vietnamese, the Persians, Sikhs, and Hindus and Muslims, the Northern Europeans and Southern Africans and the South Americans, until there was no more distinguishing between us all. We became one people, one planet, but still we were plagued by false and meaningless illusions of separation. We had work to do and I saw it so clearly during my long walk in the darkness.

I was born a healer from a long lineage of healers, but I became even more. I became the crushed spirit and voice of a once beautiful land and its valiant and hard-working people who had been betrayed once more. Yet another treaty was struck between the white man and the peasants of the land. Another written promise by the bankers and the government to the people, but once again it was nothing more than the lie of the rich and powerful. The sugary sweet deceivers who bring false hope and promise to desperate souls in exchange for something we hold that is sacred…our souls. But this time the treaty was made between white on white and everyone else with the promise that our land would become strong and our people prosperous if we but let the rich bankers guide our business and monetary interests. We believed in the American Dream so we signed on to that treaty. And so we find ourselves today alive, destitute and heart-broken upon the once proud land of the free and the brave. And I found myself carrying that wound for us all. The Chiron wound of the wounded healer.

So, at first I lived the life of programmed survival we are all taught to fit into the white conqueror's world here. The world created by and for white male authority figures, not for all the rest of the world of people. After all, I had been programmed to be the kind of woman they wanted who was always ready to appease men - blonde, busty, beautiful and blue-eyed. How disappointing for them that I also turned out to be intelligent, soulful and powerful. No wonder they had to crush me. I was programmed to agree and to defer to their wants, needs and system despite having a vision so far beyond anything they could conceive of in their comfortable, ego-centric worlds. That vision no one wanted to hear. Any mention of it brought more derision and laughter, and sometimes abuse, down upon me. "You want to heal people?" I heard them snicker. "You think a new paradigm is dawning with people waking up? You see a vision of a healed society where people work together in cooperation and good will? You want to help build it? Good luck. Just get a job, shut up, work hard and don't make waves. That's how you will survive." They advised me. The Dean of the University I attended was especially cruel to me, laughing at my career aspirations, spiritual practices and humanitarian efforts. "Ha-ha, I'll bet you stare at your navel all day don't you? You bring food to poor people, big deal. I know about women like you. And we don't want your kind at our institution. After all, you're just a woman. Just get married and keep your man happy. You've got the body for it. That's the only way you'll survive." I remember this arrogant, well-paid, highly esteemed Dean of the University I attended with the lives of thousands of students in his hands telling me as I was being advised about my future career. But I didn't want to be a sex object or just survive; I wanted to thrive, to grow, to create, to heal, to expand, to love. But those opportunities were denied me. I was a woman, a sex object, a sex slave. I couldn't fight that reality then. I wasn't yet whole. So I withdrew inward and gathered strength.

I found that the energy it took to hold back the pain and suppress my true, divine, powerful self was so great that it left me exhausted all the time. I did not have my full resources at my command. They were compromised, stolen and partitioned off still. And I still didn't know.

So, I limped along like that through many years of growth. During that period I was sick a great deal. I had always had migraines, which are a sure sign of buried sexual abuse, and stomach issues like nausea and indigestion. But as I moved into the thick of the transformation I began to get much sicker. The mental, physical and emotional toxins of a lifetime of abuse were emerging. The onset of the worst of it was my separation and divorce, which was devastating to me. Everything changed in my life then. As I grieved out my husband, I first got pneumonia which led to Chronic Fatigue Syndrome. My immune system was weakened by all this and flus were common. A couple of years later I experienced the viral meningitis episode, triggered by the memories of sexual abuse, which changed the direction of my life completely and placed me upon the path of the healer/shaman. A life-threatening illness is quite often the initiation of a healer. So is being born into a lineage of healers and having a shamanic dream that guides you to heal. I had all three several times over. After already having multiple initiations, it turns out I had many more to come. Each one brought more lessons, more vision, more healing power and more wisdom. Chunks of my old self were falling away. The new pieces were being rearranged into a new and more powerful person. Someone who was becoming whole.

But first you have to integrate the energies and the lessons. When moving through what I call a **Soul Transformation***, you go into survival mode. Everything becomes very challenging suddenly. Your previous life comes to an end and something takes you over. You are powerless to stop it, you may not understand it, but some kind of process is underway. You know something is happening and it's probably frightening to you. And you have no idea how long it will take. Suddenly, all your energy is needed elsewhere. You can only do minimal tasks. Non-essential activities are discarded. House-cleaning drops to the bottom of the list as do all things that utilize too much energy. You don't have the energy to go out and do social activities with people because your body and soul are moving energy around. And it takes energy to move long-stuck and toxic energy up and out. You never know how you're going to feel. You never know if you will be sick the next day very suddenly. And you can't be sure you won't have a panic attack or a wave of horrendous emotional pain hit you suddenly. Chronic Post-Traumatic Stress Disorder is the order of the day. As the healing progresses, waves and waves of ancient wounds come to the surface to be healed. Some of them are physical, so you may get sick or very tired. The symptoms are varied and hard to pin down. Rashes, vomiting, exhaustion, dizziness, shooting pains, you name it, it could be anything. The energy is on the move after having been stuck throughout your life. Doctors won't be able to figure it out because it doesn't fit into their allopathic view of disease maintenance. They will tell you "It's all in your head" or "There's nothing wrong with you, or "you're being overly emotional." In the meantime, you are in constant pain, can't eat or sleep and are having panic attacks.

Some of the waves are emotional, and they sometimes make you sick. But those wounds can cause crying jags, emotional outbursts, and torrents of strange emotions you are unfamiliar with that debilitate you but have to be processed out. Some of them are mental, words spoken harshly, verbal abuse, toxic belief systems, bullying and the lies of a culture steeped in violence, racism, sexism and classism coming to consciousness. You will feel them coming out, maybe even see them. Your soul is rejecting the lie and the confinement and reclaiming its space to be whole. Those energies have to be sorted out, examined and rearranged into a holistic, awakened and cogent way of thinking that respects your soul's journey. And finally, spiritual wounds from ancient traditions of religious separation, worn-out creeds and beliefs that judge others, keep you down, and separate you from God. All these energies will surface during a Soul Transformation and will swirl around all at once, forcing you to constantly meditate, ponder, rest, cry, isolate, release, heal and transform these experiences. You are given no quarter, no break and often, no compassion from others. But once it starts, there's no turning back.

Here is an amazing story of transformation and love –

<u>Jared's Reiki healing story</u> – I met Jared when I returned to college years later. He was in the counseling program with me. By then, I had an active, busy healing practice and was working all over town in various capacities. I began working at the Gay Resource Center as one of their staff counselors. I taught group therapy, couples therapy, addiction recovery, codependency recovery, and individual therapy. I was the only straight counselor there, but that was never a problem. I loved LGBTQ people and they loved me, and it had always been that way. Jared and I became friends there. His partner, Stephen, was also my friend. Jared had AIDS and had been plagued by a series of complications and illnesses common to the illness then. One day he stopped coming to school and there were rumors he was very sick. I left messages for him but didn't hear back. After a while, I received a call from Stephen. Stephen and Jared knew I was a ReikiMaster and respected my work as a healer, minister and counselor. Stephen told me Jared was very ill and in the last stages of AIDS. He said Jared was in the hospital and wasn't expected to live much longer. Jared was asking for me to come to see him in the hospital. Stephen asked me to come down to give him his last rites. I agreed to come to the hospital.

Upon arriving at the hospital, I was told that Jared had slipped into a coma. The doctors did not expect him to wake up and said that today was probably his last day of life. Stephen nodded and said that's what they were telling him. He asked me to give Jared a Reiki treatment, make him comfortable and help cross him over to the other side. The doctors were fine with it. I went inside Jared's hospital room to be with him in his final hours.

What I knew about Jared's life and family was that his father was a fundamentalist Christian minister, all fire and brimstone and bellowing God's word. He was well-known in town for feeding the homeless and helping the less fortunate and was a humanitarian. He was a good man. But his fundamentalist Christian faith prevented him from accepting Jared's sexual orientation and lifestyle. He refused to believe Jared was really gay and thought that somehow he could convince him otherwise before he died and save his soul. Right up to Jared's deathbed scene his father sat there trying to get Jared to convert and repent. This just made Jared sicker and lose hope. Like so many gay people, he was dying of rejection and lovelessness. I suggested to his father that this was the time to just love and accept Jared and that that was what he needed to hear most from his Dad before leaving Earth. His father just broke down and cried. He said to me, "I love him no matter what, but I just want him to make it to Heaven. I want Jesus and God to love him." I replied, "Don't you think they already love him? Isn't that what God promises us? After all, God made Jared and Jesus loved all the sinners. It's just you who's struggling with it. Try to just accept Jared as he is. God has made a place for him at His side. Jared needs to hear you say you love him anyway because he really loves you." I never believed Jared or any other gay person to be a sinner, but that is the belief system of Jared's father so that is the language I had to use to break through to him. His father burst into tears and said, "I'll think about it. Please help him." And he left.

Inside the room, Jared was in a coma. I took my place at his head to begin a Deep Soul Reiki Treatment, Mental and Emotional. I began to give Jared a mental treatment. Earlier, he had told me how painful it had been throughout his life to be gay in his father's house. He had to keep it a secret and he knew it would hurt his parents, whom he loved dearly. He had told me many stories and cried many tears about humiliation and judgment he had suffered at their hands. I remembered these stories as I began working on Jared. I asked his soul to release all untrue statements and to embrace its divinity. I asked all the hurtful memories and words to leave Jared and to leave him free and in peace. I asked love to return to his body, mind and spirit.

I continued on treating Jared in silence for about a half an hour more. My eyes were closed, I was meditating and asking God to help Jared. Suddenly, I heard Jared's voice speak softly to me. "What are you doing?" he said to me. I was jolted out of my concentration and opened my eyes. Jared was awake and out of his coma!!! "Jared!" I nearly shouted. "What's happening to you?" He said, "I don't know, what are you doing to me?" I replied, "I'm removing negative thoughts and feelings from you Jared. What's happening for you?" Jared spoke back to me so softly, "I can see thousands of harsh, angry, negative words and statements floating up and out of my head! It's amazing! You are removing all the hurtful things people said to me. It's like a long string and it's coming out of my head and going up to Heaven. I feel so much lighter." I jumped for joy at hearing this. "That is so fantastic! Let's keep going then. Maybe we can get rid of it all." I kept working on Jared a long time while he told me what he was experiencing. He told me that as extra hurtful statements were leaving, he felt an increased sense of peace and less physical suffering. He said he could see all the words exiting from his crown chakra. That was right where I was working on Jared. After a while, Stephen came into the room. When he saw Jared was awake, he was overjoyed. "I can't believe it!" he exclaimed. "Teri, what did you do?" "I gave him a full Soul Reiki Mental and Emotional Treatment, Stephen. The works." Stephen started to cry.

Long story short, Jared stayed awake. In fact, he improved quite a bit because of the mental and emotional relief achieved during the Reiki treatment. Reiki had removed the energy of the feelings and thoughts that were causing Jared so much internal suffering. He told me those were the feelings he had carried his whole life that had hurt him so. Now they were gone. The doctors were shocked and even asked me what I did. I told them about Reiki, what it could do and what had happened to Jared. Jared got well enough to go home. He was well enough to enjoy another 3 months of life with Stephen. And he enjoyed those 3 months in relative peace, without the agonizing emotions and thoughts tormenting him. They were the happiest 3 months of his life he told me. His Dad even told him he loved him.

Jared passed after 3 months, but he didn't even need

to go back to the hospital. He was doing well enough to stay home. He left Earth in peace, quietly in his sleep one night, without the lifelong agony of the judgment of others. Reiki had solved another life problem, even if it didn't save the life.

Jared had actually begun a Soul Transformation some time earlier. He used to tell me about it. He wanted to become a different person entirely. He had always been so timid and self-effacing. He wanted to leave the past behind him, the way people treated him, the church that judged him, and be a more confident, self-loving person. That's why he had begun going to school. He had begun making some of these changes anyway, but his illness caught up with him. He changed his beliefs, thoughts and actions but it wasn't going to end the condition he had been carrying for many years. In some cases it does, but not this time. He did, however, go through a very dramatic inner change during the time I knew him. A Soul Transformation can take many forms. Some of them end in recovery; some of them end in leaving the body behind. But the end result is the same. The transformation is achieved, the soul has changed course and is walking towards union with God. Sometimes that has to be completed after leaving the body. I was able to accomplish that and stay in my body. In Jared's situation, he accomplished enough change to be able to go home with his partner and have a joyous three more months of life. Sometimes that's enough.

If you have entered a crisis of some kind, it's likely you have begun a Soul Transformation. Whenever dramatic change is upon you, the Universe is asking you to change direction. You are off course of your life's Dharmic purpose. You are being redirected to the correct path for you. This is where all the criticism begins. People who have not begun a Soul Transformation will not understand what is happening to you. If their lives, their jobs, and their finances are stable and comfortable, they will not be interested in your suffering or your journey. They are enjoying their lives. Their egos are in a comfortable place. They will find your actions and experiences to be odd, and sometimes frightening to them. Perhaps even threatening. They may judge you for even going through what you are going through. They will give you tons of advice cached in standard cultural wisdom and clichés, most of which comes from the perspective of their comfort, and usually won't be helpful. They may even be arrogant about it. If you can, forgive them. They cannot see that you have begun a Soul Transformation because they have not yet begun one. You will enter into this journey largely alone. There will be a few beautiful souls along the way who will stand by you. They may stay a long time, or it may be brief. But treasure them. Like an oasis along an endless, dry, desert caravan, they are great gifts along the way. Know that they have been sent by the Holy Spirit to help you endure the transformation and awakening of your soul. Nevertheless, prepare yourself for rejection at this stage. Many will abandon you. Your old life will fall away. A chasm of the unknown now faces you.

You have entered the ***Garden of Gethsemane****.

For those of you keen to have a spiritual awakening, I caution you. Awakening is very traumatic. Change requires sacrifice, and the death of the ego is the price you'll pay. It won't be comfortable, but it will be incredible. I'll share more about my journey from time to time. But from here I move from my story into the Universal story of humanity, a story far more significant than mine. It's a hero's and heroine's journey, the path of the hobbled soul entering into yet an-other sojourn in human form, attempting to shed the illusion and awaken to the truth, the journey everyone is taking. This story started with me. But over time, with the continual death of my ego, it became more and more about us all. The "I" started disappearing as I began to merge with the Divine Mind, the Oneness. There are many incredible stages to this grand opening of the sacred lotus self. So, here we go.

Change requires sacrifice, and the death of the ego is the price you'll pay.
~ *Salini*

At some point in your Soul Transformation, if you keep working at it, you will arrive in the Garden of Gethsemane. Once there, like Jesus discovered, you will begin to find yourself alone with your journey and in solitude with your suffering. Because you are moving out of the dualistic mind, those around you still living in duality will naturally walk away. There is no place for them in the Oneness you are realizing as long as they perceive in duality. You will be speaking a foreign language to them. They sense that you are rising in consciousness, but will likely not understand it. It will make them uncomfortable because you are changing the rules of how you inter-act with them and the world. They may not be ready for this. They may even try to stop you from growing and awakening. They will probably silence you and tell you that you're "negative" or a "downer" or "can't you just have fun". They won't want you to change unless they plan to come with you. And few of those from your past life will want to come along. Feeling the pain of the world that accompanies the One Mind is not something very many will choose. Just accept them as they are and keep going. Always love them unconditionally if possible. If and when they are ready, they may join you. But you are already on your way and must not tarry behind where the old beliefs keep you in bondage to the illusion. If you do, you will find you suffer much more pain.

But the most painful part of the Garden of Gethsemane is when the betrayals begin. You must understand, you have begun a journey to spiritual awakening. No, you aren't just sick for a little while. No, you didn't just get a divorce, have two car accidents, go through bankruptcy and lose your job all at once. You're having a Soul Transformation. You're waking up. Your true soul path is unfolding before you. Don't be afraid. Surrender to the process and allow the river of transformation to take you downstream.

In some cases, loved ones will have legitimate cause to be angry with you. You've changed. Maybe you've let them down. Maybe you lost your job, got sick or couldn't help them anymore. Maybe you broke a promise to them even if you couldn't help it. As much as you love these people, once you enter a Soul Transformation, you may not be able to fulfill some of the promises and obligations you made to them. You may no longer have the energy, the resources, the time or the ability to do so. This will be the hardest part of your journey because you will still love these people. But you will have to move on to save your life and your soul. This will be very hard to explain and rationalize. They may walk away and never forgive you. But listen to your inner soul's guidance anyway and keep going. Ask for understanding and forgiveness. Tell them you love them and be ready to talk to them when they are ready to try to understand your journey.

The crucial question is – Will you be betrayed
by others or will you betray yourself?

If you ignore your soul's urging to change and grow, you are betraying yourself. How many times can you do that before this lifetime is over? Hopefully you will stop betraying yourself and step into your divinity.

In the Garden of Gethsemane you will try to bargain. You will bargain with your friends. You will bargain with your family. You will bargain with God. Like Jesus, you will ask that this cup pass from your lips. You won't want to taste the bitter taste of the shedding of the ego that is coming. You won't want to lose the old life, the dear friends, the family members. Those still firmly entrenched in their egos will think you insane, a loser, deluded, a "conspiracy theorist", a fool, lazy, spoiled and many other epithets you can expect to be hurled at you. But you are none of these. You are simply in the midst of a total rearrangement of your soul, mind, emotions, personality and life. Your friends and family will not recognize you because they remember you as you once were, with your ego intact, interacting with them in the same old way. But you can't help it. You aren't that person anymore.

You may still try to hang on to your old friends. You'll want to bring them with you. This is a path you don't much want to walk alone; there is terror and the unknown along the way. Some of them will come, for a while. Some of them will stay because they love you even though they don't understand what you are going through. Those are the purest of gold friends. Nothing deters them. They will be there when you emerge at the other end as well. And rest assured, you will emerge. Bless them. But many of your dearest and closest people will suddenly, and quite harshly, betray you. They will toss you on the pavement like last night's garbage. They will erase your phone number and tell you never to return. They will judge and laugh at you as they do this. You will feel the blade of the knife enter deep into your heart where it will stay forever. Your heart has been ripped open. You thought these people would always be your friends. But your love for them made you vulnerable. You've experienced the **Great Wound of Compassion***. The same wound Jesus took for us. This wound will either open you to unconditional love or harden your heart. If you pass this test, and all these trials are tests of spiritual awakening, you will become the door for many others to cross over into awakening and unconditional love. So, do you wish to be an open door or a closed door? This is what is being asked of you by God. Those who betray you are giving you that great test by ripping open your heart so it can expand to unlimited proportions and include everyone, dark, light, bad, good, whatever judgments you place upon others. Unforgiveness closes down the door to your heart. But forgiveness will lead you to the open door. Try for that door. Behind it is peace.

When I passed through the Garden of Gethsemane I could never have believed that people whose lives I had saved, who I had given money to, healed them, loved them, nurtured them, given them everything I could give them, would turn on me when I was at my very lowest. As I dropped down into the transformation, I started to lose everything. During these times none of those friends stepped forward, they all walked away in judgment and scorn. Instead, it was strangers who helped me. People out of nowhere would come forward to assist me, obviously sent by God. They would guide me to new homes, new jobs, and new opportunities. And soon, I realized the fair-weather friends were not missed, because the new people stepping forward were solid and made of God's stardust.

The Garden of Gethsemane will last until you have died the death of the ego of that part of your life. People fall away who cannot follow you where you are going, some of whom are **energy vampires***, or who want to hurt you. Let them go. You are being prepared for something else. You are shedding your old suit of clothes and adopting a new lifestyle. Once you have fully made that shift, the betrayals die down. They may continue here and there, but not usually as powerfully as the first one. If you aren't making the transition into your higher self, the Universe will have to get your attention. Sometimes a strong Garden of Gethsemane is the way that happens. A sudden and sharp betrayal, like the disciples with Jesus in the Garden, a loss of power and friends, a stripping of your life and substance, a swift kick in the rear into a new life. This is known in shamanic circles as a **dismemberment***.

A dismemberment event is a common and well-known experience in indigenous tribes throughout the world. When this begins happening to a tribal member in some of the African tribes I studied, they prepare a place for that person to go heal and pass through it, sometimes for years. In one tribe, all teenagers go through this and often live in a hut together for 3 or 4 years until they finish their transformation. In America, if you begin to have some sort of transition that appears to be a breakdown, you are often taken to a mental institution, hospitalized and drugged. The dismemberment is then interrupted and the soul cannot complete its transition into its true soul purpose. The appearance of a shaman and true healer into a tribe is often marked by a breakdown, an illness, an epiphany, a crisis, a tragedy, change or a huge trauma. This is that soul's moment of trying to integrate new wisdom, power and purpose directly related to the culture they are living in. It should never be interrupted, judged or suppressed. This person has arrived to help save the consciousness, heart and soul of the tribe. In suppressing this rising shaman, you cast a death sentence over that person and block the healing of your tribe.

The onset of a dismemberment is a moment of joy, honor and excitement to awakened people in indigenous tribes the world over. In America, the appearance of a true **shaman*** is not honored. We crush our shamans and healers and relegate them to the edges of society while the rigid, unawakened medical and professional authorities reign. Their ignorance has left our culture in shambles while everywhere there are real shamans and healers among us who could heal our American tribe. Although this is changing for the better, it's not changing fast enough to outpace the destruction being done to Earth. I know many gifted healers and shamans who are ready, willing and able to heal our tribe. Let's celebrate and welcome them home and place them in positions of authority and honor. Let's pay them well and house them and bless them. In other nations they are given housing, food and are respected. In Native American tribes, they are the most respected member of the tribe. Although I have been consulted by doctors, counselors and other professionals, they don't often wish to pay for my healing work or wisdom. Our services are not valued. By and large, shamans remain exiled on the outskirts of a society dying of a mortal illness we have the cure for. I pray you allow us inside the circle of your hearts before it's too late.

I remember when I had my dismemberment vision. I went to a shaman for a journey. This is what I saw:

Salini's dismemberment story - *I was doing a **shamanic journey*** with a powerful shaman. There were no drugs involved. She had the drumming going in the background as I lay on a sheepskin surrounded by feathers, stones, crystals, smoke and other shamanic tools. She sent me to travel down deeply into the underground hole at the base of the tree of my subconscious mind. Alice's journey in Alice in Wonderland is a metaphor for a shamanic journey. I found myself suddenly in the company of many people. I was at some kind of fire ceremony. I was on the ground for a while until I "awoke in the dream". When you awaken in the dream, you awaken in your subconscious mind. This is where your true soul purpose is held. You may not know it consciously, but you will know it subconsciously. As I moved through my subconscious, I saw a road ahead. I began walking the road. Suddenly, a group of monkeys flew towards me in the journey. They came to me and landed on my shoulders. They each grabbed an arm and ripped it out of its socket. There was no blood, this*

was in my subconscious only. I kept going. Soon, other animals came and each animal took a body part off my body until I had no human form anymore. I was just a spirit walking through an unknown land.

I saw my True Spirit, beautiful, etheric, an energy field that extended far beyond human boundaries. I felt its power and strength as I walked. Then I saw a Native woman walking towards me. She was wearing a long, white buffalo skin dress with fringe, a beaded breast-plate, feathers in her hair, a buffalo skin and pheasant feather shawl around her shoulders and a crown of beads, stones, claws and feathers. She carried a pipe in her arms and was surrounded by a great aura of power. She summoned me to sit with her. I approached and she bowed to me, I bowed in return. We sat on a bear-skin rug facing each other. She pulled out the pipe she was carrying and began to pack it with something. No words were spoken. She lit the pipe and began taking deep breaths in, holding them, and then exhaling. She did this several times until the pipe was hot, fiery and glowing golden. She then handed it to me. I took the pipe gingerly and placed it to my lips. I felt the smoky heat on my mouth as I placed it on my lips. I inhaled deeply and felt the energy of power enter my being. I held the smoke in and saw a vision of myself.

I was riding on the back of a large white female buffalo that grounded me to the Earth. On either side of me were two male lions as guards. In front of us were two wolves, male and female mates, who went ahead to scout the path. Above me was an eagle to see far beyond into the vast unknown. On my shoulder was an owl which helped carry my wisdom. And behind me was a vulture which cleared the energy. There were many foxes, rabbits, mice, bobcats and other small animals trailing behind, part of the earth family. Then I heard the woman speak into my consciousness. She said, "You are one of the White Buffalo Women who have come to heal the Earth. Wherever you go, you will clear a wide path of negative energy away. Many will heal who cross your path. Your words will be powerful. The vultures behind you will eat up the negative energies and digest them into the ethers. You are needed to heal Mother Earth. Just keep walking forward. You will be shown where to go and what to do."

I exhaled the smoke and as I did, the vision disappeared. I looked up and the woman was still there but was slowly vanishing. She looked back at me, handed me a feather from her crown, and was gone. Suddenly I was back at the fire. There were shamans chanting and drumming and dancing around me as I lay on the ground. My body had been reassembled. I felt the vision be drummed into my soul. I lay there awhile until soon I was walking back up the hole in the ground at the base of the tree. I emerged back onto the Earth. Then I heard the human shaman speaking to me. "Are you awake? Are you with us now?" And I returned to this time and to this world. The journey had ended but the vision remains with me forever.

This is the essence of a dismemberment. I experienced this during the worst of my transformation. Every time I did a shamanic journey, it helped to re-seat me in my body and back into my true soul purpose. Then Reiki would smooth over the transition. Utilizing both techniques, I did many such journeys. And I have conducted many such journeys for many clients as we all awaken to our true soul potential here on Earth. When you are experiencing trauma and transition, you need to go on a shamanic journey. It is there you will be guided as to where the path next leads you and helps to heal your soul and body.

But perhaps the hardest part of the journey of dismemberment includes being eaten by the *spirit-eaters**. What does that mean? As you are being dismembered and rebuilt, you will be eaten by the vultures of life, people and spirits who exist as parasites off others. Vultures have their purpose too. They are needed to clear the dying matter to make way for the new. Your old self is dying; it must be discarded like a dead body. But it is an *energy body**, not a human body. The vultures will come for it. Sometimes spirit-eaters are part of the dark side who are attempting to take over your soul. This is distinguished from those spirit-eaters who are here to help you transform. There is a difference. Learn what that difference is and you will be in charge of your own power and being. If you can help it, do not be afraid because fear attracts the wrong kind of spirit-eater. Even if you have to leave your body, do not be afraid. It's part of the process of awakening. But if you hold fast to your spiritual practices, you will rise from the death of the old self into your new self and will remain here. It will be a joyous event. It will be a resurrection.

But during the time of the feeding of the spirit-eaters and vultures, you may well be at your lowest point. I remember when I had breast cancer. I was too sick to deal with business or make much money. I was desperately in need of help from somewhere to help me with finances. There were many wealthy people I had helped who could have assisted me. Instead, while I lay near death, people close to me came and began to devour my assets for themselves. I begged for their help, instead they stood by to see if I would die. I was too weak to resist so they took all of my assets and property and I was left bankrupt. It happened to me several times during my

Soul Transformation. Like someone injured but alive lying by the side of the road after a car accident, I saw people come one by one and take my things. They fed off me thinking I was dying. It seemed like a living Hell. But then when I survived the cancer, they ran for the hills thinking I would come for them. Little did they know I had gone past them. I saw them for who they were finally - desperate, tragic figures who believed they had to take the last dime from a sick woman to survive. They continued to live on in their dark dungeons with their gold like Harry Potter's goblins hoarding their wealth. That is the time of the feeding. You will be stripped of everything. The vultures will come and feed and you will hate them, for a time. Then eventually you will move even past them. And maybe you will even come to pray for their awakening. Because at some point, you may have been like them too.

It is at this time that you will begin to awaken to how this experience is repeated throughout our culture over and over and over. The merchants of death who run our nation and the world and have set up the death machine around us for their profit. They will ensnare you and strip you of your money, resources and life force. You will pass through many types of near-death experiences until you learn to rise up beyond them. This is a time of powerful lessons. You must bring up your soul power that has lain dormant. Stay awake. Embrace the lessons and you will gain power.

As I awakened to the realities of life in a culture that blocks consciousness, I began to exit the matrix. There was little for me there. My ego was dying. I no longer craved recognition, possessions and monetary gain. I began to long only for peace, love and serenity. When this happens to you, know that you are in the middle of the death of your ego, a Soul Transformation. The world no longer holds attraction, desire and stimulation for you. You are beginning to identify with the One Mind.

The penultimate stage on the journey of the walking dead will be the crucifixion. This is the great lesson Jesus' life held for us. Regardless of your beliefs, and every religion has such a metaphor, Jesus' life can be a perfect example of this journey for everyone. He brought love, truth, healing and God's power to everyone. Yet he is betrayed and sent to be judged and punished. His love is rejected; his truth denied. He is taken to be judged and sentenced by his fellow mankind, people who have yet to experience an awakening, never to have entered into a Soul Transformation. When love or truth is not accepted into a culture, a society, a tribe or an individual, the person who offers them will be either punished, exiled or crucified.

Honesty towards your brethren is the highest form of love, yet often the most reviled. To tell someone an important truth is an act of love. Your honesty brings healing to that person and shows how much you really love them. Yet prepare to be reviled for this. Of all the gifts offered in the world, love is the one most hated, punished and crucified. Especially if it's love in the form of truth. Should you arrive at the point where you are ready to love everyone unconditionally, prepare to be crucified first. This is what Jesus' life showed us. This is what a Soul Transformation is all about. Unconsciousness. Pain. Death. Rebirth. The cycle continues. But the final lesson, the most important of all, is still to come. The moment when you are resurrected into the whole being you really are. That is the true goal of this long journey through the dark night of the soul. If you survive the tests and trials, it is resurrection you will achieve. But before we go there, let's examine the many obstacles, lessons, truths, lies and insights along the way.

Chapter 5

Initiations

Nobody is more indoctrinated than the indoctrinator.
We worship the Gods of our fathers who indoctrinated us.
~ *Da Vinci Code*

As an American shaman, I began to recognize the vast illness in our culture. Like an indigenous Native, I was born, bred and raised here. Like them, I came from the soil here, the canyons, the seashore, the mountains, the plains. I felt the heart of Mother Earth beat in my chest. When she cried in pain, I felt her tears in my heart. I held old-fashioned American values. I loved baseball, apple pie and Christmas. I marched in parades…I loved my country and my people - of all races, creeds and religious persuasions. I had hopes, dreams and respect for our country and our people of all creeds who worked so hard to build this land. I was still a child then. But a healer was being born.

We had become so out of balance, so violent, so obsessed with material greed, so focused on war and unconscious to those around us who were destitute, homeless, diseased, addicted, lost and orphaned. Only the rich, warlike and powerful were heralded. The rush to "make it" as the next trendy millionaire, or billionaire was on, like the Gold Rush of the 1850's. Stocks, Wall St., corporate takeovers and mergers, endless military maneuvering, hostile business wars, were the order of the day, and all for money. The dead, dying and environmentally raped lay by the roadside of the corporate American "dream", or more accurately the American nightmare.

A new form of slavery began to emerge. I realized it long ago when I first began writing this book over 20 years ago. I realized it long before it became trendy to speak of it, but the impact of awakening to this was so traumatic I fell silent for a long time. And I was threatened. The persecution I was experiencing for telling the truth was frightening and crippling. I couldn't break through. Everyone ran on a circular treadmill within a small cage built for them by invisible megalomaniacs, soulless bankers and greedy opportunists. But it led us nowhere except deeper into striving for expensive nothings, with no substance, that were never paid for, and never reached. I saw no end to it as we all worked harder and harder for less and less. It began to make my soul very sad, outraged and despairing. And, as a healer and empath, I began to absorb the sick energies of our American tribe. It wasn't just my family's dysfunctional sickness, it was everywhere in American society. We weren't working as a team like African tribes do. We weren't sharing everything like indigenous South American tribes do. It was dog eat dog, every man for himself, may the strong survive. Half of all Americans had cancer. More than one third of the country was addicted to cigarettes, alcohol or drugs. Our young people were being brainwashed by video games and television. Mothers were all working and children were home alone. People were disconnected from life. Everything was breaking down. And I felt all their pain. Because I never separated from my tribe, I kept on loving them. I kept on holding them in my heart. But it hurt too much to do that. As our culture broke down, I broke down. I was the microcosm of what was happening to America.

I needed a rest from all the pain. I didn't know where exactly it originated from. So, I stopped striving and began to just feel, listen and go inward. It was there I heard the great mournful wail of the heart of the Mother, and I knew she was suffering. But no one was listening. Was I the only person who heard Her? This was more than twenty years ago when I passed through the depths of my Soul Transformation. No one was talking about it. When I tried to discuss it, everyone silenced me in fear. Do not speak of it, they whispered, for fear of …..what? So, I observed, and I documented and I felt it all.

As a shaman of your tribe, you will know what to do to heal your tribe. But will the tribe accept your remedy? Other tribes will, but so far, not ours. I realized that the process of breaking down our clear thinking, our powers of observation and our intuition had begun a long time ago. People had become desensitized to violence, pain and suffering. Chemicals were dumped into our bodies, minds and foods. We were being lied to, deceived and brainwashed. But just how did they do this to so many of us? Where did it begin? One of the unexpected pieces of wisdom obtained during my enslavement was learning how people were initiated, brainwashed and mind-controlled. Once I healed myself, I realized it was happening to everyone else without their knowing. Here is where you first began to lose your power. Here is where the initiation into the abuse of power begins. Here is where and how they've planned the takeover of your soul.

Edward Bernays was a famous psychologist, observer of society and was Sigmund Freud's nephew. He was also Freud's follower in the study of the human mind and how to manipulate and control it. Dr. Freud, however revered, was sadly mistaken about so many things, especially his theories on women, sexuality and the roles men and women play in society. Even brilliant men like Freud succumbed to the ancient patriarchal notion that women were inferior and hysterical due to the huge inequality in power and status of the genders during his time.

But his work, and that of his nephew Edward Bernays, point to an underlying desire for power over others that is a theme throughout history, and continues on in the chronology of understanding the human mind. This theme runs deep in the hearts and minds of aspiring dictators, corporate CEOs and megalomaniacs everywhere. We are facing it again today in new and more tyrannical forms and incarnations of the abuse of power.

If we understand the mechanism and motives of the group mind, is it not possible to control and regiment the masses according to our will without their knowing about it?
~ Edward L. Bernays, "Propaganda"

Bernays became known as the father of public relations, or more accurately, propaganda. Many marketing techniques today are based on Bernays' work. And even more compelling, the intelligence community utilizes his techniques around the world today. Even Adolf Hitler and his propaganda master, Joseph Goebbels, used the propaganda techniques of Jewish Edward Bernays, to further their fascist agenda. The desire for power knows no politics when searching for geniuses to manipulate.

In his famous book, Propaganda (1928), used by dictators worldwide, Bernays argued that the manipulation of public opinion was a necessary part of democracy: *"Those who manipulate this unseen mechanism of society constitute an invisible government which is the true ruling power of our country... ...We are governed, our minds are molded, our tastes formed, our ideas suggested, largely by men we have never heard of."*

Whether or not Bernays intended this to be used by dictators or was simply explaining the realities of life is uncertain. Nevertheless, his work and writings became the Bible by which Goebbels, Hitler and the Nazi Party formed their plan of domination. And even after the Nazis were defeated in World War II, Bernays' principles were recognized as powerful and effective and a new generation of despots and dictators adopted them, driving them further underground and into the secret recesses of the human mind. Few today realize we are being manipulated by these principles every day of our lives.

You may think this isn't an important topic to address. But think again. For many years I had no idea that my experiences as a child sex slave were still in control of my life. But they were. I couldn't have imagined that I was still dealing with the effects of the mind-control program that I was put through so long ago. It was so effectively hidden, locked away and silenced that even I didn't realize it was still operational. I didn't know that many of those programs were still sabotaging my life as an adult. But once I realized it, I set about dismantling and deprogramming them. But even more shocking than that, once I began dismantling them, I realized that many, many, more programs were in effect all over the world that were affecting people negatively without their knowledge. The discovery of my own programming gave me a window into the vast, secretive world of psyops, or the mental programming of all Americans, and people throughout the world. It extends far beyond my experiences and permeates the lives of everyone today to one degree or another.

If you don't allow yourselves to become aware of this and protect yourselves, you will definitely become a victim of psychological warfare, or mind-control, in some form or another. Mind-control is the new battlefield of today. Controlling how people think, what they buy, how they vote, what they believe, how much information they have and how unaware or willing they are to be controlled is a sophisticated, secretive, billion-dollar business. Knowledge is power and withholding knowledge from the masses for just the elite few is one of the main ways they control you.

Few people stop to question how power is being utilized over them, yet every single day of every person's life there are programs designed to control you in effect. If you aren't thinking about what power you have, whether or not you have control over it, or who else might have control over it, than you aren't thinking clearly or powerfully. If you are not aware of your own power and how to use it, I guarantee you others are and will use it against you effectively and secretly without you ever knowing it.

As I mentioned in earlier chapters, I was initiated into several different disciplines of healing as a child by my mother. I was taught Reiki at a very young age. I was given instruction in meditation, prayer, Buddhism, Christianity and other forms of spirituality. In some of these situations, I was given spiritual initiation. For example, I was initiated into First Degree Reiki as a young girl, then later the higher degrees of Reiki. This enabled my healing abilities and increased the power of my energy field. I was also baptized as a Christian as a child in the Methodist faith. This placed my feet upon the path of Christ and connected me to Divine Protection and God's love. Later I was blessed by the Holy Mother Mata Amritanandayi on the path of the Divine Mother, an all-inclusive universal path which I now teach. This further opened and healed my heart so I could love and heal others. But inbetween I experienced other initiations, like graduating from high school, getting married, giving birth and becoming a mother. Each of these experiences is a form of initiation into a stage of life. Each of them carried certain power and wisdom along with them. Those were the positive initiations.

Initiations are a vital part of being alive and of having and managing your power. They mark stages of growth, passages in life and moments when power is bestowed upon someone. Passing through various initiations is a vital part of establishing one's position in the tribe, the amount of power they will have relative to their skills, their work, their value to the tribe, and their future within the tribe. Most cultures have multiple initiations throughout the lives of their members, especially early in life when the child is about to become a man or a woman. In America, we have very few initiations of real power, except maybe weddings and graduation day. We are a blended culture of many tribes and after many generations don't often know what traditions our ancestors had. Additionally, American culture does not value or honor the initiation process as seriously as other countries, cultures or tribes do. Whatever initiations we do have come from other cultures with a few exceptions.

So, we've left the back door open so to speak. Without initiations into our personal power, our soul power and our spiritual power, we are vulnerable to others who have been initiated into power. But that doesn't mean they've been initiated positively. On the contrary, they've been trained to take power from those who aren't paying attention. If we don't claim our power, someone else will. It's that simple.

Positive initiations that bestow power upon a culture are, for example, the Bar or Bat Mitzvah, the Jewish faith's celebration of a young man or young woman coming of age. This is the most important ritual of initiation for young Jewish men and women. They gain power as full-fledged men and women of their culture. I was struck by the sense of community and respect and the way they gave that young person purpose in life through the ceremony of initiation. Power, discipline, direction, connectivity to community and self-esteem is gained during this initiation. Sadly, we have no such ceremony in standard American life. Our power is left raw, exposed, undisciplined and unguided. And ripe to be picked off by predators.

In Hispanic, Native American or other indigenous tribes, initiations and rituals are extremely important to the maintenance of the culture of the tribe. One North American Native ritual is known as the Sun Dance and is practiced by the Plains Indians. The Sun Dance is a sacred power ritual. In the Sun Dance Ritual, men are fastened by rawhide thongs to a pole, which is then attached to the skin of their chests. They pray, chant or dance during the ritual. They do this as an offering of sacrifice for their families and to gain vision and power. Indigenous peoples have many other rituals such as the Sweat Lodges,

Prayer Ceremonies and Coming of Age rituals too. All of these mark important milestones in the lives of Natives and others that give them power, direction, faith, support from nature and from the Universe, connection to their ancestors, protection and help for their tribes, and even rain for their crops.

I once attended a Hopi Rain Dance Ritual with Kachinas on the hilltops above the plains where they grew their crops. The ceremony was outside the kivas on the Hopi Reservation where the Hopis prepared and went into an altered state, emerging as Kachinas. The Kachinas, who were all men, danced for three days without speaking to anyone. They were inbetween worlds gaining power, favor, gifts and information for their people. This ritual was for bringing down rain on their parched crops. After the 3-day ritual, within an hour it began to rain hard on the colorful, dry, patchwork squares of corn, vegetables, sunflowers and other basic crops the Hopi survive on. The Hopi Kachinas had contacted the Nature Spirits and brought down the rain for their tribe. All true shamans know how to do this kind of ritual. I was honored to be asked to participate in the Hopi Rain Dance Ritual as Mother Earth while the Sacred Hopi Clowns performed their part of the ritual. It was an unforgettable experience that deeply moved me. Afterwards I was showered with gifts by the Hopi people, all handmade items and foodstuffs. I felt the power of their unity enter into my body and earthiness of their souls touch my soul. I am proud to be part Cherokee, but nowhere in my white culture did I ever see or experience such magic and power, except with Reiki, which isn't white or American but is universal. It made me sad to know that we had lost so much as white pioneers as we settled the land and carved out the American empire. Now we must all find healing.

Each initiation or ritual is significant to the interconnected structure of the people of each tribe. Like a spider's web, we are all connected by a matrix of energy. Maintaining that matrix is vital to keeping the community intact, the world functioning and sustaining people's character and souls. It is important to our cultural health that we find rituals that help us heal, grow and receive power and strength. If we stop having rituals and initiations, others will step into the void and take our power.

Those are the positive initiations. But there is another kind of initiation entirely that is far more prevalent today throughout the world than people have ever known. It is the other half of the energy field of the world and it's going on under your noses. Few people will ever learn of these rituals yet they are often ruling their lives. These are the rituals that are kept secret from everyone and are practiced and taught in dark rooms, dusty basements and silent graveyards. These are the dark rituals and initiations of power. This is how souls are stolen.

Unless you have experienced it, it will be hard for you to believe just how powerful, far-reaching and frequent they are. Yet they go on somewhere in the world every single day. These kinds of rituals are bestowing another kind of power on those who participate. And this is not a power you want to have anything to do with. Yet for many, they are affecting their lives without their knowledge because someone you know was initiated into them and brought that energy into your life. These are the rituals that are destroying the very fabric of America and of the world and are tearing us apart as people. It isn't random, it's organized, and they have a clear agenda, to steal your energy, your soul, disempower you and eventually push you off the planet. This energy has become a huge part of the structure of our society. It's time to bring them out into the light of day. Only then can we understand, disempower and dismantle them for good.

Lessons Learned in Sex Slavery & Mind-Control

Since I was privy to both the dark and the light initiations and saw how powerfully they were affecting the world, I knew I must share the information with everyone. I was too young then to understand what was happening or the significance they held. Nevertheless, once experienced and learned, they become buried in the psyche of the inductee and are often forgotten. Yet, they will direct and guide that person for life. These people then go out and influence our world. Many of them are in positions of power and are acting unconsciously. But, once you are aware of what rules you, you have the power to end it. And if you wish to fully awaken, you must end it and clear yourself of these energies.

So, in order to help you rid yourselves of these ancient energies, I will explain them in detail. They range in degree of severity from harsh to lighter, but unless you know they are there, you have no power over them. But they will continue to have power over you.

The basis for all dark initiations is to induct someone into a covenant of fear and shame and separate you from God. Although the initiations may differ, they all have the same intent, to diminish you and bring you under their control. Once they have terrorized or convinced you that you are separate from God, they begin stripping you of your power and life force and either keep it, or give it to whatever dark entity they worship. You are nothing more than fuel for their power games. In some cases it's whoever the little God of that particular group is. In others it's just power and money. Still others have occult attachments, and others are focused on sex. Some are demonic. But some are just corporations, cults, organizations, religious institutions, fraternal organizations or families. Sex is a major part of many of the dark initiations because it is where power is seated in the body and how group leaders gain domination over others. So, below are the various types of initiations and how they affect someone. You may not think they apply to you, but often these can be done secretly to people or when they are too young to remember, or while someone is unconscious.

As I grew old enough to reason, I began to observe and take note of the initiations and how they were impacting people. I noticed that there were very rigid types of behaviors, rules and circular patterns inside the rituals that were a required part of how they were enforced. They brought this programming out into society and used it on people everywhere. They all fall under the category I call the **Covenant of Shame***, or initiations into shame and separation from God. Once initiated, they form a group and it becomes a group shaming covenant which can go on for life. Once you are shamed you become bonded by the **Shame Core***, an energetic field of shamed words, thoughts and experiences- like a spell - that keeps you trapped in a lowered state of shame consciousness where your power is lessened. It keeps you even away from God because with a strong shame core, you don't feel worthy enough to let God into your life. And if they can keep you from God, they have you. Once you realize your Divinity, you are free. So, these are the lessons of liberating yourself from shame, fear, suffering and hatred.

A perfect metaphor for this is the Blue Crab Syndrome.

There is a large bucket filled with blue crabs sitting on the seashore. Inside the crabs are cramped and crawling around on the bottom of the bucket. One day, one of the crabs decides to try to climb out of the bucket. He begins his climb. He nearly reaches the top but whenever he tries, the other crabs pull him back down to the bottom of the bucket. He tries again and again but every single time they pull him down into the bucket. "Why do you keep trying?" the other crabs ask him. "Because I want to see what's outside of this bucket we all live in," He answers. "There is nothing outside of this bucket. This is our world and it is the entirety of it," The other crabs tell him. "You need to learn to be content just living here with us in the bucket." They told him.

"Maybe, but I'm going to keep trying," says the lone crab. One day he makes it to the top edge of the bucket and falls to the sand outside. He looks out at the open ocean stretching as far as the eye can see and smiles a crooked, crab smile. He swivels one crab eyeball back a moment at the bucket and ponders what to do. He realizes he can't tell the other crabs what he's discovered because they have accepted their reality inside the bucket and cannot see what he sees. He turns and walks towards the ocean and slowly disappears into the sea. A whole new life stretches out before him.

This is the reality of those trapped in the Covenant of Shame. They are surrounded by naysayers who laugh at their aspirations and beliefs and sap their power, preventing them from reaching their potential. But if one blue crab can make it into the vast ocean of possibilities, so can you.

Because we are one unified field, one human consciousness here on Earth, when one person, ten persons or 10 million persons have been affected and shut down from functioning due to unseen programs of control, it affects us all. And it impairs the overall functioning of society, even if we don't know about it. It becomes our responsibility to help our fellow men and women overcome these issues so our society returns to healthy homeostasis.

We begin with the more severe initiations and work back to the lighter initiations to help you understand the power these have in our culture. The worst of these initiations are the shaming covenants, which endeavor to terrorize the person, or child. These groups are primarily satanic. They exist everywhere and are very well organized and secretive. This is going on around you all the time whether or not you realize it. The child will be forced to witness ceremonies of death and rape and be told that they are part of it and they caused it. They will be told if they don't cooperate that they are next to die. This is called trauma-based mind-control or **Satanic Ritual Abuse, SRA***. But all sexual trafficking organizations and pimps utilize this technique as well. And it will continue until the child or adult exhibits the personality traits and thinking desired by the group abusing them.

Terror and trauma are continually introduced until the child or person is sufficiently traumatized, which likely isn't very long. They have created a **Traumatic Shock***, or **Traumatic Event***, so severe that it stops normal brain function, and freezes and imprints the event into the person's mind. It blocks the neurotransmitters from firing in the brain and breaks down the energy matrix that spans the brain and keeps it functioning and communicating. The person will lose memory as the connections break down. This effectively disables certain brain functions. These experiences will likely be so traumatic that the child's brain will partition them off separately outside of conscious awareness. This is the genesis of bi-polar thinking and behavior. And this is a survival mechanism the mind has in place to keep a person alive during a life-threatening event. The programmer does this intentionally to create multiple personalities that are easily controlled. When the powerful, unified energy of the brain matrix is divided this way, it lessens the power of the brain itself and makes it easier to control. It's literally a matter of reducing the brain wattage, or dividing its forces, to a low enough level to make that person's brain malleable. A mind-controlled slave of some type is being created.

When an event is traumatic enough to cause split off fragments of memory to develop, this is the onset of the **Traumatic Trance***. With a Traumatic Trance, a frozen state of unconsciousness is permanently locked into the moment of the traumatic event. The greater the trauma the deeper the amnesia. All future behaviors, actions, perceptions and feelings from then on will stem from that traumatic event. But it will be unconscious to the entranced individual. Defending the suppressed memory of the trauma becomes the goal of the entranced individual but they won't know why. They do not want to remember or re-experience the trauma; that's how deeply The Traumatic Trance then becomes the trigger and focal point for manipulation of an entranced individual because terror now holds sway over the person. And that is when someone begins being mind-controlled. A person can stay in a Traumatic Trance for life, or it can be shattered by another traumatic event, an epiphany or a Soul Transformation. But for a mind-controlled or bi-polar person who has had this experience, only a true spiritual intervention and awakening will heal it. Counseling will never be enough. It requires spiritual force to unravel the programming and reassemble lost parts. This kind of experience is the precursor to a spiritual awakening, so a ReikiMaster, shaman and or spiritual teacher should be brought in to guide you through it; someone familiar with healing *Soul Trauma**, *karma** and spiritual issues. Until their trance is shattered, they will be manipulated and mind-controlled by the person/s orchestrating the trauma. Sometimes they are sent out into society to act out, commit crimes, etc. and are controlled by handlers.

This state of mind will begin to create a bond with the abuser that is known as the *Traumatic Bond**. A Traumatic Bond is a close relationship formed with your abuser based on the taking of your power and the adjustment of your thinking to align with your abuser's desires. Your mind has once again slipped into survival mode and if getting along with your abuser is the only way you can survive the situation, you will bond with the abuser. This is common with battered wives and children, prisoners of war, hostages, sexual abuse victims and victims of human trafficking. This condition is known as the *Stockholm Syndrome** and is a form of mind-control.

A perfect example of a Traumatic Trance and Traumatic Bond, or *Traumatic Trance-Bond**, is the kidnapping, imprisonment and subsequent transformation of heiress Patty Hearst.

Patty Hearst's Story - *Patty Hearst, the grand-daughter of newspaper mogul William Randolph Hearst, was kidnapped in 1974 by the Symbionese Liberation Army, called the SLA, as an act of revolution against the wealthy establishment. The SLA demanded Patty's father distribute $70 million dollars' worth of food to the poor of California for her safe return. Her father distributed $6 million dollars worth of food. But instead of returning her, Patty was subjected to physical, sexual and mental abuse and mental programming while locked in a small closet. She was deprived of food and water and given LSD in an effort to mentally re-program her into thinking as a revolutionary. After a long period of this kind of mental and physical abuse, Patty began to exhibit signs of bonding with her captors. She joined them in a bank robbery and even shot up the front of a store with a machine gun to cover the escape of two SLA members after they robbed the store. All of this is classic mind-control and TranceBonding.*

She was captured in 1975 and tried for bank robbery. She identified herself as "Tania" when captured and declared herself a revolutionary fighting for the liberation of the poor. It wasn't until Patty was safe and away from her captors for a period of time before she finally returned to her former self. She then described the brainwashing and abuse and tried to explain to people what it was like surviving in a situation like that. She was still found guilty of bank robbery and sentenced to 35 years in prison until President Jimmy Carter commuted her sentence. She married and returned to a normal life without incident and recounted her ordeal in books and film. In 2001, Bill

Clinton pardoned her completely. But she remains a textbook case of TranceBonding.

Once a person is terrorized to a degree beyond where they can protect themselves or control their self-image or their power, they are malleable and their power can be stolen. As this process progresses, the mind is completely rearranged, split apart and controlled until you no longer know who you are. This is why they begin the initiations in early childhood, to control the young mind before it can decide for itself. These types of initiations are known as **Fear, Shame and/or Sexual Initiations***. All activities conducted within these initiations are directed at shaming, scaring and dominating the child/person. The act of shaming a child or person successfully is when the power is stolen. That stolen power is then used against others to further control and dominate people.

Sexual trauma is usually part of these types of initiations. Sex is the most powerful way to completely disempower someone and render them under your control. This is done because they understand that if you enter the chakra system and forcefully take power, the person and that chakra is open, weakened and vulnerable and forever marked and enslaved. It is through sexual initiation that most of the magical power is extracted. An invisible energetic connection is made between the abuser and victim and the victim is marked for life. That energetic mark is recognizable to all other secret society members. Individuals in these groups are well aware of how to use sex magic and how to take it from an innocent person. In fact, it is innocence they are looking for to refresh their polluted, dead souls.

So what we are talking about here is nothing less than the stealing of souls of humanity. It's going on every day. It's spiritual warfare and it's very real. This may seem incredible, but look around you at those battling their "demons", and the kind of corruption taking over our nation. That is spiritual warfare. We are all challenged to stay strong in our good intent and avoid temptations around us. Every day you are faced with choosing good actions or negative actions. Each choice you make determines the amount of positive or negative energy that comes your way. If you choose to aspire towards good actions, more good energy will surround you. If you choose to participate in negative actions, that energy will gravitate towards you.

You may be thinking, this doesn't apply to me, it never happened to me. But the truth is there are millions of Americans who went through some form of trauma-based programming. The reason this applies to you is that of those that were members of special groups or secret societies and especially trained, they were placed in positions in society for the purpose of controlling world events from their jobs and positions of power. Some of them are judges, lawyers, doctors, military personnel, teachers, politicians, stockbrokers, counselors, media people, businessmen, college deans and any number of careers. They were placed where they could be the most effective at controlling the actions and thoughts of others to shape the world they envision. You simply need to know this is going on if you want to maintain control of your own power. If you don't, they will use your unconsciousness against you.

There are many more initiations such as, religious initiations, drinking initiations, gang initiations, fraternity or fraternal order initiations, family initiations, money initiations, business initiations, emotional initiations, military initiations, intelligence initiations, government initiations, artistic initiations, physical initiations, tribal initiations and power initiations. These initiations range from light to very serious. Some are simply a fraternity initiation where you have to get drunk and run naked through the street before becoming a member of the fraternity. Others are more serious such as gang initiations that involve murder. Inbetween these well-known types of initiations are the secret initiations into secret societies. And even deeper, are the initiations into mind-control and sexual slavery. Those who graduate from the latter category and go on to work in certain jobs will not know that they were pre-selected and trained to go exactly into that type of work. They will not know they have been prepared through mind-control. But they will follow their masters, whoever they may be.

Many of you may have seen the old movie, <u>The Manchurian Candidate</u>, with Frank Sinatra, Laurence Harvey and Angela Lansbury, released in 1963. The story centered on a young man, played by Laurence Harvey, who had been mind-controlled by his mother to assassinate a political candidate. Frank Sinatra was trying to unravel the mystery and help Harvey get free of the situation. Harvey was completely unaware of his programming which was triggered by the use of the playing card, the Queen of Diamonds.

This movie was a very accurate portrayal of the kind of standard mind-control that has gone on in America since after World War II to the present to millions of Americans. Then CIA Director Stansfield Turner admitted to a Senate investigating panel on August 3, 1977, that the MK-ULTRA mind-control project was very real. He went on to report that the CIA had spent millions of dollars on mind-control research. Director Turner further disclosed that the CIA had been conducting mind-control on huge numbers of unsuspecting victims for years, since World War II, without their knowledge or consent. These CIA mind-control operations were carried out with the partic-ipation of a least 185 scientists and at least 80 American institutions, including prisons, pharmaceutical companies, hospitals, and 44 medical colleges & universities. Many of America's most prestigious institutes of medical research had cooperated with the CIA. Many big name corporations also allowed mind-control experimentation to take place within their organizations. This report by CIA Director Stansfield Turner is a matter of public record now as all these secrets are being revealed. Only recently are the victims stepping forward to report on what they experienced, saw and learned through these horrific programs.

Another form of initiation is that of the **scapegoated** or **targeted child.** The scapegoated child is the child that is expected to carry the family's pain so the rest of the family can go on living without any pain or consciousness of the suffering of the family as a whole. That child is expected to be accountable for the emotions and sick behavior of entitled, unconscious family members. Sometimes it's intentional, other times the whole family is unconscious. But in every instance, the family remains in total **denial***** that anyone but that child has a problem. Every flaw falls to that child. It's usually the weakest or youngest child of the family with the least power or position. The targeted child will be the punished child. That child will live up to the family's expectation of them being the loser, the bad child, or the black sheep because that is what they were told they were to be, however subconsciously. Once a scapegoat is chosen, whether that be in a family, in a culture, or in a nation, the punishment begins. The scapegoat in any system can expect to be blamed, mistreated, exiled and ridiculed. In cases like with the Jewish people, or African slaves, their fate was obviously far worse. They were at the bottom rung of power. Those above them had free rein to project their pain upon the chosen scapegoat.

I remember one family where their youngest of three sons and three daughters was always punished for everything more than the other children. He was yelled at, beaten, punished and blamed for things out of his control and for his parent's rage. He saw himself as the bad child and often said it out loud. He ended up going to prison and never really became functional. The treatment he experienced was an initiation for the purpose of keeping the family functional. He portrayed a role for the family, a role that might even have had a certain place of honor because it made it possible for other loved ones to function. The rest of the family has to go on making a living, raising kids, maintaining the house, etc. so if there is a targeted child around, the pain that impairs their progress can be laid upon this child and they can keep going. This child will develop illnesses and problems throughout life. That child may even die young. They could have entered counseling of course, but few families do. This is an ancient and common initiation, known as the scapegoated or targeted child.

In many families whose members do not wish to be accountable, the mother will be blamed for everything. This is a very common and subtle initiation/myth in our culture – *Mother-Blame**. This myth is a vital cornerstone of the patriarchy which exempts males/fathers from any responsibility for their contribution to family problems or bad behavior, enshrining their entitlement and lack of accountability like a golden rule. It's right up there with blaming women victims for getting raped instead of males being held accountable for their own lustful behavior. These are cultural myths and initiations into an unbalanced, patriarchal society. And they hurt everyone, especially women.

In families, there are always special initiations related to family, to their national origin and to their specific family legacy. Like Irish families where drinking on St. Patrick's Day is a time-honored tradition. Or children expected to follow their parents into the family business, common amongst immigrant families. This is a business/money initiation that is common amongst families that own small businesses and wish to pass them to their children. Even more business initiations are parents who teach their children the specific trade the parent is in, like the construction industry, or entertainment parents who bring children in to show business. An even more dangerous initiation is that of teaching your child to become a sharp business practitioner, or to learn the trade of white collar crime, which can be easy to get away with. This crime has become an acceptable money initiation in our twisted, greedy society. Boys, or even girls, who follow their fathers into Wall St., hedge funds, corporations, law, intelligence positions, arms dealing and other similar business learn the art of *Collateral Business Murder**, or destroying the lives of others for your own financial gain. This is a financial initiation for which they are rewarded. Amongst wealthy, entitled males, this is an honored practice, even if people die as a result of their business dealings.

The accumulation of wealth has come to supersede all other principles of life in America to the expense of the planet, its inhabitants and the very soul of humanity. This is what's destroying the world, the worship of the god of money rather than the true God of life and love.

~ Salini

We've all seen the wreckage in the lives of people whose life savings were stolen by the Bernie Madoffs of the world. Collateral Business Murder is on the rise globally with corrupt corporations and billionaires raping the resources of the world, and is now resulting in mass deaths of whole cities, nations and villages of people for profit. I am not referring to the many good men and women who run legitimate honorable businesses to support their families and raise their children. Business with integrity is something to be proud of and to teach your children. Large corporate business for profit at the expense of humanity, nature and your soul for riches galore is not a goal to aspire towards. We must take a hard look at how greed has infected our soul's morality like a toxic virus and made us callous to the suffering of the less fortunate the world over. If you choose to run large businesses, make sure the profits made are not from the sweat of some 7-year-old's brow working 12 hours a day to make your phone, your clothes or your coffee. Make sure you haven't poisoned the water supply of some community or taken over their land so they cannot grow enough food for their own villages. Make sure you aren't planting GMOs which kill off future generations. Because if you do not, you are soiling your own nest and poisoning the society you live in by bringing your torture home to our culture. Remember, your every action is carried with you in your Akashic Record into your next life. That which you do on Earth boomerangs back to you, be it good or bad.

Female initiations can be like little beauty queen preparation for life to turn you into a seductress and money magnet. Or for women, they often receive the emotional initiation where they are expected to be the emotional baggage carrier for the family. That female child will soak up all the hurt feelings of family members and sometimes becomes a healer. But before that, they will often get sick from carrying the emotions. Or they can be sexual, where you become the objectified sex object for males and are used for your sexual abilities which extend into prostitution and trafficking.

But what's really happening here with initiations is that the energy baton of some career is being passed to the next person. If it's a power initiation into dark power, the initiate will be expected to do something that creates receptivity for the dark power. When the initiate submits, they are submitting to the power of another. Their power is taken from them. But later, after they have demonstrated their allegiance to the power and willingness to get more power for their master, they will be promoted and power will be given to them. When this happens, an energy baton is passed. This occurs in most all initiations of men in power in various organizations. All allegiances will be to the dark power organization, never to their jobs, families or country.

When the energy baton is passed, they then are authorized to take power from others. When this occurs, a new leader is born who goes out and wields their dark power in the world. This is happening all around us all the time. The people in positions of authority in our government and other institutions are filled with a mixture of well-intentioned people and people who have been initiated into darkness. Of those initiated into darkness, they have been given assignments to strip people of their power through television, video games, the law, courtrooms, taxation, breaking unions, lowering wages, imposing unnecessary and unconstitutional laws, controlling the media and other forms and methods of slowly and methodically taking away your power. This is happening to you right now every single day. If you do not make an effort to stop it, you will be initiated into slavery and lose your power, resources and position in life.

That's the bad news. The good news is that for every dark initiation, there are twice as many positive initiations into the light, into God's grace. The initiations I experienced into healing, love, light, meditation and God, were more than enough to counteract the dark initiations I experienced. My energy field was filled with God's healing energy and it worked its magic on my soul and my heart. These are the kinds of initiations we need to work towards. Going into spiritual practices, praying daily, meditating daily, chanting a mantra, visiting a holy temple or church of some kind and joining in with other worshipers, reading spiritual literature, and most of all giving selfless service to those who need it. These kinds of actions initiate you into God's grace, heal your energy field and restore you.. You will be protected, loved, healed and guided.

But none of this is possible if you don't know that you are being manipulated by other forces. Finally, our society has become infiltrated with darkness of all types - physical, mental, emotional and spiritual - and all of these dark toxins are controlling and diminishing your power. We have chemtrails poisoning our soil, air and foods every day. We have a mind-controlled television and media service that is training children to be dumbed down. The movies have become increasingly violent and sexual and when this happens, we are desensitized to violence and sex in a way that makes it seem acceptable to children. Now we have entertainers that are brainwashing children to be over-sexual at younger and younger ages. This is a direct effect of pedophilia in entertainment and these pedophiles came out of mind-control programs. They bring you pedophilia daily in your TV and movie programs. They are creating a violent culture of violent young men who go out and kill for thrills, do school shootings, and can't distinguish between a video game and real life.

There are chemtrails, fracking and environmental destruction, all designed to diminish life. There is chemotherapy, which was developed from the leftover byproducts of chemical warfare from World War II and was developed to make money only, not to heal you. And we have pharmaceuticals, all designed to suppress immunity, not heal you. These are the byproducts of an underground system of initiates who learned all this as children or as young adults. They worship the Gods of their fathers who indoctrinated them and they are pushing this agenda into your lives, your bodies and into your souls.

In fact, their main belief system is that death is more important than life. They believe they have the right to take life, to manipulate life and to end the lives of all who get in their way. This is why you **MUST** know they exist. Their goal is to take your power, diminish your life and eventually take your life through one of the death systems they have developed and brainwashed you into thinking you need. Don't believe them. You have more power than that. And God has more power than that.

This is why I urge you to find a spiritual path that suits you. A path that has deep practices and that celebrates life, love, respect for nature and all people, that is sacred and treats women, children and nature sacredly, and one that gives service to humanity. Once you enter this path, everything will be returned to you. All power stolen will be returned, all betrayals healed, all losses restored, all pain relieved. It may take a while. It may not appear as you wish it to appear. But a new life stands before you when you look square in the face of darkness and take back your power and mean it. Turn to your heart and to love and let the light stream into your life.

Everything I have just told you is about spiritual tests along the path of spiritual awakening. I failed some of these tests. But I noticed that when I did, that test would reappear in a different form over and over until I mastered it. Until I surrendered to my Divinity. Even as you are being tested or raked over the coals by the dark, you are held by the light, just waiting for you to realize they are there loving you. As harsh as the dark initiations are, they can be doorways to your divinity. Everything is in divine order, happening at the right moment for your awakening.

The initiations into light are ALWAYS more powerful than the initiations into the dark. Remember to call upon God and the Angels, call Jesus, call Divine Beings and whoever awakens your soul to come into your life and protect you, heal your energy field and surround you with the light so you may clear and overcome any past connections or losses related to contact with individuals from these programs. Together if we do this, we will change the energies that have prevailed here into energies of light, love and healing. Together we must reclaim our world and heal it.

Many of those initiated into the dark long for release from these worlds and these persecutions that they are also experiencing. Some of them were initiated from birth and could not find a way out. Remember to ask God to heal them too and to provide a way out for them should they realize it's time to come to the light for a new initiation. I urge you to practice forgiveness whenever possible, however difficult it may be, because it opens the channels to even more light, love and energy to flood in for everyone to heal.

Prayer for Deliverance from Darkness

By the power of the Holy Spirit within us all, I call for healing for all persons and all souls ever trapped in the dark energies of persecution, occult practices, confusion, lies, fear, hatred, shame, abuse,

vows, contracts, oaths and other forms of bondage to darkness. We pray for your surrender to the light and the relinquishment of your allegiance to darkness. Deliverance is yours upon your willingness to open to love. We will be praying for you.

Chapter 6

The Sacrifice

As my sufferings mounted I soon realized that there were two ways in which I could respond to my situation -- either to react with bitterness or seek to transform the suffering into a creative force. I decided to follow the latter course.

~ *Martin Luther King Jr.*

Dr. Martin Luther King Jr. was one of my life's greatest inspirations. I remember watching him on television as a child marching through the South in front of thousands of civil rights marchers and surrounded by police, dogs and jeering racists. I was a small child but I watched in horror as the police unleashed water hoses, vicious dogs and violent men with clubs onto these innocent marchers. It was a searing lesson for a child who believed in justice, equality, respect, law and America. Why were black women being dragged and beaten by white policemen and then arrested? Why were small black children being screamed at by enraged white adults and protected by National Guardsmen just to attend school? This all seemed unfathomable to me as a child who loved everyone equally.

I asked Mom if we could help them. "Can we go down there and walk with them, Mom?" I asked plaintively. Mom replied sadly, "No honey, it's too dangerous, we could be killed." "But couldn't they get killed too?" I worried. "Yes, people will probably be killed and it's a tragedy." She cried. There was nothing she could do of course. But as an innocent loving child, I felt the sting of injustice, the grip of fear and the heat of hatred in my own chest and inside my heart, as I saw these helpless people being beaten. Then I saw a young teenage girl get slapped and dragged through the streets by a white policeman. Her shoes were ripped from her feet and her already ragged cotton dress was torn even more as she was dragged until her shoulders and back were bloody and pitted with gravel. And I started to cry, and I cried hard for their pain, for the disrespect and for the fear they must be feeling. My heart hurt a long time then. I silently apologized to them for how they were treated. I knew what it felt like. Then I whispered a prayer to God to please protect them. But then I suddenly felt a jolt of shame come my way, something I had grown accustomed to when around others in silent emotional pain. But where was it coming from? As it moved through me I could tell it came from the white Southerners involved in this and I realized they felt bad too, in their own way, for some reason unknown to me then. I felt their deep inner shame and hurt. They were projecting their historical pain out onto the easiest, most vulnerable scapegoats, African-Americans. The cycle of shame and violence from their own suffering was repeating itself again. So, I prayed for them too. I prayed their pain would be healed so they could love themselves again. I prayed they could feel good about life and let others feel that way too. I don't know if it helped, but I prayed that way a long time when I was a little girl.

Then I saw Dr. King come on TV. He was talking about freedom. He mentioned a dream. A dream of all of us sitting down together and loving each other. I felt inspired. And then I saw him speaking at a church. He talked about going up to the mountaintop and seeing the Promised Land. He talked about faith in what's ahead. His voice was explosive and his words reached deep into my soul and gave me hope and inspiration. He was the kind of person I wanted to emulate.

A person of character and courage. And I realized that the horror I was witnessing was a group of people seizing back their power from oppression. I saw that this man had been tasked with leading them there. And I realized that it took courage, faith, perseverance and COMMUNITY to get the job done. Even as a little girl, I promised God I would try to be that kind of person. Someone who cared enough to put my life on the line for what's right in this world. I saw that God was speaking through Dr. King in that moment. That the power to change was present within his soul, and all our souls....if we but came together and seized it.

But there was one last great sacrifice during those dark days, the one that finally turned the tide in favor of integration and freedom. One sad April day in 1968 I turned on the TV to see scenes from the murder of Dr. Martin Luther King in Memphis, Tennessee. I was older then. And the enormity of what we were experiencing as a nation was just beginning to sink in. Like Abraham Lincoln's assassination was the sacrifice for the end of slavery, Dr. King was sacrificed for the establishment of long overdue rights for African-Americans. How many more would have to die before we could give birth to the true principles our nation was created for? It was then that I began to see and understand the imbalances that plague our nation and the world. It was then I started seeing the sacrifices made everywhere. And it was then my soul longed for a solution and a desire to bring healing to the situation arose within me. Like Dr. King, I wanted to create a spiritual force that healed our nation. Through my tears I promised him I would carry on that healing, creative force that day. And that has been my torch and touchstone ever since.

I realized that in every situation, especially when a new era dawns upon us, there are those who are sacrificed. And in some tribes and nations, these sacrifices have remained the same for centuries. Often those that are sacrificed were done so simply because they were powerless and held no status in their tribe or nation. I saw the inequality, the imbalance, the injustice. I felt the sexism, racism, classism and religious intolerance all over again right here in my country, a nation founded to end those problems.

In America, since its inception, the peoples readily sacrificed to build our nation were African-American slaves and Native Americans. Both races were routinely killed or sold like sacks of potatoes for commerce, greed, ambition and power. Even the white women of America had no say in what went on. They couldn't even vote. This was cultural, endemic, racist, misogynistic, classist sacrifice for the purposes of building our nation. We were founded on the sacrifice of many souls. Even white pilgrims and settlers, immigrants, Chinese and others who came to make a new life for themselves here were sacrificed. There were thousands of Irish slaves sold by the British to the New World, too. Sacrifice lives in deep recesses of the ancient souls of humanity but brings shame upon our cultural soul every time it happens. It's a product of imbalance and compromised souls, from an old paradigm.

Sacrifice plays a huge part in all cultural rituals, traditions and initiations. We can trace this to earliest tribal times when virgins, children or virile athletes were sacrificed to please the Gods and better their tribe's standing. The Legend of Troy from Euripedes' tragedy, **Iphigenia in Aulis**, tells us that King Agamemnon and Clytemnestra's eldest daughter, Iphigenia, was strong and brave. Once, Agamemnon killed a stag in a grove sacred to Goddess Diana. Angered, Diana stopped the winds so that the Greek fleet could not sail to Troy to reclaim Helen, Menelaus wife, from Prince Paris. The seer Calchas announced that the Greek fleet could sail only if Iphigenia was sacrificed. Agamemnon refused, but under pressure, he gave in and agreed to the sacrifice. Beloved, loyal Iphigenia was sacrificed for war and the spoils men wish for their ego power.

Agamemnon, Iphigenia and his battle with the Trojans that ended victoriously when their Trojan Horse was brought inside the majesty of Troy's impenetrable walls, is the stuff of myth and legend. But the tradition of sacrifice is, sadly, a brutal reality deeply imbedded in ancient history…..a reality that has continued unabated throughout time. In ancient times, groups of people were sacrificed according to whoever was in power.

Sacrifice is practiced first in war and the taking of power. This ancient tradition has become embedded in the belief systems of cultures throughout the world. But perhaps Iphigenia's sacrifice had deeper meaning, and retains a powerful symbology for today's times. As a female, Iphigenia's value to Agamemnon and Diana lie only in her relationship to her father the King, and his love of her. She wasn't a soldier, a King or a man. Even though she was considered strong, brave and loving, she was the one sacrificed simply because she had no other usefulness in their day. She was not a man. And so it has been for women throughout history. The sacrifice of the female is the one of the biggest, darkest of all ancient traditions still to trouble our world today. A woman's gifts were so little valued that she was always the first to be sacrificed. And still she is sacrificed today.

Along with the sacrifices of life, there are other types of sacrifice within cultures where there is an imbalance of power. There are the **Denied*** and the **Exiled***. People who are denied are not allowed to partake in society for one reason or another. People who are exiled are sent away for some reason. Sometimes it's legitimate. Other times it's as simple as telling the truth when truth is not wanted. Where the balance of power rests upon unfair rules being followed, anyone who is outside those rules will be exiled or denied participation in the culture. Often though, the exiled person is the person the tribe most needs to heal and grow. Shamans, healers, mystics and **Truthspeakers*** are historically the ones most likely to be exiled, yet they are always the ones every culture needs to embrace to move forward. They are the ones who see, the ones who heal, the ones who prophecy and the ones who advise wisely. And an exiled master is a sacrificed one, because his or her wisdom and power are never utilized for the good of the tribe. Female shamans, mystics, healers and leaders have been exiled for centuries leaving our world bereft of sacred feminine energy. It has brought us to the brink of global destruction.

When ignorant men come to power, wise ones are exiled.
~ *Salini*

There are many famous examples of exile that point towards how leaders can miss out on their most powerful advisors when they fear the truth. A famous long-time exile is Aung San Suu Kyi, the Burmese Democracy leader. Her father negotiated the liberation of Burma from the British in 1947 and became its first democratically-elected President. Soon after, he was assassinated. In the meantime, Aung San Suu Kyi married an English scholar of Tibetan history and had two sons. She went on to the University to study philosophy and politics but returned to Burma to care for her mother in 1989. Because she was a powerful political voice and had run for President, an office she legally won and should hold today, she was placed under house arrest and kept there for nearly twenty years. Her voice silenced, no letters allowed out, no family visits allowed. Her husband died while she was imprisoned and her sons were not allowed to visit. While there she was awarded the Nobel Peace Prize, and she wrote inspiring speeches and letters to her followers worldwide. Finally her house arrest ended in 2010. She continues to fight for national healing and democracy in Burma, but the military junta refuses her assistance. She remains the political and spiritual leader of Asia, but in a form of exile. She lost her family to save Burma. The Dalai Lama is another famous exile. As the spiritual and political leader of Tibet, he came under fire when the Chinese annexed Tibet, claiming it as part of their nation. He fled to India and has remained there in exile but continues to speak out against the Chinese occupation whenever he can. His power increased in exile. His wisdom is even more available to the world as an exile where he is frequently seen on media everywhere.

Perhaps, the most notorious exile/sacrifice currently is whistleblower Edward Snowden, who took the unprecedented step of copying, securing and revealing the vast extent to which the United States has spread its tentacles of surveillance and how that is affecting the world today. Snowden's revelations may actually be the ones that save the world from total oppression and tyranny. They have been so far-reaching and explosive that it has changed the interaction between the United States and the rest of the world, as well as how we interact with one another here. Everyone is now more aware of how we are surveilled every moment of every day. Big Brother is watching, but now, thanks to Snowden and Julian Assange, we're watching back. These men put their lives on the chopping block to do a service for the world. Yet they remain outsiders in their own land. They should be honored, not sacrificed.

The exile is the person best positioned to see what's wrong with a system, an organization or other group, and make beneficial suggestions. A person dependent and entrenched within a system cannot do that effectively. But when you stand outside looking in, you see the blemishes more clearly. The wisdom of an exile should always be taken into consideration to improve the health of any tribe/culture.

Other scapegoated exiles appear in the medical field which is monopolized by profit-centered allopathic physicians who have effectively suppressed all proven, natural treatment modalities. One such hero was Dr. Royal Rife, a genius inventor who invented a frequency machine that gave off healing frequencies that matched those of pathogens in a sick person's body. These pathogens responded to the healing frequencies in the Rife machine by dying off. Dr. Rife began using his Rife Machine to heal cancer patients and was wildly successful. As a result of this simple machine's success at healing cancer, he became the object of a smear campaign. His machine was cutting into their massive profits at managing but never healing disease. He was harassed, discredited and driven out of the United States. Dr. Rife died in obscurity and his work was confiscated. Now you can obtain a Rife machine under various names. I have used this machine on several occasions and it works magnificently to heal disease. But of course, I have Reiki and my hands do it already. Dr. Rife was sacrificed on the altar of medical profits.

Another scapegoated hero worth mentioning is Dr. Stanislaw R. Burzynski, the famed Polish cancer physician who has a cancer clinic in Houston, Texas that successfully treats hundreds of patients. Dr. Burzynski advocates alternative cancer therapies and NOT chemotherapy or radiation. He is the first medical doctor in the United States to survive a more than twenty year long assault and harassment by the entrenched medical system attempting to drive him out of practice. He has been ridiculed, attacked, discredited, lied about and sued. He fought back year after year and during his ordeal of attacks his patients continually recovered. Many of his patients have brain cancer and he is one of the few doctors to successfully treat them. Dr. Burzynski's success is a powerful statement against all the unsuccessful, immune-destroying therapies out there. He is a scapegoat whose wisdom and knowledge will break down medical ignorance and stonewalling and bring us closer to healing cancer. And he is one of the few exile/scapegoats to emerge victorious.

But these are the classic examples we know about. How about the ones we don't know about? Did you know about the gifted shamans who live amongst the indigenous people all over the world who can heal you of many illnesses? I've met many of them. I am one myself. When I lived in Santa Barbara, doctors who were secretly sympathetic to holistic cures would call me on the phone for advice for their patients. They asked to remain anonymous, but several of their patients got well from healing secrets I shared with them. And of course, I never got paid. I also met a Native shaman from Montana that creates a paste that heals cancer from herbs they grow somewhere in their native lands. They perform ancient, sacred chants over the herbs, and then prepare them for the patients. This is an ancient indigenous herbal formula that has worked for centuries.

Then there was the ReikiMaster/shaman/magician from Germany who was raised in the Black Forest of Germany on the borders of the Alsace-Lorraine. He learned the secrets of healing from many different teachers and was by far the most magical person I have ever met. He saved my life from breast cancer. It was he who removed my cancerous nodules through Reiki, prayer and blessings day in and day out. Will he be rich and famous? No. Will he be welcomed and heralded for his work? No. But I will never forget him. I saw him do so many incredible and magical things that I learned that the physical laws of the Universe do not apply when dealing with someone aligned with and channeling the Holy Spirit into someone's body for healing. Miracles happened around him every day. He was a Catholic and learned exorcisms from a Catholic priest. Demons fled in his presence. His heart was wide open to love and his power was always present, but ever humble.

I met a Mexican curandera in Baja California that could dispel curses, demons and illnesses with simple prayers and holy water. Her house was a temple to Jesus Christ and Mother Mary and the forces of God were with her. These are the unsung, unknown, exiled healers and shamans that can heal our human tribe. We must welcome them in to our temple, our hearts and our lives for they are the ones who will heal our troubled hearts and souls during these dark times.

Blood of the Innocents

~ ~ ~

The Sacrificed Children

These are the exiles that can be known. What of the sacrifices, exiles and scapegoats that you never hear about? The ones most torturously exiled are the literal sacrifices, the children sacrificed in films and rituals - the sexually trafficked children. Children who are sold by their parents, snatched from the streets or bred for sacrifice and sexual enslavement. And the ones like myself, who were held in the secret society Virgin program, the Monarch sex slave program or the MK-Ultra program. All of us were used by people who wish to steal our divine life force for their own strength and power. We were the innocents, it was our blood and life force that were sacrificed for the lust and fuel of the machine that runs the **Secret Holocaust***. And add to that all the people who are trafficked as prostitutes for the modern day slave trade. These are the true sacrifices of our day and you will never hear of them. The statistics are staggering. There are at least 30 million people in the West who have gone through trauma-based mind-control, programming, rituals and various types of programming. Many do not remember that they experienced this. ***That 30 million represent those that are still alive.*** There are millions more who didn't make it. Those still living are in various stages of mental, emotional, physical or spiritual illness. No one is helping them. They work in positions of power and authority and make unhealthy decisions over us every day. They need intervention and treatment, and sometimes arrest. We need to bring this out into the light of day and create solutions not more secrets. It's time to release our fear and long held secrets.

Here is a healing story of hope after tragedy –

Chrissy's healing story *- I met Chrissy in a support group. She had been battered by her boyfriend and mandated into counseling by the court, as was her boyfriend. She was a Christian, was very devout and had two sweet boys. Their father was in prison and she was on her own, they never married. She was able to see spirits and angels and often commented on what she saw. She said she could see Angels around me. We began working together and did some Reiki healing and counseling work. After working with her a while, she was able to begin talking about what had happened to her in childhood. Chrissy was abandoned by her parents when she was young, maybe 9 or 10 years old. Her father sold her to a group of people who began using her in child pornography films. He sometimes participated. She was forced to perform sexually for years during her childhood.*

One day, Chrissy was rescued by the police after someone tipped them off there was a ring of child pornographers living where she was being held. The police came in, arrested the traffickers and interviewed her. They then took her out of the situation. She thinks she was 14 or 15 years old then, after having been forced to do this for five years at least. She was placed in foster care and given counseling. She suffered from severe Post-Traumatic Stress Disorder, alcoholism, an eating disorder and nutritional deficiencies. She had been beaten repeatedly and showed bruises and scars from old beatings. She was fearful and stressed all the time, but had a strong faith in God. The police saved her life.

Chrissy blossomed in group and in therapy and began overcoming her issues. She got a job and supported her sons as she went through the stages of recovery. Living in California had become too expensive for her, so she decided to move East. She was preparing to go. One day she called me to tell me she had met someone special and wanted me to meet him. I met them for lunch and she wanted me to check him out. I spoke with him privately and asked him if he could treat her right since she had been abused her whole life. He cried and said he loved her and hoped he would be given that chance. I spoke with her at length and she said he treated her well. I gave my blessing. They ended up leaving together to go East. A year later Chrissy called to tell me they were happily married and doing fine. She was sober, the kids were in school and they were both working. She thanked me for standing by her during her recovery. She told me she could not have made the right decisions without the female support that I and other women gave her during her critical transition from abused sexually trafficked child…to woman, mother and wife.

Reiki, group therapy and counseling, plus a strong faith in God, gave Chrissy the necessary foundational structure she needed to recover from her childhood abuse and sex trafficking. Her faith protected her from giving up and from her soul being lost completely. She was stronger than she knew but needed healthy women around her to find herself again.

In 2013, sexual traffickers made $32 billion dollars in profit. $10 billion dollars of that was in the United States. There are more than 100 websites that traffic children for pornography, sex, or

sale. More than half of those websites originate in the United States. There is a huge market for children for ritual sacrifice, sexual murder and snuff films. Every year in the USA, between 35,000 and 80,000 children are kidnapped and taken into sexual slavery, pornography, sacrifice or snuff films. Thousands of children are killed during these activities every year all around the world. These are satanic ritual practices and must be stopped. These are our littlest sacrifices.

The U.S.A. is the capital of the Sex trade.

100,000 people a year in the U.S.A. are kidnapped into sex trafficking, including children.

50% of the children will be used as sacrifices or in snuff films and will never be seen again.

Sex trafficking is a $32 Billion dollar a year business.

Trish Croace.

And then there are the school shootings. The blood of the innocents, just like in ancient times. These are clearly sacrificial in nature. No other nation is experiencing the volume of school shootings as America. ***This is a staggering sign of severe American cultural illness.*** Violence is taught, not something we're born with. We've become a nation of bullies, brown shirts and bullet addicts. And like any illness they develop from an imbalance within the psyche of our culture, with a clear origin that must be addressed. Brainwashing, patriarchal systems and the many cultural toxins are contributing to it. And as they increase, they signal the overt rise of dark power. **It will take all of us working on it, and shamans of all types to heal it.**

The Economic Policies of Death

Finally we arrive at cultural sacrifices deemed normal or acceptable to a society, tribe or culture. Like centuries ago in foreign lands when it was considered normal to sacrifice a virgin to please the Gods, we have our modern, accepted sacrifices. These we all participate in, these we must finally recognize and face. Today we see the rich sacrificing the poor so blatantly and so openly, almost like in Rome when Christians were sacrificed to the lions to appease the Emperors. It doesn't matter what color you are anymore. If you don't have money, you are sacrificed in the world of the entitled 1%. Our basic freedoms, needs and rights are going down like dominoes and many are falling by the wayside. These are cultural sacrifices deemed okay by 1%'ers, fat cat politicians and their wealthy corporate sponsors.

Let's take it a step further. In the late 1800's, a new college degree specialty was introduced as the industrial revolution boomed. It was called the Master's in Business Administration and it originated in the United States. This special area of studies focused on seeking to discover the *science of business management*. Studies were devoid of any holistic, natural or humanistic approach to creating business. There was only one major focus – making a profit. If all other concerns were *scientifically* stripped from the study of making a profit, they could teach young people to myopically focus only on the goal of making money. No concerns for how this would impact nature, how it affected the economies of towns and cities and nations, or how this might affect individual people. It was reduced to a scientific formula on a blackboard of how to create profit only, the rest of the world be damned. All the while forgetting that we live within a unified field, as one living organism known as Earth.

A great civilization is not destroyed from without until it has destroyed itself from within.
~ *Will Durant*

Since all life is interconnected, focusing only on your profit will still affect everyone on Earth. Creating this degree was like cutting the heart and brain out of someone and installing a computer to run things without any human qualities whatsoever. It's what they wanted, it was efficient, and hey…it was **cost effective!** The MBA degree became highly sought after as the greed factor took off in the United States. Gordon Gekko was king; greed was good. Making a profit became more important than living life, than loving humanity, then protecting our natural resources. This way of thinking became like a disease, a scourge upon the Earth and everyone was affected. Everywhere we looked were more and more corporations springing up with MBA degreed people running them. And what was the result? The breakdown of global societies, infrastructures, communities, jobs, homes, lives and ultimately families. People starved for someone's MBA profit. People lost their homes for the enrichment of CEO MBAs. Villages went into poverty for someone's MBA dream. In short, people died everywhere for profit as the economic policies of death superseded reverence for life. There was a massive loss of connection to humanity, community, life and nature. Profit over life. Money over humanity. And it was planned that way. So this is where we find ourselves today, in a global soul crisis that now has all of us in its grip. And it's a death grip. **Everyone** is eventually sacrificed. We must free ourselves from this.

In India, where there are thousands of small farmers whose families subsist on small plots of land where they grow yearly crops for sale, the farmers were sold GMO seeds. Soon, their land wasn't producing crops because of the terminator seeds given to them. And soon, they could not support their families anymore. Since there is no system for welfare or unemployment in India, there was nowhere for these farmers to turn for help. As a result, thousands of poor Indian farmers killed their families and committed suicide rather than leave them in the streets to beg and die. These farmers were sacrificed for profit. And that's just the tip of the iceberg. There are a million more stories like this. This is now beginning to happen in America where GMOs are forced upon us and farmers are going bankrupt.

What this all boils down to is the sacrifice and parasiting off of the weak for the gluttony, pleasure and enrichment of the rich. It is immoral, unsacred and violates Divine Law and Natural Law. Those with their law degrees and bought off Congressional seats and Court appointments talk about special interest law, and how right it is to have laws like Citizen's United where corporations are more important than people. This is what the Masons built America for, special, white, entitled interests. Or how they are entitled to more than their share because they found a loophole to use to get away with white collar crimes against the poor and middle class to enrich themselves. Today, most of the corporations shelter their money offshore in tax shelters and pay no taxes whatsoever, yet they complain about wages and unions while we pay their taxes for them. How much longer are we going to tolerate the wholesale corporate globalization of poverty, illness, death and evil for profit? Like in the movie, The Matrix, they see us as batteries to fuel their profitable schemes only to be discarded in a death heap when our usefulness runs out. How bad must it get before we stand up and refuse to participate in their plan for global genocide? Not long is my prayer. Not much longer brothers and sisters.

Finally, there were a few more sacrifices I wanted to mention. Perhaps you remember these guys....Martin Luther King Jr., Robert F. Kennedy, John Lennon, Malcolm X and John F. Kennedy? These men gave us hope, inspiration, faith, spirituality, love, joy, wisdom, strength, artistry, truth, power and the hope of freedom. These are the kind of men and women we need leading us, people of truth and honor. All that was taken from us when they were sacrificed on the altar of power and money. And what did we get in return? A world on the brink of destruction sucked dry by the same vampires of devastation and death.

I call for an end to the sacrifice of innocents. I call for an end to the parasiting off the sacred, humble, worthy, truthful and divine. I call for those who live for death to stand down. I call for honor for the beloved Divine Feminine once again.

I call for new leaders of honor, vison and truth to replace them. Let their sacrifice not be in vain. I call for new hope and faith, a renewed vision and a transformed world. I call for the restoration of hope, love, faith, cooperation, brother and sisterhood, mercy, truth, vision, respect, honor, creativity, sacredness, the divine feminine principles, safety, trust, opportunity, abundance, sharing, joy, community, sacred rituals, and an end to war and persecution.

As a healer, minister, shaman, visionary and teacher, I announce that time has arrived. A new world is born, with new leaders and healers of heart, soul, vision and power. I make a path for them to step forward. I honor them, bless them and initiate them into their positions to lead us. I open their hearts and the hearts of all who choose to come forward for healing. Bless us as a nation and as a global community of souls committed to love and light and resurrection. Let those who were sacrificed and their work not be in vain. We now take up the torch where it lay and carry on into the light of God's love.

Chapter 7

The Secret Holocaust

If money and power were the only path to happiness, there would be no hope for billions of abused, disenfranchised souls alive today. Instead, love your own soul unconditionally. It is then the doorway to abundance and opportunity will open wide to everyone.

~ Salini

There was so much to say about the dark, secretive nature of the old paradigm. It was everywhere I looked. My mind was reeling with the expansion of consciousness that comes with truth hitting my soul. That which I did not want to remember came flooding into my awareness. As I moved through first my personal, then the massive global awakening currently taking place on Earth, I realized this global tragedy was just the tip of a great melting iceberg of awakening that was occurring. The dissolving of the collective ego, the dismantling of the demonic forces, the truth exposing the lie and the thunderclap of waking up the sleepwalkers to the dawn of a powerful new paradigm of cooperation, love, equality and harmony were all happening at once. And together it was both exhilarating and frightening. But from my perspective as the exiled shaman, I see the emerging paradigm arising from the ashes of the old one. The consciousness is rising, people are throwing off oppression and we are emerging as a unified global community.

But first, you need to know what they are doing behind your backs, with your lives, your energy, your money and your future. Only when you are fully equipped with the truth can you turn and use it as a laser-like weapon to vaporize the lie they are feeding you every single day.

This plan began as far back as the time of the Pharaohs. Perhaps further back. There were many secret rituals of power, priestly classes and secrets passed only to the chosen ones to initiate in a class of people to rule us. Power was concentrated in the hands of the few, the class divisions were extreme. This power structure kept getting repeated in different times and places throughout history until today when the structure of society had transformed dramatically from serfs and lords...to workers, families and bosses. With the industrial revolution and the passage of fair laws protecting workers, we grew a thriving middle class which created a strong economy. We had some rights, freedom and personal power. But as this secret agenda began to take hold, it's brought us to the brink of destruction.

What we now know, is that our history is a lie and was manufactured to control our thinking and power. Historical amnesia created by false programming and carefully controlled, selected images created to saturate your mind with lies, deception and a false history is now the norm. In school, we were told the Indians were bad and the Cavalry was good. We were told Christopher Columbus discovered America and was a good guy who opened up the new world. In reality, Native Americans were slaughtered by the Cavalry in massive acts of genocide, known to indigenous peoples as *The Trail of Tears**, to facilitate a land grab. And 500 years before Columbus came Leif Ericsson and his Vikings and the Chinese. Some historians believe a group of Hebrews even made it to New Mexico a thousand years before that. So we were sold a bill of goods. And Columbus? He never even made it to the shores of America. He stopped in the Caribbean where he is credited as being the original slave trader and human trafficker. And that is where our American history takes a sharp turn towards being crafted by the white slavemasters of today. They wrote what fit their view of the world and truth had little to do with it. As a result, our history is warped and largely false. But it served them well to keep us docile…for a while.

After eliminating all those who came before Columbus and white-washing his slave trade history, they created their first false hero. He was simply a man who did a brisk business in human trafficking for his Queen, just like traffickers of today. He sold children into sexual slavery. He was financially successful and killed off entire tribes of indigenous peoples to establish a foothold in the Caribbean Islands. For this he was rewarded in history as a conquering hero. Incredibly, we still celebrate a holiday in his name. In order to honor someone as despicable as Christopher Columbus, there had to be a **Collective Denial*** amongst the power elite who established this recognition. So a bubble of lies was created to legitimize his actions. And that is where today's false structure all began. After centuries of repeating the lie, it has taken hold.

Some of those following Columbus were lucratively financed and asked to set up businesses and financial structures as an early infra-structure for the arrival of the upper classes who meant to rule us. And the groundwork was laid. In order to build this nation as the secret society founders envisioned it, it required free slave labor. So, slavery was not abolished in the founding of America or written out of the Constitution. This is the real reason why Columbus is honored today; he is the man who laid the foundation for the modern day slave trade that provided centuries of free labor to wealthy plantation owners. This is how the wealth of America was built. And collective denial made it possible to keep the gravy train rolling.

Never underestimate the power of denial.
~ *Lester Burnham, American Beauty*

As we moved beyond the Civil War and into the Industrial Revolution, the Steel Men came forward – Alfred Hunt, Andrew Carnegie and Charles Schwab. And then the bankers – J.P. Morgan, John D. Rockefeller Jr. and Andrew Mellon among them. It was the early big bankers, steel magnates and business tycoons who were shaping our economy. There was a gradual move from an agrarian economy to an industrial economy. An alliance formed between the largest of the industrialists, the biggest bankers and the newly forming militaries of the West. This became known as the Military-Industrial Complex. Together they formed a powerful force of weapons of war, businessmen who sold them and the bankers who financed it all. Everyone scratched each other's backs. Wealth and power began to be concentrated in their hands. And once it was in the hands of a wealthy few, they began devising plans of how to further concentrate it and gain greater control over the populace. This was the beginning of the modern-day Secret Holocaust.

With the rise of business, corporations and central banking, nations began to be run more and more as corporations. By the 20th century we saw the institutionalization of the corporate state and central banking. The turning point towards loss of individual freedom and the destruction of America was the establishment of the Federal Reserve, a private banking group of wealthy global bankers who charge interest for making and handling our money, in 1913. The Federal Reserve is not a federal agency, but a private business run by wealthy individuals to reap a huge profit off unsuspecting Americans.

Another piece of distorted history accompanies this tragedy in our national history. In exchange for financing and support for his Presidential campaign, Woodrow Wilson agreed that if he were elected he would establish the Federal Reserve and turn over the reins of America's finances to the central bankers. He knew this would destroy America's strong financial base, but he did it anyway out of his burning ambition for power. And the likelihood he was a member of a secret society bent on global domination and following their instructions. On his deathbed it was reported he said he felt great shame that he had "sold America down the river". And he certainly did.

The bankers wasted no time in moving to seize control. Within a year, they engineered the onset of World War I, harshly impacting Western civilization because it ushered in Communism, the Great Depression, Fascism and World War II. This would never have been possible without the passage of the US Federal Reserve Act and the Income Tax Act in 1913. It was the American taxpayer who was stuck with the bill for financing both sides of the conflict. And debt slavery in America began.

After demoralizing the West and exhausting their resources in World War I and the Great Depression, the follow-up agenda put forth by various secret societies, factions and bankers was to wear down the steadfast and good-hearted American character of honor, freedom, goodness, hard work, discipline, faith, love, family and belief in the American Dream. The breakdown of society was orchestrated carefully by global think tanks whose policies reached like tentacles into every single organization, local government, school, city, state and family everywhere. The vast nature of the plan was staggering and included intellectuals, institutes and other respected organizations.

But first, there was another World War to fight. World War II was simply an extension of World War I. The elite had grown filthy rich on the first war, but had failed to accomplish their ultimate goal of creating a One World Society dominated by the elite. They had pitted and financed both sides against each other, but here and there were individual megalomaniacs like Hitler or Stalin who had their own plans. They couldn't quite control them all. Another war was needed to bring in the society envisioned by the elite where everyone else was enslaved to their machine. So, World War II was launched with more devastation and finally, the Holocaust. After World War II they proceeded in earnest to move towards their goals of world domination.

But surprise, the American people were not demoralized. We were strong, proud and hard-working, fought hard in the war, came home and started lives, families and built a strong nation. Two wars weren't enough to destroy the souls of generous, freedom-loving Americans. It was going to take more than that. They were going to have to destroy our hearts, our health, our careers, our families, our economy, our education, our minds, our faith and our souls. And that's exactly what they set out to do. It was **Spiritual Warfare*** this time. They launched a battle for the souls of humanity.

But they didn't take something into consideration. The Holy Spirit rules here.

Those involved in this plan are so entrenched in their ego games that they failed to notice that it is the Holy Spirit who runs the show down here. This is God's domain; all things here are created by God, even them. All life is interconnected. Everything here is part of the Oneness. There is no separation. They have lost sight of the beauty of their own souls, of life, of family, of community and of nature. Their Machiavellian nightmare has overrun our American Dream. They fail to recognize the awakening taking place before their eyes. They see only their own ego, and perhaps the faces of the Masters they serve. They cannot lead us anywhere because they are morally and spiritually bankrupt. Their paradigm is dying. We must strike out on our own.

> *Man did not weave the web of life; he is merely a strand in it. Whatever he does to the web, he does to himself.*
> ~ Chief Seattle

But there is a much bigger reality overlaid upon this small-minded drama playing out right now. And that reality has been laid out for us by Masters, teachers, mystics, preachers, lay persons and the many Holy men and women who have walked the Earth for ages. That is the ***Divine Blueprint of Global Awakening****, a scenario now playing out before our very eyes. No matter how much havoc they wreak they will never change the evolution and eventual awakening of everyone on Earth. Even themselves. They have no clue that what they are currently doing they do to themselves. But even they have the choice to wake up. We all do. That Divine Blueprint was laid out so beautifully by many of the great spiritual teachers of Earth throughout history. Like the Mayans more than a thousand years ago. Their Master Calendar delineates every stage. We've passed through the final stages and are on our way to full spiritual awakening. Here's the breakdown.

> *The forces of light on Earth shall overcome*
> *the forces of darkness. Complete spiritual*
> *enlightenment on Earth will occur.*
> ~ *Edgar Cayce*

The grand awakening and end of the Mayan Calendar, the long-awaited turning point in world evolution arrived on Oct. 28th, 2011. The Mayan Calendar is a very complex mathematical and scientific object that divides the evolution of our planet into a 16 billion year cycle, with 13 distinct segments that represent each stage of the development of life, from the first cell to today's advanced consciousness. The longest cycles are the first ones, covering billions of years and slow stages, like cellular development, then plant development and so on. As the vibrational frequency of Earth speeds up, the consciousness of life on Earth also accelerates. When this occurs, cells evolve into higher species with more advanced consciousness.

The Earth has now passed through all 9 waves or 13 Ahau cycles and passed the very last day of the Mayan Calendar, Oct. 28th, 2011. Each cycle was faster and shorter, each leap in awareness more profound than the last. This last cycle began on March 9, 2011 and concluded as of Oct. 28th, 2011. It was intense, energetically challenging and very rapid. What this means is that the consciousness of Earth is no longer operating from a place of separation, or duality consciousness, but has accelerated in frequency to a place of Oneness, or total Unity Consciousness. We have evolved to one united organism. It's going to be harder to operate the way we have been under the oppressive system we live in. The old paradigm is not supported energetically anywhere in the Universe. It's going to get grander, more transformational, more liberating and more spiritual than you could ever imagine. The bad guys don't stand a chance.

It's explained in the Vedas, the Bhagavad Gita and Mahabharata and many other spiritual documents as well as prophecies from advanced individuals throughout history. The procession of the Yugas explains the evolution of the eras and what happens during each one. We have just emerged from a long Kali Yuga, which is the darkest of the dark ages. During Kali Yuga there is a strong focus throughout the world on earthbound dark activities, such as war, murder, corruption, slavery, greed, etc. We just moved into Dwapara, a middle stage before we get to the Sat Yuga, which is a long period of peace and enlightenment.

And of course the Bible and the Christian faith tell of the return of Jesus Christ to bless and heal the world. That promise aligns with other faiths which tell us that a period of peace and oneness is coming; only each is explained in the terminology of their religion. Whatever you believe, know that the Holy Spirit is at work here creating a massive global transformation. Arming yourself with truth while the world wakes up and the old system dies out will make it easier to navigate the changes.

After World War II, we saw the solidification of the union between industry, military and bankers. Only now, they added in the scientists to make the mix even more deadly. Nazi scientists working for Hitler who survived the war, were secreted into the United States via Operation Paperclip. The same scientists who made weapons to kill Allied soldiers and commit genocide in concentration camps, were now employed by the USA to develop even greater weapons of mass destruction - biological and chemical weapons - and hundreds of other secret programs. Among those programs were the mind-control programs developed by Dr. Josef Mengele in the concentration camps. All of these programs were brought to the United States after the war. And it's these hundreds of programs that have infiltrated our daily lives and are breaking us down today.

It was discovered during scientific and Nazi experimentation that people's minds could be controlled without their knowledge. So, they began to implement it in society. Boundaries of testing had to be exceeded to reach their goals. In order to make it possible to perform these experiments, the people enlisted to perform the tests had to be emotionally disconnected from their test subjects and from their personal value system. This required the scientific testers to also be mind-controlled. As a result, whole groups of people were prepared in childhood to enter into these scientific programs chosen for them by the elite. A vast schedule of indoctrination began in earnest of scores of people destined for their role in the grand plan. *These are the people running the show here right now.* We need to understand their pathology to regain our power.

Those individuals most responsible for foisting upon the world a destructive agenda of devastation, disease, etc. are themselves initiated, indoctrinated, and mind-controlled into a mental state of service to their masters. Many of society's most highly placed individuals have been forced to go through these initiations as a way of compromising their integrity. They don't all wish to be a part of it;

many of them long to escape the grip of this agenda. But if you've been brought in unwittingly or very early in life and initiated, it's difficult to leave. In order to understand what we are undergoing in the world today, we must understand the nature of mind-control, spells and trances and how they work to keep us enslaved, even if we are not part of any secret societies and have only the best intentions.

We'll know our disinformation program is complete when everything the American public believes is false.
~ *William Casey, former CIA Director*

Programming the minds and psyches of world leaders has been going on for centuries. The goal has been to create leaders who can control societies and cultures of their day. It has grown more sophisticated over time with secret rituals and practices of controlling and blocking the energy of people, and of the Earth itself, added in continuously. But additionally, all patriarchal cultures that featured violent, dictatorial rule have a common denominator - the absence of the Sacred Feminine within their culture. They were largely male warrior cultures like Attila the Hun's, or wealth/power cultures like Rome. There was no respect for the female energy that heals, loves and nurtures thus creating a death/conqueror energy devoid of compassion plundering the Earth. The excessive male/yang energy was too unbalanced and became continuously aggressive. This unconscious, ego-based mindset led to the development of mind control and occult practices to consolidate dark power. Modern leadership hierarchy takes it a step further. Even darker, more oppressive global leaders became the norm. The upper echelons of secret, sociopathic global leadership have received multiple layers of the same programming used by Dr. Mengele years ago.

The common factor in developing sociopathic tendencies is deep shame, which cripples the self-image, the soul power and the heart and locks in pain. Too much pain creates a spill-over effect greater than most individuals can contain. The point where the pain becomes too much to bear is when the mind splits into projection. Projection is perhaps the greatest denied issue in human behavior today. Everyone is projecting at least one of their denied painful issues out onto someone else. But when someone is mind-controlled, their pain is goal-directed and shaped to be directed towards specific situations and people. When pain becomes unbearable, it is then projected unconsciously outward as a release valve, usually towards the source of who came in contact with their stored denied pain. In love relationships, when someone's pain is contacted, they will likely project it outwards onto their partner unconsciously causing pain for both parties. And if it's pure divine love that has entered the painful place, great pain will be instantly liberated, shooting out towards someone close by.

But targeted, trauma-based pain and the resulting projection can happen to anyone anywhere in any culture raised harshly and expected to obey without question. When something is done universally to everyone at a very young age, it becomes unconscious. It then becomes a group mindset. If all children are raised with the same abuse common denominator, it doesn't stand out and becomes buried in the cultural subconscious. Traits of innocence and compassion can be abused out of children over generations until you create a generation of soul-dead youth. We are now beginning to re-experience these effects in the world around us today as children shoot children and go to war as children.

In order for men to become violent enough to be willing to commit genocide or torture, there has to be enough childhood or adult torture to completely wipe out any normal compassionate tendencies, respect for humanity or the ability to feel pain and to make it seem routine. *Enter the practice of trauma-based mind-control.* Conditioning is performed to cultivate sociopathic people to carry out a violent agenda that serves the profit-driven, soulless system of oppression.

When great suffering is inflicted upon someone, whether physically or psychologically, their feeling self has to escape to safety. And the soul must leave the body to survive. The mind is an incredible instrument. It has a strong survival mechanism that kicks in during an experience of this nature and will compartmentalize a portion of brain memory and function into a separate unconscious part of the brain. That brain portion will hold the painful memories in an unconscious state so they do not have to be re-experienced on a daily basis. The memories will be totally inaccessible to the trauma victim, except through being triggered either intentionally or unintentionally. This is how a split personality is formed. When the trauma is continually repeated, different personalities are formed. The split-off brain portions will accumulate pain and trauma that fill up and gather at the edges of that portion's consciousness. Later, when properly triggered by handlers or certain events, the split-off brain compartments of traumatized individuals can open the floodgates of pain and strike out at targets they believe to be threatening, but which are nothing more than their own pain projected onto someone else. Often occult rituals are included to call down demonic forces.

But amazingly enough, even those afflicted by darkness come for healing.

Here is one of my amazing, true Reiki case histories as an example. Names have been changed and specific details eliminated to protect the innocent and living –

Edward's Reiki Miracle - *Edward came to me as a client in one of the addiction recovery programs I worked in. He was a long-time alcoholic and it was his third time in for treatment. He was 70 years old and retired. He promised his wife he would get sober. His record said he was career military but when we began treatment, a whole different story emerged. This particular treatment program utilized Sodium Pentothal, better known as truth serum, to dredge up painful histories from clients to work out issues more quickly that might be causing addiction. During Edward's Sodium Pentothal sessions, he strangely didn't reveal much but said odd, disjointed things that I had never heard anyone say before. All other clients would always truthfully reveal everything they had ever done under truth serum. These statements were very bland and sounded scripted. It was clear he had been programmed to say certain things, even under Sodium Pentothal.*

During therapy Edward revealed he was actually a career intelligence operative but retired quite a while. He said that his retirement was contingent upon his willingness to undergo trauma-based mind-control to wipe his memories of his life as an intelligence operative. He said they programmed him to say certain things under truth serum in case he was captured. He remembered his job, but not the details. I asked him why the programming was necessary given he was committed to secrecy anyway. He said he had been involved in very sensitive, high security operations that they wanted him to forget. He also told me he would have left it alone but that he loved his wife very much and that she was the reason he was coming for treatment. He said he was unable to stay sober due to the painful nature of his memories and the level of trauma inflicted upon him. He drank to self-medicate. He said he was willing to remember whatever was so terrifying that they had wiped his memories of, if it meant staying sober and keeping his wife. His recovery hinged upon his willingness to face and heal his trauma and memories.

I offered to give him Deep Soul Reiki Treatments to help him heal his inner pain. He agreed. We did a series of Reiki treatments. Immediately upon the second treatment, Edward began remembering his days as an undercover operative. Edward was able to describe his years performing black operations. He said he was mind-controlled prior to certain assignments and then again afterwards. He said he was seduced with women, alcohol and money to go deeper into the work until he lost himself completely. He said the final closing trauma-based mind control program at retirement lasted six months and was the worst of all. Edward said he was given LSD and other drugs to wipe his memories. He said when he left he barely remembered anything, the anxiety and fear stayed with him always but bits and pieces of memory crept back in as he got older. As he shared each memory of operations he was involved in, Edward went through a process of deep shame and grieving, a sign he was telling the truth, and would get physically sick with each release of memory. We continued this process until the memories flowed freely and the emotional trauma was coming to the surface. I was impressed by Edward's courage and perseverance. He did a lot of difficult personal healing work for someone his age with a long history of alcoholism and trauma. Few do this much work with less painful histories, but his love for his wife motivated him. It was beautiful to see how much love healed Edward. I came to learn that it's really love that heals us all.

After about a month, Edward began to recover and

was no longer tortured by his memories and the trauma of the programming. I was able to connect him to a strong after-care program and counseling for his return home. I advised him to adopt a spiritual practice. When Edward left treatment, he had three months sobriety. He called me regularly to tell me that he was staying sober and was in therapy and was praying every day. Edward stayed sober until his death years later. Had he not received the Reiki treatments, spiritual connection and restoration of his faith, Edward would likely have died of alcoholism and the trauma-based mind-control he received. But no one would have known the true cause. Edward was able to prove to me that he worked for the intelligence services. His wife verified many of the details of his life as well.

Trauma-based mind-control programming responds well to high-level Reiki treatments by a properly trained ReikiMaster with additional training in shamanism and counseling. Sobriety is mandatory to liberate the trapped memories. Standard counseling is not enough because there is no energetic healing of the amnesia that is induced through the programming. Only spiritual intervention can accomplish that. It's a very deep process of healing that takes many years, but can be achieved through adopting a spiritual path, surrendering the old ways, doing your personal work and sincerely asking for spiritual assistance. The right counselor/healer/spiritual guide will be needed.

Like Edward was drawn into his intelligence work through addiction, trauma and shame, so were the German people seduced by Hitler because he triggered their pain. He reinforced the *collective denial* of a people unwilling to remember the dark traumas they had universally experienced as children and who were unable to heal their cultural pain. Hitler stepped it up by increasing the number, ferocity and visibility of savage public traumas that tapped into existing terror placed like a ticking time bomb in the souls of the German people. Such is the nature of trauma-based mind-control and ritual abuse. It can even control a nation of people.

Their unhealed trauma, when triggered by the right traumatic event, froze the German people into a **massive traumatic trance** where they were willing to standby and allow their power to be stolen. They had been entranced by a skilled black magician of the occult who knew just how to manipulate them. They were living out a real-life national **Stockholm Syndrome** where a nation was held hostage to a madman by his ability to energetically control a whole people by threats of more trauma and death. This can only happen when sufficient trauma has already occurred that robs the person of their personal power and they are unable to access it later. This energetic matrix is laid down in people usually during childhood and sometimes throughout later life. It becomes the glue and the fastening foundation for a nation based in trauma, terror and violence. A true shaman can see this clearly, a traumatically entranced person is too compartmentalized and in a **forgetfulness spell*** to realize what's being done to their souls and their lives.

Does this sound familiar to anyone?
It's happening to all of us right now.

When the Nazi scientists were relocated to the United States to continue their projects, they brought their Nazi mind-set and beliefs with them. No accountability, no charges, no trials, no transparency, no amends and no justice were required of them. On the contrary, they were given new identities, homes, jobs and incomes and they continued on as they did under Hitler, creating death and destruction. That is when the covert programs began in earnest and the push for mind-control commenced. The Cold War was also born and Russia and other nations also had their spies and mind-control efforts going on. This reality is not just a United States issue, it's a global elite issue. Everyone is spying on everyone. Many Americans carry high ideals and wish this to end. But without the clear understanding of how pervasive this is entrenched into our culture, we can't unravel the spider web.

The newest and most terrifying threat of all though is the ***weaponizing of corporations*** * to strip the world of its resources, freedoms, economies, food and seeds, land and link everything into a global corporation. It's like a giant Pac-Man devouring everything in its path and leaving nothing but death and destruction in its wake. A new invisible post-war empire rose to replace the Third Reich....***the Fourth Reich****. And this one is far more diabolical because they have mastered the art of killing us secretly without our knowledge or resistance. They have made us love our enslavement.

> *The road to power is paved with dead bodies.*
> ~Frank Underwood
> House of Cards

And so here we are today, living within this new world order. How do we turn this around? Well, first we must make the methods of our enslavement visible. Like an invisible cage, there are bars, locks, restrictions and energetic barriers placed upon us that must be broken down so our true divinity and beauty can shine. ***And it absolutely can be done, peacefully and non-violently.*** Most people don't want to harm anyone. Yet through the structure set up for us by the ***Merchants of Death****, we are doing just that every day unconsciously. Now we are in a state of collective denial of how we are harming others by the way we live, what we consume and how we treat others in less developed parts of the world. Yes, many are waking up, but we have far to go still.

One of the most common methods of mind-control is disinformation. Disinformation works by utilizing the truth to insert the lie. Here's how it works – A public spokesman wants to make a false statement about an event that occurred to cover for someone. They carefully craft a statement that cloaks the false statement with several true statements. The false statement is bookended by the true statements that are often well-known facts. The true statements cover for, and lend credence to, the false statements merely by association. Like guilt by association, there is truth by association. People will believe the lie because it stands with the other true statements. Hitler used this often, so do government and intelligence agencies. That's the easy stuff.

Most of the world's great scientists over the last 100 years have experienced their work being co-opted by governmental powers that be for purposes of power games. Nikola Tesla is an early example; Albert Einstein is another example. More recently, Dr. Patrick Flanagan, inventor of the Neurophone, and Dr. John Lilly, inventor of the Lilly Wave, are two scientists whose work was co-opted by the government.

John Lilly developed a method of bypassing the brain's subconscious defense mechanisms that resist programming. The waveform he is credited with inventing is called **The Lilly Wave***. It puts the brain in a neutral, receptive state whereby information can just flow in without resistance. Dr. Lilly's intention was for healing, peace and bringing people to a higher state of consciousness. Instead it has been used for global mind-control and is currently in use in all Western countries. The process works by piggybacking the mind-control data onto the Lilly Wave as it enters the mind. The mind-control information comes in just above 60 degrees kHz AC riding in on top of the Lilly Wave much like a tracking cookie rides in to your computer and is stored there when you surf the net for goods or information. The 60 degree kHz is in every single home in America, in all your appliances, and is undetectable. The mind-control data is pumped into your TV during all your favorite programs, without your knowledge. It's in your Wi-Fi, microwave, your power grid and anything that can carry the waveform energy. You are being mind-controlled daily by your habitual patterns of TV, electricity, cooking with microwave, video games and whatever else you may be doing electronically and electrically.

Another form of mind control is the standardized music frequency 440 kHz used around the world. It has been discovered that the vibration of love is 528 kHz. That is the same vibration of green plants in nature, of the center of the sun and of your heart chakra, so it's clearly a divine frequency. Music played at 528 kHz will open and heal your heart chakra sending the love vibration throughout your body. The scientists of the global elite also realized that that the Universe was run by sacred geometry and math. This information was likely passed to them by earlier adepts of their orders in mystery schools but kept secret. They realized the power and patterns that numbers had to manipulate the energy of the Universe. And so they set out to do just that. The musical scale we use to create beautiful music aligns with sacred geometry. But one note on that basic scale is dissonant, 741, or the **Devil's Tone*** as it is called.

This tone, F# on the musical scale, translated into kHz, or **Kilohertz***, becomes 440 kHz and creates a chaotic, dissonant sound often used in musical compositions to create a sense of fear, dread and danger. It was discovered through extensive studies that when all music is tuned to this frequency it creates disharmony, chaos, stress and fear and made people more subject to control. This frequency also suppresses the heart chakra and focuses on the head and the mind, making love inaccessible and mind control easier. Because of this discovery, it was decided amongst the global elite that all the world's music would be standardized to 440 kHz, the Devil's Tone.

After requests to make this frequency change were turned down by British musicians in the 1930's, Josef Goebbels, Hitler's propaganda master, went to London to convince British musicians to change. He was successful in convincing them, and the other nations of Europe as well. And this was on the very eve of the start of World War II. Soon, the 440 kHz frequency was standard all over the Western world. And when rock and roll was introduced in the 1950's, all its music was tuned to 440 kHz for maximum chaotic impact. Hence the moniker the "Devil's Music", for rock and roll. Rock and roll was then played to young people continuously to bring down their spiritual vibration and create chaos amongst them. This tone has helped to fragment and disturb human consciousness causing reduced awareness in humans globally. The solution is simple… re-key all music to the 528 kHz frequency of love. Rock music does not have to be played at 440 kHz and can be re-keyed.

One of the basic principles of mind-control and world domination is that it is to be carried out so incrementally and imperceptibly in tiny doses that you don't realize you are being controlled, your energy stolen and your power curtailed until it's too late. Like the proverbial frog in the cooking pot being boiled slowly, you don't feel it until it's too late. Now, our children are being mind-controlled to be violent, dumbed down, Godless, overtly sexual and disconnected.

Even more sinister than that is that the programmers can control your emotional reactions to the point that if they wish to have you act out violently, commit suicide or be fearful, they know the frequency signature of these emotions and can program them into you unknowingly. These emotions keep the populace divided, fearful and under control. This is the programming you are currently being subjected to.

So, they are programming you to feel fear and creating a national collective traumatic trance, just like Hitler and Goebbels set out to do in Nazi Germany. Only now they have fine-tuned it so it appears normal. If every day you have 100 violent images and only one of a rose or an animal in nature, the energy of the prevailing images will override the one or two good images. A mindset of trauma develops, a trance-state sets in, and you become numb and unconscious to the chaos around you. More murders on TV, more TV programs that focus on death and murder until you are desensitized to death and violence. This is how they slowly traumatize you. And a traumatic trance-state makes it possible for them to commit crimes and violence against you because you are frozen, numb and scared by the chaos around you. Like Patty Hearst shooting a machine gun at the store to cover her friends while standing there alone, instead of just taking off with the gun and the car and turning herself in. This is a traumatic trance-state and trance-bond. She didn't even think to leave because she was so traumatized by the physical, mental and emotional abuse that had created her fear. The same thing occurs with an abused elephant that is tortured from birth until nothing but a thin rope tied to a chair is enough to hold it. This is what is happening to all of us, we are all boiling frogs in a New World Order stew pot.

They have layered it all in one event at a time until we live as a nation constantly traumatically entranced. It's a spell being cast that includes the TV mind-control programming, the cell phone, the Wi-Fi towers, and the advertising, all designed to create a false illusion of a fake reality and to distract you from your highest self. There are even certain trigger words used repeatedly to create fear triggers within you. You don't need their fake world; you have everything you need inside. You are Divine. The whole Universe is within you, you are more powerful than you realize. ***But you must break your traumatic trance and your trance-bond***. You must break the spell and wake up before you are boiled alive.

The number of programs designed to strip you of your power, your health, your freedom, your mind, your homes, your jobs, your economy and your souls are far too numerous to mention. I name just a few to give you a more well-rounded view of the situation because it permeates every single area of your life. And these were scientifically engineered *intentionally* to kill you slowly. I'll start with the medical system and the food we consume, which is now unnatural and too toxic to sustain life but actually harms the life force and is designed to weaken you without you knowing it.

Food has become a weapon against humanity and is the perfect delivery system for genocide. The amount of chemicals, toxins, poisons, additives and killer substances routinely inserted into our food on a daily basis has created a crisis of health globally, but especially in the USA. And it's done intentionally to wear down your health so you then have to turn to doctors and pharmaceuticals to manage your many diseases that result from toxic food. Medicine is very profitable and they have created a system that combines ill health with an unnecessary allopathic system of health services to turn a huge profit. The cancer industry is built on that while the cure for cancer was found 80 years ago and suppressed.

One hundred years ago we had natural holistic techniques everywhere. In the early 1900's, the allopathic physicians hijacked our health system for their own profit. Naturopathic physicians, osteopaths, acupuncturists, nutritionists and other natural health practitioners were driven out of the USA. Today, there are at least 60 medical doctors offering alternative cancer treatments in the USA, and all are under attack.

Here's how they hijacked your food. We have vast amounts of mass produced junk foods stacked with chemicals we have no knowledge of, yet are often carcinogens, neurotoxins and pathogens. One of these toxins, aspartame, has been found to be a causative factor in diseases such as multiple sclerosis, blindness and brain cancer. Results of these studies prior to the FDA's approval of aspartame bear this out. Dr. Russell Blaylock, assigned to study the effects of aspartame states, "*This particularly nasty substance should have never even been approved for human use. In fact, had it not been for some fancy footwork by those in power in the FDA, it never would have. Early experiments using low, medium and high doses with aspartame all found dramatic tumor increases in test animals. These included brain, pancreas, and breast tumors.*" Toxic ingredients like sodium nitrite and aspartame are formulated to work at sub-acute levels so they don't cause people to drop dead right away. Instead, they cause the chronic, long-term degenerative collapse of body and mind, leaving behind a wake of results masked as diseases such as cancer, kidney failure and mental disorders including psychosis. It then appears people die of a disease when in fact they die of toxic poisoning. Yet aspartame is now included in all our foods and beverages as an artificial sweetener, but with a new name.

America is also experiencing an epidemic of obesity. This can be attributed to weight-gaining food additives put secretly into foods on purpose such as hormones and steroids. After all, weight loss programs are big business. Food additives have been found to be causative in autism and other physical and mental conditions such as ADD and ADHD as well. The United Kingdom's Food Standards Agency conducted a study in 2007 showing that the consumption of foods containing dyes could increase hyperactive behavior in children. Another glaring issue is the meat and poultry industry. Factory farmed animals bound for slaughter have been polluted by steroids, hormones, antibiotics, ammonia and other chemicals designed to combat disease commonly found in factory farms but which are toxic to humans. Salmonella, staph and other serious diseases are found in these meats regularly. Parasites can also be found in meat and fish. Avoid all processed meats that contain sodium nitrite, such as bacon, hot dogs, sausage, ham, deli meats, pepperoni pizza and even beef jerky. Don't eat factory farmed meat. This is just a sampling; the list goes on endlessly of toxins in your foods.

Your body's energy frequency needs to be at a certain level to maintain health. Kilohertz is an energy measure. A minimum range of 58-62 kHz in your body is what it takes to maintain good health and strong immunity. Below that number, colds, flu and disease develop. Every food has an energy frequency. The higher the frequency, the healthier your body will be. Here is a short list of foods, essential oils, etc. and their energy frequencies.

Canned and packaged foods	-	0 kHz
Fresh vegetables	-	15 kHz
Dried herbs	-	15-20 kHz
Fresh herbs	-	20-27 kHz
Essential oils	-	52 - 320 kHz
Spiritual frequency	-	92-98 kHz
Forgiveness oil, Frankincense	-	320 kHz
Love oil, Rose	-	320 kHz

So, as you can see, eating low vibratory foods can lower your overall immunity.

Next up would be GMOs, which are genetically modified not to feed the world, but to limit the world's food supply. GMO seeds are intentionally engineered to be sterile. They are known as terminator seeds. These seeds not only do not reproduce, but gravitate towards neighboring fields. When this happens, all crops grown die out and a farmer's ability to continue farming also dies out. Farmers lose their farms and global famine becomes a very real possibility, something the world is waking up to today. Another example is GM corn, engineered to grow a deadly toxin inside each and every grain of corn. This deadly toxin is then consumed by all the people, including your children, who unknowingly eat genetically engineered corn crops in their breakfast cereals, corn tortillas, corn chips, popcorn, etc. This mass poisoning of the population is clearly intentional, as it is deliberately engineered into the crops which are grown for the sole purpose of human and animal consumption.

Fluoride was sold to us as a boon to our dental health, so they put it into the water. But that, too, was a lie. Did you know that during the Holocaust they gave the Jews fluoride to make them more passive while in the concentration camps? In scientific studies, fluoride was found to create a docile, malleable personality and make resistance lessened. Fluoride accumulates in the body's organs and pineal gland and causes deterioration, especially of the male reproductive system.

> *Denial is a powerful sedative for*
> *the pain of transformation.*
> ~ *Salini*

But by far the most obvious reason to fluoridate the population brings the discussion back around to the priestly classes, the elite and mind-control. For thousands of years the initiates into the secret mysteries have known that the pineal gland is the doorway to higher consciousness. Once a person has opened and can see from her/his Third Eye/Pineal gland, they awaken spiritually and transcend the physical plane. All spiritual power, known by many names such as the Holy Spirit, Reiki, chi, Qi or Kundalini energy, travels up the spine and enters the pineal gland thus awakening and enlightening human consciousness. When it arrives there permanently, the person/soul becomes awakened and is no longer controllable. Their life force has been liberated and they are free to ascend to God.

Adepts* of occult practices soon realized that fluoride had the power to destroy the pineal gland and reduce mental capacity, as well as control natural resistance to persuasion. If the pineal gland could be kept diseased and withered, higher consciousness could not be reached. Here was a powerful tool at their disposal for controlling the masses. So fluoride was added to many of our commonly consumed foods and in many processed foods so it becomes undetectable.

Chemtrails* are the trails of smoke you see trailing behind jets in the sky these days. They differ from contrails in that contrails disperse and chemtrails do not. Contrails are also thinner than chemtrails. Chemtrails are filled with chemicals they are dropping into our air, our topsoil and onto our homes for the purpose of further damaging your immune system. One of the purposes is to lower your alkaline balance, a precursor to serious disease, through dispersing heavy metals.

Two metals have been found consistently worldwide during analysis of chemtrail residue - barium and aluminum. When they're released into the upper atmosphere, the particles could retain their nanoparticle size and be easily absorbed as they filter down into the lower atmosphere and into our lungs and vegetation. Since nanoparticles are much more inflammatory to tissue than other forms of environmental aluminum, dispersing them through aerial spraying is very dangerous to human health. Dr. Russell Blaylock, neurosurgeon and neurotoxin expert, explained that aluminum nanoparticles can enter the brain and spinal cord quickly through the lungs and nostrils causing severe damage. He sees a connection between chemtrail aluminum deposits and the rise of neurodegenerative diseases, such as Alzheimer's and Parkinson's disease. Dr. Blaylock also expressed concern over the saturation of plant, crop life, and water with aluminum nanoparticles. It becomes necessary to constantly drink green drinks, spirulina and other health products to ward off the effects of heavy metals in the body due to chemtrails.

So that's the bad news. Just a touch of it anyway. There are thousands of toxic programs currently in place throughout the world and right here at home in America you need to know about while distracted by TV, work, and the hamster wheel of life. What's critical to understand is that we live in a constant state of trauma and denial – *a collective traumatic trance** – that blinds us in a spell of forgetfulness to the genocide being committed upon us currently. Which is exactly how they designed it and want it to be. Go docilely to the ovens please while we steal your soul and pick your pockets.

Do not lie down in the sand. I say, damn well don't let them do this to you. It's not too late, we can turn this around. Let's reclaim our souls, our lives and our world today.

The Story of the Crushed Souls and How They Got That Way

One day, when I was staying at the Navajo and Hopi Reservations years ago, a Hopi Elder said to me, "See that drunken Indian over by the kiva?" I looked over in surprise to hear him use this term. We had been discussing the problem of Native Americans and alcoholism. He went on to tell me this, "We hold the Drunken Indian in a sacred light. He carries within him the Spirit of the Wildness we once had and once were. He may be troublesome, but he refuses to submit to the authority of the white conqueror and he hides his power behind his drunkenness. This is how he is left alone by the white man. Otherwise, they keep coming to take our power. But he is not conquered." I thought about this a long time after that and I realized there was truth in his words.

I know alcoholism is a serious problem in many cultures, especially among Native Americans. I don't minimize this problem in any way. But the Hopi elder was referring to a soul survival technique, a way to hide the True Self from destruction. Until the soul of a tribe is recovered, someone has to hold the power for the tribe hidden from the thieves of souls until it's safe to return to their true selves. In Native American tribes, perhaps this is one of the ways. This is not to excuse the ravages of addiction but only to add to the understanding of what happens when a tribe's soul is tampered with, crushed and denied. People become ill sometimes as a survival mechanism. The True Self and Soul Power go into hiding for protection from the predator.

Addiction is a symptom of the crushing of the human soul.
~Salini

The more I thought about it, I realized it was true for other groups as well. As a raped woman, I have observed in others and felt inside myself, a great tornado of rage that swirls inside of us. It's always with us. This tornado is filled with the unhealed energy of soul violation, a suppression of spiritual power. That violation often becomes the trigger for an inner transformation that takes place alchemically inside every rape victim, every Native American and every culture where power is stolen. Sometimes it lashes out in pain at its trapped, unhealed circumstances, scaring everyone nearby. The rage of a raped woman is a very powerful thing. It builds over time until it either becomes an illness or a force that storms the fortress of her denied Sacred Feminine self and rescues her own maiden energies long-held hostage by the magicians of plunder and darkness. An angry raped woman within is the warrior you need to make the alchemical change and reclaim your power. It's time for all our inner warriors to rise.This truth translates to the Irish and the Highlanders who have been so long oppressed by the British. They hold their long sorrowful oppression inside their addictions as well. Yet within them they all carry a powerful inner Braveheart. The days of the Highland wars are over, but that alchemical fire still burns within the heart of a Highland warrior and an Irish rebel and is capable of transforming lost power into alchemical transformation and awakening. Their deep magical roots can liberate them from their long initiation of pain. If they use their magical power from a place of light, the separation can be healed and the power restored.

Every culture has a similar allegory of oppression and the potential for healing. Perhaps the best example after all is said and done are the Germans. The total annihilation of their country and people became the ashes from which their Phoenix of healing arose. They have rebuilt themselves into a beautiful, peaceful nation filled with natural healers, homeopaths, mystics, Goddesses, and geniuses, all devoid of the former soullessness of the Third Reich and free of the desire for war. Their fiery death became their brilliant resurrection. And a hope for us all...

This is the journey we're all on. Keep going. If you make it to forgiveness, you've won the war.

Chapter 8

Exiting the Matrix

Myths are part of every tribe. And every culture is swallowed by its tribal myths. If you want to be part of the tribe, you have to buy the myths. Or, you can choose to exit the matrix.

~ Salini

The list of Western myths that have swallowed our consciousness and power is endless. I named a few. It dates back thousands of years to the point we hardly know the truth anymore. The saints and spiritual teachers have told us how incorrect our history is as they tried to awaken us. This is how we lost ourselves. Who are we really? Where did we originate? What are our true historical stories? What powers might we have that have been withheld from us? Many mysteries still remain. So more than ever, it's time to return to the truth because that is where our power lies. They have held us hostage in the **maya*** *(illusion)* long enough. We've reached the tipping point of delusion, lies and corruption. It can only tip towards the truth now or we're lost. But when a culture becomes inured in the lie, it's very difficult for it to grow beyond the decay and disease that develops when a lie takes over a culture. ***That is when the sages, mystics, visionaries, healers and shamans are most needed. To bring us back to the truth, to our center, to our wholeness.... yes... we need our Western shamans.***

I quoted William Casey's infamous statement that *"When everything Americans believe is false, we'll know we've accomplished our goal."* And what goal is that? The total stealth of your power, soul and Dharmic path so your life is not your own and you have no idea who you are as you walk to your programmed death. This outrageous statement is the reality of where we are at today....led by people who believe there is something to gained by this demented viewpoint. How did we get to this point? ***By persistent, consistent disinformation, deception, repetitive trauma, illusion, black magic and sustained mind-control.***

I was wondering where this began in modern times. It's an ancient plan, but I came across Charlotte Thompson Iserbyt's recent work. Charlotte was born into a secret society family but as a woman was not part of the inner circle. She knew nothing of their programs until she became an educator and began to observe the destructive nature of the educational system. She began documenting what she saw as a clear plan to destroy the American education system and harm children. She is the author of <u>The Deliberate Dumbing Down of America,</u> a bestseller about the elite's plan to lower the standards of education to make Americans stupider and easier to control. A plan that is now in effect and is working well for them. The vast, well-thought out program to turn our children into worker drones has been planned for over 100 years. In 1910, a well-known foundation created a think tank to find ways to lower the mental capacity and free will of Americans. Charlotte was on board to watch them be implemented as a senior policy advisor on education to Ronald Reagan in the 1980's. The central program around which others rotated was B.F. Skinner's famed ***Operant Conditioning****, which is a process by which humans and animals learn to behave in such a way as to obtain rewards and avoid punishments. This was used to force children to react in ways desired by educators to reinforce obedience, stupidity and brainwashing. The goal is to squash individualism and create a docile workforce for the corporate New World State. Free thought was discouraged and brilliant children told they were odd or outsiders and should be scorned. This was the basis for 60+ years of brainwashed children and a dumbed down America. Lucky for us we had good teachers along the way to subvert some of these programs.

Charlotte states that even more sinister programs were developed that aimed at mind-control through today's computer software programs. These programs began in the 1970's and are now fully implemented. Among the mind-control programs were video games and other software all which introduced violent war games for children to create virtual warriors and violent-minded teenagers. We see the outcome of that with the school shootings of today. There are also software programs to control people's emotions being utilized without our knowledge in social media today.

But there is one more vital detail that was included and began long ago. That small detail is the intentional and utter absence of the sacred feminine principle in all global elite teachings. Over the course of the last 10,000 years, the feminine principle and its corresponding yin energy, has been banished from the world's power structure, even from society altogether, certainly from education. For centuries we've seen powerful women banished to convents, whorehouses, burned at the stake, sent to live in caves or monastic environments somewhere but rarely included in the conversation of power. Their vast wisdom, sensitivity, power and nurturing love has been lost on the development of the Western world.

As a result, ego-centric, violent, insensitive, angry and emotionless male leaders and warriors have ruled the world causing centuries of destruction and evil. This has culminated in the two World Wars of the 20th century and the rise of fascism with the resulting massive tragedy of the Holocaust. With no feminine yin energy to temper the violent, aggressive male yang energy, the world leans towards aggression, war, murder and violence. All the dominating philosophies of the last two thousand years are totally devoid of any positive, loving, wise, sacred feminine principles and are top-heavy with emotionally dead, clinical, stern, harsh and overly-analytical belief systems that gave rise to the egoic notion that men are superior and that they have the right to experiment on and control the minds, bodies and lives of other humans because of their superior status. It's a form of **Patriarchal Eugenics*** whereby men believe they have the right to control the lives, and even deaths, of others, particularly women, minorities, the poor, the young, the sick, the disabled and the elderly, making life-changing decisions for whole groups of powerless individuals. It is an exclusive, rather than inclusive, form of structuring the world and all its life forms to suit elite groups. It is this pure yang, purely ego-based consciousness that is now destroying the world.

There is much illusion around us causing us to be separate from one another. Yet we all live under the same God and walk upon the same Mother Earth. We all have beating hearts that flow with red blood and are all part of the same ecosystem and energy matrix of Earth together. Somewhere along the way, we became split in our consciousness. It's time to heal the split they've created and exit the false matrix. As you heal this manufactured split in your consciousness, you will naturally begin to love yourself. This will begin to generate love for humanity within you and you will naturally gravitate towards harmony and oneness with your fellow brothers and sisters on Earth.

One barrier in overcoming the split in consciousness is the rise in philosophies that tell you never to talk, think or look at anything that is "negative" for fear it might take you over somehow, or that you might "create" it. This spreading belief system popularized today in various sub-religions, a hit film, and popular seminars about "positive thinking", has actually done more harm than good and has vastly helped the secret society movements to gain ground. But I make a distinction here. There certainly isn't anything wrong with thinking positively, living positively and trying to be a good person who holds solid wholesome values. Most of us aspire towards those goals. I support that and believe we must move towards love and positivity. But that is not what I'm referring to here.

I'm speaking of something more insidious and actually very psychologically dangerous. I'm speaking of denying your shadow self completely and excusing that by saying it's "negative" to even talk about it or acknowledge it exists. It's the elephant in the living room that is destroying our world. To deny it is to embrace a distorted sense of reality of only half-truths about our world which actually contains dark and light, yin and yang in everything. To ignore the shadow aspect of life is to not be fully conscious. It's real, it exists, and it has to be faced to change things here.

Denying the shadow can translate into extreme forms of the shadow like racism, addiction, violence, abuse, sexism, crime, classism, greed, murder, rape, separation and apartheid. When people fail to acknowledge their own shadow, they are missing a vital component in spiritual awakening and power. When you acknowledge the shadow self, reclaim the lost power and embrace it, you have the potential to transform, recharge, rejuvenate yourself and emerge whole. There is much suppressed power and truth in the shadow self waiting for expression in our world today. To pretend it isn't there and say that we have to be "positive" all the time is to blind oneself to the whole of universal consciousness. Forced optimism…fake happy face…the pain still deep inside. It's a judgment to force others to assume false happiness. A form of denial and mind-control. It's a brainwashed reality we've been force fed. And it silences a vital part of our inner voice.

Those who do this are teaching separation, not wholeness. The term for this is called *Wetiko**. Wetiko is to fall under the spell of denial of the wholeness of the self. It's to deny the reality that there is a shadow world. Wetiko is also to project that denied shadow out into the world onto others and then attack them or hold them to blame for your own imperfections. In doing that, you allow the shadow free reign to rampage through our world, creating havoc, destroying the planet, starting wars, practicing sick rituals and harming humanity gravely. In doing that, you create separation in the world. But when you turn and acknowledge your darkness and claim your full-fledged spiritual power, you can stand up to the shadow world and tame it. Once tamed, its power becomes your power. This is something ***every single person on Earth must do immediately in order to save Earth. We cannot exit the matrix until we know the full extent of its existence and the boundaries between it and our true selves.***

To avoid consciously engaging your own shadow self, and everyone on Earth has one, is to walk around with a split consciousness. By turning away and believing you might "create more darkness" by putting any attention on it, you are reinforcing the very evil from which you are trying to flee. As long as you keep your darkness unconscious, it still has power over you. As long as we avoid looking at the larger darkness in the world today, it also still has power over us. That is what evil depends upon for its existence. It laughs at us for our unconsciousness. But if we claim our true spiritual power on Earth as children of God and inhabitants of Earth, and turn and face our dark tormentors, we can take back our power that they have taken from us, reclaim our planet and begin to heal it.

If you insist on seeing only one aspect of reality, you reinforce duality and strengthen evil. Do you really believe your own inner light to be so weak it cannot face down darkness? Do you have so little faith that in the moment of contact your soul will fail to channel God's power to deal with and transform the darkness within yourself and the world? Do you realize the darkness around us we created, is part of us and we have to power to end it? Do you think so little of yourself and your Divinity? God doesn't, so think again.

Your soul is a microcosm of the whole Universe and contains everything God ever created. You HAVE THE POWER TO DISPERSE

DARKNESS COMPLETELY. You will not be taken by the dark unless you allow it to happen. Deepen yourself; go within to the vast reserves of power you have never tapped before. Go beyond the rules and outside the box. Take the journey inward and see what kind of stuff you're made of. You might be surprised how brilliant, vast and incredible your power is. You only need to call upon the forces of light within and around you to disperse the dark and they will be there. First you must acknowledge you have darkness and that it also exists in the world. Then let your light expose the dark and its shadow disappears. The light consumes and unites with the dark. All that's left is light. We ALL must begin to be fearless about facing humanity's vast shadow that now looms over us or we ABSOLUTELY DO risk losing our individual and collective souls.

I know that some of the illusions are tasty. We all love to eat, drink and be merry, and sometimes that's ok. They may be fun, they may be exciting, and they may be interesting. But they also may create desire in us. The dark knows well how to do that and that is how they trap us. I've been tricked, I've been trapped, and I fell for desire. I know how tantalizing it all can be. But so much is taken from us there. Don't let those illusions trap you in a corner. Your soul is worth a lot to them but is destined for a higher good here on Earth. The battle is underway to gain it from you. Be the instrument of good in the world not the unconscious helper of evil.

As I said earlier, your denial of your own power weakens your inner magnetic field. When that happens, and you have denied more than half of yourself, your soul is in danger of being lost completely. At that point, you may have completely forgotten who you are and how to regain your spirit and divinity. They will endeavor to keep you in a state of forgetfulness, satiation and desire. There you are easily controllable. There they can use you and your body as a battery for their machine. **You must turn and face your shadow and reclaim yourself. We all must. This is what it will take to save the world.**

This is why I had to write this down. I was taken into their world as a small child and tortured, teased and told I had to walk their path and give up my goodness for their use. But I was born with power, wisdom, purity and God's grace. No amount of their profanity, violation and filth could take that from me. I may have become confused awhile, but I regained my footing and reclaimed my power. I also saw my mother sacrifice herself to save me from darkness whenever she had the strength to do it. I felt my sister give me her sweetness, love and God's light to show me something better. They taught me about love, healing, God, meditation, prayer, spirituality and the goodness that is possible in God's world. Mom knew it was possible because she healed many people herself. I watched her goodness in action and knew that was the path I wanted to take. I chose to honor what God gave me, and what my mother and sister strengthened in me. I believe my dual initiation gave me the unique perspective of both roads, both paths and allowed me to understand the seduction and grip of the dark and the deep soul power of the light and what it takes to save one's soul. I knew that many would not be given this information to make that same choice. I knew few would be shown how frightening it gets and the damage that will be done to you when you choose the wrong path, and that few would be shown the power of God that is at your fingertips if you but ask as I was shown as child. And I saw that many did not make it out of the grip of darkness simply because they didn't know how.

So, I share it with you now to help you make your choice. It's up to you, no judgments. Every soul gets to choose its lessons. But if one person can wake up and heal someone, we all can. If that one person wakes up a few more, soon there are 20 souls working for good. If those 20 wake a few more up, then there are 100. After that, those 100 can bring a thousand to the God, and so on. And when I say God, I'm referring to the one God that loves us all equally throughout the world no matter what religion you are. There are no exclusions here.

The true story and theory of the 100th monkey goes like this:

*There were a group of anthropologists who were conducting a study of monkeys living on a string of islands. The islands were too far apart for the monkeys to ever swim across or interact, so they had no contact. But the anthropologists were in constant contact as they observed the lives of the monkeys. One day, one of the monkeys on one of the islands went to the water's edge and began washing his food. The other monkeys on that island watched him and some began washing their food too. After a few days of this, the number of monkeys washing their food increased. The anthropologist on that island reported the food washing to the other anthropologists. They reported no food washing was occurring on their islands. Then one day on the original island with the original monkeys who washed their food, the 100th monkey washed his food. That very day, when the 100th monkey washed his food alongside the other 99 monkeys, all the monkeys on all the islands began washing their food simultaneously. **Critical mass consciousness*** had been reached. Because all consciousness is connected throughout the Universe, when a critical mass of consciousness is reached, it exponentially and rapidly spreads to the rest of the universal web of global consciousness. It is for this very reason that the forces of darkness endeavor to separate our interconnectedness with one another, our consciousness, and our connection to God and truth. They know that our power is so universally great that nothing can stop us once we connect the strands of our consciousness to God, each other and the power of the Universe.*

So, we must be the 100th monkey wherever we go awakening, healing, strengthening and loving one another back to wholeness and power. We can completely banish the woes of this world if we do that one simple thing and connect the web of consciousness to everyone. What's going to change this is the melding of the ***yin and yang energy****, primarily the opening for the flowing in of the divine female intuitive intelligence into the heart of the male dominance structure. Males in power should create openings for empowered, gifted women wherever possible, and make room within themselves for the sacred feminine to flow in and allow the integration of consciousness, and the halting of the destructive yang force. Only when the fragmented cellular particles of our damaged cultural consciousness of duality and self-hatred are re-joined, and the split is healed and infused with the love of the Divine Mother once again, will we step away from the ledge of global annihilation.

We've entered a new era, a new paradigm, one that requires new thinking and action. As Einstein said, *"We cannot solve our problems with the same thinking we used when we created them."* The problem is that most modern thinking evolved from duality thinking, a type of thinking steeped in patriarchal values and the exclusion of matriarchal forms of intuition, power, creativity, innate wisdom, receptivity, ebb and flow, and all the opposing forms of thought and creativity that mark balanced thought. It's virtually impossible to come to a place of harmony while these are the prevailing thought forms. What literally must happen is the dissolution of those thought forms, which have matter and power to rule us, or the penetration and integration of such thought forms with more than 50% sacred feminine energy so the yin energy can heal the yang energy.

The issue at stake is that yang energy, when in an unbalanced state, is primarily action energy-thrusting, taking, using up, and conquering. When yang energy is present in more than 50% quantities in any energy field or thought form, it becomes the prevailing force and then becomes corrupted. When power is absolute, it then corrupts absolutely, which in turn, corrupts the energy field. This energy then takes and uses up all resources without creating new energy because it only contains half of the truth of the structure of the Universe. Without yin energy, it isn't whole, unless it steals energy from the yin field (and it does steal yin energy. That's what rape and the stealing of natural resources is.) which is against **Natural Law*** and **Divine Law***. Thus in an unbalanced state, it is finite & destructive in nature. This is the same principle as in the process of cellular oxidation, which creates free radicals in our bodies, the underlying cause of disease. With too much yang and not enough yin energy, the electro-magnetic field of Earth is destabilized. This has been occurring for a long time globally, thus the planet has gone into an extremely unbalanced state. So, what we face today is the possibility of total depletion of resources by forces made up of unconscious yang energy without providing an alternative for creating new energy. In addition, the byproduct is a diseased environment.

> *We are called to be the architects of*
> *our future, not it's victims.*
> ~ *Buckminster Fuller*

By contrast, yin energy is inherently creative and possesses an inexhaustible supply of Divine Energy. What has become the dominant form throughout the world is the suppression of more than 50% of the creative energy force in favor of a small percentage of yang forces literally eating up the world alive. This is a thought form, a pattern of energy grooved upon the energy matrix of Earth that we have been living out for thousands of years. It's brought us to the point of destruction so it must be removed. The key to solving this problem is the restoration of the balance of divine energy, and the renewed respect for the provider of resources, Mother Earth. We must stop all forms of suppression of natural energy, whether it's human or fuel energy.

An additional vital issue that must be integrated is the current lack of spiritual consciousness inherent in any system, thought form or action that uses more than its share of resources provided by Mother Earth at any given time. That guarantees the total exhaustion of all Earth's resources without consciousness of any kind. In other words, these unconscious forces are not operating from either Natural Law or Divine Law, even though these are the systems of order that actually rule everything here on Earth. Human law does not prevail here because it differs from culture to culture and generation to generation and cannot be universally applied. Only a universal principle of law encompassing everything and everyone can be the standard by which we measure and apply harmony everywhere on Earth. It is the fair and compassionate application of Divine Law in combination with Natural Law that unites us, and our energy, in harmony.

What does this really mean, and mean for us living through it?

What it means is that those of us who are awakened to the problem, to whatever degree, are on a crash course with the prevailing unconsciousness that rules here. Because this is inevitable, we must prepare our own bodies, minds and spiritual consciousness to be fit enough, awakened enough and united enough, to prevail in whatever conflict arises on the horizon soon. We must all become spiritual warriors, and we must primarily work in unison within that warriorship; we must become one united consciousness. To do so multiplies our power synergistically, making us an unstoppable force.

Remember the physics question, "If an unstoppable force meets an immovable object, what happens?" Well, what happens is an endless transfer of energy….!!!! Yes, exactly. We must become an unstoppable, united force of awakened energy that does not back down in the face of an immovable system that abuses its power and the Earth's energy field. Once we collide with them, and I promise you we will, all their energy will be transferred to us. When you stand in your power and face them with the full force of your spiritual power, their power will transfer to you. We must be prepared for this momentous event.

At that point, we begin using it to transform and heal the Earth.

And how do we accomplish that? Become the 100th monkey and bring the spiritual power of your soul to others. Quite simply, if there is no spiritual awareness, or incorporation of some spiritual path, those of us endeavoring to preserve the Earth will be mowed over by the sheer size and power of the forces arrayed against the rest of us. This cannot be accomplished through intellectual discussions, obtaining higher levels of education, money and job power, although those may be helpful to a lesser degree. *We must mobilize our spiritual power... now.*

No, what must happen is a mass spiritual awakening, a mass apostasy, where all previous ways of doing business, war, consuming and living our daily lives are abandoned, and we all adopt a culture of living totally spiritualized and totally infused with Divine Energy. In short, a spiritual revolution in thinking, action and perspective towards Earth must occur, and it must occur today. Once enough people realize that we are standing upon, and disrespecting the Mother who feeds us, the consciousness shifts. Once the consciousness shifts enough, the Divine Feminine can enter our cellular structure and transform our entire being top to bottom, crown to root. We literally become the vessels by which the Divine Feminine re-enters the Earth and the consciousness of humanity. We must allow it to happen.

They've served you a large portion of terror pie and it's become a sedative to your soul's power. We're choking it down as we watch ever-increasing images of violence, sex, sacrifice, war, school shootings and so on. We're living in a traumatic trance where we've been mind-controlled into denying our feelings, our souls, our power and our truth. You are only as enslaved as you are asleep or afraid. Walk through the spell of fear they have cast upon you and take back your power NOW! If you do not, they will take our souls, this nation and the world.

Do it. You will be amazed at how powerful you are.
When this occurs, all resistance to love, compassion,
Divine and Natural Law, and harmony with Earth will
fall away. This is the true beginning of Earth's Divine
Transformation……and it's already underway.

It may not be easy, and it won't be instantaneous. First you need to know the codes of transformation. In the following chapters I explain them. Find an experienced soul healer with deep spiritual awareness and counseling experience. They should be shamanic, awakened and holistic. Once you feel you've found someone you can trust, enter your Soul Transformation. The Universe will likely guide you to the right person. Let's walk through the stages of healing together. But first we must once again honor the women, the exiled Divine Mothers and Goddesses and restore them to their place of sacredness. It is their loving energy that will love and heal us back to life.

Chapter 9

The Rape and Resurrection of The Divine Mother

In all early civilizations where the first great breakthroughs in our material and social technology were made, the peoples of those civilizations where those breakthroughs were made all believed God was a woman.

~ *Riane Eisler*
The Chalice and the Blade

There was once an era, lasting for more than 10,000 years, where people lived peacefully together in cultures ruled by females, sharing harmony, balance and abundance, and co-existed respectfully with Nature. These Goddess cultures were discovered and precisely documented by the pioneering work of the famed Lithuanian archaeologist Dr. Marija Gimbutas when she disputed the male-domination theory of history and proved that all world cultures were not always male-dominated and warlike. She proved that prior to the spread of war-like male-ruled cultures, there were hundreds of villages and tribes that existed in Europe that were matriarchal in structure, and ruled benevolently and fairly by women, where men were peaceful and cooperative. Gimbutas pioneering work shows a society that spread across Europe from the North Sea to the Danube. Women were held in high regard with men and carried equal status. This culture existed for thousands of years peacefully without war in an equal and balanced fashion. Goddess figurines were found everywhere. Other art discovered honored the regenerative powers of nature such as sculptures of birth-giving goddesses, pottery figurines of bird-headed deities and sacred serpents representing the power of **Kundalini***, the divine life force that travels up the human spine and awakens us.

The Goddess in all her manifestations was a symbol of the unity of all life in Nature. Her power was in water and stone, in tomb and cave, in animals and birds, snakes and fish, hill, trees, and flowers.
~ Marija Gimbutas

In fact, in these and in all early civilizations where the first great breakthroughs in our material and social technology were made, all the people of those civilizations believed God was a woman. Religious practices involved worshipping the sacred hoop, creation and nature. These cultures were free of war, famine and poverty. Women leaders practiced fair tribal rule that kept life in balance. Men were taught to respect Mother Energy and worked in harmony alongside women.

This was also true in ancient Egyptian culture for a very long period of time. The most famous of the powerful female Goddesses who carried the full power of the Sacred Feminine was Isis. Isis, the Divine Mother of Egypt, was a goddess in Ancient Egyptian religious beliefs whose legend has endured for centuries, yet few understand her true purpose. She is known as the Goddess of Motherhood and Fertility and the Protector of all of Egypt. She was worshipped as the ideal wife and mother, goddess of nature and magic; friend of slaves, sinners, artisans, and the downtrodden. The Romans spread her worship throughout their empire right up until the time of Christ. Many of the Egyptian deities became Greek and Roman gods and goddesses, but the Romans changed their nature to become increasingly male and infused with the Roman Christian patriarchal view, and less of the matriarchal female Egyptian view. A few remained relatively unchanged. Isis stands out for her unparalleled power and historical position, and retained her unique Egyptian nature while also being worshipped in other cultures.

Isis married her brother Osiris, a common practice to preserve royal bloodlines. Together they had a son, Horus. The long buried truth of Isis' power was her ability to resurrect her husband, Osiris, after he was murdered by Seth. Her skills with healing and magic are said to have been used to restore his body to life after she gathered the body parts that had been strewn about the earth by Seth. Isis came from the High Priestess sects who had vast powers which have mostly been suppressed and lost until recently. Stories were told throughout history about women's natural healing abilities and powers which upset the stranglehold of established Christian power. Isis had to be wiped from history. Only now are we rediscovering her ancient healing techniques.

Eventually, Sacred Feminine power proved too threatening to established male-dominated cultures and theologies. The church and political leaders began forming beliefs and practices that demonized women and fostered their persecution in future centuries. But the Egyptian Goddesses and Pharaohs, such as Isis, Hatshepsut and Nefertiti, were unparalleled in how they were allowed equal stature with men of their time, even the Pharaohs. Only Egypt maintained this tradition of powerful women long after other cultures had become hopelessly patriarchal. But sadly, even Egypt gave way to the desecration of women. When later Pharaohs came along and were envious of powerful women such as Hatshepsut and Nefertiti, the suppression and obliteration of female power began. When Nefertiti's mummy was recently discovered, it was found her power symbols, including her face, arm and royal jewelry, were desecrated and her memory erased from history. Nefertiti is now being restored to her former glory. Isis stands as the great suppressed Goddess, where the beginning of the loss of female power occurred.

Dr. Marija Gimbutas' findings reveal an ancient widespread matriarchal culture which flourished throughout Europe between 6500 and 3500 BCE in the era historians call the Neolithic. This civilization was nothing like the warlike images we've seen of men fighting battles across Europe nor did it resemble the history we've heard of Kings, warriors and conquering gods ruling the lands as we've been told. To quote Gimbutas, "*This was a long-lasting period of remarkable creativity and stability, an age free of strife. Their culture was a culture of art that featured women.*" So, what happened to the truth? Once again, the conqueror erased the history of powerful women Matriarchs to represent *his-story* instead of *her-story* of the world. All cultures that featured female leaders were sanitized to reflect a new version of history, one that was male-dominated, to serve new masters, the patriarchs. Did you even know that there were hundreds of peaceful, abundant villages led by women for thousands of years throughout Europe and Northern Africa? Did you know they all believed God was a woman and worshipped as such? These were successful, benevolent societies without the kind of breakdown we're seeing now in our modern, wealthy Western societies. There is no excuse for this other than the imbalance of the patriarchy which is responsible for all the world's crises today.

> "*The main theme of Goddess symbolism*
> *is the mystery of birth and death and the*
> *renewal of life, not only human but all life on*
> *earth and indeed in the whole cosmos.*"
> ~ *Marija Gimbutas*

Dr. Gimbutas remarked often that much of the evidence of ma-triarchal cultures was either ignored or thrown out by her male con-temporaries who couldn't accept the existence of any matriarchal cultures anywhere. Sexism extended even to science. Her own re-markable history proves her point. Despite reams of evidence, years of painstaking scientific research and documentation, photographs and worldwide accolades for her outstanding work, as soon as Dr. Gimbutas passed, the male archeologists began dismissing and dis-paraging her work. Big male egos overtook scientific minds and real evidence. Eventually, one of them erased all records of her work, then claimed he was the one who actually discovered it. Today, she is laughed at by many of these archaeologists, but only those steeped in arrogant, patriarchal views. Their day is drawing to a close. Wiser scholars who understand the importance of the sacred feminine as-pect of our world and how it's been suppressed have tried to restore her work to prominence. Soon they will succeed.

Throughout my research I found that women in all fields who accomplished great works, especially in the field of science, were often brushed to the side, dismissed or blocked outright from receiving any recognition or reward for their lifelong contributions to their respective fields by their male counterparts. Selfishness and ego are huge factors in the science world. But as I explained before, when the mind is in duality, as most people's minds are, they perceive the world as us and them. For entrenched patriarchal sexists, who are accustomed to power, privilege and entitlement, there is no way they will ever accord a woman her due. It simply goes against their beliefs or willingness to share power. For a patriarchal male sexist, sharing power with a woman is a sign of weakness that is too shaming to their outer ego, especially if they have a pronounced shame core. Additionally, the sexist male is usually one with a larger than life narcissistic ego attached to their shame core. They will not surrender their power or accolades for fear of exposing their inner shame. Their competitive spirit will kick in to the max in defense when a powerful woman steps forward.

Other examples of outrageous sexism are these magnificent women. Rosalind Franklin was born in London, England in 1920. Franklin obtained a degree in chemistry from the University of Cambridge in 1941. She undertook the task of cracking the code of the DNA molecule, the leading biological problem of the day. She and a colleague worked on it night and day and were the first to discover the structure of the DNA molecule. They wrote a paper on it but before they could publish it, their paper was stolen by two male colleagues who claimed they had written it and took credit for the discovery. They were awarded the Nobel Prize for this act of thievery without mentioning her development of it at all. She was devastated by this treachery and died at 37 of ovarian cancer. These false pretenders are still listed on the list of Nobel Prize winners for her discovery. It's important to note that a high number of women who experience abuse and sexism die of cancer of their breast, ovaries or other female parts.

Lise Meitner was a German chemist during the Nazi era. Despite her brilliance, she was hamstrung by the sexist German male chemists around her, and by Anti-Semitism. After fleeing to Sweden to escape Hitler, she continued her work and eventually was the primary discoverer of nuclear fission but shared that information with her employer, Otto Hahn. Since he was still powerful in Germany, and the times made no room for women, the Nobel committee awarded the Nobel Prize in Chemistry to Hahn alone with no mention of Meitner. He did give her a nod in his speech. Despite her work being the main contributing factor in the very important discovery of nuclear fission, which soon came to the United States, she was overlooked in history.

Perhaps the most glaring example of a woman overlooked for her great achievements in science was, Mileva Maric Einstein, Albert Einstein's first wife. Mileva was an outstanding science student, a math genius and was advancing in graduate school at a time when a woman going to University was unheard of. In fact, she was the only female student there. Einstein, on the other hand, could barely pass his exams and flunked math in high school. It's likely he was dyslexic, but he did not obtain high enough marks to be accepted to the advanced graduate levels at the University where he met Mileva, so she interceded on his behalf to get him into graduate school. At that point in their careers, she was far more advanced than he was. During the time they were together in school and in their early marriage, they both worked on the theory of relativity together. Mileva's contribution was equal to Albert's, something he acknowledged throughout his life privately to his friends.

When man is completely infantile...he does not need and does not have an understanding of the outer world. It exists for him merely as gratification or denial.
~ *Walter Lippman*

Mileva Maric Einstein was so learned that she became a colleague of Nikola Tesla in their early years and informed many of them of the work both she and Einstein were working on. The Tesla Memorial Society has unearthed evidence that indicates Mileva is indeed the co-author of the Theory of Relativity. Physicist Evan Harris Walker claims the basic ideas for relativity came from Mileva. This is borne out by research done by biographer Abram Joffe who saw an original manuscript for the theory of relativity which was signed, "Einstein-Maric" together. Einstein himself concedes this in numerous letters and missives privately, but never publicly, expressing remorse and regret about how he treated her. When Einstein received the Nobel Prize for his body of work, primarily a nod to the Theory of Relativity, he gave his wife, Mileva Maric, the Nobel Prize money saying you deserve this more. But he never publicly acknowledged her scientific involvement in his work.

What happened to Mileva is what happens to all women, even

today. The early birth of Mileva's and Albert's first two children, one out of wedlock, prevented her from progressing in her work, and stalled Mileva's career. She was forced to take a leave of absence to give birth and care for the first child. Subsequently, she gave the child to her parents to raise and returned to school. But the nature of her and Albert's relationship was so passionate that she became pregnant again, and he married her. She had a son and tried to continue her studies but was burdened by the child and the marriage. Nevertheless, they continued to work on the Theory of Relativity together and exchanged numerous notes and conversations developing it.

However, Einstein was a typically stern German husband who, once married to Mileva, reverted to old-school authoritarianism to control her and her intelligence. She played the role of the dutiful wife and allowed him to take the spotlight and stood in the background while he took credit for their joint work. Upon the birth of their third child, another son, Mileva stayed home to care for the children and let Albert take all the accolades. They submitted the Theory of Relativity but only under his name and he took the credit. From there, Einstein's career took off and he began traveling and speaking.

Mileva's predicament was one of the most glaring examples of patriarchal values that arrogantly squashed a woman brilliant enough to be a contemporary of Nikola Tesla, and prevented her from receiving credit or acknowledgement for her vast body of work and knowledge. But then, neither was Tesla recognized, until now. The Tesla Memorial Society has taken it upon themselves to honor Mileva Maric and legitimize her work.

But before all the great women scientists struggled to be seen and heard, what brought down the balanced, egalitarian matriarchies of ancient times was the rise of the Roman Empire and their ultimate quest to destroy *paganism**. Many believed that all pagans were devil worshippers and worse. In reality, paganism was also the seat of the worship of creativity, nature, the Mother and the sacred feminine where women shared power with men, were honored, or even led tribes. It was during the crushing of paganism that the demonization of women began in earnest. It's true that there were those that practiced human sacrifice and devil worship amongst the pagans but not all of them practiced these rituals. The truth is that amongst Christians and pagans alike, there were people who were sacred and people who were profane, no matter what their beliefs. In fact, they both took turns sacrificing humans and practicing evil, like when the Romans sacrificed the Christians to the lions. No one had the right to pass judgment in such times.

But with the arrival of Emperor Constantine on the scene in 312 A.D., the tide turned toward Christianity and against the pagans. Emperor Constantine united all of the vast Roman Empire into one collective state. He was a monotheist who believed in Sol Victus - the Sun God, an anthropomorphized masculine projection of man onto God. Constantine issued the Edict of Milan in February of AD 313. The Edict of Milan forbade persecution of all forms of monotheism and offered tolerance and rights to Christians throughout the empire. The Edict of Milan was one of the most important laws ever passed in modern history as it reversed the entire trend of paganism to monotheism establishing the beginning of Christianity in the Roman Empire. From there, the persecution of pagans began. The Emperor was divided in his beliefs because although his mother was a Christian, his father was a pagan and had taught him the ways of magic, so he tried to allow both religions to coexist. Constantine utilized seers, magicians and **Druids*** in his court as soothsayers throughout his reign. It was Constantine's sons who were largely responsible for launching the massacres of all the pagans, **Celts*** and Druids and the decimation of the **Sacred Groves*** throughout Europe and wiping out paganism. With the crowning of Emperor Theodosius, the legalization of destroying paganism reached its apex. For more than a thousand years, the Roman and French Inquisitions raged, with vast religious persecution throughout all of Europe. Women were especially targeted by Rome because they represented the Sacred Feminine power they were now crushing.

But it was Emperor Constantine's mother, a devout Christian, who pressed upon him throughout his life to establish and legalize Christianity as the state religion. She also urged him to create a document that deified Christ and would be the official "book" of the religion of Christianity. Until then, there were only loose collections of stories about Jesus' life that were told here and there but not bound together or officially recognized. But on her promptings, Constantine convened the Council of Nicaea in 325 A.D. The Council was a gathering of local bishops, political figures and other prominent individuals of the day from throughout the Roman Empire who convened to adjudicate all the official issues surrounding Christendom. It was there, upon a vote on each section and story, that the modern Bible was created. It was also there that all reference to women as equal, powerful or even significant was eradicated from the Bible. The decisions made during the Council's tenure were not based in spiritual beliefs or truths handed down from Jesus. They were decided upon political expediency and personal preference.

Much of the decisions made surrounding the birth of the Bible were made during a time when women had no power and would never have been included in a gathering as prestigious and important as the Council of Nicaea. Additionally, Emperor Constantine himself was a believer in the Sun God, Sol Victus, which is a staunchly patriarchal religious perspective. It wasn't until his last days that he converted completely to Christianity. His power at that time in history, where he was even called the Messiah and the First Pope, was so great, that anything he suggested would have been taken with grave import. Consequently, Constantine infused the Bible, as did others at the gathering, with solely patriarchal stories, beliefs and viewpoints. It was Constantine who decided to spin the story of Mary Magdalene as a prostitute rather than as the noblewoman and powerful High Priestess she really was.

The men of that day feared the power of women, and especially of women like Mother Mary and Mary Magdalene, who had the power to heal, restore life and create magnetic energy for manifestation. They also feared Jesus' mystical teachings from his time in the Far East such as reincarnation, mystical vision and yogic practices. These, too, were eradicated from history. This is why we haven't moved forward in consciousness. We're missing half the story and half the power. We can't become whole as a people without the whole of the wisdom and power of our world intact. Without the feminine magnetic energy to drive the awakening in consciousness, we remain partially aware in a state of half-consciousness, but only the patriarchal half. Men then and now did not understand the true power and purpose of the yin feminine energy. But the Gnostics did. The Gnostics knew Jesus' teachings included a more holistic explanation of the nature of the Universe. But they were silenced. When it came down to describing the Holy Spirit in the new document to be known as the Bible, they even wiped the feminine principle out entirely and used solely male terminology. They came up with the Father, the Son and the Holy Ghost to describe the Holy Trinity. And where in that equation is the Divine Mother, embodied by so many saintly women over time such as Mother Mary and Quan Yin? Where are there references to the mother, daughter and all the billions of women of Earth who make up more than half of the population here? Are we to pretend they have no part in creating life? All reference to women was erased from history that day and every day since. And Christianity is the only creation story in all the Earth's cultures that does not include a woman as creator of life. Even though we all know that to be the truth of life on Earth.

Because we have eliminated half of the truth, we've stayed stuck at a reduced level of consciousness where the patriarchal ego rules the day. And that is where we've been for 2,000 years. The glaring truth and irony of this is obvious in the fact that although it was Emperor Constantine's own mother who drove the founding of Christianity as a global religion, taught her son to be a Christian, gathered the stories, and inspired the Council of Nicaea where the Holy Bible was created, women were still eliminated from history. Constantine didn't even include the great story of his own mother's awakening to God and Christ.

Mary Magdalene was overlooked, denied, exiled and suppressed throughout Christian history not for the trumped up reasons we've been told, but for a power play by men to steal power from powerful women and deny them their proper place in history and at the table of leadership. According to Gnostic texts, it's likely that Mary Magdalene was Jesus' wife and never a prostitute. It's also likely she was a wealthy noblewoman and supported the disciples financially during their travels. The lies they concocted are the myths still perpetrated by the Christian patriarchs, that a woman powerful enough to earn Jesus' love and be given his secrets, had to be turned into a prostitute to diminish her true power in the Church. It is said that she was the person he left the Church teachings to. But look where we are today, a patriarchal form of Christianity that still derides women.

The time has come for all religions and governments
to end their stealth of the Sacred Feminine
energy for their own use and abuse and restore
the sacredness of the women in their cultures.

~ *Salini*

Much of the early history of Christianity, which included many stories of the powerful women of Jesus' time, was discarded and likely destroyed. Not until the discovery of the **Dead Sea Scrolls*** and the **Nag Hammadi Scriptures*** in the 20th century did the holistic truth of Christianity come forth. These codices lay hidden for 2,000 years until a time when modern scholars could objectively analyze them without the fear of ancient Inquisitors who might kill them and their families or imprison them.

It's highly likely that scholars, initiates and monastics who knew that they were about to lose sacred, ancient teachings that more accurately represented the truths of Jesus' life and the people who birthed Christianity, intentionally hid the Dead Sea Scrolls and Nag Hammadi Scriptures far away from the men making decisions at the Council of Nicaea. They must have known this was their only chance at preserving sacred truths and the power of the divine feminine from the monodimensionally myopic patriarchs of their day.

All reference to the teachings of Isis and the Temples of the High Priestess were eradicated at the Council of Nicaea. These teachings would include how to heal energetically and how to reach enlightenment through sexual practices. There is no discussion of the fact that Mary Magdalene performed the same rituals of healing, purification and magnetism on Jesus that only Jesus is credited with. All powers that Mary Magdalene was said to have demonstrated in her time as a leading High Priestess of the day were wiped from history. Instead, we are left with a woman who is described as nothing more than a prostitute wiping Jesus' feet, to be pardoned and allowed in by Jesus out of the generosity of his heart. This is a blatant projection of patriarchal and sexist values projected onto perhaps the most powerful woman of her time, Mary Magdalene, to steal her power and wipe her from history. It's obvious to anyone with common sense that Jesus would never have allowed someone of low character who wasn't awakened and noble that close to him during his mission and crucifixion. Further to allow her at his feet during crucifixion and to dress his body after death are only tasks assigned to advanced initiates, not former prostitutes. The truth is, she was an advanced spiritual initiate with accelerated spiritual powers of her own. We now see this kind of character assassination has been done to dozens of powerful women throughout history right up to today. The men of the Council of Nicaea knew well of the powerful deeds of Mary Magdalene and Mother Mary, both Temple High Priestesses. But they were intentionally wiped from the Bible at the command of Emperor Constantine. And it is a crime that has reverberated throughout history, damaging all women, and men too - robbing them of their wholeness, sensitivity and sacred feminine energy.

Among the additional 155 important Gospels and codices left out of the Bible but found with the Dead Sea Scrolls at Qumran were: The Coming of Melchizedik, Hur and Miriam, Phases of the Moon, Meditation of the Fourth Day of Creation, The Lives of the Patriarchs, the Secret of the Way Things Are, An Aramaic Horoscope, The Book of Secrets, The Healing of King Nabonidis, Commentaries on the Psalms, The War of the Messiah, Enoch and the Watchers, The Charter for Israel in the Last Days, The Parable of the Bountiful Tree, The Last Words of Joseph, The Jubilees and the Book of Giants. The codices from Nag Hammadi that were discovered also bear vital information about the Sacred Feminine role in the development of early Christianity and in the world. Among them are: The Gospel of Truth, The Gospel of Mary, The Secret Book of John, The Gospel of Judas, The Gospel of Thomas(known as the Fifth and most important Gospel), The Concept of Our Great Power and Melchizedek.

Additionally, there was the **Apocrypha***, or the <u>Missing Books of the Bible</u>, meaning *things hidden away*. These chapters were left out over centuries of translations of the Bible but were once required to be included in all Bible versions. Among the missing Apocrypha are: The Book of Judith, The Wisdom of Solomon, The Rest of the Chapters of the Book of Esther, The First and Second Books of the Maccabees, The History of Susanna, The History of the Destruction of Bel and the Dragon and The Prayer of Manasses. Other vitally important Gospels that have been intentionally or accidentally lost that refer to the Sacred Feminine nature of life are: The Gospel of

Mary Magdalene, which refers to her close relationship with Jesus in more detail than we hear in the Bible, The Gospel on the Nativity of Mary, The Gospel of Nicodemus, The Gospel of the Egyptians – which refers to ancient Egyptian practices of higher consciousness, The Essene Gospel of Peace – which refers to Jesus status as a member of the Essene Community, The Essene Book of Revelation, The Sophia Wisdom of Jesus, The Treatise on the Resurrection, The Dialogue of the Savior and The Lost Gospel of Peter. Many of these may be considered the Gnostic Gospels but for more exact information I refer the reader to the master work by Elaine Pagels – **The Gnostic Gospels***.

When a ruling class is structuring their view of the world, part of the process includes re-framing history and those people of history who were power players, male or female. Additionally, mind-control, even ancient mind-control, requires a uniformity of thought, belief and obedience to certain set beliefs of the day even if they are incorrect, dysfunctional and destructive, as we are seeing clearly today. Finally, those who favor patriarchal stances will further endeavor to minimize the efforts and achievements of great women past or present. Another woman who suffered this fate was Nefertiti, the Queen of Egypt and King Akhenaton's wife. Considered very beautiful and powerful, she ruled Egypt alongside her husband for twelve years. They started a new religion, monotheism, and changed the direction of Egypt. After their reign, they disappeared from history. It's thought her successors wished to blot her memory out due to her great power so all carvings, statues, pyramids and writings about her were destroyed until a bust of her was found in 1921.

Then came the great persecution, the Dark Ages, when millions were killed in the name of Christianity. Anyone suspected of pagan practices was executed. Women were especially persecuted and tortured. The Catholic Church even wrote an especially vile book, the **Malleus Maleficarum***, which trained Inquisitor priests in how to capture and kill a woman/witch. The figures are impossible to measure accurately but it's said that between 5,000,000 and 10,000,000 women were put to death by the Church. The charges could be nothing more than having herbs, being a healer, having wisdom and so on. The pendulum swung the other way, the purge was on. Unfortunately, this lasted for roughly 1400 years, until Napoleon brought it to an end.

Soon, the Renaissance began, and with it slowly came the return of the Divine Feminine but only in artwork, music and other forms of artistic expression. The Renaissance painters began painting in symbolism about the Sacred Feminine in their works to guide us towards the truth. These artists were Leonardo DaVinci and his masterworks, The Last Supper, the Mona Lisa and the Vitruvian Man….Michelangelo and his incredible painting on the ceiling of the Sistine Chapel, his sculptures of David and the Pieta, Botticelli and his famous Birth of Venus painting, and Raphael and his great work, the Sistine Madonna, all pointing us towards the truth of the power, beauty and sacredness of the female and the Mother. As consciousness rose, slowly we felt the return of Mother, but not into her full power. Still, within the last 2,000 years there has been endless persecution of the Mother energy, the Divine Heart of the Female, and of the female form.

No one sought her wisdom, nurturance, love, intuition, magnetism or creativity. She was left to live her days out in caves, monasteries, in forests and nunneries, her voice silenced, her power suppressed. She cried for generation after generation - *Who will hear my voice? Who will believe my wisdom? Who will accept my gifts? Who will recognize my power? Who will take my hand? Who will accept my love? Who will protect me? And who will love me as I am?* But no one answered. She was denied, for centuries, and it was the denial of what she needed to sustain herself that held the energy of suppression in place. Then she was scapegoated, for the fall of humanity, for all the children, for tempting men and many other things **she never did**. But the greatest wound she received was that when she spoke her truth, shared her pain and asked for help, she was judged, rejected and sent into exile away from love, into the **Dark Field***. And all the predatory patriarchs received abundant love and support despite what they did to her, while she was expected to live without any. It was the ultimate betrayal. They expected her to be vulnerable and give love. They expected her to open herself, and when she did, they plunged the knife of betrayal, gave her their pain to carry, took her divine creative life force for themselves and sent her away in exile for life. A world still living in denial would not look at the pain they had inflicted upon her. So, she was left to live with it inside the dark field, where little is known of the energy there, and much was feared. She had to find her way alone. She had to find her sacred **Alchemy***.

But she was bonded to them by their betrayal of her. They took a piece of her with them and she wasn't whole anymore. She had to get it back to be free. And that is where the Heroine's journey began for her. She was broken, but she had to breach the **Betrayal Bond*** ***that began with The Magdalen and Isis, both so terribly betrayed in*** ***history***, and go out and search for her broken self, and reassemble her soul parts into a new and stronger woman. It was a hard mountain to climb, especially while wounded. And even harder is reaching the place inside herself where she loves herself more than she loves them. She had to ask for more than the crumbs they threw on the floor for her. She had to say no to the betrayal which looks and sounds like love. She had to believe there was something better for her. And there was.

The betrayal bond is the one that holds you the deepest in bondage. Because it's always someone you really love. Their betrayal is a traumatic bond that holds you close. It may not be violent physically, but it holds your heart hostage a long time. You keep hoping you will hear the words I still love you, I'm sorry, let's make up, or I didn't mean it. Sometimes, a betrayal is healed. Especially if the person who betrayed you really loves you, was unconscious to their actions and didn't mean it. They were unhealed and unconscious them-selves when the betrayal occurred. It's possible they may have grown and healed some themselves. Those are healings that can take place. Congratulations if someone in your life is able to heal that wound be-cause it is then you will really learn to trust again. But often you will hear nothing. When you break that bond, it's going to hurt because it's likely you did love them. To heal the betrayal, you have to break the old connection to make way for a healed new one, sometimes with the original person, sometimes not. But the person you really be-trayed was yourself, by allowing that kind of energy into your heart. Forgive yourself, forgive them, break the betrayal bond and move on. Once you do that, a space opens up for real love to enter in. And the most important love to allow in is self-love. Make sure there's plenty of that to go around before you allow anyone else to love you. Or else another betrayal bond is waiting for you.

Somewhere in there is when the split in consciousness first took place. There is a quote from Plato who said, *"Zeus talked about hu-mans having too much power, so he decided to split them in two by putting them in a trance, then dividing them. When they awoke, they spent all their energy looking for their missing half, thus wasting their power."* Whether real or a legend, because of this split we expend our life force in the struggle to find ourselves, then are reborn endlessly until we realize we are one and reconcile the two broken halves. One cannot live without the other; the yin cannot be without the yang, and vice versa. The feminine yin is the life energy that animates the male principle, and the male yang in turn creates action in the world. They work as a team. And this is why we are here now, today, to heal this split once and for all. And we are about to do it. It is the Divine Feminine energy that will accomplish this.

It is best described in the Wisdom of Sophia who tells us from her place of isolation that she is the exiled, abandoned and persecuted Divine Feminine. She tells us that she feels wounded and abandoned by her masculine polarity. And when there is a wound on the psyches and bodies of women, there is a corresponding wound on the culture itself, and in Nature, which is feminine. Sophia tells us what it feels like to be in the very center of her pain and still try to love, both herself and others. Nearly impossible to do, yet it must be done. This is the path all women walk at some point or another, if not in this life then in the next, in order to become the Goddesses they really are. She unknowingly and innocently entered into the most difficult initiation of them all, the initiation through the dark night of the Feminine soul. She lives in the dark field yet to be acknowledged, the field still not understood by science or theology, the place of mystery and magnetism. She holds great wisdom and power there, waiting to be expressed into the world for its healing and awakening.

There alone in the isolation of the dark cavern of your pain, where you live inside the wound, is where you finally find the deepest of chakras, the **Holy Grail***, the **Womb Chakra***. All women carry within them the Womb Chakra, all men are permitted to enter if they have acquired sacred respect. It is the Holy Grail, the place of renewal and it is uniquely feminine energy that provides this renewal. If it's wounded there, it carries your initiation into the heart of unconditional love. But it is a harrowing journey. Within the Womb Chakra, you will find the places within yourself that you don't love. The places where you hoped another would love you so you didn't have to. But you have entered the inner chamber; there is no turning back now. The energy there must be healed and transformed. The alchemical transformation is now underway. You must learn to love yourself. In doing that you will discover your internal opposite and become whole. If you are male, you will find your sacred feminine, if you are female, you will find your internal sacred male. This is what the dark field is made up of and where we will find unity and resurrection. Once unified, your opposite self will come to your aid if necessary.

And when you are whole, you will be the door for others to walk through to wholeness.

When you have lived a while in the dark field, the place of exile, as I have, you come to see the interconnectedness of everything. There are rich gifts within it to be obtained. A great wisdom is imparted when you spend time in the field, because so many long held secrets of science, power, consciousness, the universe and truth are still suspended there waiting for release and recognition. The dark field is not a place to fear. But it is a place where you have stored your fears, your shame and the unloved parts of yourself. The Mother has kept them there for safe-keeping until you were strong enough to heal them. It's a place where you have sent those women who signed on to carry your darkness for you. And sometimes men. There are men who reside beside us, especially gay men and women, who have been demonized for holding both halves of the whole consciousness. They have been placed there until we fully understand their purpose. And the truthspeakers – men and women both. All of us reside there, exiled and in pain, holding your suffering for you, lovingly, until you can return and do your personal soul work. But in the darkest part of the dark field are many women, shamed throughout history for their gifts, exiled until everyone wakes up. Their bones rattle and echo through the vibration of the field, crying out their painful stories and calling for love, healing and companionship. All of us women live there, the Goddesses, the wise women, the sages, the healers, the crones, the Mothers, the mystics and the shamans. The time has come to let us out so we can bring healing to humanity. That lost wisdom is about the ebb and flow of the deep and powerful Feminine Energy that brings forth and sustains life, blessing all who revere Her. She brings forth the healing we desperately need. There is nothing to fear, it's going to be a beautiful thing.

There are many mysteries and long held secrets that need to see the light of day. These secrets will help to heal us all. Among them is the mystery of **parthenogenesis***, or women's long lost ability to self-conceive. Buddha's mother conceived her son when in a state of blissful meditation under a banyan tree. Mother Mary was part of a Sacred Feminine Goddess group that practiced parthenogenesis where it is said she conceived Jesus. It's believed that Leonardo DaVinci, Joan of Arc, Moses, Zoroaster, Plato and other brilliant geniuses, visionaries and healers throughout history came about this way. Den Poitras, Divine Feminine expert, states *"Many of the lower species can and do conceive parthenogenetically. So it's easy to postulate humans can too. Why isn't science looking into parthenogenesis? More than a hundred years ago famed biologist, Jacques Loeb realized that the male is not necessary for reproduction. A simple physio-chemical agent in the female is enough to bring it about."*

In the Mother Cell begins all living things. The Creative Principle is feminine. The highest divine mystery is Brahamana, the feminine of Brahma.
~ The Veda

Dr. Walter Timme, eminent endocrinologist, presented evidence in his paper, "Immaculate Conception - a Scientific Possibility", to prove that Immaculate Conception is physiologically possible. The parovarium of the female reproductive organs, he claims, in some cases can produce living spermatozoa capable of impregnating eggs in the same body, causing them to develop without male fertilization. They've been known to appear in young girls, from age 8 to 16, and that have their hymens intact. Unbeknownst to them, one of their eggs had parthenogenetically been fertilized and then had stopped developing, got trapped in their fallopian tube and had to be removed.

Indigenous tribes have long known how to conceive parthenogenetically. In the Ojibwa tradition, wise women looked for certain young maidens that possessed a great degree of grace, intelligence and compassion. Then she was encouraged to dance for hours and hours around a fire in a sacred women's lodge built far away from the village. Throughout her time of dancing she would attempt to enter a state of bliss, a physio-spiritual orgasm if you will, during which according to the Ojibwa wise-women's knowledge, it would be possible for her to conceive. They knew that a child born this way could become a great leader, healer, or visionary.

The Great Spirit, it was thought, would know what gifts the child should have in order to match the current needs of the tribe. In the book, PARTHENOGENESIS: Women's Long-lost Ability to Self-Conceive, it says, "*I believe this is what happened among The Essenes who once lived along The Dead Sea over 2,000 years ago, and from which Jesus originated. The Essenes had either planned his birth, or somehow had known in advance, and had made the necessary preparations. Supposedly, Hannah - Mary's mother - conceived Mary through parthenogenesis. It was prophesied that Mary would conceive Jesus in the same way.*" This powerful, ancient process is still overlooked in modern society.

But a new time is upon us. **On Dec. 21-23, 2012, in fulfillment of a 6 billion year Mayan prophecy, the staff of world leadership was passed from the masculine to the Divine Feminine.** This was never the end of the world or a huge apocalypse. It was simply a transition from a period of repression, darkness, half-consciousness and patriarchal control to a new and better paradigm. This is a return to an ancient time long forgotten when Matriarchs ruled the world. The old paradigm's death will be the mulch for the birth of the new paradigm. The time has come to return to Matriarchal leadership and restore Earth to a desperately needed balance. With the Divine Feminine leading the way, war and genocide will begin to fade, and people will remember caring for one another, building community, and sharing. A concern for collective needs will return because Matriarchal beliefs are circular, everyone is included, and everyone's needs considered. All life is considered sacred and is respected. Men raised in these beliefs choose to nurture life and respect the Divine Feminine rather than wage war.

> *The repression of the feminine*
> *has led to a planet on the edge*
> *of collapse. The re-emergence is*
> *going to be a dance to behold.*
> ~ Clare Dakin

But before we can go there, we have to tackle the issues of the denied, damaged, destroyed feminine that still resides within each one of us like a ticking time bomb. Men experience it too when their sensitivity is destroyed in this harsh environment. It's vital to nurture a boy's sacred feminine within because that is how he grows into a loving, holistic man who respects women. When fathers attempt to "beat the sensitivity" out of their boys, they are condemning them to a half-life of broken consciousness and likely poor marriage prospects. Maybe even violence and crime.

But it's the women who get the specialized treatment to prepare them for their lives at the bottom of the pecking order. And if they are an ethnic minority, the enculturing is deeper. There is a soul-murdering process that takes place, not for all women, but for most. Yes, it's much better than decades ago, but even today women still earn about 77 cents to every dollar a man earns. *In 2014, the entire Republican U.S. Congress voted down the measure stating that women should be paid equally to men.* **Did you catch that? Not 1914, in 2014 they voted that way!** The level of inequity and selfishness by patriarchal males is off the charts. It is outrageous, abusive and unacceptable. Many of the same issues plague women that have for centuries. We must create a new mental paradigm, ladies. It's vital for women to begin to weed out of their psyches the mental thought forms of self-hatred, submission, unworthiness and slavery they learned that have recreated oppression in their lives for centuries. It's equally vital for men to weed superiority, entitlement, greed, sexism and narcissism out of their psyches. Face your shadows, pull up the weeds, clear the path for abundance, joy, equality and freedom to take hold. Create the mental space for wholeness to take root and blossom.

We also are seeing a rise in the mistreatment of women in the Middle East as fundamentalism takes hold there. It's the issue of extreme religious beliefs that seem to bring out the worst in all religions. Honor killings are on the rise. Young women who choose their own mates are frequently killed by their families. Rape has increased in India to record numbers. Women there are taking self-defense classes and arming themselves. In many countries, if a woman is raped, she is expected to kill herself. Recently in Iran, a young woman was raped. This young woman was <u>tried for being raped</u>. When she stood up for herself, removed her hijab (headdress), and said the man who raped me should be tried, she was sentenced to death for speaking back to a man. Elsewhere in the Middle East we see girls like Malala be shot at by the Taliban for wanting to get an education and graduate from college. She survived, went on to write a best-seller and is now the 2014 winner of the Nobel Peace Prize. Here at home, we routinely see the rape of high school girls by football team members who often go scot-free. That happened to my mother in college, where she was an honor student, #1 student in school and on a full scholarship. After being drugged and date-raped by the football captain, she was expelled from school and returned to poverty while he was rewarded with a full scholarship ***after they knew he was a rapist***, with a job waiting for him when he graduated. He went on to become famous. In another case in Pakistan, Mukhtaren Bibi was gang-raped by the town elders. Afterwards, she was given a can of gasoline and told to commit suicide. Instead she pressed charges and in a first-of-its-kind victory, she won and was awarded a sum of money. She used that money to open a co-ed school for children to teach respect of women and equality. Some of the children who attend are children of the men who raped her. We're **_still_** working on the basics of equality.

It goes deeper though. In the matrix of secret societies that make up much of the world's underbelly infrastructure, the female is valued only for her sexual and procreation abilities. The female is viewed as profane not sacred and are always over-sexualized and raped in that world. The archetype of the selfless, pure, loving Mother figure is ridiculed except as to how they can corrupt and change her into someone for their purposes. An attempt to kill the sacred Mother energies is made during the mind-control of society. Images of young girls having sex or being sexualized begins early. They show this as more powerful than the image of a pure Mother loving and guiding her family. Girls are encouraged to have sex before marriage instead of holding their sexual energies sacred for marriage, or even parthenogenesis. Mothers are pressed into service as worker drones, unpaid volunteers at churches, charities and other events, and in general are not encouraged to develop themselves. However, young girls are encouraged to expose themselves physically and sexually to get gigs on TV and elsewhere. If you agree to this, you will be expected to compromise yourself in every way, including sexually.

These are the attempts to murder the soul of the Great Mother who nurtures all life. Once a woman becomes a mother, she is then scapegoated in society for all its ills and anything that is wrong with the children. Even if the patriarchs are harming or abusing the children, the mother will be blamed. The power of the Great Mother is minimized, even laughed at in a diseased culture. Cultures that are whole and healthy place the Mother at the top of the pyramid of power because she is the life-giver, the nurturer and wise woman. No one else can ever fill her shoes. But overly sexualized girls who are exploited will be discarded by the lowest males in our culture when their shelf-life ends at 30 years of age. The age of wisdom for a woman does not even begin until 50 years of age. All female tribal leaders were past 50 years of age. The cultures that honor their women are the African cultures, the indigenous cultures, the Hispanic cultures and many others. Even Mohammed was a feminist and married a much older powerful woman with her own business who taught him the ways of business and life. He had great respect for her and did not take another wife until after she passed.

In the Iroquois Nation, the indigenous collective of Native American tribes that our Constitution is based on, men ruled equally and harmoniously with women. This tribal group was prosperous and harmonious for 1,000 years in New England before the Revolutionary War. It was the tribal women and mothers who held the most power in the Iroquois Nation. Their Iroquois Constitution, known as the Great Law of Peace, which ruled their great Native empire, is the basis of our U.S. Constitution. Thomas Jefferson, Ben Franklin and other founding fathers studied it, and spent time with the Iroquois, learning the secrets of their harmonious rule. Their success was based upon the fact that females ruled the families of the Iroquois Nation, which were made up of these six tribes - Oneida, Mohawk, Cayuga, Onondaga, the Seneca and Tuscarora. They had a strict tribal struc-ture and living arrangement in long houses with the eldest females ruling the tribes. The men met in the Council House with their male Chiefs making decisions, but it's the women who chose the Chiefs and made all decisions regarding who would be their leaders and who had forfeited that right. When the time came for a new leader to be chosen, the women went into their Council House and chose the best male for the position who would most peacefully, wisely and harmoniously lead their tribes. The women were consulted on all decisions and were never lorded over, overlooked or oppressed in any way, shape or form. Their power was sacrosanct and they were recognized, along with nature, as Creators of the Universe and all life. In fact, there are few cultures on Earth that fail to recognize the female as the Creator of the Universe. The primary one is white Christian culture.

When our founding fathers drew up our Constitution, they included many of the principles of the Iroquois Constitution. But due to the strictly patriarchal, sexist nature of our founding fathers and the aggressive culture they were building, they chose to eliminate all reference to, or power inclusion of females. The females were canceled out of all segments of our new American society, yet we were sewing the uniforms of the Revolutionary soldiers, feeding everyone, caring for the men and the children. This is where America went awry, right at the outset. The moment they negated the vast power and potential of more than 50% of the population who carry unique gifts no man has, they set us off on a course limping towards our eventual decline. And that doesn't even mention the exclusion of African slaves, indigenous cultures and other races. The tight circle of the patriarchy, which is a totally exclusive all-white male club of power brokers, have assured the destruction of America in their founding structure. On top of that, few realize that underneath this founding structure is the Secret Society structure which is all male and worships other Gods entirely, even Satan. Yes, there was more freedom than in Europe. Yes, there was freedom of religion. But the Secret society structure was designed to bring us to the New World Order we are currently struggling with that is destroying the world.

The time has come for the INCLUSION of all people of all races, genders, creeds, and classes. The time for an egalitarian society based harmoniously on Divine and Natural Law. But in the meantime, the divine feminine has been left in exile in the dark night of the soul. An attempt to isolate and drive the Mother crazy or into exile has occurred throughout the last 2,000+ years. Know that this is part of the satanic grand plan to strip us of our power. No one survives without the love and respect of the Mother. She is the Creative Force of the

Universe. We must return to a sacred culture and a sacred reverence for the Mother again.

Even deeper rituals take place amongst the secret societies where they actually try to kill the creative force of the Mother within the Earth through violent fracking, drilling, strip-mining, clear-cutting and other destructive acts against Mother Earth. The Earth is a living organism of feminine yin energy and design. When violent machines or weapons go digging into Her soil, it affects the entire energy matrix of the planet. The strips of ore, metals and minerals that snake through the body of the planet are part of the electro-magnetic grid of Earth. To strip-mine them harms that grid. Fracking is cracking open the tectonic plates that act as a skeletal structure over the Earth's core just to get some natural gas we can live without. This is tantamount to giving someone a skull fracture so you can probe around in their brain for goodies. The result is a massive increase in earthquakes wherever fracking occurs. Weather anomalies are a result of the government's attempts to control weather all over the world with HAARP and other secret technology for their advantage. As a result, we've seen the Japanese and Haitian earthquakes and resulting tsunamis causing the Fukushima disaster now threatening all life on Earth. These are all violations of the divine feminine energy of Mother Earth.

Because of all this, a great traumatic heart-shock is experienced by the Mother as her vital energy was attacked over time. She was placed in a near death-like state. This trauma still lives within the dark field and on Earth, but is currently healing alchemically through a great *Earth Soul Transformation**. This has been a concerted effort taking place energetically amongst the adepts within secret societies, to kill off the very powerful Mother core life force and take the energies for themselves. The stealing of feminine power is a major issue on this planet in all systems from religion to entertainment to families to school systems because the Mother energy is the creative life force and the dynamic love force that runs the world. It isn't money that makes the world go round, it's love. And the Mother's love is the strongest of all. If they can separate women from their divine grace and love, they can overtake the souls of the children who rely upon them. Getting children more interested in IPads, IPhones, TV, video games, movies, pop stars, sex, drugs, etc. than in the directives of their parents or spiritual practices is a technique to undermine the power of the Mother on the family and in the world. These attempts are more than just patriarchal, they are satanic in nature. This thread is present underneath it all and spreads into all the systems in place currently. The goal is to replace the sacred with the profane, and they will stop at nothing to achieve that. It's a global effort and it's deep in the heart of all the secret societies actions. But the Mother is rising, and we must help her.

The task of the woman rising in power is to cleanse herself of all violations, mind-control, dark energies, negative attachments, lies and predators within herself to restore her sacredness. She must be the one to believe again in her sacredness. She must reach for her sacred self that dwells within. She must find her inner power and call it up. She must do consistent and persistent inner homework. She must fight off the temptations to give up, be profane, become prey for men, disrespect herself, lose her power, and be seduced by various groups, offers or individuals. A process of deep inner cleansing must begin that includes prayer and/or meditation, chanting sacred chants, reading sacred literature, avoiding profane situations, detoxifying mentally, emotionally, physically and spiritually especially from mind control, taking care of her health, keeping fit with exercise/yoga and the like. She must remove people and situations from her life that bring her into predation that lowers her vibration and power. She *MUST* separate from patriarchal men who seek to suppress her power and truth, block her from self-actualizing, lower her self-image and steal her divinity, however subtly. However painful and difficult, the time she spends shattered in the dark field is a sacred time. It is the time her soul is allowed to reclaim and reassemble her fragmented soul parts and rediscover her lost power. It is a time of inner mysteries and wisdom being revealed to her that she has carried within her for eternity. That wisdom has been denied. She must claim it now and step forth with her truth regardless of how it is received. Much is going on at an unconscious level. Even the suffering of exile and isolation can be a boon when deep introspection during solitude leads to awakening and redemption.

Now if a woman has been a long time in the dark field of exile, she will need to relearn self-love in the strongest ways. It's vital for a woman who has been prey or has been exiled and ridiculed for her True Self to create a safe sacred space around her. She will have to learn to create a boundary within which she can live where she is safe instead of constantly seeking safety with new predators. It must be a place where no predator can enter and take her power. An energy field where no one can diminish her verbally or harm her physically. These are stages in the process of self-love that must be attained. Some only have one or two, some have more. But she will have to dig down into her psyche to find the thoughts, behaviors and beliefs that shelter the predator, abuser, the death merchants, the self-hatred and weed them out. She will have to banish the fatigue that comes from once having had your power stolen, especially if it's been through ritual abuse. That takes work and health rituals, but she must force herself to rise again and remember who she was, fierce, strong and true. There can be no enabling of the abusers. No denying their offense towards her if she is to reclaim her sacredness and power. To deny the offense to her soul, is to become complicit in self-abuse. She must be her own greatest protector and champion, she must call up her inner sacred masculine to do this.

She will have to speak her truth loudly and be prepared to be rejected for it. She will have to learn to stand alone against those who dishonor her truth and believe in the lie. She will have to be willing to be the only person who loves her and still be ok with that. She will have to be ready to have no fear about standing in her truth and her power even if other powerful people don't like it. She will have to be very comfortable with who she is and what her truth is because many may dislike her truth. She will have to face, embrace, heal and integrate her shame core because that is how they keep her power down. There will be demons stored there like sentries guarding over the power they have stolen. She will have to fight them to regain her integrity and inner peace. She will have to regain her trust in the Universe after having been betrayed over and over. That can only be accomplished by walking into fear with faith at your back and courage in her heart. She will have to reclaim her soul's purpose from the dungeon they have placed it in. And her body will have to be strong enough to hold the power that is coming. It's a monumental task that takes time. Once she reaches that milestone, she is ready to claim her power.

The discussion of the rape, persecution and resurrection of the Mother wouldn't be complete without including *Lilith** and *Eve**. Lilith and Eve are major missing puzzle pieces in the over-arching holistic view of sacred feminine history since so many myths that have swallowed our culture are based on them. These ladies got a bad rap. Lilith was Adam's first wife so the legend goes. She and he were said to both be made from the Earth's dust equally. When Adam demanded she submit to him, she refused saying she was his equal and was to be respected, honored and held sacred and equal to him. He banished her from the Garden of Eden and Lilith went into exile. And the first patriarch was born.

According to Genesis in the Bible, Adam then pulled Eve out of his rib and demanded she submit to him. Eve agreed. But the myth that continues to swirl around her is that she brought the downfall of mankind by listening to the snake, eating the fruit of the forbidden tree of knowledge and then tempting Adam to eat the fruit. This explanation reeks of patriarchal projection of blame for male desire onto the woman. Something we're still dealing with today. The clear explanation for Eve's situation is the metaphor she represents. The snake is the Kundalini, the great sacred snake of divine power that lay dormant at the base of the spine, only to be awakened by sacred sexuality. The fruit is woman herself, who is desired and bears fruit of another kind through sacred union leading to awakening. Eve offered this to Adam, giving him the spiritual awakening into Nirvana through Tantric sex. Eve offered Adam the chance to move out of his patriarchal half-consciousness and embrace his own divine feminine. Somehow, the lesson of Kundalini awakening was not embraced and was lost along the way. Humanity fell alright, but not because of a woman. It was because of embracing a patriarchal half-consciousness. And that is where we have remained.

It is this experience that can awaken a man's heart and soul to divinity when properly and sacredly conducted with love present. Eve represents the Divine Feminine come to bring unconditional love, healing and awakening to Adam from our Creator. She is not the seductress portrayed by Christianity any more than Mary Magdalene was. These are religious myths that have swallowed our culture but are doing great damage to women and men both, and scapegoating the female gender for everything. It's part of duality and the patriarchal half-consciousness that prevails here. And women lose their power in such false myths of inferiority, blame and male entitlement. It's equally catastrophic for men who lose their hearts and souls in the constant denial and castigation of the sacred feminine. In doing that, they condemn themselves.

The current archetype that is known as Adam is a representation of all patriarchal males who cannot take responsibility for their own sexual desire so they project that on Eve and blame her for the entire fall of humanity. Certainly all men are not like this and things are improving. But not everywhere. We still have male-dominated cultures placing blame for their own behavior onto women. Do we want to continue to engage in this kind of unconsciousness, projection and sexism? No, it's time to admit it. Eve was framed. Men need to step up to the plate and take responsibility for their part in duality. Meanwhile, Lilith was rudely exiled into the dark field and has not forgotten her betrayal and heartbreak. There she has remained throughout history, alone and unloved, carrying the unhealed pain of thousands of years and millions of women. But, now her time has come.

> *The world will be saved by the Western woman...*
> ~ *Dalai Lama*

It is at this moment in world history that Lilith steps forth to be heard. She has three forms in nature – Asteroid Lilith, Dark Moon Lilith and **Black Moon Lilith***. We are feeling the presence of the Lilith energy right now and will continue to for some time. She is the exiled, powerful, brilliant Goddess not allowed to express her power. She is capable of so much yet left on the sidelines throughout the game while men destroy the field. In her exile, she has developed extra-strong inner powers of perception, intelligence, strength, perseverance, endurance, truth, outspokenness, confrontation, and anger. Her voice is like a whip that cracks at the lie. She can draw blood when she voices her truth. The powerful Black Moon Lilith Goddess is an energy vortex that cuts through the veils of illusion with the sword of truth. It is this energy that is coming to Earth at this time to liberate us from our bondage within the illusion. All formerly suppressed sacred feminine energies, within men as well, will stand up now to face down the demonic patriarchal forces now destroying Earth. What was once a kindly Father Knows Best or Ozzie Nelson type of man has morphed into corrupt Wall St. banksters, corporate criminals, sex traffickers, political hacks and more. These are not the men of the past we could at least talk to. These are cunning predatory men, and sometimes women, who require great strength and wisdom to confront and deal with. We have to pull up all our reserves to hold the line against their constant violation of sacred energy. There can be no backing down. Only after they have been subdued can we begin the process of healing Earth.

We must adopt a non-cooperation policy with evil whenever and wherever we find it.
~ *Salini*

I call out all the Black Moon Liliths wherever you are. Stand up and be heard. Unveil your power. Speak your Truth. Shine your Light. Step out and be seen. We are ready for you. The Earth needs your power, strength and truth to cut through the illusion and release the toxic energy so long held within our breasts. Lead the charge and the rest of us will follow. We honor you today and forever. Your beautiful voice we long to hear. Your time has come. We welcome you back into the fold of humankind.

Healing the Patriarchs and Predators

Soon the time is coming for the healing of everyone. That includes even the patriarchs and predators, for remember, we are all connected. They live in the shadow of our unclaimed soul power. What you deny in the way of your soul's power, they make use of. But when you claim it, they are forced into the light of day. They await our arrival into our full Goddess power to bring them healing. They cannot do this themselves. When the female has reached her full readiness to claim the unconditionally loving Mother within, she is ready to heal the patriarchs and half-conscious men. This is the Great Initiation of the exiled Goddess. The hardest initiation of all. She must bring back the ravaged heart of humanity, in spite of her betrayal and wounding at their hands, and restore it for everyone, not just for women. Because we've done this to each other over and over and over. And it needs to stop here....now.

But first we must honor those who were lost along the way. While in the dark field I heard the voices of the Matriarchs and sisters long gone who had lost their lives in the oppression, torture, exile, abuse and murder during the great persecution of women. My mother, sister, cousin and best friend were among them, crying out to me for justice. Like the spirits of Native American ancestors visiting the tribe around the council fire, these women spoke to me, bringing me their suffering, seeking relief and healing, and asked me to speak for them. Their stories speak to the great wrong done to women throughout history in the name of greed, ambition, power, conquest, ego, and all things patriarchal. Their suffering can never be forgotten. In honor of them I call for justice, recognition, respect and the restoration of sacredness for the millions of abused and oppressed women everywhere who then and now had to live through the misogyny, sexism, horror, rape, torture and murder of the patriarchy.

But now, those energies have flooded through me and seek transmutation. I spent 40 years healing the extreme pain of what was done to me, but I always knew I was doing this for many, many others. I always felt the ancestral suffering of so many passing through my energy field. Because I witnessed so much suffering of women, and of abused men as well, I began to see the loop of pain we were all trapped in. I saw many generations of victims and perpetrators, some in this life and some in other lives. I saw the men who once abused us become the women who were now abused. I saw the women who long were victims take up the sword against people in other lives and I saw the cycle of birth and death played out time and time again with the same sad story of revenge, unforgiveness and suffering. I saw the thread that connected us all. As I passed through the alchemical transformation up my chakras and in my heart and soul of the lead of suffering to the gold of awakening, I knew what I had to do. The time to cut the ancestral cord to the past paradigm of war, rape, murder, revenge and terror had arrived. It ends now. The door has opened to begin the process of healing and forgiving the patriarchs. But they must lay down their ways. And we women must be in our highest Goddess selves to accomplish this task. These men will be tough customers. Women will need to be standing as Warriors, strong as steel, but with love in your hearts. Healed men must stand at our sides to speak to their brothers of love and healing. The steel only comes down when the patriarchs and predators have fully surrendered their swords of darkness and willingly entered their healing.

In the mix of healing will be our gay men and women. These people have brought forth both halves of consciousness to help us heal our split. When I hear the judgments against them my heart breaks because I know it's an extension of the persecution of the sacred feminine. Gay males are here to show us the presence of the sacred feminine within men that has been destroyed. Gay women are here to show women the strength they deny. Embrace your whole self as they are showing you and become whole and strong. You don't always need a man to do it for you. And men, you can take care of yourselves.

Are you ready ladies? Can you hold your power and love our predators too? Are you ready proud men, to lay down your machismo in favor of a tender, loving heart? We offer you love and healing for the many lifetimes you've lived in pain as a warrior, a worker peasant, a soldier, a father supporting his family. In the Democratic Republic of the Congo, and likely other African nations as well, there has been an epidemic of young boys being kidnapped into armies and trained as soldiers and rapists. Their sweetness and humanity is beaten out of them. They are told their families don't care about them and to forget them. They live in the wild with their army leaders and then turn on their former tribes and rape, and sometimes kill their mothers and sisters. It's ravaged their villages and continued on a long time. So the women formed a plan. In several of the villages in the Congo, the women of the tribe have joined together to form healing groups of women. These groups of women have begun welcoming the boys back into their midst and are healing them through love, forgiveness and mothering. Their courage, forgiveness and love is staggering.

This is a difficult and scary proposition but works largely because of the nature of tribal community principles and long-standing tribal structure. I doubt this would work here in the broken down, diseased West now until we return to our tribal roots and live once again as loving, cooperative communities. But maybe we can begin by using the Congolese women as an example, much like the Iroquois women of the past, as powerful forces for leadership, healing and change. We female shamans, healers, ministers, kahunas, grandmothers, mothers and medicine women can lead the way. What have we got to lose? After all, right now, all we have to look forward to are increasing numbers of Americans going to jail, a woman being raped every 2 minutes somewhere, black men being gunned down in the street for no reason regularly, the rich stealing our life's blood every day, brutality on the rise on both sides – police and gangs, corporate and political tyranny, and you know the rest. I think we can do better than that. Let's see what we can accomplish as a people, as a team of sisters and brothers working together.

Know that it isn't just Black Moon Lilith, or Isis, or Eve or any other of the cultural myths and legends that are rising now. No, it's much bigger than that. It's all of you, all over the world. Every oppressed woman, man and child. Every patriarchal man who longs to be heartfelt again. Every secret society man who wishes he didn't sell his soul for money. Every long-abused woman who is ready to become powerful again. Every disenfranchised Third World resident raped by the corporations. Every child working in an Asian phone factory for .50 cents a day. Every sexually trafficked child who yearns to break free. Every sexually trafficked adult who is searching for a way out. Today is your day. Release your Divine Feminine Power. She lives within you and longs for freedom, set her free. Stand up. Break your chains. Throw off your bondage. Escape from your slavery. Walk free. Above all, reclaim your hearts and share them with the world. The world is waiting for all your sacred feminine power to be transformed into a massive healing wave of love and creativity. Together we can heal the world.

RISE EVERYONE AND SHOW THEM YOUR TRUE POWER AND GLORY. WE CAN HEAL THIS PLANET IF WE WORK TOGETHER WITH LOVE TO DO SO.

AND SO LET US BEGIN

Chapter 10

Energetic & Emotional Anatomy

Matter is nothing more than trapped energy waiting to be freed. Feelings are another form of trapped energy within the body. When they remain trapped, they become denser and denser until they form illness. Love releases it.....

~ Salini

In order to reclaim your power and health, you need to understand how your energy body works. The energy of the human body is given to everyone at birth by our Creator. From day one it is yours to utilize how you wish. It belongs to no one but you. It is divine in nature and is called differently according to the language of different cultures. The Chinese call it chi, the Japanese call it Reiki, Hawaiians call it mana, Hindus call it prana and Christians call it the Holy Spirit. But those names all refer to the same thing.....God's divine energy. The energy itself is made up of unconditional love and has unlimited powers of healing.

Your divine energy system is like a series of rivers inside of you that flow everywhere and permeate all systems of your body and all aspects of your being. Its origins are the Universe itself. It is intended to flow unhindered within an internal orbital pathway known as the microcosmic orbit which is made up of hundreds of tiny vein-like channels and thousands of processing stations known as nadis. There are 72,000 **nadis*** of energy points connected to your nervous system within this energy matrix. Also within that system are 77 chakra centers positioned throughout the body to receive and distribute energy where it is needed. Additionally, there are 5 primary chakra centers and 2 magnetic poles, one at the crown and one at the root. The chakras act as the main fueling stations for receiving and distributing energy and the magnetic poles keep the yin/yang Kundalini energy charge in balance and traveling up and down your spinal column and throughout your nadis. The main orbital channel passes through your primary chakra system and around your body in an oval, passing from top to bottom and back up again. Your chakras capture your energy as it enters from the outer etheric field and distribute it to each endocrine gland within the endocrine system. The endocrine system in turn distributes the energy to the rest of the body's organic system, through the energy channel system, according to the body's needs.

The energy distributed by the endocrine glands becomes fuel for daily organ function. A free and powerful flow of this divine energy throughout the body is the natural healthy state all humans are intended to dwell in. If your energy remains strong and unhindered, a healthy body is the result. However, many forces and interferences can alter or block the flow of this energy within our bodies. Some I've mentioned earlier. If our energy flow becomes blocked, lessened or diverted, disease can result.

It's important for people to understand that they continually exist within an energy field, or aura, which empowers them, and that their energy field stores every single experience, memory, shock, emotion, event and trauma that occurs as a form of energy. If those experiences are frightening, toxic, violent or shaming, a distorted form of energy enters the field and remains there. Your energy field then attempts to process it like your stomach processes your lunch. If it's too difficult to digest, break up, or process out into other areas of your field and body, the aura will store it in a safe place within your body until a time you can process it out. If it's too toxic to process, it becomes a stagnant host for disease.

Dr. Masuro Emoto, a Japanese researcher, conducted a series of incredible experiments with water showing how energy, words and thoughts affect water molecules. He applied a series of words superimposed on the water, spoken to the water or thoughts directed towards the water. He also experimented with different types of music played towards the water molecules.

Dr. Emoto's experiments show that water molecules are profoundly affected by even simple words spoken to them. How seriously then can our cells and bodies be affected by repeated onslaughts of negative energy, angry emotions, cruel words, violent trauma and toxic energy entering them? Especially since our bodies are approximately 80% water?

Creating an unhindered flow of divine energy within your body should be what we aspire to. This is part of our self-maintenance like brushing our teeth and exercising. Many factors can occur to block the energy flow. The obvious culprits to avoid would be smoking, drinking, drugs, and junk food. But it's more complex than that. When you introduce GMOs, processed foods or synthetic pharmaceuticals into your body, you are interfering with the body's natural abilities to heal itself. The body has to respond to the synthetics that have been introduced. Most of them are stored in the lymph, liver, gall bladder or kidneys where they remain as part of your toxic load until cleansed out. But this type of pollution is more well-known and health information on this topic can be found in many other books on nutrition.

Let's concentrate on the energy of emotions. Emotions have a particular force of their own. I'm sure you have felt the energy of anger rise up in you, perhaps fear pounding in your chest, or sorrow in your heart and eyes. These are the very palpable energies of emotions. They can also become blocked or lodged in the body depending on their origin and how they were imposed or experienced by the individual. These emotions can also impede the flow of divine chi energy. Some people express emotions easily, others do not. Women are more likely to express and release their emotions because it's culturally acceptable. Men are often shamed into holding in their emotions or risk being branded a sissy or weak. Holding in painful emotions for long periods of time is never healthy.

If there has been trauma to the body of any type - physical, emotional, sexual, psychological or toxin-related, the body's energy system becomes distorted, diverted, polluted, blocked or drained off. Then in turn, your immune response is affected. Due to the largely misunderstood nature of how trauma and karma affect the development of disease, allopathic medical doctors often attempt to track down disease pathogens and organisms to find the origin of illnesses. They are looking monodimensionally at the body and see disease as primarily physical in nature. This is incorrect.

The body is actually holistic in nature with four primary systems – physical, mental, emotional and spiritual – all of which must be addressed to heal someone. In some cases, it's a simple physical issue, like a broken leg, but most often it is a larger holistic issue going on. And even with a broken leg, there are underlying soul issues at play, like in the example further on in this chapter. When the energy system of the body maintains a healthy, strong flow of divine energy throughout all systems without interference, diseases are kept at a minimum and immune response is strong. This is called homeostasis and should be everyone's goal, including doctors.

If there has been trauma at some point in life, especially in childhood before you have developed the mental and emotional capacity to process the experience, the body will store painful or frightening emotions and experiences somewhere within the tissue and energy body, often without the person's knowledge, where it can remain for life like a ticking time bomb. At this point the energy flow of the body becomes distorted and begins to divert or partition off the energy. Energy stagnation can begin. It can be stored there as toxic energy within the body's tissue for indeterminate periods of time where it can develop into disease or until the individual chooses to release and transmute the energy, or dies.

Certain diseases are related to the type of emotional energy blockage that has occurred. Often, some kind of trauma has triggered an intense emotional response. When trauma and emotions are present together, the trauma will seal the emotion in place. The trauma itself acts as a binder and barrier because it freezes emotions in place. The trauma is able to bind these emotions by using one of our basic emotions as a binder/barrier. That emotion is fear/terror which is strongly engendered during a traumatic event. Just think of how you feel when you are terrified, you freeze in place and take in a sharp breath and hold it. The trauma acts to stop the normal breath and flow of energy. Then we breathe in the shock of the event. That is when the fear is frozen in place in your *cellular memory**, with an in-breath. Terror is the deepest fear response. Because of the feeling and belief that your life is in danger, terror will trigger the body's response mechanism to block off the traumatic event and seek safety, even if that's only in your mind. So, when terror is present, it stops normal mental, physical and emotional energetic flow and activity and gathers all the body's energy to itself, seizing control of it, effectively walling off access to the stored traumatized emotions by blocking their return to conscious memory. Then the calm, centered consciousness can return to managing daily activities.

If enough terror is present, amnesia accompanies the process to protect the conscious mind. Thus we forget that we are holding painful emotions. We can become unconscious to our pain. These emotions can then be held there for many years without our conscious knowledge. If painful, traumatized emotions are held in place long enough, they develop into stagnant pools which are disease hosts.

Because so much energy is stored in these stagnant pools and is required to hold the fear barrier in place, we have lessened access to our body's divine energy. This then creates a lowered immune response. An additional side effect of these raised levels of fear as barriers is they also act as barriers to love. Love is what heals, but fear is what blocks it from entering. This is the eternal struggle we face in life, the internal battle between our cells and our minds, and the overarching battle between good and evil on Earth.

The chart below shows some areas where the body usually holds certain emotions. There can be variations and exceptions to these listed below, but commonly you will find these emotional energies in these places within the body. Empaths, healers and medical intuitives can see and feel these blockages and have accurately mapped out emotional anatomy for centuries. Certain specific illnesses will be associated with this stuck, toxic emotional energy. The actual cause of the illness is commonly the stored emotion or the stored trauma connected to the emotion. They work together to create disease. These illnesses will vary in severity and type according to the length of time, intensity of trauma and depth of emotion held there.

In addition to carrying current emotional pain in specific body parts, the soul brings karmic material from other lifetimes to process out in this lifetime. That material is part of your Akashic Record. You can literally be born with a condition or disease that is a result of karmic actions in another life. This can be one cause of young children and infants with serious illnesses such as cancer.

Unless you have an *Ayurvedic**, *Holistic** or *Chinese physician**, it is unlikely your doctor will discuss karma or trauma with you, since they believe in a disease maintenance model, not holistic prevention or cure. Chinese doctors have a vast training and knowledge that includes Chiropractic, herbal remedies, surgeries, medicine and *Chi Gong**, which is similar to *Reiki.* They are fabulous healers, but don't necessarily discuss karma. Ayurvedic doctors have the deepest of all healing knowledge and training about disease, origins, treatment and their karmic roots thus they make the best doctors. Regardless of one's belief, karma is always present in nearly all disease conditions, because the body is predisposed at birth by past karma to develop such a condition. The soul's energy from the last lifetime is carried over into the current lifetime. If there was an imbalance in that life, it is brought forward to the new body to be resolved in the current lifetime. This will continue until the soul resolves all imbalances and is restored to wholeness and wakes up. These imbalances can be mental, spiritual, physical or emotional, or a combination of all four quadrants.

Similarly, emotions are also present in all disease conditions in the form of energy. These two factors are rarely if ever addressed in traditional medicine and are being overlooked as main causative factors in today's chronic illnesses.

Cancer is a case in point. Cancer is the wounding and separation of the parts of the self. When one is unable to love the entire self, or when the energy of love is somehow blocked from being present within the whole being, the parts that do not receive love can be become diseased. As mentioned earlier in this chapter, when trauma walls off emotions and traps them within a certain area of the body, it also blocks love from entering there to heal the wound in that part of the body.

Cancer is a direct byproduct of a diseased culture that feeds on others and Mother Earth. The USA has the highest rate of cancer in the world, a relatively new phenomenon. If their theory of "cancer genes" was accurate, the rate of cancer would be universal and stable globally. It isn't. What we have instead is cancer growth proportionate exponentially to the increase in toxicity of our society mentally, emotionally, physically and spiritually.

Americans have very high rates of cancer currently, around 50% of the population, and more and more children are getting cancer. It isn't necessary to spend billions on searching for fruitless "cures" for cancer when the cure has been readily available for eight decades from multiple sources. The true cures were suppressed decades ago to support the burgeoning cash flow of the cancer industry. They keep the lie going to drain your bank account and your soul's energy. Don't let them. So let's begin to look at some of the true causes.

Cancer is the somatization of cultural disease and trauma with a dash of karma. It is caused by several main factors - toxins, lifestyle, karma and a deep emotional/physical trauma, including cultural trauma. Being exposed to radiation, asbestos, toxic chemicals, smoking or other toxins contribute of course. But to suggest someone gets cancer because their mother or grandfather had it is absurd once you understand the causative nature of disease, which always includes trauma and karma. Ancient Vedic texts from India confirm the true nature of illness as karma, trauma and imbalances.

Additionally, cancer is primarily a modern disease not common in earlier times. Supporting data suggests fewer people got cancer 100+ years ago; so how could everyone be inheriting it now? The *New England Journal of Medicine* states that in 1900, cancer and heart disease accounted for 18 percent of all deaths. Today, that figure has jumped to 63 percent. Obviously, the rise in toxicity in our environments in our foods, our homes, our jobs, radiation, pollutants, heavy metals, chemtrails, vaccinations, etc., contribute to the increase in cancer. But the deep emotional trauma & suffering occurring around us today in our very deeply violent, oppressed, disconnected society is also causing our bodies and immune systems to shut down, divine energy to stop flowing and cancer to develop.

Here is a story of how the power of Reiki to heal and transform someone proved the presence of God's divine healing energy around and within us -

Jessie's Reiki healing story – *Jessie came to me sick and in a very broken down state, fearful, upset and crying. She had been given a diagnosis of adrenal and kidney cancer. The doctors had already removed one kidney and one adrenal gland. She was working full-time, was sick and very stressed out. It showed. Her anxiety would dissolve to tears in a moment's notice. She had been to a number of doctors other than her surgeon who performed numerous tests on her. Some of them gave her less than 6 months to live. One in par-ticular said to her while I was working with her, "You came too late; there is nothing I can do. You probably won't make it to Christmas." Doctors love to play God, and give the death sentence. This just added to her stress. I knew that any disease could be healed when God was brought in, no matter what stage someone was at. She was in late stage cancer and the doctor's vision was limited to his knowledge. I kept encouraging her to believe she could heal herself and win this battle. We prayed and meditated together.*

When she told me her story, it was clear what was causing her illness. She was experiencing severe family issues that created enormous emotional stress for her, causing her adrenals and kidneys to shut down. After a prolonged period of extreme stress, she became ill. All of the toxic energy concentrated in her adrenals and kidney. She had become so nervous and jittery she collapsed with stressed adrenals. Her case was not one of toxin exposure at all as she lived in a beautiful, healthy environment. Her emotions had worn down her body specifically in her adrenal response area. One of her adrenals became malignant, as did the adjoining kidney, and both the adrenal gland and kidney on one side had to be removed.

This is how emotions can affect the body powerfully.

She had to relearn how to live and react to life in a calmer, stress-free way. Among other things, I gave her Reiki, taught her meditation and then taught her to self-heal with Reiki. We did a lot of emotional release work and soul retrieval, all elements of Soul Transformation Therapy. She learned to access her power, her past lives, her healing abilities and her will to live again.

Over the course of the time I worked on her, I could see inside her body where the kidney had been removed. Although I could see where the surgery had taken place and the organ was gone, I also saw something amazing. It appeared to me that a new kidney was growing where the old one had been! Every time I looked intuitively, it appeared to be a new kidney. I can't prove that of course, but I know what I saw. With God, miracles are always around the corner. While doctors were telling her she wouldn't make it to Christmas, we were working on healing her, on how to relearn her responses and getting her back on her feet. Instead of his dire prognosis, she's healthy, cancer-free, back to working full-time and gives herself Reiki every single day. Jessie learned to access the divine energy of Reiki in her body and move it where her body, mind and spirit most needed it to self-heal. You can too.

There are many more like Jessie who are given only a physical diagnosis, then sometimes the death knell instead of searching for the true cause. While we suffer with these diseases in denial, medical arrogance and lack of compassion, people are dying of stress, toxins, trauma and abuse. This book is dedicated to all of them that they might find their way out of this impasse of healing. There are so many so-called "incurable diseases" caused by buried trauma and abuse.

Those who pass from them are listed as deaths from Cancer, Lupus, Multiple Sclerosis, Fibromyalgia, Rheumatoid Arthritis, Lou Gehrig's disease and other diseases, but they really die of something else. Are you holding in any secret, denied trauma? I hope not, because that toxic energy could be the basis for you to develop a life-threatening disease.

After many years of working with trauma victims of various types of suppressed trauma, I have discovered that large portions of unconscious deep trauma are usually stored in the brain stem. The worst types of trauma that include violence, especially sexual abuse, beatings or war trauma, are stored in the brain stem unconsciously directing thoughts, actions and life decisions through the brain, creating an **unconscious split*** in awareness. In order to survive severe childhood abuse, a child's brain will compartmentalize painful and traumatic experiences due to the lack of mental and ego strength, or understanding necessary to process such an experience. This becomes a split off portion, or fragment, safely compartmentalized away from regular daily brain function. It is these energy fragments that I frequently deal with in healing trauma and disease victims. They emerge during healing and recovery to be **re-membered***, processed, integrated, and embraced.

If a person is able to reach the stage of peaceful integration of the traumatic episode early enough, it's likely they will recover from whatever they have, but only after intervention by skilled energy healers. After witnessing this phenomenon in so many of my clients, I suggest that a malignant brain tumor in the brain stem, especially a glioblastoma, should alert medical professionals to the likelihood of early sexual trauma, or other severe trauma. Energy healers, medical intuitives and counselors should be brought in at that point to give a clearer diagnosis and understanding of the holistic issues involved and to assist in trying to save the person's life. The traditional allopathic methodology and practices, as well as the ego of the medical professional, needs to step aside and let higher knowledge in. Many doctors today are beginning to understand this and bring in healers and other alternative practitioners to help.

Migraine headaches are also a marker for this kind of trauma and should be immediately addressed with Reiki, Cranial-Sacral Therapy or other natural energy-based therapies before disease or tumors can develop.

Additional locations of buried sexual trauma are the root chakra area which translates anatomically to the tailbone (coccyx), anus, sphincter, psoas muscles, erector spinae, thoracolumbar fascia, other deep low back muscles and lumbar vertebrae, all of which absorb the energy of violence and sexual trauma and store it there. The difference from the brain storage of trauma is that there is no brain memory of the experience to process and think about. This type of traumatic memory is stored in the tissue and felt in the body as pain and stiffness usually. This is how trauma, emotions and thoughts are **somatized*** into illnesses such as Rheumatoid Arthritis, Lupus, Fibromyalgia and Multiple Sclerosis. Bodywork and Reiki should be employed to release and heal it while simultaneously changing diet and lifestyle. Yoga is very helpful, if you can do it. Easier energy practices that are very helpful are Tai Chi or Reiki.

Additionally and most crucially, is the function and capacity of the sacrum to store, protect and process the body's divine energy. The sacral bone acts as a shield protecting an unseen well or chalice that stores the body's divine energy. When looking at the sacrum from an anatomical design, the area inside appears to be a void. In actuality, that area is an energetic chalice, **the sacral chalice***, where divine chi energy is stored as it is processed in from the chakras and endocrine glands. It is a storage well, similar to your vehicle's gas tank, where divine energy (chi) is stored until it is needed somewhere in your body. Like your car, when it gets empty it needs to be refilled with more divine energy. It is specifically designed to be near the reproductive organs of both the male and the female for the purpose of creating life, thus it is considered the divine life force energy.

Inside the sacrum, there are nerves that enter and pass through the holes inside the sacral walls. There are also small muscles deep inside the sacrum. These can all be traumatized during an abuse event and transfer intense traumatic energy to the sacrum and on up the spinal column to the brain stem where it gets stored in brain tissue. This area is highly prone to trapping traumatic energy, especially sexual trauma, and must be released by a trained professional such as a Cranial-Sacral practitioner, MyoFascial Release practitioner, Chiropractor or Reiki practitioner. I caution individuals and practitioners to take care when working with trauma victims on this area. It can trigger the release of traumatic memory and a download can begin which in itself is very traumatic because you re-experience the original trauma. Additionally, the individual can become very sick from a sudden release of toxic traumatic energy. Worst of all, a person can experience ***Kundalini psychosis**** if the traumatic memory travels all the way up the spinal column and into the brain. Kundalini is the coiled, life force energy at the base of the Root Chakra that provides each human with the potential for spiritual awakening. It has the power to wash away past karmic traces from the person's mind and body. But it also may stir up a lot of repressed feelings and traumas from the unconscious. A premature Kundalini awakening may cause psychotic episodes in individuals with severe early traumas. I have had to work on people who were improperly triggered by unskilled practitioners and were experiencing Kundalini psychosis. Kundalini psychosis is life-threatening as a person can go insane and commit suicide. So, do this kind of work slowly and in intervals, not all at once. Make sure the client is ready, willing and can handle it.

Additionally, the Dura Mater, or dense, white, inelastic, fibrous connective tissue, covers the brain and spinal column ending in the coccyx. This tissue ends in the sacrum and carries energetic memory throughout the nervous system and spinal column up into the brain. Trauma occurring in the sacrum is stored first in the sacral/coccyx area, then transferred back and forth up the spinal column to the brain stem, and finally into the brain where it can interfere with brain function. If there is severe continuous trauma to this area, the tissue surrounding the spinal column and fluid will develop a constricted fabric pattern which in turn, creates a stagnant, blocked energy flow. This can be the cause of severe back, sacral, spinal, and muscular or neck pain.

Add to that the other layers of thin fibrous body tissue, known as *fascia**, that line the inside of and overlay all the organic structure of the human anatomy, which can also store trauma and other troubling emotions, and you have a recipe for pain and disease. Fascia is an interconnected web of thin, spidery fibrous tissue connected like a piece of fabric that covers the entire internal structure of the body, especially the muscles. It holds certain bodily structures together and allows others to move freely as it assists with the internal support structure of the human body. It also carries messages electrically throughout its nadi tissue points and can transfer trauma messages as well.

Bodyworkers know that any trauma to the body is often held in the fascia and muscles which must be released for people to fully heal. Diseases such as Fibromyalgia and Lupus can spread this way due to the trauma being stored in the fascia all over the body for long periods of time and causing migrating pain, weakness and fatigue. Don't waste time with drugs, find skilled energy and bodyworkers to help release stored trauma. This illustration shows what fascia looks like in the body as it covers your muscles and organs to protect them and help them stay in place. But the vast area that it covers makes the fascia the connecting tissue that also carries the messages of pain and trauma and deposits them into the muscles and organs.

thoracolumbar fascia

TRISH CROALC

Finally, perhaps the one muscle most profoundly affected by trauma due to its pivotal location is the Psoas muscle, known as the muscle of the soul. I have seen so much pain in this area from sexual abuse survivors that it's important to mention the Psoas' crucial role in overall healing. This muscle is often closest to the original traumatic event thus takes the sharpest blow. Since it is a large muscle that connects all the way from the back, inner body cavity and spine, through the pelvic floor and down the inside front of the leg, many areas and opportunities for movement are dramatically affected. The psoas is crucially placed and is vital to body movement and function.

The Psoas muscle is the deepest muscle of the human body. According to bodyworker and Psoas expert Liz Koch, it isn't just a muscle but an organ composed of bio-intelligent tissue that perceives. The Psoas is the primal messenger of the central nervous system. It is the only muscle that connects our back to our legs and is responsible for lifting our legs to move, walk or even run from danger. The Psoas is also connected to the diaphragm through fascia which affects both our breath and fear reflex. These reflexes are part of the reptilian brain which is directly connected to the Psoas muscle. The reptilian part of the brain, which includes the interior part of the brain stem and the spinal cord, is the most ancient part of the brain, existing before our advanced brain developed. Known for its survival instincts, the reptilian brain maintained our essential core functioning. The Psoas muscle still holds these survival instincts. For this reason, trauma stored there affects the body and daily life profoundly, but unconsciously, since the reptilian brain is unconscious to the conscious mind except through the fight/flight/freeze response, also known as the fear response.

If the Psoas muscle becomes chronically constricted, it will continually signal your body that you're in danger and eventually exhaust the adrenal glands. This, in turn, will deplete the immune system. Additionally the Psoas muscle acts as an energy conduit, sending messages to and from the muscles, spine, nervous system and brain, then on down to the earth itself helping to ground us.

Traumatic energy can be inserted intentionally or accidentally. Whatever the genesis, tumors and cancers often grow in the areas where the trauma is stored. When this happens, it remains there until it is released. Similarly, when women are repeatedly sexually abused in their genital area, it is not uncommon to see cancerous tumors grow around the cervix, uterus, ovaries and vaginal areas. Toxic, angry energy entered there and lodged within the tissue. ***Body part cancer* is a marker for the site of the wound/trauma.*** The location of the cancer is where you were energetically attacked or where you hold the emotion of the traumatic event, whatever it was. If it's a bodily system that's affected, such as blood (Leukemia) or lymphatic cancer, it's a deeper wound and deeper toxic energy that has taken hold.

Body Part Cancer can be self-diagnosing in that if you remember your original wound, you know why it has lodged in that body part and you then have more power to remove it.

**Larry's Reiki healing story** – _One day I received a call from a man who told me he was given a dim prognosis for recovery. He had been diagnosed with prostate cancer and was about to have surgery. He wanted me to try to assist him further. Larry decided to have his prostate removed before coming to me but told me he didn't yet feel well and was afraid he was going to have a recurrence of cancer. The doctor warned him it could travel to his testicles, liver, or worse, even after prostate removal. Larry wanted to try Reiki. I began working on him. Then he asked me to teach him Reiki as he began to feel better since beginning with treatments. He said it was the best he felt during his ordeal._

I started teaching him First Degree Reiki and soon after his first attunement, Larry had a huge breakthrough. He began to cry during class. We had to work together after class to understand what he was experiencing. I did shamanic healing and Second Level Reiki on him to open his mental/emotional pathways. Soon I was hearing a frightening story that clearly was the source of his cancer. Larry's father had been a violent batterer of his mother throughout his childhood. This was surprising news given how gentle, kind and loving Larry was and happy his own marriage was.

But Larry spelled out the whole story in racking sobs. After decades of abuse, Larry's mother had moved out into an apartment of her own finally. She was a librarian and had a good enough job to live on her own, *and was still working into her 70's. His father was in his 80's. One day, as Larry's mother was leaving work, his father lay in wait in the bushes outside the library for her. He carried a shotgun under his arm, cocked and ready to shoot. When she rounded the bend of the driveway, Larry's father shot and killed his mother in broad daylight. She wasn't going to leave him he declared. Then he killed himself. Larry was called to identify the bodies and file a report with the police of the long history of violence between them. Within the year, Larry came down with prostate cancer.*

In Larry's case, the wound he received was from his violent father killing his mother, a deep soul wound, so it lodged in the male body part – the prostate. His mother had always been kind to him. Either watching his father beat his mother, or receiving beatings himself, Larry developed a suppressed immune system over the years and buried a great deal of trauma within his body, especially in his male organ, the prostate. This all came roaring forth during his Reiki sessions with me. After a few months of sessions, and learning First and Second level Reiki, Larry began to bounce back. He gave himself Reiki regularly and spent a lot of months grieving for his mother especially. But as he grieved, he grew stronger. And by the end of the year, there was no trace of cancer in his body. He had done a huge piece of Soul Transformation work, triggered by a great tragedy. He told me it brought him closer to his spiritual self. He began to pray and meditate daily and a couple of years later he called to tell me he had a whole new peaceful and happy life. He had come to terms with his parent's marriage and his father's violence. He released *the pain and it resulted in restored health for him. This is an example of **body-part cancer** caused by stored physical and emotional trauma.*

The problem with simply cutting a cancerous tumor or organ out is that if you don't deal with the underlying root cause, the deep emotional wound or thought gnawing at you daily, it will regrow elsewhere. Our thoughts are powerful and can manifest disease anywhere in the body if concentrated on daily. I've known people who did not want to heal emotionally but just wanted it cut out, end of sentence, no discussion, move on. Many of them grew new cancers elsewhere in their bodies because they didn't look at the emotional core wound.

When you disconnect from your emotions, your heart and your compassion for yourself and others, you begin to numb yourself to what you and others are feeling and become increasingly disconnected from the world around you. Eventually you will fail to notice the source of your dis-ease. And that is exactly what is happening to you…..dis – ease….you have become ill at ease….thus diseased. As this happens, your emotions become partitioned off in separate and distinct parts of the body without the energetic connections necessary for the free flow of healing energy. They effectively become separate cells that are unaware of other cells in the body, like secret terror cells waiting to attack your healthy cells without warning. Thus begins the secret host and genesis of disease.

Let's look at some of the common conditions and their related emotions. There are three main tiers of emotional energetic structure, each with increasing depth and subtle perception to the human eye, or to the third eye, known as the pineal gland. First there are the basics of emotional anatomy that many of us know. We all know that when you experience the end of a deep love affair - you become "heart-broken" - your heart literally hurts. What most people don't know is that that broken-hearted, hurt energy stays in the heart forever, or until some kind of resolution occurs. When you really deeply love someone, that never goes away, or it sometimes turns to hate. But the energy is still there. Or perhaps one day you love another, and you feel that painful energy begin to leave your heart, or change to forgiveness because someone new has come to love you. These are the ways we resolve heart pain. But sometimes, the person we loved betrays us, or goes away without explanation, and we have leftover, hurt and unresolved feelings which can last a lifetime and weaken the tissue resulting in disease.

It's been said Joe DiMaggio, the Yankee slugger who deeply loved and married Marilyn Monroe, never got over her after their divorce. They were rumored to be on the verge of remarrying when she was found dead in August of 1962. He left red roses on her grave every week for decades and never remarried. Those who knew him said "he had a broken heart, and it eventually killed him. His love for Marilyn was so deep it hurt him so." This is the energy I am referring to…. an energy so powerful that it can empower or harm someone. We all know how powerful love energy can be.

Or I'm sure you've known someone who became very fearful and anxious about something and reported feeling "the adrenalin pumping". This would be their adrenal glands excreting adrenalin based entirely upon an emotional response. Too much adrenal hyperactivity and excretion of adrenalin can result in adrenal overload and malfunction.

Let's take a look at where emotions are stored in the body. This is where the genesis of a disease can begin if the trapped emotions are not processed out and dealt with. Here is the primary level of emotional energy. The emotional patterns increase in intensity and depth in following charts. I give acknowledgment and respect to Louise Hay for her landmark work. However, all of this new data came solely through my own spiritual wisdom and revelations, from my personal clientele or my personal healing experiences.

Here are the basics of emotional energy anatomy and where it gets stored in the body.

EMOTIONAL ANATOMY

Anger (by degrees)	Light	Bladder (pissed off)
	Serious	Liver (silently enraged)
	Solidified	Gall Bladder (bitter)
Grief		Lungs, Heart
Loss		Heart, Lungs, Pancreas
Guilt		Brain, Heart, Gut
Fear		Kidneys, Brain, Adrenals
Sorrow		Pancreas, Heart, Lungs
Hatred		Brain, Gut, Heart
Confusion		Brain
Acceptance		Digestive Tract
Ignorance		Eyes, Brain
Joy, Love		Heart
Life Force		Bloodstream, Heart, Endocrine System, Nervous System, body whole
Energy		Nervous system, Adrenals, Endocrine System, Cardiovascular System
Processing emotions		Stomach, Intestine
Deep grief/fear		Diaphragm
Extreme trauma		Brain Stem, Sacrum, Coccyx
Dissociation		Entire Brain

~~~~~~~~~~~~~~

But how about more subtle energetic effects? The next energy tier would be the body part and its related disease, as the unresolved emotional/mental energy begins to solidify into a toxic mass. A common example we are all familiar with would be a person who is always upset, nervous and anxious about everything and constantly worrying. Soon, this person has developed an ulcer. The ulcer is the real physical manifestation of the energy of worry, an actual open sore inside your stomach lining due to constant emotional energetic tension held there silently by someone. This is how emotional energy works inside your body to actually create disease. If this intense toxic emotional energy continued on unresolved, the person could develop intestinal diseases such as diverticulitis, or even stomach or colon cancer, if the emotions are held deeply and for a long enough period of time. All diseases have a portion of their origins in thoughts and emotions. This is why all disease is holistic in nature and must not be addressed as a physical condition only. A medical intuitive or empath can detect this energy and notify the healers involved where to work in the body.

With this in mind, let's look in depth at the list of illnesses created by various emotions and traumas. All of this data came through spiritual revelation or from my personal clientele. This is a partial list only.

Body Part	Emotion	Related Diseases
Lungs	Grief, sorrow, betrayal Suppressed abuse/trauma Massive unexpressed loss & despair	Pneumonia, Lung Cancer
Heart	Feeling unloved, betrayal, Broken heart, despair Suppressed abuse/trauma	Heart illnesses, Heart Attack, Arrthymia, Heart

Body Part	Emotion	Related Diseases
Liver	Unresolved conflict & anger Mind control programming Suppressed abuse/trauma	Cirrhosis of Liver, Liver Cancer
Kidney	Fear, holding in paranoia Unrealistic fears and terror Suppressed abuse/trauma Mind control programming	Kidney infection, Blockage, Stones
Bladder	Lesser anger, powerlessness pissed off"	Bladder infections, Blockages
Stomach	Holding in all emotions	Ulcers, Indigestion, Cancer
Spleen	Releasing anger	Inflamed spleen, "Venting spleen"
Gall Bladder	Long resentments, bitterness	Gallstones, Gall bladder disease
Intestines	Holding on to emotions	Colitis, Candida, Colon
Intestines	Cannot digest truth	Cancer, Intestinal blockages
Brain	Not integrating trauma	Brain tumors, Aneurysms,
Brain	Stubborn refusal to grow, Unwillingness to "re-member" Separation of mind/body/spirit	Stroke, Seizures

Body Part	Emotion	Related Diseases
Brain Stem	Trauma storage center	Brain tumors, withered pineal Migraines
Bronchial tubes	Inflamed environment	Asthma, Chronic Bronchitis
Skin problems	Vulnerability, Protection Extreme stress/Toxins Fear of the world	Eczema, Shingles, Rashes Psoriasis
Pancreas	Joy, sweetness of life, excess	Pancreatitis, Cancer, Diabetes
Blood	Life force, joy and power	Leukemia, anemia
Throat	Suppression of the true voice & Creativity, not allowed to speak your truth	Throat, tongue & thyroid cancer, nodules, thyroid issues.
Thymus	Love, or lack of it, regulates Life force	Immune related diseases, AIDS, Chronic fatigue, lupus, etc.
Thyroid	Speaking truth, creativity, joy	Throat cancer, early aging, Thyroid problems
Pituitary	Stubbornness, refusal to grow	Brain tumors, senility

Body Part	Emotion	Related Diseases
Pineal	Spiritual vision	Eye problems, brain function
Adrenals	Fear, survival, energy storage Codependency, work addictions Success/money addictions, living on fake energy (coffee, power drinks)	Cancer, exhaustion, energy illnesses, e.g. chronic fatigue, adrenal exhaustion
Gonads	Sexuality, creativity, power	Cancer, Endometriosis, Impotence
Male organs	Cultural wounding to masculinity,	Prostate Cancer
Male organs	Denial of Sacred Feminine within and without, Sexual abuse	Impotence
Breast, Female Organs	Wounding by patriarchy to the Divine Feminine, No respect or nurturing of Feminine self, Sexual abuse	Cancer, Cysts, Tumors Endometriosis
Psoas Muscle	The Soul Muscle, deepest muscle in body, balances body, stores trauma	Back problems, hip problems, spine problems
Lungs	Deep grieving	Lung cancer, Pneumonia, Pleurisy
Colon	Not letting go, base of the problem	Colitis, Colon Cancer

~~~~~~~~~

The final tier would be the deeper issues and emotions and how they infiltrate our bodies and tissue more thoroughly to solidify and create even more serious forms of body dysfunction and disease. These are much harder to spot unless you are a skilled medical intuitive, clairvoyant or energy practitioner with training and experience. All of my life I have been able to feel the feelings of other people, even when they aren't always able to feel their own feelings. This hasn't always been well received as even as a child I knew what people were feeling and would sometimes say it out loud.

Sometimes, right when a person walks into a room I know exactly what they are feeling. If they are ill, especially if they are on my table, I can often sense what emotion they are holding and where in their body they are holding it. Quite often, my own body begins to ache right where the person is experiencing some pain or illness. So, my body becomes a diagnostic tool for getting to the source of the issue without expensive medical tests. And this is where this knowledge came from and what I teach my students to do as well.

I'm not suggesting you never go to a doctor and never get medical tests. Sometimes we need to get some hard data on what's going on in our bodies. Sometimes they can be helpful. But there are many things medical tests never pick up, or that a doctor misunderstands because he has no concept of energy medicine. Learn to trust yourself and listen to your intuition. It will give you many answers no medical professional can ever give you. Then combine all the data you've gathered and come up with a safe and healthy path to follow for your health. Educate your doctor. They need to know this information to be better healers. Find alternative doctors as well.

I am what is known as an empath, sometimes called a medical intuitive. Medical intuitives, however, can usually give a clear medical diagnosis as they often can see inside the body as though they had x-ray vision. As an empath, I don't necessarily see, it's usually more about feeling, although sometimes I can see conditions. As an empath, I am able to pick up much subtler energies people don't see or understand, and often don't even feel. When I pick these up in relation to a condition they are experiencing, I can help them release it and prevent further illness from developing. If you happen to be an empath, you may be picking up the emotions of those around you without realizing it. If you are doing that, you can develop illnesses from the emotions of others. It's important to discover all your spiritual gifts, not only so you can use them, but so their power isn't used against you.

In creating this next list, I have chosen those illnesses where I have seen the proof with my own eyes. I've clearly been able to feel the emotion the ill person was holding inside their body, inside their area of disease or in their energy field.

But first, here is an example of how I see energy within the human soul and aura and how it translates to illness or something else -

Trevor's Reiki healing story - *A dramatic example of the power of unseen but felt energy, was when I was consulted on the case of the 11-year old son of the mayor of the town I lived in. His father, who was raising his three sons alone, was a busy man who didn't have much time to spend with his sons. Trevor was the youngest of the three sons. I was called in when Trevor came down with a very bad case of the flu that he contracted while skiing with friends. He was too sick to come see me so I worked on him from home with* **Long Distance Reiki***. *All they told me was that he had the flu. So, I began working on him and his energy field from a distance. I saw the flu in him, which wasn't so serious, and began the process of moving the sick energy out. While I was doing this, I saw something more* *urgent on his left thigh. I kept seeing a red hot flaming energy coming from this thigh. It looked as though the thigh was ripped open and flames were coming out. I thought perhaps he had also injured his leg skiing and they didn't tell me either to test me, or because they didn't know.*

It was not clear to me then what the flaming energy represented for the boy because it didn't carry any emotional, mental or physical content at that time. But it did appear as fire, which often denotes anger. I worked on Trevor, including his leg, and finished the treatment. I got the distinct feeling he was going to recover from the flu, but that the leg issue was more serious. I reported my impressions to the father who said as far as he knew, Trevor's leg was fine. Trevor recovered from the flu quickly after my treatment.

During the following week, Trevor's father took a trip to Washington D.C to meet with President Clinton regarding his work as mayor. Exactly a week after I worked on Trevor, while his father was away in Washington, Trevor was struck by a car and his left thigh was severely injured! Just as I had seen, ripped open and a bloody energy emerging! Upon further working on Trevor but without any further information about his state of mind, I sensed he was very angry at his father for leaving him to go to Washington D.C. He subconsciously wanted to force his father to return home, and managed to manifest a car accident to get harmed enough to make that happen! Because the angry energy was still suppressed in Trevor earlier and not fully manifested, it appeared to me just as flames the first time. But when the car accident happened and the energy had actually manifested as an incident, I could sense Trevor's anger in full force. I told his father what I sensed occurred and why.

A few weeks later the Mayor called me and confirmed that Trevor finally shared with him how angry he was at his Dad for always being so busy with his job as Mayor. Trevor had been having a series of accidents and illnesses, but after I reported everything I saw and sensed, his Dad began spending more time with Trevor and including him in city events. After this change occurred, Trevor had no further incidents. The energy of Trevor's anger was beginning to manifest in his leg a full 8 days BEFORE the car accident even happened! I could see the energy, but it was not yet fully defined enough for me to recognize and explain it to Trevor's father. Trevor himself could not articulate it. By the time of the accident, the energy was clearly felt as anger to me and I was able to counsel the family as to how to proceed.

The human aura does not lie. It carries all the real emotions, thoughts, experiences and memories of the person whose energy field it is from the beginning of its inception. Even energy we may not remember or feel. It's all stored in their Akashic Record. Unresolved emotional, mental, physical or spiritual energy remains in the person's energy field after death and is carried into the next life to be resolved.

The examples below represent some of the cases I've had where I sensed the emotions within the person which were causing a disease. Or, it represents repeated case studies where I have seen the same illness connected to the same emotion over and over and over. And sometimes both of the above.

Once again, I am not discounting or overlooking the effects of toxins on the human body and in the development of disease. I know these are very real factors, e.g.- smoking, alcohol consumption, GMOs, toxic foods/junk foods, toxins in the environment like radiation, asbestos, pesticides or other chemicals known to cause disease. I am simply pointing towards the missing puzzle piece of disease genesis that so many have overlooked in the form of emotions and thoughts.

Here are some of the deepest issues that are seated at the base of many of today's common illnesses and health problems.

~~~~~~~

The Energies of Disease

Disease	Emotional energy	Energetic cause
Lupus	No self-love, suppression of True Self, suppressed trauma	Child abuse, Battering by a loved one, trapped in an unloving and abusive situation - emotionally, physically or mentally, spells, magnetic field interruption
Cancer	Unresolved pain/betrayal Medical system based on greed Disconnected medical professionals Cultural blocking of true healing	deep emotional wound, financial hopelessness, no healing love offered, exiled shamans & healers, True healing blocked in our culture, Engineered disease for profit

Disease	Emotional energy	Energetic cause
Cancer	Accepting cultural lie about disease Toxic culture infiltrating our bodies	Somatization of trauma/ abuse by NWO, spells, magnetic field interruption
Breast Cancer	The loss of ability to nurture Theft of female energy (yin) by Patriarchal culture & abuse Fear/no love for our female forms self-mutilation/ dismemberment Self-hatred	Systemic abuse and sexism towards women, cancer fear, cultural programming, Sexist disease programming, Programmed to cut out body parts unnecessarily, Engineered disease for profit, Sexual abuse, magnetic field interruption
Diabetes	Hopelessness, sorrow	Toxic food system, additives & synthetics, false culture creating sorrow, loss of goals due to cultural suppression
Eczema	Self-protection	Creating armor for protection
Fibromyalgia	Lack of energy Chronic Pain Inability to move around Advanced disease state	Restriction of yin energy Holding in forbidden feminine emotions and experiences,

Disease	Emotional energy	Energetic cause
Cancer	Mental fogginess	Cultural restrictions on sacred feminine power Belief in your unlovability and worthlessness, hopelessness,
Fibromyalgia		No path for you in society, satanic intrusion Infiltration of foreign thought forms, emotions or energies, toxicity in environment/food, chemtrails, vaccinations psychological abuse & programming, magical spells, suppressed trauma, magnetic field interruption
Multiple Sclerosis	Feeling crippled	Stored and suppressed abuse & trauma, magnetic field interruption, satanic spells
Viral Meningitis	Paralysis, fever	Introduction of viral thought forms & energies into the system to paralyze and steal life force, satanic spells

Disease	Emotional energy	Energetic cause
Immune Disorders Rheumatoid Arthritis Chronic Fatigue, Lupus	Suppressed trauma & emotional pain	Suppression of true self, magnetic field interruption toxic thought forms, stored trauma and abuse
Stroke	Pain and confusion	unprocessed life experiences, lack of self-love, poor diet and self-care

~~~~~~~~~

Another vital issue to discuss that is often overlooked by doctors is something now called ***Magnetic Deficiency Syndrome**** by many holistic practitioners. Everyone has both an electrical field and a magnetic field, known as the electro-magnetic field. The electrical field is the male yang energy. The magnetic field is the feminine yin energy. Together they make up a balanced energy field that empowers your aura and your body. There has been a steep rise in cases of Chronic Fatigue, Fibromyalgia and other immune-suppressive and energy-related diseases over the last 30 years. Fibromyalgia is a severely debilitating disease with symptoms ranging from lack of energy, chronic pain, mental fogginess, emotional suffering, and various other symptoms such as rashes, indigestion and depression. Doctors are generally baffled and used to tell people that only women get Fibromyalgia and we don't think it's real, just in your head. Then men started coming in with it. I remember an African-American male client of mine telling me that when he was diagnosed with Fibromyalgia that the doctor told him only white women get Fibromyalgia, even as he sat there in front of the doctor with it. Then another person I know used to be told by numerous doctors that it was "all in her head", "there's nothing wrong with you" and "take some vitamins", thousands of dollars later with no treatment and no results.

Finally, I myself had Fibromyalgia and it worsened dramatically at one point. Even Reiki alone was not enough to dispel it because I gave myself Reiki regularly. What I discovered is that in the electro-magnetic field, the dark yin field vibration was suppressed, blocked and reduced by various factors, including power poles, computers, electric boxes and the denial of the sacred feminine in society. This then impacted the energy field, leaving it unbalanced. I discovered this by sleeping on a magnet pad. After years of intense body pain, especially my back, someone convinced me to try a magnet pad. After sleeping on the magnet pad for two weeks, 90% of my body pain was gone. One month later, it was all gone. I've been sleeping on a magnet pad ever since, only now I don't need it as much anymore. I have more energy and need less sleep. My electro-magnetic balance has been permanently restored. This is the essence of Magnetic Field Deficiency, or Magnetic Deficiency Syndrome.

Because of all the environmental issues I discussed earlier, electrical wiring, cell towers, computers, TV's, microwave, HAARP, chemtrails and many other technological devices, the electro-magnetic field of Earth is interrupted, blocked and impaired causing many imbalances such as in the weather. It is also impaired in individuals. Too much TV watching, computer time, driving in cars, not being in nature, eating denatured foods, and all the unnatural things we do cause the reduction of the electro-magnetic field. Once this happens in someone, their body's energy field becomes imbalanced and disease can begin. Reiki heals most diseases anyway. But I found that the energy diseases in particular needed a re-balancing of their energy fields with magnets as well as Reiki. Magnet pads combined with Reiki can heal it all. I loan my magnet pad to my cancer patients who recover quickly. They all tell me they can feel the difference immediately. There are many magnet products to choose from for different issues. You can get knee braces with magnets, elbow braces, back braces, etc. I also drink magnetized water and I use a magnet sometimes for emotional release work on clients. And I have a magnet pad for my office chair. I no longer have any pain.

Finally, and most importantly, is learning **Reiki**. Of all the techniques I've tried, and I've tried so, so many, Reiki is the most powerful healing tool I've ever utilized. After teaching someone First Degree Reiki, I often see all their life issues begin to heal, along with their health. Their backs align, their emotional upheavals begin to die down, their life path straightens out and they find work, and so on. Reiki is the aligning of your divine life force that resides within you, with the same life force that resides everywhere in the Universe. Most people have lost their life force alignment somewhere along the way and are searching for re-connection to it. Reiki is much more than just an alignment; it's a path to spiritual awakening. It's more than a healing tool; it's a form of resurrection. Your health crisis is the gift that brings you to your Soul Transformation. Reiki is the tool that will take you there.

Here is an illustration to show you the vast power of Reiki and its omnipotent place in the Universe and nature:

A Reiki Nature Miracle - *My former husband was a commercial diver and we owned a small dive boat for fishing. We decided to take our two daughters out to the Channel Islands for a weekend of swimming, fishing and diving. I promised them we would see dolphins. After two days, we hadn't seen any dolphins and were heading home. It was at least a good hour before we would reach the harbor of beautiful Santa Barbara, so I decided to try to summon the dolphins. I sat down on the deck of the boat and began meditating. I held my hands up and drew the Reiki symbols in the air silently. I also drew the symbols into the ocean water. I began to call to them in a special chant silently to myself. I told them we loved them, wouldn't hurt them and wanted to greet them. I asked them to greet us too. I continued drawing the Reiki symbols.*

After about 40 minutes, my husband said "Here come my buddies." I was seated and couldn't see so I thought some of his fishermen friends were coming so I asked, "Oh which of your fishermen friends is it?" He replied, "No, it's my dolphin friends." I jumped up and looked out across the sea and there were hundreds and hundreds of dolphins swimming towards us. They had been swimming parallel to the coastline and had picked up my signal and made a sharp 90 degree turn towards our boat. You could see the corner they were turning on. They reached our boat and swam around us squeaking and jumping in the air at least in a vast circle as far as the eye could see. They looked at us and even waved flippers at us. I asked my husband how many dolphins he thought there were. He said over a thousand. I took pictures of that momentous day. I realized then that Reiki was a universal language that all species could hear. It is a divine and sacred energy that is defined by love and interconnectivity and the Oneness of life. It healed us all in a great circle of love that day.

The two biggest unexplored regions on Earth are the energy field of Earth and the human brain. The most overlooked causes of

disease are the human energy system and its spiritual, emotional, and mental components.

Einstein tried to tell us but was ignored. I'm telling you again

We are living in a world of trapped energy in the form of mass. WHEN ALL TRAPPED ENERGY IS FREED BY LOVE, THIS WORLD ENDS.

Chapter 11

The Trauma Codes

*Do not hold in awe those who have
taken your power from you.*

~ *Salini*

We are living in the midst of a massive secret that is so big, all-encompassing and all-pervasive that we don't even realize we are walking around inside of it. The secret has been made invisible to you so you won't realize you are being held captive. Like your computer system, it even has its own code. I call these codes the *Trauma Codes**. They are the brain codes that are traumatically imprinted onto brain function patterns during collective or individual, overt or covert, private or cultural trauma that control your reactions, feelings, beliefs, power and behaviors. These are the codes that traumatize and paralyze the divine energy of an individual or system. These are the codes we are living under today.

But just as there are trauma codes, there are also awakening codes. I know that most people don't want to look at the dark side, either in the world, or within themselves. I understand, I wanted to skip this part of my Soul Transformation. Yet it is present in both parts of your life every hour of every day, impacting you. If you don't face, embrace and integrate your dark side, it will remain in your subconscious mind where you are unaware of it. From there it will run your life and diminish your health, your happiness and your prospects. You will believe you are free and acting independently, but you will be held hostage by one or more invisible systems or energies. In order to move into the awakening codes and have them work abundantly for you, you must understand and dismantle your personal trauma codes. One never works independently without the other. They are an interconnected part of the web of life. For this planet to fully heal, we must face, embrace, heal and integrate its dark side and those perpetrating it. Secrecy, invisibility and unconsciousness/forgetfulness is the cloak under which they can best operate to control you. As their methodology is exposed to the light of day, their power over you diminishes. Many of them will also choose to heal their dark side and step into the global awakening. After all, that's where the love is. Everyone is welcome, if they are willing to do the work of awakening. An important part of that process is to uncover your own personal traumatic codes and weed them out of your life, psyche and energetic field. Eventually, the separation heals, your consciousness unites and you are free to awaken.

You may think this doesn't apply to you, that your life is always positive or that dark things are far away from you. The opposite is true. Someone dying in Africa from starvation when many of us in the West are overweight is an imbalance and a karmic blow to all of our souls. Since we are one energetic matrix of wholeness, it impacts our energy at the soul level. Someone secretly manipulating the economy and the stock market behind your back can harm you right here. Or the impact on the energy field of Earth from a war is astronomical. You live inside that energy field. If bombs, chemical weapons, or other toxins are released into the atmosphere somewhere else in the world, it's going to affect you here. All toxins make the rounds of the environment. So, to turn away, to hide our heads in the sand, is to live in a bubble of illusion and pretend darkness isn't happening. What must then happen to awaken you and open your heart, is that darkness comes to your door and knocks upon it to tell you, "I'm the pain in the world you won't acknowledge…… I'm the 7-year-old child who died sewing brand name clothing in a sweat shop in Bangladesh or who committed suicide while making electronics in Asia for the West…I'm the poverty-stricken children from Central America on your border suffering through your global war on our resources." If it remains unacknowledged, it has more power in your life because it's free to run rampant through the world. Eventually, like a home invasion, it will bring down your house and threaten your life. You must eventually turn and face the darkness and transform it into something healed. The dark part of you and this world carries great power, suppressed power that has the potential to heal the Earth. It's currently trapped in unconsciousness waiting to be claimed. That power has been seeking liberation. It is also seeking love. That is why it is raising havoc on Earth. The more love you give your darkness, the more it calms down and transforms. The more you embrace all aspects of the self, the more transformation you bring to the world. And eventually you are having an impact on the world's darkness. And the more love you offer those trapped in the dark, the more souls you will liberate to the light.

So, let's begin to understand the codes of trauma and awakening so we can integrate them into our lives and become whole. In doing so individually, we assist the collective whole to transform and the Earth to heal. You are far more powerful than you realize once you unlock the codes of your inner divinity. And that is precisely what they don't want you to know.

> *I freed a thousand slaves. I could have freed a thousand more if only they knew they were slaves.*
>
> ~ Harriet Tubman

One of the main goals of those who seek to deny us our freedom is to block our divine energy from rising up to our brain stem, also known as the **Mouth of God***. If a person is allowed to arrive freely and unhindered at a higher state of consciousness, they cannot be controlled and enslaved unconsciously. For this reason, much research, time, energy and effort has been made throughout the ages to create programs to specifically suppress the rising of human consciousness. Centuries of practice have gone into developing programs of suppression, destruction and division of human consciousness so that humans won't realize they are divine, powerful and part of God's divine plan, born fully empowered. The primary goal is to separate consciousness so it's power is diluted or lessened. If they can break apart sections of the soul and insert doubt, fear, terror, shame, paranoia or hatred, they can succeed in taking over the life force, capturing it and using it for their own means. It is very much like a hostile corporate takeover or a virus in the body - it is a malicious energy that takes over something in a weakened state. This is accomplished in the soul and psyche through trauma and is the main tool of satanically-based secret societies. If done in childhood, the child's psyche has no defense against it due to its lack of ego and mental development. If enough terror/shame is inserted there, the soul will either capitulate and join with evil, die or fight back. To fight back requires great spiritual strength, commitment, presence of mind and courage not often present in children.

> *By means of gradual, treacherous systematic abuse, this system has put every person into a spiritual prison…every people deserves the regime it is willing to endure.*
>
> ~ The White Rose Society,
> Student resistance group
> opposing Hitler in WW2

Earlier I explained the nature of the Secret Holocaust where there was a clear and precise underlying plan that drove the war, suffering and chaos of the 20th century – a plan for a New World Order. To fully understand the Trauma Codes, and how to dismantle them, it's vital to know the philosophy that gave birth to them. In the early part of the 19th century, leading thinkers, philosophers, doctors, scientists and social scientists, most of them members of secret societies, began meeting in think tanks and universities to discuss how to shape future society. Some of these men were the leading thinkers of their day and in positions of power. They created dozens of organizations whose aim was to shape a trauma-based society. Perhaps the most important and central to these organizations was the creation of the field of psychiatry.

Psychiatry was created specifically for the purpose of creating traumatized individuals to carry out objectives of their global plan and was birthed from observing the effects of war and trauma on soldiers returning from World War I. They conducted studies on how war trauma damaged the psyches of soldiers, causing shell shock, **Post-Traumatic Stress Disorder*** and the infamous **Thousand Yard Stare***. This gave the Secret Society men the idea they could transfer this trauma to society in general by simulating or threatening war continuously. Then they came across their biggest star, Dr. Sigmund Freud. Freud was fascinated by how the human mind broke down and went crazy, and as a result came up with many theories, most of them now discredited. Unfortunately, his theories were widely respected at the time and became the basis for the future trauma theories still used today. The architects of these plans were all secret society initiated men who were looking for better ways to achieve their goals. They began to listen to and study Freud's speeches and writings.

It's speculated that Freud was an abused child himself during his childhood in Austria and may have abused his own children. As I mentioned earlier, there was a strong culture of abuse and authoritarianism in Austria and Germany back then that was likely a part of Freud's childhood too. He was a product of his time when only men were empowered and entitled and he had distinct theories about people's societal roles, especially women. Oppressive, authoritarian males were the order of the day. He was obsessed with those topics and came up with some bizarre theories about them. One of them was about the human breaking point through trauma, which was transplanted into the world of psychology, and the new science of psychiatry. Freud's theories worked nicely to justify and direct the goals of the Secret Society members. Whereas psychology began as a healing method for emotionally and mentally disturbed people, the birth of psychiatry was the morphing of the field of mental health into a delivery system of mental chaos, shock, trauma and psychiatric medications. Not all psychiatrists maintain that goal or harm clients today of course. But earlier psychiatrists did so during decades of shock treatments, drugging and other outrageous methods practiced routinely. This was the genesis for the field of psychiatry even if psychiatrists today don't implement it that way. Their goal was a conditioned public ready for programming into the controlled society they envisioned. Freud, and his disciples, such as Carl Jung, unwittingly helped them develop the program they would implement over time.

> *When the body experiences trauma, it stays in the cellular memory. It's difficult for the mind to let it go. Therefore healing must include mind, body, emotions and spirit.*
>
> ~ Salini

Two of his theories in particular, the Trauma Breaking Point and the Polarity Pattern Process, a series of lectures Freud delivered, which went in depth into the dynamics of the psyche and collective unconscious, became touchstones for the future mind-control of the masses. Although Freud is celebrated for his original concept of the Id, the Ego and the Super-Ego, staples of modern psychology, his theories also became the foundation and cement of modern mass mind-control. It's an interesting side note that his nephew, Edward Bernays, expanded upon his uncle's work to create his widely used theories of propaganda and persuasion, also fodder for Nazis and other mind-control freaks. Enter the era of the **Subliminazis***, doctors and psychiatrists whose sole aim was to perfect the art of mental separation, breakdown, chaos, compartmentalization, mind-control, personality disorders, multiples, and the labeling of individuals to further break down their self-image and self-esteem. This was a mental power play at its finest and most subtly devastating.

Voila, the birth of modern psychoanalysis and psychology, all trauma-based personality theories that do not even acknowledge they were birthed from trauma. More historical forgery and collective denial that was transferred to future innocent students of psychology simply wishing to help people. Once you understand the origins of modern psychotherapy, you realize that conventional therapy hides the truth behind personality disorder theory. Theories of personality in modern use today were CREATED by *traumatizing patients or watching already traumatized patients*, then by creating explanations for why they behaved the way they did. Then later, the source and context for these theories were divorced from the curriculum in modern universities so that no one would know that the trauma behind them was intentionally inflicted. This was done intentionally to hide the real agenda for these theories and treatment procedures which were created by adepts and secret society members to control human behavior. Modern students remain in the dark of the causes of these personality theories. Only recently are professionals beginning to credit trauma with the genesis of a personality disorder and it's still considered a controversial theory. Instead they treat it as a separate mental disorder that just independently springs up and labels the client according to the current DSM-IV or V manual. As a result, a client gets a diagnosis label and is likely to be pushed into pharmacological treatment rather than holistic and spiritual therapy, which is what they really need. Personality disorders nearly always result from some form of trauma, whether it is psychological, sexual, physical, mental, chemical or induced invisibly by brainwave mind-control through the Lilly Wave, or other experimental brain techniques practiced secretly. The exception to that are genetic birth defects, karma and sudden damage done by some accidental form of trauma such as a car accident or fall. The mitigating factors are, of course, the well-intentioned and sincere therapists who become licensed professionals and try to do good work anyway in spite of a flawed system. Thank God for the wise counselors who do exist. Most of them are gifted counselors by birth before even going to school and becoming licensed. And many have long transcended the outdated theories of personality system. But in our society, you can still get labeled with one or more personality disorders. And if that happens, scapegoating, surveillance, drugging and exile are sure to follow. We can transcend this system in our quest for wholeness. But first, it's time to understand the toxic roots of a widely accepted system to realize that it's part of the sickness within our society.

There is no longer room for denial and disbelief for evading the grim reality of SRA (satanic ritual abuse). Solid scientific inquiry does not allow that luxury, neither should Christian conscience.
Dr. James Friesen – Journal of Psychology and Theology

Nevertheless, the subliminazis entered the mainstream and initiated dozens of programs to break down the mental state of society such as television, psychiatric drugs – which have had a devastating effect on society, chemicals in our water and food that affect brain function such as Fluoride and Aspartame, street drugs, sensual temptations now common in TV and movies, images and trigger words designed to create fear and separation - such as TERROR ALERT, violent video games, engineered poverty programs, endless wars, and many more scientifically engineered programs designed to break down families, our minds and our society. Their formula for creating a continuous and mass state of sick pathology is rooted in deception, dissociation, brainwashing, conditioning, trauma, terror, trance-formation, spells, energy manipulation, mind-control, soul abuse and constant surveillance. These are the origins of the Trauma Codes. And they are doing vast psychic damage to us, and especially to our children. And our current population has lived through more of it than any other generation in world history. The people who perpetrate this atrocity on humankind are the thieves of the heart and souls of humanity. They hold our hearts hostage with their trauma conditioning while we live on in a collective traumatic trance. It's time to bring this to an end. And we will. That formula is forthcoming here and is surprisingly simple.

But there is much more to explain about the codes first as it's a vast matrix of interconnected negativity and trauma poisoning our own energy fields. As I started out this book, I mentioned how I was silenced and could not tell this story. That went on a very long time in my life. I couldn't understand how I was so effectively silenced. Until I began to access the deep mind-control programming. There I discovered a suicide program laid down within me to prevent me from ever speaking my truth. Placed there were **thought forms*** of suicide that if I move into my power, I must kill myself. This was both a suicide and a silencing program. Advanced mind control programming always includes a suicide program in the event you break your programming and remember it. The last piece of programming is that you will kill yourself before you reveal the program. Thought forms are concepts, statements or beliefs that when repeated constantly, can take shape in your mind and become permanently held beliefs. Once they become solidified in your mind, they carry the energetic power to heal, to create illness or to awaken according to the nature of the statement. Many such thought forms were placed in my mind during my trauma conditioning which anchored in beliefs that I was unworthy and unlovable. They attempted to keep me in a low shamed status and low energy frequency. In fact, each statement and emotion carries its own frequency and when that frequency is activated constantly, that is the brain wave pattern that is created in the brain and the corresponding belief or emotion is then firmly implanted there like the root of a tree. It takes hold and grows, either towards empowerment or shame according to its frequency. You can see how powerful this is for mind-control technology.

To explain further, the neurons of the brain contain interconnected mesh structures called axons and dendrites that connect across synaptic gaps with other neurons. Dendrite and axon connections stretch out holographically forming the neural network of the brain. Neurons have hundreds of dendrites connecting to other neurons performing the varied functions of sending messages to the brain and back. When we think repetitive thoughts or perform repetitive habits, certain well-used dendrites get more established and patterns develop within the neural network. These neural patterns, when used repeatedly, form grooves within the brain because they become like a well-traveled road. These grooves also function to encourage the brain to return to those same neural pathways, like a horse going back to the barn stubbornly follows a certain pathway. This can create repetitive negative thinking or positive thinking, depending on which path you choose. Other potential dendrite pathways within the neural network of our brain may have atrophied due to lack of use. So, like exercising a flaccid muscle, it's going to take repetition and time to create new positive thought forms and patterns of thinking that replace the negative ones.

Dark power functions in secrecy and holds its power in secrecy. Dark secrecy only develops from the deepest of shame and the violation of a person's self, boundaries, privacy and modesty in some way. Some form of perversion has occurred in secret and locks in the dark power. Secrecy then occurs when we lose our sense of natural shame and go to the extremes of shame. What we are given as a birthright, which is natural shame or modesty as I would call it, becomes transformed into toxic shame from the perverted act. This is the way the shame core forms, a perversion of natural shame. The shame core has enormous power over people to have them act in very sick ways. The abuser gives his toxic shame to the innocent child during the perverted act to process and there the sickness begins to form in the child. It's a ritual of sorts, sometimes intentional, sometimes unconscious. The child is held hostage and scapegoated energetically while the abuser walks free with their power. An energy exchange has taken place, a very toxic one. The child carries the abuser's shame and the cycle begins again. It's the silence and secrecy that gives it more power. Therefore revealing it all is mandatory. Like slimy worms under a rock, shine the light hard on whatever the toxic shame is. Once revealed, it withers in the light of day and loses power. The same is occurring to everyone in society every day to a lesser degree.

As I began breaking the programming, more and more truth surfaced and like a giant jigsaw puzzle, the pieces began to come together. But you will find that those still mind-controlled are kept in place by the intense fear programmed in alongside the suicide program. They are threatened with being killed if they reveal anything. They will defend their programming vehemently even while harm is done to themselves and their loved ones. This programming so early in childhood effectively controls the many still programmed. This is one of the main reasons so many of them have yet to come forward for healing. Many therapists are not knowledgeable or trained in dealing with this kind of programming. And it's far more prevalent than they realize.

As I recovered, I discovered a vast array of codes, secret words and trigger words used in secret programming as their world is posited in cryptography and their secrets held in hidden languages and codes. Then I saw that the terms were sprinkled throughout our society to deceive, program and confuse us. So, I created the **Glossary of Terms** to help people understand their language better so it would lessen its power over you. Many of the terms there I have coined and have no other precedent in modern language. Learning them will help you understand our cultural and collective programming.

I have an interesting story on this topic.

> ***A Secret Society Story*** - *I had won a small claims lawsuit against an insurance company for a car accident where I was rear-ended. The female judge awarded me a few thousand dollars. The insurance company appealed. When my lawyer and I returned for the appeal, there was a well-known corrupt male judge sitting on the case. The wealthy insurance company had two slick lawyers representing them. Mind you, we're only talking about a few thousand dollars. Yet as the appeal proceeded, we witnessed the lawyers flashing signals surreptitiously to the judge, who either returned them or nodded each time. My lawyer alerted me to this telling me those were secret society signals as we went through the case or I wouldn't have known. As soon as we finished the case, the judge immediately nullified my award. I saw him wink at the lawyers for the insurance company.*
>
> *This is how our system functions, or at least in some cases. Even for a few thousand dollars, which would really have helped my children and I, they sent in their wealthy, programmed secret society men to cheat on the case. That's because the foundation of secret society law is to keep all money for themselves at the expense*

of all others in society. Even unto the death of others. It's rooted in their ancient history as Knights Templars when they were stripped of their money and power, and persecuted by the Pope and King of France. This event on Friday the 13th in 1307, effectively ended the Templar run of power, sending them underground. It was then the Templars were infiltrated by the other secret societies who ultimately took over. Because they lost all of their money, land and power, they vowed to keep everything within their secret order from that day forth.

The secret societies are present in law, judiciary, teaching, medical, all fields of service. They will compromise the system and themselves for money and for each other. Their allegiance is not to the law, to the common man or to justice but to their secret society and to the God of money.

The Trauma Codes include the actions and policies of the secret societies but are not exclusive to them. They include any and all traumatic experiences that create a trauma pattern or cycle in someone. But generally there are many code words, coded handshakes, coded sentences, gestures, glances and other forms of secret communication used by secret societies to inform their members of various things. The entire English language is a patriarchal language created by conquerors with words that suit their view of the world. To fully explain the modern day mental slavery we live in, I would need to translate our entire patriarchal language but that is not my purpose here. So, I give you the basic and most vital introduction into the mental and emotional codes we are held in slavery to.

Each programmed person, and I don't mean full-scale mind-control, just standard life programming, has trigger words that work to trigger pain stored in memory and in the body. When done intentionally, it's to create certain emotional responses. If it's unintentional trauma, certain words will have the effect of triggering an emotional reaction in someone. These serve to activate the compartmentalized portions of the programmed person's mind and personality. It's like the Excel computer program. In that program there are cells that are programmed with a function or a logarithm. Those cells are the master cells that control the other cells. When it's activated, it can order the other cells to function according to how the master cell is programmed but without knowledge of the master cell's programming. Therefore one secret master cell can control all the other cells without them knowing it. That is the essence of compartmentalization. It's the same with compartmentalized mind-control. The programming is specifically designed for that person. For example, if you use the word "Holocaust" when speaking with someone of the Jewish faith, it will probably elicit a strong response. So, often trigger words are woven into our dialogues, media, etc. to elicit certain emotional and mental responses. There are also trigger words and code words for our country, our culture and the world. These words indicate to members certain plans or agendas coming up that they need to know. When it comes to our country, the code words for triggering trauma are inserted into our media to mind-control us into fear. Words like "Terror Alert", "kidnapped child", "murder", "rape", "jihad", "illegal immigrants", and so on are trigger words for our national collective subconscious towards fear, which creates separation consciousness. They may have dual meaning to our controllers as signals for something else. But it's written into a nice story on the news that seems benign. But that is precisely how secret messages have gotten out to the world for centuries, through coded messages. Now, it can be done through television, radio, the internet, movies, and in new and more dangerous ways to program your thoughts and create negative thought forms in your mind which can create depression, illness, etc.

Additionally, they use forms of speech and tone to control a person's power. When trauma is planted in the mind, trigger words and behaviors are used to bring the pain back up to elicit a certain response. Ridicule is a powerful method. For powerful truthspeakers, they will ridicule them to diminish their power. First they try to drive them crazy. They might be called a "conspiracy theorist", a false term invented by the intelligence community. The greater the numbers of people saying this, the greater the energetic force of denial the person is up against and the more likely they've struck a truth nerve. It's tough to stand in your power against group denial, but you must. You're being gaslighted. If that doesn't work, they try to make the person look crazy. This will take the form of a series of statements, attitudes, and shaming gestures. Sarcasm is a way to try to steal another's power or to shame a person into silence. Bullying and sarcasm have become a serious problem in our culture and is a learned reaction to the abuse of power prevalent in the world today.

Once it's been identified that there is programming and its breaking down, or trauma and it's releasing, there should be a spilling out of intense emotions, fear and revelations. Sometimes dissociation will occur, a sign that a compartmentalized multiple sits before you and is experiencing healing of her/his fragmented self. That is if you've had the kind of mind-control programming I've described, or profound sexual trauma elsewhere. If it's not as severe, you will still break through and discover trapped pain and emotions stored behind the walled barriers of the programming. Even television programming can do this to someone, or video games. It will be found in differing stages, levels, layers and varying degrees of intensity. Be prepared for a long haul of emotional and mental healing work with the individual, or with yourself. A shaman may well be required to call back lost soul parts, something you don't learn in psychology training and can't learn in traditional educational settings. You are unraveling and re-integrating portions of lost, fragmented soul parts that are meeting each other for the first time. It takes time.

Most of today's epidemic of bi-polar people are results of the mind-control experiments, trauma or other forms of rampant secret deviant sexual abuse going on today, often from satanic groups. Some of it is chemically-induced by food toxins, some of it is psychiatric drugs, some of it is mental programming through media as I've explained, some are spells and some of it is trauma-based. Whatever the cause, you have to proceed slowly, carefully and realize that conventional therapy with labels of personality disorders will only hurt the person and send them away and back into their split-off self. To label someone bi-polar in today's society is to stigmatize and ostracize them from the real help they need. It also draws in the predators to potentially isolate the person in a toxic treatment facility or other place where they may be drugged with psychiatric medications. Medicating a split-off personality type is risky and can result in further splitting occurrences. It also always attracts entity attachments, like what you see in homeless people walking and talking to themselves. But in some cases, medication can be helpful depending on the individual's tolerance to it and personal situation. Sometimes people are too far gone and need to be medicated. But those decisions must be made individually. Unless the person is severely mentally ill or psychotic, a holistic and spiritual approach to healing is best. That is where I have found the most success.

So, let's move through the trauma code rules and explain the traumatic trance again. It's repeated terror and fear that keeps conditioned tyranny in place, and it's held in place by the traumatic trance. It doesn't have to be the extreme version I experienced, it can be cultural trauma – like 9/11, domestic violence trauma – like witnessing Mom get beaten as a child, war trauma – seeing death all around. It's the unconscious state of living in the trance created by the traumatic trance-bond.

The traumatic trance-bond, or traumatic bond, is the toxic bond that exists between one person and another person, or a group of persons, or a traumatic event that remains in place unconsciously and dictates the actions, reactions and feelings of that person for life, or until it becomes conscious. The creation of the traumatic trance is necessary to endure the pain of the original traumatic event and persists long after the event took place. The traumatic trance is characterized by compartmentalization and extreme denial of the traumatic bond/event, and related abusive behaviors. In fact, most people living in the traumatic trance are still traumatically bonded to their original abusers, or someone very similar to that individual, and are continually re-enacting and re-living facets of their original wound unconsciously.

The Traumatic Trance is frequently accompanied by one or more addictions to anything from alcohol to sex to money or to adulation/power, and on to things like food, possessions, control, etc. Any forced or unrequested attempt to break a traumatic trance will result in fiercely defensive behaviors by the entranced individual who is protecting the possibility of having to re-experience the original wound. So, many of their techniques are designed to keep the fear response stimulated, such as today's news programs, constant reporting of murders, school shootings, non-stop war reporting, violent movies and similar fare. They've mastered the art of inducing terror and trauma and even tried to trademark the term, "shock and awe", during the Iraq war started after 9/11. They were attempting to institutionalize and corporatize the art of shock, terror and trauma. The effect on our psyches and energy fields from constant war, trauma, terror alerts, fear, etc. is to reduce our immunity and our serenity to a permanently fearful, demoralized state. This lowers the vibration passing through our brain and our energy matrix, which in turn inhibits consciousness. It also creates mental separation and then we are easily dominated.

But how can an event that happened years ago still be controlling the lives of people? Many people even question the credibility of women who stay with battering spouses, those who keep choosing sick partners, or sabotage their lives in other ways. But often, no solutions are offered to these people, only judgments or criticism. And judgments and criticisms never work, but are certain to deepen the trauma of the wounded person and the denial in our society. If you don't understand, seek to understand it, because it's happening around you all the time. Shaming those who are suffering further deepens the divisions in our world. And we can't afford that.

What has happened to them is simple but invisible to others. During traumatization, the person's energy becomes linked with the cause of the trauma in a permanent way. There is energy leakage towards the source of trauma. It's also done partially through black magic and spells they have mastered over time and use during their rituals. These spells latch onto your energy field and drain off power. As power escapes, it becomes inextricably linked and leaked towards the person or event that traumatized them. An ***amnesiac barrier*** * is intentionally created so that no memory of the event exists, only the suffering remains. A traumatic trance has been created. From there, the person begins their life inside of a traumatic trance. And that can go on for life. An amnesiac barrier is similar to and supports denial in that the amnesia functions to support your denial system. Once denial of your ***True Self*** * has crossed the midpoint of your consciousness, you have denied more than half of yourself. And once you have denied more than half of yourself, your magnetic center, which is what your True Self is made up of, is now weaker than the denial. You are weakened by self-denial because you are denying the very source of your own power. Much like the amnesiac barrier withholds the truth from your conscious mind, the denial of self withholds your power from you for you to use in life. The reclamation process against the vast power of your inner denial is difficult. There will be three forces vying for power within you, the lie and those who tell them, the truth and your soul's urge to awaken. It's a battle for your very soul and you must undertake it. If you don't try to reclaim what you have lost step by step, you slip into permanent unconsciousness or permanent denial. If that happens, you will have to return for another life to accomplish it, if you are given that opportunity. If you have harmed others in your denial, you may have to live out many lives of unconsciousness.

If a person is traumatically entranced, they will begin to pass through several stages, each of which can last years. It is known as the **Pattern of Trauma***. The patterns of trauma become coded into the body and into its energetic matrix. You begin to see the body change along the lines of the pattern of trauma. You begin to see the emotions change along the lines of the pattern of trauma. And you begin to see the mind change towards the encoded trauma pattern. Your mind, body and emotions become distorted. People sometimes walk bent over, react suddenly or think obsessively within their trauma pattern. Finally, you see the loss of soul purpose and a permanent trauma code inserted. Depression, despair and aimlessness can then set in.

Below is an extreme example along the lines of ritual abuse, but it illustrates the whole pattern very clearly. And it's more common than you might realize; it's how a sociopath is made. We begin as innocents... babes in the woods, bringing our purity, love and innocence to the world. This is what a predator wants most. So, they seek it and when the find it they go about taking it. And that can also be a business predator, a spouse predator, a co-worker predator, a friend predator. It can take many forms, not just extreme forms. So, it begins with the traumatization, which is a frozen-like state that can go on a while. This often begins in childhood when the child shuts down completely for survival and enters into **Programmed Survival***.

During the stage of traumatization when the person is frozen, the beginnings of stealing the soul is undertaken. A person's defenses are down or have not yet developed. The gradual breaking down of the core personality begins which weakens their spiritual resolve. They are probably not asking God for help or protection, especially if they are a child. The trauma breaks open a hole in the auric field, energy begins to leak towards the abuser, and the soul loses footing within the person and often leaves the body. When this occurs, a soul is turned towards evil or another being can enter the person and take over. Then comes the open wound, which is a very difficult and painful state where the wound is felt but not seen by the victim. The wound cannot be addressed properly because the origins of the wound are not available to the individual who is still traumatized and cannot remember. During this period, the person's life force becomes fuel for those that have traumatized them. It's literally the vampiring of your life force. People often become ill during this period. As the person weakens, the emotional appeal begins. They ask for help from someone. But if they don't find it, they weaken further. If the proper help and healing does not arrive at this time, this is when the soul can be lost. Only if the individual is strong enough to fight for their own soul can this be reversed at this stage. If that does not occur, the death of the heart and the emotions begins. When that happens to a man traumatized by other men, he experiences the death of his sensitive, emotional self, his feminine yin self. This is when their inner sacred feminine is lost. They split away from their innate yin/yang balance and become abusive, aggressive, narcissistic and patriarchal. These kinds of men are running the world. And this diseased pattern has been going on for thousands of years.

NWO Mantra

I survive on your energy
I please myself at your expense
I satiate myself on your lack & suffering
I relieve my pain on your body

I escape by scapegoating you
I profit by your addiction
I support my lie on your illusion
I gain by your enslavement
I enrich myself by your illness & death
But I die a dark soul death to do it
And will endure the same suffering
A million and one times over
Until I surrender to love…

~ Salini

At this stage, extreme programming can occur which further deadens the person. Eventually, through sustained trauma, the death of compassion occurs because it becomes too painful to feel anymore. Then a long silence begins and everything shuts down and is compartmentalized. The rage and pain are stored out of memory. Then ultimately comes the rise of magical transformed fury, the damaged person rises. And this is the goal of programming, to bring out the magical being of great rage and power. At that point, the person begins to project his pain out upon others. The final stage is sadism and the birth of a dark soul has been completed. A sociopath is born. This is an illustration. For most people, it never goes this far. Maybe it's simply a few trauma episodes when someone was small and then a lifetime of buried unknown emotions. That is much more easily reversed and repaired than the former. ***However, healing can be accomplished, even for the most evil, if they agree to lay down their former path completely.*** **Love is always the key**. **And the presence of the Holy Spirit**. It's important to understand the pattern of trauma even if you never experienced or met this kind of person because it can happen in smaller increments to anyone.

During the traumatic trance phase, the ***Core Self****, or your true healthy personality, is severely damaged and it's the ego that performs the daily functions of life. It is just a shell of your personality on the outside. This shell holds only a few personality traits covered over with a thin veneer of narcissism, false ego, charm and other socio-pathic traits we all carry to some degree to function in a diseased society but are exaggerated in a traumatized individual. The *True Self**, or pure soul, has left the body for safety and must be found, healed and re-integrated. This is the work of a good shaman, or shamanically-trained counselor. The degree to which the core self is destroyed varies widely depending upon one's experience, but it can be seen more and more today with people who are broken down, drug-addicted, video game addicted, violent and sensually over-stim-ulated. Maintaining family structure, good values, spiritual beliefs and practices, a loving family system and avoiding the toxic culture is paramount to turning this around.

The process of losing the core self takes many forms and avenues. West African tribes know that to be harsh with a child is to cause its soul to retreat from its body, sometimes many days walk away. So harshness with children is forbidden in those tribes. In the case of the advanced secret societies, they *aspire* to cause the soul to leave the body so it can be replaced with entities of their choice related to their beliefs. They endeavor to turn off traits of innocence to bring the child into the fold of darkness. This is done through violence and hatred, which is all we see in the news and the television now. The number of shows that concentrate on murders or sex is staggering. This is done specifically to demoralize and sexualize children and bring them into acceptance of violence and depravity. Through generations, you can inculcate hatred and remove innocence entirely, and that is what you see in cult families, hate groups and extreme religions. And now we are seeing it more and more in regular society. This is the spiritual warfare we are faced with, saving souls from darkness here.

The effort to break through the soul's divinity and steal their soul was first undertaken through sustained ritual abuse, and now, even in our everyday society. This occurs when the abused person's auric field and power are so completely penetrated and vampired that they can no longer defend against abuse and unconsciously choose to surrender their power to the perpetrator-vampire. If the abused person does not choose to address, face, feel and heal their own personal experience of abuse somewhere in the mid-course of life, one of three outcomes will occur. Either the person being traumatized will die of the abuse and their life force will be cannibalized by the abuser/predators, or they will choose to join the abusers and become one of them, thus sparing their life and losing their soul, and begin to vampire off of the life force of others to survive. The third option is the hardest, but the only way out. You must fight back. That may not happen until you are much older. You may carry the energy around a long time. But there will come a moment when you know you have to reclaim your soul or totally capitulate. The moment you make the decision to do so is the moment a spiritual battle begins. You must seek spiritual help at this time for only an empowered spiritual guide can help you at this point.

So, the imprint of the abuser upon his victims is total and complete. If you can't escape from your tormentor, you endure until the trauma begins to seat itself permanently in the body. The energy is finding its resting place. You are open and vulnerable to the wounding. You have no safety, it flows in easily. When the traumatic bond is indelibly sealed, that is when the wounding occurs. Like a baby animal following its mother, the abused victim who has fully internalized the abuse without fighting back will eventually mimic the behavior. If the abuser goes unchallenged and the victim unhealed, the victim will eventually become the abuser and remain traumatically entranced and in denial for life. Their power has been stolen, they live in an amnesiac traumatic trance, and they have been rendered submissive thus are tools for the abuser to use to abuse others. This is how Manchurian Candidates, Sex Slaves and Operatives are made.

But it's also how a society is enslaved and a population is controlled and manipulated towards a goal. It happened to the German people in World War II, now it's happening to all of us.

Your situation may not be as severe as this though. But you may be struggling with simpler issues such as helplessness, depression, fear, loss of direction, etc. These can come from a **Cultural Trance***, a suppressed society, invisible forms of mind-control or buried trauma. The level of helplessness you demonstrate in your life is directly proportionate to the amount your power and defense system was compromised at some point. It's the breaking of the will, like the breaking of a horse. You learned helplessness somewhere, from someone, or in society as a whole where your soul is suppressed. A traumatic bond develops at this point with the person/s breaking the spirit. A common example of this are soldiers, many of the most elite of whom must go through traumatic initiations to bind them in honor and obedience to their military leaders.

In ancient times, all male warrior tribes were initiated very young through sexual initiations passed down from Canaan and Babylonia. This creates a powerful shame core which facilitates obedience; it also locks the energy field under the control of their military officer or handlers. To make a fierce warrior, you awaken powerful rage through pain, sexual initiations and trauma. This wound coupled with rage can then be triggered and released upon whomever your leader wants it released upon. This is how warriors are often prepared for battle even now in warrior cultures. A lot of the violence we see around the world today was initiated in early life or recent trauma-based training to prepare them for war. They have been prepped with trauma and are ready to inflict it upon the "enemy", whoever that may be, but who is really just a projection of their own pain. Many of these soldiers, and other trauma victims, also become addicts and alcoholics. And it's buried trauma that anchors all addictions, so look for trauma in all your addicted clients. A side note to recovering addicts and alcoholics reading this. In your recovery practices, ask God for the pain of your trauma to be lifted just as you ask for your addiction to be lifted. If you don't release the trauma at the onset of your sobriety, it will draw you back to your addiction to numb the pain. You must work on your trauma healing alongside your addiction healing simultaneously.

Another major trauma code is the breaking of trust with oneself. In order to gain control over another, someone must first break your trust with yourself until you have no more credibility, even within yourself. The loss of trust in oneself bars the way to a full life and blocks the flow of life energy. There are several ways it's done, but sexual abuse is one of the strongest. If there is enough of a shame core, you become incapable of bonding with yourself. You literally are ashamed of yourself even if another caused it and you cannot approach your inner being. It's an unconscious thought form that develops and takes hold. Your conscious self will distance itself from your core self and your divine self. You will be set adrift. Then you are ripe for manipulation. The right con man comes along and you'll buy the Brooklyn Bridge from him, or let him do a $700 billion dollar U.S. Treasury bailout for his bankster friends on Wall St. To do that also requires verbal trauma. A steady breaking down of self-esteem through verbal abuse, planting lies, tricking and deception, grooming, disinformation, and doubt. Eventually, you've been won over, then they go in for the kill, and you find yourself with a wallet full of moths or worse, they've taken your soul.

Another stage of the trauma pattern is the loss of the will to live during sustained abuse over time. A sense of hopelessness sets in. A piece of the soul dies off or fragments away whenever its been asked to carry more than it can handle of terror or trauma. Parts of the spirit die out and there are mini-deaths that occur. This can lead to illness later on in life. But this also can lead to a resurrection and a new life. One of the stages of my profound soul transformation was the uncovering of the many mini-soul deaths I experienced throughout my

18 years of child abuse. As I faced intense hopelessness, despair and suicidal feelings, each instance took me through another round of illness. Every time I got seriously ill, I would call God in and say, "How do I overcome this? You know how, but I don't." And God would show me how to recover and restore myself. Each time it happened, I would have a rush of divine energy flowing in that would heal, patch and restore these broken parts. On more than one occasion I saw a physician who would always tell me I was going to die. Those were his beliefs. I had much more faith than that. But I could see I was having another round of death/rebirth/cleanse/resurrection. The thought forms I held in my head of death, the beliefs of death taught to me by a diseased culture, were surfacing and dying out. I no longer believed them. They took with them dead tissue and left me with another near-death experience. But I arose from my deathbed yet again, minus the old self. A new resurrected person was born each time, another lost soul part had returned home.

The Four Directions of Trauma

After trauma has set into a pattern and is trapped behind the amnesiac barrier, the survivor's life begins to be directed by the trauma unconsciously. Most all of the victims decisions will be centered around one of four actions, although they will have no inkling that they are following this pattern. They are attempting to escape in one way or another from the inner pain of their situation. These are called the *Four Directions of Trauma**. These four directions are as follows: <u>seeking safety</u>, <u>seeking numbness</u>, <u>seeking release/death</u> and <u>seeking transcendence</u>.

The first three of these are the first actions the victim will seek. And most often, safety is the first one. In seeking safety, the victim will look for people and situations that make them feel safe from the buried trauma. They won't realize they are making these choices, but they will be choosing safety rather than empowerment. Perhaps they will choose a mate that seemingly provides the comfort, love and safety missing from their childhood. They have idealized that person as a protector and projected all their early childhood needs onto them. They will attempt to solidify that situation to lock down safety in their lives forever. Or they will pick a work situation that makes them feel the safety missing in their lives. These choices will provide a temporary false veneer of safety, for a while.

After a person realizes that having sought safety did not bring relief from the inner pain, they often go looking for some form of a drug. Like amnesia is protection from the truth, addiction is protection from the pain. The drug can be anything, but it serves as a sedative/pain killer from the searing internal pain they are carrying around. It is not unusual for a serious drug or alcohol addiction to come into play at this point. The origin of the pain is inaccessible, the chosen safety nets didn't kill the pain, something stronger is called for. As an Addictions Counselor, I've seen the array of drugs and substances people become addicted to and they are more and more favoring the Oxycodone/Heroin type drugs, especially for suppressing buried trauma pain. This is a very gripping addiction that can be a lifetime habit, or can take a person a long time to overcome. It is also a killer. Other big ones in our bottoming out culture are crystal meth or crack. Both drugs have devastated an already devastated population. Both drugs stand as another manipulation to initiate the breakdown of our culture and our inner strength.

But many other addictions are used to induce numbness as well. One of the primary ones is sex addiction, an addiction that destroys marriages, families and lives. Shopping is also a serious addiction as over-spending becomes uncontrollable. Since consumerism is encouraged in our culture, you see people over-spending constantly as a form of instant gratification. Food addiction is similar that way and another huge sedative. Since food is an accepted drug in our society, we can choose our poison there. Even more destructive is a gambling addiction which wreaks havoc on people's lives, wallets and family stability.

And more ways to numb out are entertainment such as television, movies, shows, strip clubs, etc. Or work addictions – overachieving in the workplace, workaholism, shutting the world out, working long hours. Or power addictions such as trying to one up people in the workplace, in business, in relationships, in sex, in life in general. You see this in our leaders, corporate CEO's, politicians, Wall St. brokers, and people striving for power/money/adulation, very serious addictions affecting our world today. Money and power become more important than life itself. Many of these people have also experienced early trauma which is buried. Other odd addictions are OCD - cleaning addictions, touching a recurring list of objects every day at certain times of the day, etc. The list is endless as to what forms seeking numbness takes. But know that it is an unconscious reaction to trauma and a deep disconnection that drives it. Eventually, all addictive behaviors that are attempting to drive out the pain will fail and trauma will have to be faced.

When the other two directions of trauma have failed, the trauma victim begins seeking release from the pain. Things are more desperate at this point and more desperate actions begin. A variety of methods of release are more common today. If the victim has not sought counseling or spiritual help by now, the more destructive options are sought. Violence, self-harm such as cutting, and finally suicide are often chosen at this stage. Fantasies of death and release from suffering are strong during this phase. But it's also a stage where healing is sometimes sought due to the severity of the suffering.

The final direction is seeking transcendence. In this stage, the person has exhausted the tried and true methods of marrying an abuser, hiding out, becoming a workaholic, drinking, taking drugs, having affairs, moving around geographically, taking on addictions and eventually attempting some form of suicide. A crossroads is reached and the traumatized soul must decide if taking their life is really the solution or if there is a possibility of redemption. This is the powerful turning point when something can enter the soul's consciousness to inspire them to try to overcome the experience and heal. They can leave Earth or seek to transcend the situation. Clearly, the last option is the best, but not everyone chooses it. ***Know that transcendence is definitely possible, no matter how severe your trauma. My resurrected life is proof of that.***

At this point, the ego has begun to collapse completely. In fact, it was collapsing all along but you just didn't know it. Time and time again I have seen the parallels between people having alcoholic breakdowns and then a spiritual redemption, and people's lives collapsing around them due to buried trauma and then watching them step into spiritual awakening. In every case there is a profound ego death. The person who was running the show was simply an outer ego shell devoid of spiritual power, depth or purpose. They had created that shell out of the broken pieces of the shattered core self after being traumatized, and now they have fallen in their effort to stay together. They were Humpty Dumpty. They were knocked off the wall and broken into pieces. And they couldn't be put together again in the old way, because that person was destroyed. The rhyme is indicative of how a person's life is after trauma. You are in a fragile, egg-like state. You are in an unsafe situation in an unsafe world without protection. You have only a thin outer shell covering your pain and fear. Falling apart is inevitable. It's a metaphor for spiritual awakening.

Humpty Dumpty sat on a wall; Humpty Dumpty had a great fall. All the king's horses and all the king's men, couldn't put Humpty together again.

~ An olde English nursery rhyme

After you have exhausted all four directions of trauma, you either reach transcendence or die. For many, this experience is a gift for trauma leads us into transcendence of the illusory world. You can never again be asleep in a world so violent, traumatic, false and dangerous. You have to wake up. You have crossed through one of the veils of illusion never to return. You may awaken, or you may die. And for some, death is transcendence.

Perhaps the most vital part to understand about the trauma codes is how they create disease and amnesia in the body. As I mentioned earlier, when we experience trauma, an amnesiac barrier is created. In secret societies, the creation of this amnesiac barrier is intentional for several reasons. This barrier is a neuro-synaptic brain barrier that is a chemical reaction and a survival-oriented byproduct of trauma, especially trauma-based mind-control. Their goal is to warp the *synaptic pathways** and natural chemical hormones. When they accomplish this, they can control your thoughts. It can get created with other types of trauma or poisons as well, like with fluoride in your water, a head injury, a car accident, a fall and so on. The event is imprinted on the body's tissue and memory forever, but if the event is too traumatic for the person to deal with in the moment, it will be stored in brain tissue behind the amnesiac barrier. The barrier will hold back the energy of the incident like a dam in a river of the amnesia-state, suppressed, until the soul is strong enough to deal with it. Portions of the brain are compartmentalized this way behind this barrier away from the conscious part of the brain. It starts in various ways with mind-control techniques. A neurosurgeon could explain it more thoroughly, but here is the simple version.

*Neurotransmitters** are chemical messengers that travel along the spinal cord to the brain and relay messages to the brain about breathing, swallowing, etc. They also carry emotional and pain messages. During the sexual abuse initiation, trauma is enacted that is specifically designed to warp the synaptic fibers and neural pathways, as well as compartmentalize the brain and memory. The base of the spine near the **Root Chakra*** is traumatized, including the spinal cord. The nerve bundles of the spinal cord are shocked and then send these repeated painful messages rapidly up the spine to the brain stem. The neural pathways are subsequently overwhelmed, traumatized and compromised in this way – the painful, shocked nerve impulses now shooting up the **axons*** into the **pre-synaptic neuron*** deposit traumatized, pain-filled neurotransmitter messages into the **synaptic vesicles*** of the sending neuron in preparation for delivery into the receptor sites on the **post-synaptic neuron* dendrite***. The neurotransmitters must then fire and make the leap across the **synaptic cleft*** into the receptor sites on the receiving neuron.

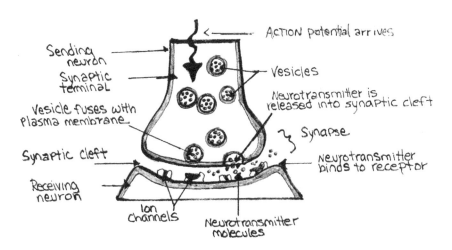

There are enzymes in the synaptic cleft inbetween the pre and post-synaptic neuron heads that can consume neurotransmitters. Since the neurotransmitter process is a chemical process, various chemical reactions occur during the transmission of neurotransmitter messages. In the case of an avalanche of shocking, painful and threatening messages up the spinal cord, whose stability must be maintained and protected for the body to survive, the chemical reaction in the spinal fluid changes to reflect a dangerous threat/fear/pain shooting up towards the brain and brain stem. The body perceives a threat to the brain, so its protective response is to shut down the neural pathways. Some of the toxic messages get through to the brain stem where they are directed at the ***amygdala****, the ***hippocampus**** and the pineal gland. Protective reflexes and chemical reactions move to block the messages from entering and overwhelming the brain so the process of compartmentalization begins.

The amygdala is the part of the brain responsible for emotional learning, memory modulation, long-term memory control, fear conditioning and memory consolidation. Terror and fear originate in the amygdala. It is this area of the brain that is often targeted by mind control experts because they know if they can stimulate terror they can immobilize someone and gain control over them. Memories of emotional experiences imprinted in the outer synapses of the amygdala elicit sustained terror by making repetitive neuronal connections to the central nucleus of the amygdala. By manipulating the number and times of the initiation to surprise and overwhelm the gates of the synaptic pathways, the amygdala's memory system can be manipulated, segmented and controlled, a terror state permanently installed, and in turn, a person can be manipulated and controlled. This is how a Manchurian Candidate is made. And to a lesser degree, how a population is controlled.

Similarly, the pineal gland, which is the gland of spiritual sight, is seated at the top of the spinal column where it enters the Mouth of God and on into the brain stem. During the initiation, the messages received are pain, fear and trauma. This causes the neural pathways to the pineal gland to shut down or warp, and the area of the brain stem that receives them to segment off the compartments where the trauma is received and stores it in the brain stem. These compartments then effectively block off access to the pineal gland and a person's spiritual sight, and the brain stem fills with trauma messages. The brain stem then becomes the storage dump for pain and trauma where it can stay for life. It also blocks access to higher parts of brain function and isolates powerful energies down in the brain stem where reptilian consciousness originates.

But there is more to the intentional trauma initiation given to those intended for mass control and enslavement that you need to know about. If you understand the basics of Newtonian physics, you know that most everything on Earth has a gravitational field. Gravity rules the day here. That is as long as the mass of an object is larger than 1/1000th of an inch. Objects larger than that obey the laws of Newtonian physics, e.g. – an apple will fall to Earth from a tree due to gravity. But objects smaller than 1/1000th of an inch dwell in the *quantum field** of all possibilities. Particles that miniscule are too small to have a gravitational field. Your spirit/soul falls in that category of the quantum field. Spirit has no mass, is not subject to Newtonian physics and is simply energy and light. Therefore your spirit is free to move without limitation into the universal quantum field where spiritual awakening occurs.

So, here's the kicker. The distance between all the pre and post-synaptic neuron heads in your brain is exactly 1/1000th of an inch. What this means is that the space between neurotransmitter heads, known as the synaptic cleft or gap, is the space inside of you that dwells in the quantum field, or the cosmos itself. And this is the key to spiritual awakening. Those who seek to awaken spiritually know that prolonged meditation on that part of the brain and consciousness, or the gaps between thoughts, can send you into the quantum field, or *nirvana** as it is called by the awakened. Science has their own theory, *quantum field theory**, for the quantum field. It's the field of physics that studies sub-atomic particles, particle physics, quarks, condensed matter physics and field quanta. Quantum field scientists attempt to study and define the movement of sub-atomic particles through the field that is absent of a gravitational field. This is essentially what happens in meditation but without the participation of the mind. If one meditates long enough on the pineal gland and the empty connecting spaces of the synaptic clefts contained therein without thoughts, spiritual awakening occurs. And contact with the Divine is part of that experience. Unfortunately, priests of the dark cabals also know this information and devised the sexual initiation, known as the **Luciferian initiation***, to warp all synaptic clefts and pathways so no seeker could broach the field of consciousness where all power, love and awakening lies. They wish to keep the spiritual energies for themselves. They wish to control the access to this un-limited power. But you don't need their permission to go there. You simply need to begin a daily spiritual practice of advanced medita-tion and if done diligently, you will arrive there. Regular meditation, prayer and chanting sacred chants will heal and open your synaptic pathways and usher you into the divine field. And there is nothing they can do about that except try to scare you. You are free to go there anytime. Your power is your own.

An additional side effect of this type of trauma-based condi-tioning is the reversal of the thinking processes of the mind. If they can warp the synaptic pathways, they can also reverse the synaptic pathways. This type of extreme trauma-based mind control is done to certain individuals who are needed for specific tasks. If they are successful at reversing the thought processes of an individual, they can create a **contrary***. A contrary is a person whose thinking pro-cesses have been severely impacted and they perceive everything as distorted and backwards. This is a common satanic initiation. These type of people have been conditioned to see the world a certain way so they can be used for specific purposes such as disinformation, reverse publications, satanic writing, charismatic lying, deceptive practices and duplicitous behavior. They often do not realize they are doing and seeing things this way. Many trauma-based sexual abuse survivors have this distorted thinking and must be deprogrammed, cleansed and re-connected to the Holy Spirit. It takes time, but with steady counseling, Reiki training, spiritual practices and a strong connection to God, the mind can be healed. The most powerful tool I have come across to heal distorted, confused, contrary thinking is Reiki. Reiki, utilizing God's divine love, has the capacity to heal mentally thus a mental spiritual cleansing process begins when a person takes Reiki Level Two.

Additionally, the corpus colossum, a bundle of nerves that connect the two brain halves, can connect or disconnect the two brain halves according to the type of stimuli recorded. If there is enough fear, it disconnects you at the level of the corpus. Further, the brain creates an amnesiac barrier there with chemical reactions that isolate the trauma away from the rest of the brain so it can complete its daily functions. A surface egocentric narcissistic personality is created to interact with the world. This is why you see so much charm in sociopaths; it's been developed over time, most often with trauma. [I postulate that most sociopaths were once trauma victims and lost connection to their true spirits due to the suffering they were experiencing, slipping into a fallen state of consciousness. This is the true goal of secret society programmers.] Thus a split-off, compartmentalized mind is created and can function quite well a long time. But in the meantime, the pineal gland, or third eye, is closed down and access to higher consciousness is limited. The pineal gland pathways must be opened again to regain spiritual sight and heal the consciousness. Brain stem compartmentalization with trauma memories is a major cause of brain tumors and migraines. If you have a client with brain stem tumors or recurring migraines, it's likely they have been sodomized with the satanic ritual abuse sexual initiation and will need de-programming with my program, or a similar one.

This is but the tip of the iceberg of mental, physical, emotional and soul manipulation utilized to steal your life force and control you. But for my purpose of showing the path to spiritual awakening out of darkness, this is a basic roadmap to begin with. The more you heal yourself, the more you will awaken and see on your own. You won't need to be told then because vast vistas of knowledge and power will open up to you.

But there are a few more pieces to add to this puzzle. One of the worst aspects of institutionalized trauma, denial, deception and corruption, is how those who commit it group together and protect one another to cover their crimes. We've all seen it with politicians and banksters who now openly steal from us without even one prosecution. The same is true of wealthy sexual predators. They have trained **Praetorians***, who are mind-controlled, in their positions of power to cover for them. But what most people don't realize is that there is a huge underground network of sexual traffickers and slavers that operate a burgeoning multi-billion dollar network of sexual slavery, especially of children. This network is largely run by Satanists and Secret Society members who keep the information out of the news and the public in the dark about how vast this problem is.

Every year in the USA, there are between 50,000 to 100,000 children kidnapped, sold or bred into sexual slavery. Are you hearing about them in the news? No, of course not, because the mainstream media was co-opted years ago by high level secret society members and law enforcement were sometimes involved. You hear about maybe 3 Amber Alerts a year. In reality, children are trafficked like sides of beef on the sex slave market every day. Many of them are sold to pornographers for films, more will be sold to make snuff films and they will be killed on camera. This is a billion dollar business folks. Where money is to be made, children are simply collateral. I tried to alert people to this issue twenty years ago and found that in California, sexual abuse and slavery were protected. The few I could speak to simply didn't believe me, didn't care or were part of the sex slavery rings which reach high into the ranks of police, law, government and politics.

What you need to know, however hard this is to hear, is that the people taken into these slavery situations, especially the innocent children, are used in satanic ritual sacrifice ceremonies on a daily basis. They live off the energy they have vampired from the children and others and it continues on secretly 24/7. In order to do their dirty work, they need to keep you in denial and unaware of their actions. The children are being flown in, raised in cult families for sacrifice and kidnapped off the streets of America. And you don't even know about it do you? This has been going on for centuries. People have been keeping sex slaves in their homes for ages and no one even knows. It's far, far more widespread than you can even imagine.

Know that when you see perpetrators get arrested and 6 boys step forward to testify to being raped, there are thousands more. They will throw someone to the wolves and keep going on. Their circle tightens around them. But they will continue to live off your energy field. All the men gather around the perpetrator and slap him on the back, and talk about how great he is, he's on our "team", etc. The real story remains untold. This is how it is in general society. Time and time again I saw perpetrators be embraced by judges, lawyers, police and other people in power who covered for them. I'm not referring to the many good policemen, judges, lawmen and lawyers who do fight to end this corruption. I met them too, and they were the greatest heroes of all. They went into dark places and pulled the children out. To them I tip my hat. But overall, the superstructure remains in place. We must expose this. We must end this. We must pull this rotten octopus of evil out by its very roots once and for all. And we are getting closer every day. The children who make it out are never the same and will need help for the rest of their lives.

Finally, the reason that this is happening and that groups of secretive people are trying to enslave us all, is they want all of your divine energy, all of the grace God gave you, for themselves. They know that if they perform certain rituals, they can capture, trap, funnel and utilize your vast spiritual energy for their goals. Think of your spine and its energy centers, called chakras, constantly channeling God's divine energy into and through your body 24 hours a day. You are like a huge Texas oil rig spouting energy all day long. Their eyeballs are bugging out with greed. When the pineal gland is activated, the power that surges through there is stupendously enormous. They know that if they can harness that divine energy before you do, they are hooked up for life and can do so much more than they could if they functioned on just their own energy. So, they are right now as we speak attempting to attach to everyone on Earth's divine power source, which is ultimately God, of course. And if they accomplish that, we are all living in pods like Neo was in the Matrix as batteries powering their grid.

The truth is that your energy is yours to use and no one else's. Yes, we are all connected, but to take energy without the consent of another is in violation of Divine Law. There has to be consent. There are huge karmic consequences for this which they will have to face. Mr. and Mrs. Einstein wrote the theory of relativity in 1905. When they stated that $E = mc^{2*}$, they were illuminating a basic spiritual principal known by Masters, sages and yogis for thousands of years, that energy and mass are equivalent and that to turn mass into pure energy releases an enormous amount of power. This is something the Dark Illusionists have always known. This is the energy they are stealing from you and this is the enormous power they wield, and it's ALL YOUR POWER, NOT THEIRS. *Now it's time for you to know it.*

If you were to split your own Divine Atom, your own molecule of Divine Energy, you would release incredible power within yourself and merge with the Divine. You would never be afraid again, have enormous personal power, always live abundantly, and be filled with love. They can't let you get there, because then you are awake and free. And when Einstein split the Universal Atom in his mind, he found within the entire Universe. He spoke of it often, *"I didn't arrive at my understanding of the Universe through my rational mind."* Einstein had a spiritual awakening. After splitting the atom and basically inventing the first atom bomb, he spent the rest of his life trying to stop them from using it to destroy the world. But they are still trying. And their future grand plan is even worse. We absolutely, unequivocally, beyond a shadow of a doubt, must take our power back, heal ourselves and restore Earth, while we still can. There is precious little time left to do this. But it's about to happen.

The intuitive mind is a sacred gift and the rational mind is a faithful servant. We have created a society that honors the servant and has forgotten the gift.
~Albert Einstein

Since reclaiming my power, I've moved through huge personal shifts in my life and in my power. We will reclaim our power, they will be defeated, we will heal this planet and everyone will wake up. But first, we have to fight the spiritual battle to reclaim our souls. We must each begin to do the work of our personal Soul Transformations.

Chapter 12

Trauma as Transformation

An illness or crisis is but the beginning of a transformation to come. Sometimes we have to breakdown...to breakthrough.

~ Salini

So where do we find ourselves as a culture today? Three main things are abundantly clear. We are living in the most oppressive period of political tyranny in world history, we are in a global political, economic and environmental crisis of epic proportions, and we as a people have lost the ability to resolve it because our power has been taken from us by corporate, political and banking vampires posing as "good fathers" who care about us. We are all so shocked and traumatized by the agenda they have implemented, that we are stressed, fearful, exhausted and have forgotten our divinity. We have forgotten that we came equipped with abundance, love, joy and a divine purpose. We don't remember that we came to help the world grow, heal and transform towards wholeness. And that is exactly what they intended to happen. I'm here to tell you that you absolutely do have that power and can make those kind of contributions, but you've been deceived into believing you have no power and no choice. We've reached a turning point and a critical mass consciousness as I previously described. But that critical mass consciousness can go either way. They are fine-tuning you right now to make it be tuned permanently to the zombie channel. I urge everyone to take critical mass consciousness in the other direction, to mass awakening.

Those who wish to be your slavemasters believe they have put all the chess pieces in place for their grand plan. They traumatized us into zombieland and a massive collective traumatic trance, and shattered and fragmented our souls. But what they didn't count on is that although shattering a mind and soul through trauma may make it vulnerable to manipulation, it also makes it possible to re-arrange the soul's mind, spirit and purpose into an even more powerful persona capable of regaining and even surpassing the soul's original power. All boundaries have been broken, the rigid walls and belief systems torn down, your divine energy can now flow free. They risked throwing down their trump card…..they split the atom of your soul to rob the inner jewel of your divine energy and consciousness for themselves. They entered the temple of your body and soul and defiled it through poisons, rape, lies, magic, violence and desolation of the spirit. They sought to unleash the vast infinite power of the Universe contained inside the human soul that was uncovered when Einstein revealed the secret formula – E=mc2. He wasn't just talking about the Universe, he was talking about everything because all energy is a unified field. He was talking about your soul's central core. It is filled with unlimited energy too.

Basically, Einstein was saying that mass and energy are equivalent, but are just in different forms. If you can release the energy inside mass, you can access the incredible power released there. This was the principle behind the development of the atom bomb. The same is true of the human soul. Within it is all the power of the Universe. If you split a human soul open, you release the power of God. But they entered the temple without permission, they robbed it of the sacred jewels of the spirit, they took the heart hostage for self-protection and they began linking to our divine power for their fuel. And they used a spell of trauma and forgetfulness to do it. We do it sacredly when we meditate, chant and pray regularly. We open those same gateways through reverence, humility, respect, love, spiritual practice and surrender. It's not to be done violently without permission. Otherwise, they have broken Divine Law and have committed **Soul Murder***.

What they may or may not know is that your divine energy matrix, made up of invisible molecules of inter-connected energy like a web of connective tissue, will always stay connected, even if it's suppressed by a spell or process and doesn't remember it's connected. Our energy field does have a unified consciousness; in Physics it's known as the **Unified Field Theory***, which only partially explains it. Some may disagree, but it doesn't matter. I understand the block in their consciousness as part of the universal split in human awareness I've described in other chapters. If a scientist doesn't say it, it can't be true according to the egoic mind. **No mystic shall be heard**. The groove in their brain is set; they can't violate the cultural truth. This is part of the mind-control veil dropped over us. Yet Einstein believed it until his dying day, that there was a unified field that featured magnetism. I'm here to tell you it's true. I see, feel and sense things that others may not. As a ReikiMaster I utilize and heal with that field. Even science can't explain how a mystic can see non-physical phenomena or explain forces of the Universe without scientific equipment. The Masters figured all this out thousands of years ago. And they all came to the same conclusion, there is a Unified Field and it works as one whole organism and is self-regenerating and self-healing.

This is precisely what is missing in the conversation, the voice of the mystic who sees the whole. I see and feel the Unified Field, as do all true healers and mystics. What science doesn't fully understand yet is that the dark field they are still studying is made of magnetic matter, which draws together the Unified Field with a form of magnetism. Physicists from Vanderbilt University have researched and verified the existence of massive amounts of electro-magnetic energy in the dark field, which makes up at least 85% of the matter in the Universe. What science also doesn't understand, but the Tao does, the Vedas do and all the great Masters do, is that this dark matter is primarily the elusive Yin energy, the sacred feminine principle of creative life force energy, which is inherently magnetic, the divine Shakti of Creation, the Goddess Mother energy. Because yin energy has been largely denied in all discussions of the Universe, it's very existence and power is denied and we have a partial view of the make-up of our Universe. Thus science flounders under its addiction to patriarchal perspectives of half-consciousness. This field of energy will be continuously straining to re-join and mesh with its disconnected parts, just like two magnets coming together. This will create a constant field of tension within the energy field as it strains to rejoin. Black magicians and secret society priests will have to constantly redo the separation and forgetfulness spells throughout the collective consciousness, or eventually a person will gravitate back towards wholeness. And eventually the entirety of consciousness will gravitate back towards wholeness because the forces of magnetism and truth are stronger than the forces of the lie and terror.

But if healing is undertaken at any point, the re-unification of the soul energy fragments will begin and the soul's original integrity and power will be restored. This is the eternal struggle between the soul destroyers and the soul restorers. But by triggering the breaking apart of your soul's energy structure, they have also unwittingly triggered the beginning of your restoration and resurrection to a more powerful being. And by enacting their plan on a mass scale as they currently are, our planetary awakening has been triggered. We can use their treachery to our advantage. As Buckminster Fuller put it, "Don't fight forces, use them." I take it a step further.

Let their global trauma plan be the cosmic wave and surfboard you ride towards your greatest power. Begin the sacred journey of the restoration of your soul.

~ Salini

Trauma can be utilized for your greatest transformation, your personal Soul Transformation. When I began going through mine, it felt like a death experience, only over and over and over again. I kept asking God, "When is this going to end?" As if my childhood wasn't traumatic enough, I began having a series of illnesses related to my healing crisis. Each was more serious than the last, and they spanned a 20-year-period. But as I released each piece of toxic energy from my energy field, I made space within my consciousness for the return of another lost soul fragment. And as each soul fragment returned, my consciousness expanded and a spiritual awakening occurred. This is now happening on a global level to everyone on Earth. The Universe is helping it along. And even the dark ones have their hand in it. Their unconscious actions that are damaging the Earth are forcing us to wake up. Surely God is guiding their hand.

It isn't going to be a war against them that does the trick. No, it's going to be the moment we realize we are inexorably connected to them in way that makes it our responsibility to awaken them. We do that by holding them accountable but also offering healing, love and forgiveness. But the gift of love and forgiveness can only be put into effect when accountability is fully implemented. Since you probably aren't going to get the Hitlers of the world to step forward and apologize, you will have to do this process within yourself. Because as you heal your own shadow, you reduce the size of the world's shadow. As you change the consciousness within yourself, you create a 100th monkey wave of awakened consciousness that impacts the world. You can do all this right inside of yourself when you undertake a Soul Transformation. You can do this by using your current life trauma as a springboard to your spiritual awakening. And if your trauma is a total shattering of the self, as mine was, you are prepped for a massive spiritual awakening. Your awakening can be the catalyst for the awakening of others, even the dark ones.

But prepare yourselves. The moment of the breaking of the

traumatic trance is often as painful as the event that originally created it. You split off to survive a traumatic event. Now you've been shocked somehow into remembering it and the shattering of the fragile protective shell of your traumatic trance has begun. Much attachment and energy has gone into keeping the shell in place. When it breaks open, your insides spill out to be healed. You may be like a lump of clay for a while. As I discussed earlier, a soul shattering is often called a dismemberment. If this happens to you, prepare for a major Soul Transformation. Your trauma has finished baking in the crucible of change and is awakening within you. The alchemy of transformation is underway. But don't be afraid, you only need a shard of the old to recreate the new whole. Only this time, it is a more powerful you. Your journey will go in stages. You have begun the Hero/Heroine's Journey to reclaim your soul.

It might start with trauma and frozen fear, an injury or the beginning of an illness. Each represents an unhealed, unacknowledged portion of your soul that has emerged on the surface to be reclaimed by you. Your soul has instigated this journey, even if you don't realize it. It's unconscious, but timed for the right moment on your life path. Now, you must go about retrieving the pieces of your broken self. You don't need them all. In fact, you should discard and transmute those that no longer serve you. Because long lost soul parts have found their way back to you for integration. Make room for the new consciousness that will flood in.

There won't be a clear, mapped out road ahead. There will be landmarks, guides, and messages along the way, but you will be entering into the void of your consciousness….an unknown place where fear is the first thing you meet and the first test you must overcome. It's a dark field, but know that Mother yin energy is there, holding you, guiding you through the dark. Then you must begin to unlock the secrets of your soul, and remember your truth, whatever that is. It will be the truth of your soul's purpose here. When you find your truth and claim it, it will set you free. As you see, in the clear blinding light of spiritual truth, who you are and why you are here, your soul will appear as a large torn-up map, a jig-saw puzzle. One by one you will reclaim the torn fragments and re-arrange them into a new person, a more whole persona than you ever were before. You will let go of what you no longer need and save the best parts of yourself. You will then begin to go through an alchemical transformation. You will experience a cellular cleansing, if you allow it, and will go through a healing crisis. All that is untrue will begin to fall away. You will step beyond the veil of illusion and see the truth on Earth. Once again you will have to take this path alone. No one can do this for you; it's your soul's work. But helpers will appear along the way.

Here is an amazing story of Soul Transformation that began with trauma and ended with Reiki healing him –

Fred's Reiki healing story and Soul Transformation – *Fred came to me with a severe rash in the area of his buttocks and low back. He had already been to several doctors who prescribed various creams and prescription medications to ease the rash. None of these treatments helped him. He asked me why his rash persisted when he had been to so many doctors and tried so many different treatments. I said we needed to find the true cause of his condition. I told him that sometimes the origin of the problem isn't physical but emotional or mental or even karmic. When he got on the table, he was very agitated and upset about the rash and told me how painful it was. I began with a traditional Reiki treatment which starts at the head. As I reached the point where I gave him a deep mental and emotional treatment, I felt his extreme agitation. I completed the mental and emotional treatment. I could*

feel the waves of painful emotions from Fred washing over me. I moved to the next positions and reached his chest and heart. When I got there and began working on him, Fred began to sob uncontrollably.

Fred began to tell me what he was seeing and feeling. He said that right then and there, while I was giving him the treatment, he was seeing and remembering scenes of being molested by a Catholic priest right where the rash was. And I hadn't even reached that area of his body with Reiki, but I had given him a mental/ emotional treatment and addressed his deep emotional issues. Fred continued to sob intensely for a while. We did some emotional release and process work. I finished the treatment and we agreed to continue with more treatments later. I urged him to stay in touch with me since he was having memories. He called me a few days later to tell me the rash was completely gone. He said it left not long after returning home from his Reiki treatment. Once the memories had been accessed, his body began to heal the condition.

Then about three weeks later, Fred became dizzy and told me he was having difficulty walking. He said he felt like he was going to lose consciousness. He went to see a doctor. The doctor told him he had vertigo, then later told him he had a brain tumor and that they should operate. Instead of having brain surgery, Fred asked me to come over and begin giving him Reiki at his home. I did so. After giving Fred several deep soul Reiki mental/emotional treatments, Fred told me he felt the dizziness and brain fog lifting off of him. He also said he had intense memories of the sexual abuse by the priest, and that they were much clearer this time. He said it had gone on for more than ten years and that it was the family priest. His family knew and didn't care. Fred had felt trapped in the situation and had begun a process of losing his spiritual and emotional center and his soul force as a child. He said he suppressed himself completely and tried to pretend it didn't happen. It wasn't until that day we began the first treatment for his rash that he said he began to feel the release take place. But first, he went through the terrifying moments of the brain fog, dizziness and being told by a doctor he had a brain tumor.

During one of the treatments, Fred experienced a soul retrieval of a past life experience. As I was work-ing on him, he saw himself in another life and another place. Fred told me he saw himself dressed in priest's robes. "I'm a priest in this previous life!" he blurted out. Fred saw the progression of the past life. I asked him to go to the point in time in that life that was connected to his current experience and bring the lesson forward for clearing. He saw himself involved in molesting children in another time and place as a priest somewhere in Europe. At some point in that life he realized what he was doing was wrong. He went to a cliff, asked for God's forgiveness, and jumped off. The memories of guilt were the last thoughts he held in his mind before death. He brought that guilt with him to this life and that was the karma he was healing now with this experience. We worked through his guilt together, helped him release his feelings, and slowly Fred recovered. Today, he is fully recovered.

If Fred had not received the spiritual healing with Reiki, he may have developed a brain tumor, or been misdiagnosed and treated for something incorrectly. The doctors would have missed the true cause of Fred's condition, the early sexual abuse at the hands of his family priest for more than ten years and the karma he brought to this life. Fred had compartmentalized the memories and didn't remember them for a long time. The rash was the beginning of the memories surfacing for healing. Sometimes, the body is the first to warn us of a deeper soul issue. We must pay attention when something appears on our body because it's really a warning message from our soul to handle something that's becoming serious. To suppress symptoms that may be telling us something we need to know is to possibly give ourselves a death sentence. Pay attention to your body and your intuition. It has much wisdom to share with you.

Fred's story is an example of a Soul Transformation. It started with a condition on his body, morphed into an emotional crisis, then became a physical crisis. But when Fred allowed himself to go the full distance of the transformation and not stay stuck on the physical manifestation, he was able to unearth deeply buried feelings that were deadly, and a past life that still held him hostage. He had felt powerless most of his life, but this crisis caused those feelings to surface to be faced and dealt with. He decided to confront the family and the priest. In doing that, Fred was finally able to call back his lost soul fragment and his power from the priest who had been molesting him. As a result of completing his personal work, he is recovered and whole.

During a Soul Transformation, it's likely you will find that you must reclaim the will to live. That may be the biggest stolen piece of soul fragment you must reclaim. It is taken from you during trauma, but it is yours to reclaim if you have the strength to do it. This can take the form of a severe illness. Or it can take the form of a huge loss and a broken heart, like a divorce or the loss of a loved one. Or it can be a mental or emotional illness, signs you are missing a soul part. These are big mountains to climb, but on the other side is a calm oasis of a peace-filled life.

Your journey on the path of Soul Transformation is a very sacred journey. Never let anyone tell you that you've done something wrong. Yes, you've made mistakes, but those mistakes are the mulch for your future growth. No one ever grew who didn't falter in their steps first. Never let anyone take your power as you navigate the path. You must always listen to your intuition as you go along. For your soul is giving birth to its true self and its true mission. Messages will rise up in the unlikeliest of places. These are the flashes of your soul speaking to you and creating exercises to make you learn to listen within. If you externalize your power at this time, onto say a doctor, a spouse, or a counselor, you lose the valuable lesson of learning how to let your soul guide you. That must be mastered along the way. That is how we stay the course in life. No one else can do this for you.

Your soul will have unique messages only for you. In heeding them, you are claiming your power. If I had listened to the doctor when I had breast cancer, I would be without breasts today and possibly no longer on this planet. His message was to cut off my female parts and undergo chemotherapy and radiation. My soul screamed NO!!! I listened to myself. And because I did, I'm here today to tell you this story and still have my original breasts, healed and whole. What I gained in that experience was not just my life, my breasts and my health, it was the certainty that my soul voice was the one that spoke the words of life over my body. I listen to that voice every day and use it with my clients as well. It's the voice that is connected to all of the Universe, to the Divine, to God itself. I allow it to flow into my consciousness to guide me. And so I can rest in the calm knowledge that I am loved and guided always. I would not have known that if I didn't have the experience of nearly dying from breast cancer. It was also one of the vital initiations into being the healer I was born to be. It confirmed my ability to restore health in people.

Dr. Malidoma Patrice Somé, an African shaman from the West African Dagara tribe, was discussing how mental illness is the sign that a healer is emerging from within a tribe, someone bringing new information and who is uniquely qualified to heal their tribe. Mental disorders are spiritual emergencies, spiritual crises, and need to be regarded as such to aid the healer in being born. The West erroneously views mental illness as a cause for drugging, incarceration and ridicule from our communities. But African and Native American tribes view this as *"good news from the other world."* The person going through the crisis has been chosen as a medium for a message to the community that needs to be communicated from the spirit realm. *"Mental disorder, behavioral disorder of all kinds, signal the fact that two obviously incompatible energies have merged into the same field,"* says Dr. Somé. These disturbances result when the person does not get assistance in dealing with the presence of the energy from the spirit realm. Western doctors and psychologists view mental illness as something that must be changed and stopped immediately when the opposite is true. There is the presence of new wisdom, perhaps a guiding spirit or an ancestor bringing healing in that must be integrated, recognized, heard by the tribe and accepted. If a person with a mental illness were to go into nature with a skilled shaman from a tribe, they would receive the guidance they needed from the shaman to bring forth the necessary information and healing. Indigenous holy men do this all the time. As an American shaman, this is the work I do as well but in a more Americanized way. I was raised in this tribe, I speak the language of the West. So, I have a Western approach to healing our tribe with special wisdom given to me for this purpose from the many initiations, teachers and spirits who have helped me grow into the healer I am today.

But mental illness is also a reflection of a diseased, fragmented culture that blocks the life force, and a wound to the psyche of either the male energy or the female energy or both. A mark of a diseased culture is the level of acceptance by the culture of violent, sick, predatory behavior by members of that culture upon other members of that culture. In African or South American tribes, they don't prey on each other, they help each other, share everything with each other and love and support each other. In our tribe, there is much predatory, violent, diseased behavior that is accepted and tolerated and ignored, so the tribe grows sicker and sicker. If sick behaviors become routinely accepted into a tribe and taught to the children, there will form a schism in the child's mind and a future split in consciousness with a ripple effect throughout the culture. For example, if a child is raised in a racist environment and witnesses mistreatment of other races, this teaches the child to harm others and to hate others which in turn teaches him to hate himself, since we are all connected. Therein is the beginning of the split within someone.

I firmly believe that the special initiation I received into dark patriarchal male abuse by my ancestors and relatives was a long lineage that was brought to me for healing. Since I was also initiated by all the brilliant healers among the female lineage of my clan, I was born with the gifts to heal the male side of the lineage. Some of the males came to me for healing, sometimes in spirit form, to ask for my help. The long history of darkness loomed over the family side by side with the brilliant lineage of women sages, mystics, healers and visionaries. These energies merged into my field and I faced them down and transmuted them. This is an alchemical process. I believe this was part of my assignment on Earth.

What's been missing for them, and for all abusive patriarchal males, is the healing of the sacred feminine within themselves, and the restoration of their hearts, which was taken hostage during the Luciferian initiations throughout centuries of abuse. Generations of these males globally have been sodomized, traumatized, chanted over, mind-controlled and turned into little robot soldiers to man the front the lines of the New World Order. Here they are today as sociopaths in the workplace, corporate banksters, CEO's, Wall St. hucksters, politicians, judges, military personnel, lawyers, teachers, police and so on. These are men with once good spirits but damaged hearts and souls. Restoration is ABSOLUTELY possibly for these people. But they must surrender their attachment to the dark side. They must be forgiven and loved, their energy fields cleansed and restored to wholeness, then they must be re-programmed with love. It can be done.

I want to emphasize at this point that the dark sexual initiation I have described differs entirely from healthy, consensual relationships between straight or gay people that do not cause the split in consciousness when done lovingly, respectfully and consensually.

Dr. Some and other healers and shamans like us understand that the emergence of new wisdom might look crazy to those still entrenched and enslaved within an old cultural system and afraid of change. But these are the very people who most need to be heard for they bring forth the healing medicine most needed at the current stage of that tribe's evolution.

I was fortunate in that my mother understood my spiritual powers and honored them. She recognized I was a gifted healer, sensitive, intuitive and visionary and nurtured it in me. Later, when my own very psychic daughter began demonstrating her abilities, I supported her emergence into her spiritual gifts. When energies from the spiritual world emerge in the Western world, our culture tends to ridicule or even demonize anyone who is able to see and understand those energies and truths. If you tell a counselor or psychiatrist that you see spirits or hear voices, you are immediately labeled as schizophrenic, bi-polar or psychotic and medicated. There is zero understanding of the reality of the spirit world, of ancestor spirits, guardian angels, demonic entities and so on. It was the counselor I had that had been a professional psychic that helped me the most. This counselor understood my journey through the splitting open and awakening of my consciousness and just allowed it to happen without judgment. That is why our culture is still so shut down and damaged; we are not allowing the wholeness of consciousness in. With no understanding of what is occurring with a person breaking through to another level of reality, the system judges the person as insane. Pharmacological drugs compound the problem and prevent the integration that could lead to soul development and growth in the individual who has received these energies and intuitive insights.

Psychics tell me all the time, and I often feel or see their presence as well, that spirits are hanging around someone to either help them or ask them for help. When we drug people, we prevent the spiritual assistance or healing from taking place. In the Dagara and other powerful tribal traditions, the community helps the person reconcile the energies of both worlds. That person is able then to serve as a bridge between the worlds and help the living with information and healing they need. Thus, the spiritual crisis ends with the birth of another healer. This is not understood or honored in Western civilization.

I witnessed this myself on the Hopi Reservation and also when I lived in Mexico on a large healing ranchero I managed. While on the Hopi Reservation I was invited to join the solstice rain ritual. It was an incredible sight to behold indeed. When the beautiful and sacred Hopi Kachinas emerge from their kivas in full ceremonial dress for the rain dance, they are unapproachable. You cannot speak to them or look at them while they are in the kivas. This is because the Hopis say they are inbetween worlds interceding with the spirit world on behalf of the tribe. When they enter their dance circle to perform the dance of rain, they chant, dance and circle the square for hours on end, for three days straight, sometimes 18 hours a day. They don't eat or drink much during this ritual but are connected to the Spirit world. They are in unison with movements and chants and their clothing is representative of nature spirits and birds. They are having discourse with the spirits of the rain, which are alive with energy, and asking them to rain down upon them. No one speaks to them for three days. An hour after their 3-day ceremony ended, it rained hard. Their call had been heard and honored by the natural world and its guardian spirits. They transformed drought into rain. This is an ancient ceremony that speaks to interconnectedness between indigenous peoples and nature. Our conqueror culture has no such connection with nature nor honors this knowledge. ***But we can learn!!!***

Similarly, when I was living in Mexico so many supernatural events happened that I will have to write an another book just on those experiences. The natural and spirit world was very much alive for me there and literally brought my soul back from the brink of death. I went there with death close at my back. I was running from it like a rabid dog nipping at my heels. I felt its sticky hot breath on my neck every night when I lay down to try to sleep. My best friend had died, my cousin died, my sister had died and my mother was dying. Four women, all of whom had been abused by violent, patriarchal men and became ill from it. Three of these women I loved so much died in my arms. I was devastated and losing the will to live. My heart hurt and my breast was aching. My soul was crying for the spirit of life to return to me and sent me here to regain it.

As soon as I moved there, magical events began happening. I had left the grid and the matrix. I was living in a Third World country; poverty and deprivation were everywhere. But a special kind of magic was there too. A magic not destroyed by "progress". I went down into the Tropic of Cancer where the energy is worlds different. The shimmering life force literally vibrates before your eyes like a rich Van Gogh night sky. I could almost reach out and touch its ridged edges. I opened to it. The natural energies of the Earth were free to flow through me, re-aligning my broken spirit. Nature spoke to me, I communed with the insects living everywhere around me, had a rattlesnake ceremony where I asked their permission to live on their land. Every night I conducted the insect ritual, which was about which giant insects had made it inside my trailer and how was I going to deal with them. How could I forget the powerful dinosaur dragonflies beating their bodies frantically on my porthole windows every evening. They were so large that they were like skinny, frenetic birds and if you looked closely, you could see their **little hearts beating inside ribcages**! I didn't think dragonflies had ribcages but these certainly did have very distinct insect ribcages! Their life force was so strong and amazing. Their little hearts would beat and flutter so hard as they strained to come inside where the faint trailer light played against the small framed windows. Like all creatures struggling for the light inside the darkness within which they lived. The metaphor was not lost on me and I observed them a long time. They would exhaust themselves with the effort and I began to worry about them and would switch off the light early so they wouldn't try. The creatures were everywhere and clutched out at me wherever I went. Some of them were dangerous. Your soul wakes up when it's in danger. I needed that then. I was fighting for my life. I had wondered if I might give myself over to the sweet sleep of death because life had become so terribly painful. I didn't want to wake up anymore. The mothers I loved killed off by the dark patriarchs, angry alcoholics around me, sick pedophiles to fend off, preyed upon financially by wealthy family members. It was too painful to contemplate then. I just wanted to slip away into the jungle and disappear and regain my wild self.

But the wild animals, insects and spirits of the desert brought the lesson home bigtime and made me ponder the essential soul question. Did I want to keep living? The wildlife sensed my quandary and tested my resolve. The insects and I had running dialogues every night while their huge bodies darted around my trailer towards my bed and mosquito netting until I no longer feared them but accepted them as friends and teachers. They would cling to my mosquito netting at night and eventually I grew used to them hanging there. I recall one day, after a long day's work, I decided to go down to the beach at the rancho and sunbathe a little. I lay down and fell asleep for a short while. I was awakened from my nap suddenly by the bite of something chomping down on my toe. I looked up to see literally hundreds of tiny crabs surrounding me in a circle, waiting to see if I were dead or alive so they could have a feast. One brave little guy had taken the first bite out of my toe; the rest were poised to chow down. I looked around me to see hundreds of bulbous little crab eyes perched on top of antenna-like sticks fixed to the top of their shells all trained on me. I felt like Gulliver tied down and surrounded by Lilliputians. I made eye contact with several of them. They freaked out and backed away en masse; I laughed out loud as they stared at me, frightened. Then I glanced up to the sky and saw that a huge buzzard was circling over me as well. So, I sat up and shouted to them all, "No way Jose! I'm not dead yet! Go find another meal!!!" I wasn't ready to surrender my body. That was the end of my sunbathing as I realized that nowhere in Baja were you ever really safe from predators of some kind, even tiny sand crabs.

As my time there wore on, I realized my hair and fingernails were growing rapidly like jagged bamboo shoots. They grew long almost overnight and my body seemed to take on a jungle-like feeling. I could feel my body more than I ever did in the U.S. I was transforming before my eyes visibly. Like a lush, tropical plant, I was sprouting up and ever so slowly inching back to life. Mother Earth was restoring and reclaiming me.

People would come out to see me and ask me why I was out there with snakes, scorpions and insects as big as my hand. I said I was never told when I took the position how dangerous it was. It seemed to be what God knew I needed but if I had known, I may not have come. Yet it awakened my soul. You have to fight for survival in the mountains of Baja California where poverty is everywhere and nature rules the day. When I asked nature and the living creatures for help surviving there, they stepped forward and helped me. They never harmed me, but spoke to me in their language. Once I was bitten by a giant centipede and my arm was paralyzed for about 24 hours. But the centipede had given me his medicine. Not long afterwards, I was giving Reiki treatments and I could feel the power go through my hands anyway. It felt like electric shocks. It left tooth marks on my arm. When I went into to town to have it looked at, the clinic doctor said few people survive the bite of the giant centipedes here. But I felt stronger.

I also experienced a visitation from two great female spiritual leaders, Anandamayi Ma and Holy Mother Ammachi. I had been meditating to them for months and reading about their lives while living alone on the desert of Todos Santos. One day, I ran out of water. It was 125 degrees outside. So, I went to get in my car to drive to Cabo San Lucas to pick up some water. My car wouldn't start and I was bone dry. I panicked a little, then closed my eyes and began to pray. Soon, there appeared next to me the two great saints. They smiled at me and emanated great peace towards me. Intuitively I knew I couldn't touch them, but still they were there and offering help to me in my mind. And even though neither of them spoke English, suddenly Anandamayi Ma spoke to me softly. "Go under your hood and I will show you what you need to do," she said to me. In awe, I lifted my hood and looked down at my engine but having no clue what to do. She began to explain which hoses were disconnected and which plugs were not working. I followed her directions while Ammachi stood by and watched, smiling. To this day, I could not repeat exactly what she said. I only know I did what she asked me to do. I finished and got back in my car and tried to start the engine. It fired up. I looked up to thank them only to see their forms slowly disappearing. They smiled as they faded away, like two beautiful Cheshire Cats floating in mid-air. It was an astounding experience. I was glowing. I drove to town and got some water and came back to ponder it all. This marked a distinct shift towards higher awakening for me and was proof the spirit world was present helping and guiding me. And that is only one of dozens of similar stories.

Western culture continues to ignore such truths and the gifted healers as they emerge with sacred information for the culture's survival. This always spells the end of a culture, when state-sponsored dogma takes over and the life force is squeezed out of a nation. That's what's happening here in the West with corporate and political tyranny. We must stand up and reclaim our souls from them.

Those who are the most sensitive will be chosen by spirit to deliver new messages, bring in new wisdom and birth new medicine. They must be honored and heard. These are the Nikola Teslas (genius inventor), the Petra Kellys (founder of the global Green Movement), the Dr. Royal Rifes (Physician and inventor of the Rife machine and the cure for cancer), the Galileos (famed Italian astronomer and scientist) of the world. People who were exiled in their day but contributed vastly to their culture. And those are just the ones we know of. Many more were exiled, killed or lost through ignorance, power plays and oppression, especially all the women. Wisdom, shamanism, sensitivity and spiritual gifts are too often viewed incorrectly as mental illness or oversensitivity. I know, I received the sting of judgment and repression for being energetically attuned and spiritually awakened. In native traditions, they are honored. Every tribe has its shaman or kahuna or medicine man who the tribe consults. In a time of great chaos, the cracking of stability and violent energy that characterize today's Western culture, we need to allow the shamans in to heal our tribe.

We live in the middle of a great machine of corporate greed that swallows up our life force, our traditions, ancestors, truths, creativity, community and freedoms. This is causing great inner disconnection and the severing of our interconnectedness with nature, true history, our ancestors and our personal power that runs through those threads. As a result, our culture is demonstrating a "disease", a societal disease that is like a cancer growing on the hearts and spirits of everyone, spearheaded by our spiritually dead leaders who are fused to that machine through greed and inner compromise. This is a disease that calls for healers and shamans, not scientists and doctors.

A deep and profound tribal healing must take place down to the roots of the source of the problem. We must root out the diseased seeds of mind-control, worship of darkness and wealth, DNA restructuring, eugenics, chemicals, poisonous principles such as addiction to materialism, classism, sexism, ageism and racism. Mystical, shamanic experts must be brought in to diagnose this problem and provide the cure and we must turn away from the emotionally dead, spiritually corrupt, half-conscious male dogmas that led us to the cliff of destruction. We are being coaxed like lemmings to follow them off the cliff to a certain death but they have a contingency plan in place for themselves. They have all the money, secrets and goodies and have made their exit plan and it doesn't include us. We as a people must not follow them off the ledge. We must create and carve a new path as a unified society without the lies, splits and dependencies of the past. We must transcend our attachment to possessions, images and materialism, the Gods of Greed, and reconnect at the soul level to powerful universal divine principles of spirituality, personal divinity, brotherhood, equality, compassion, mercy, sharing, nature and respect for the Divine Feminine.

And this can be accomplished by allowing the truth to flood into your consciousness. How is that done? Well, let's explore the healing of *The Split** and the splitting of your personal atom…the divine jewel of your soul, full of light and divinity. It begins with the *Pineal Gland**.

The light of the body is the eye: if therefore your eye
be single, your whole body shall be full of light."
Matthew 6:22

The Pineal Gland

The pineal gland is one of the family of endocrine glands whose job is to process and regulate the flow of divine energy into and throughout your body. The pineal gland is located in the **Sixth Chakra, or Brow Chakra***, and is about the size of a grain of rice. It is part of the epithalamus deep in the brain and is constantly bathed in cerebrospinal fluid. Unlike the rest of the brain, the pineal gland is not isolated from the body by the blood–brain barrier system. It has a profuse blood flow. It is believed to have an eyelike structure and to function as a light receptor. The pineal gland is the source of melatonin, a hormone derived from tryptophan that regulates the circadian rhythm (sleep cycle). Additionally, the pineal gland manufactures trace amounts of the psychedelic chemical dimethyltryptamine, or **DMT***. This chemical in the human brain is believed to play a role in dreaming and other mystical states. DMT-containing plants are used in several South American shamanic practices. DMT experiences can be life-changing awakenings such as journeys to paranormal realms, time travel, encounters with spiritual beings, profound time-dilation, and or other experiences that put one in touch with their spiritual power. So, this is another power experience the black magicians are blocking for us.

The pineal gland just might be the most important of all the endocrine organs. It is believed to control the flow of memories into consciousness. Obviously, this makes the pineal gland the key to controlling one's mind and a prime target of sophisticated mind-control techniques. René Descartes, a 17th-century French philosopher, believed the pineal gland was the seat of human consciousness and the soul. Today, modern corrupted scientists and dark priests have perfected the art of controlling the flow of cerebral-spinal fluid, blood and nerve impulses to the pineal gland to diminish its powerful function and segment consciousness. They don't want the pineal gland to function properly because it is said that when the pineal gland is awakened, it can awaken our mind's ability to see God. Some believe that supernatural powers will be initiated with pineal gland activation. Besides increased psychic awareness, pineal gland activation will help the third eye act as a stargate that can see beyond space and time. It acts as a link between the physical world and the spiritual world.

The pineal gland is multi-faceted and produces hormones that perform vital endocrine tasks. Many neuropeptides and neurotransmitters are present in the pineal gland so it has a function in the transmission of messages to the brain. It also produces serotonin, which creates calm and well-being in the brain and assists with mental and emotional stability. These can be affected by improper stimulation, diet, chemicals such as fluoride (the biggest culprit in destroying the pineal is fluoride) and mind-control. A calcified pineal gland cannot be utilized properly because it becomes like a stone. So, it must be de-calcified as part of your cleansing and awakening routine.

The pineal gland is sensitive to all types of magnetic fields, including geomagnetic fields of the Sun's solar storms. The pineal gland secretes melatonin, which is believed to contribute to our well-being and regulates our sleep/wake cycle. Melatonin is also believed to fight free radicals that can damage neurons. The pineal gland is also extremely sensitive to tissue calcification, especially when exposed to fluoride, which is also magnetically attracted to the pineal gland, causing a number of mental disorders.

The healing of the split begins with the unification of your consciousness. Because your pineal gland, or **Third Eye***** as it is often called, has been intentionally affected and polluted by the corrupted system here, you must cleanse it and awaken it to bring the broken parts back together. And they are fixable, because the energy field is always unified. It's like a corrupted part of your hard drive. It has to be cleaned or replaced. You must cleanse out the negative thought forms, break the amnesiac barrier, de-calcify the pineal gland, and begin to re-unify your thinking. If you are ready to awaken and heal yourself, then these are the first steps you should take.

To de-calcify your pineal gland, here are the basic steps to undertake which will necessitate a lifestyle change, mostly in the form of elimination of toxins. First, eliminate fluoride from your life. This will include fluoridated toothpastes and other bathroom products, showering without filters, red meat, inorganic fruits and vegetables, any sodas and artificial food and drinks and tap water. This may seem impossible, but start slowly and clean out your life and you will see results.

Herbal detoxifiers are - Chlorella, Spirulina, blue-green algae, Iodine, Zeolite, borax, vitamin D3, Bentonite clay, chlorophyll and ginseng. Essentials oils are also good for stimulating the pineal gland and facilitating states of higher awareness. The best oils for the pineal gland are - Frankincense, Lavender, Parsley, Pine, Sandalwood and Pink Lotus. Essential oils can be smelled, burned in a diffuser or nebulizer, and added to bath water. Lemons are nature's detoxifier and cleanser and can be used in pure water or other natural beverages or simply used as potpourri around the house for detoxification.

Foods that detoxify fluoride are cilantro, seaweed, raw cacao, watermelon, hemp seeds, bananas, goji berries, honey, coconut oil, and noni juice. Raw apple cider vinegar is amazing for so many things, including weight loss, but for detoxification of pineal it works well. Get raw apple cider vinegar as the others don't work. A great recipe for a detox is - 1 Quart Mason jar with Ionized Alkaline water, 8 tablespoons of Bragg's Apple Cider Vinegar and 2 tablespoons of raw, local honey. You will experience much more than just a detoxed pineal gland if you use this recipe. Garlic is another full-body detoxifier.

Sungazing* is one of the truths the elite didn't want us knowing about so they undertook a century long disinformation campaign telling us that too much sunshine caused cancer and that we needed to stay out of the sun and cover up. In reality, sungazing prevents cancer, if done moderately, and vitalizes the pineal gland. We also need Vitamin D from the sun to stay healthy. The best times for sungazing for the greatest impact are during the first 15 minutes of sunrise and last 15 minutes of sunset. This alone will begin to activate your pineal gland. Start slowly, like 10-15 seconds at a time and work your way towards longer gazing times.

Adopt a meditation, prayer and chanting routine that centers you on your spiritual core every day for at least 15 minutes. Chanting causes the tetrahedron bone in the nose to resonate and this resonance causes the pineal gland to be stimulated to secrete more beneficial hormones. An additional benefit from chanting is serenity, better sleep and a more youthful appearance. There are dozens of prayers and chants that heal the body. The **Buddhist Heart Sutra***, *Gate Gate Parasamgate Bodhi Svaha*, is one of my favorites chants. It means "Going, going, going on beyond, always going on beyond, always becoming divine." Chanting ancient Sanskrit chants helps to unlock God's power in your body, mind and spirit. Another chant is the sound **OM*** which is the Hindu symbol of the Absolute Omnipotent God and is the perfection chant which restores the purity and integrity of the body simply by chanting it. It activates the **Heart Chakra*** at the center of your chest. Chanting or playing an OM CD opens your consciousness up to a more universal and unified awareness.

A sacred Muslim prayer of protection is this simple and beautiful phrase –

Hasbunallaahu wa ni'amal-wakeel,
or in English –
Allah is sufficient for us and the best of those on whom to depend.

Here is a Jewish prayer often spoken - *You shall love HASHEM, your God, with all your heart, with all your soul and with all your resources. Let these matters that I command you today be upon your heart. Teach them thoroughly to your children and speak of them while you sit in your home, while you walk on the way, when you retire and when you arise. Bind them as a sign upon your arm and let them be tefillin between your eyes. And write them on the doorposts of your house and upon your gates. May the pleasantness of HASHEM, our God, be upon us - may God establish our handiwork for us; our handiwork may God establish.*

Here is a beautiful Sufi prayer for peace –

Prayer for Peace

*Send Thy peace, O Lord, which is perfect and everlasting,
that our souls may radiate peace.
Send Thy peace, O Lord, that we may think, act,
and speak harmoniously.
Send Thy peace, O Lord, that we may be contented
and thankful for Thy bountiful gifts.
Send Thy peace, O Lord, that amidst our worldly strife
we may enjoy thy bliss.
Send Thy peace, O Lord, that we may endure all,
tolerate all in the thought of thy grace and mercy.
Send Thy peace, O Lord, that our lives may become a
divine vision, and in Thy light all darkness may
vanish. Send Thy peace, O Lord, our Father and
Mother, that we
Thy children on earth may all unite in one family.
Amen.*

And the Lord's Prayer is one of the world's most powerful chants and is actually known as the Exorcist's Prayer. It protects the body temple from intrusion by disembodied entities and forces and can be spoken every single day to assist the pineal gland as well as the entire human body, mind and spirit. Since the Sacred Feminine was written out of the Bible, I always add the Mother into the prayer to honor the sacred feminine and make it whole again…

> *Our Mother and Father, who art in heaven and on Earth,*
> *Hallowed be thy Names.*
> *Thy Kingdoms and Queendoms come.*
> *Thy will be done in earth,*
> *As it is in heaven.*
> *Give us this day our daily bread.*
> *And forgive us our trespasses,*
> *As we forgive them that trespass against us.*
> *And lead us not into temptation,*
> *But deliver us from evil.*
> *For thine is the Queendom and Kingdom,*
> *The power, and the glory,*
> *For ever and ever.*
> Amen.

Saying the Lord's Prayer, and all prayers, connects you to the Holy Spirit and activates a great protective energy around you. Nothing can penetrate God's Divine protection. Every religion has a prayer, chant or meditation to help with clearing, protection and cleansing the pineal gland. I support all faiths and efforts to reach God and your inner Divinity. No one is left out of God's heart.

Crystals can be helpful to detoxify the pineal gland as well. The most powerful crystal for this is the amethyst. A large amethyst around the house is going to help immensely to detoxify your pineal gland. Quartz crystals are good for clearing as well.

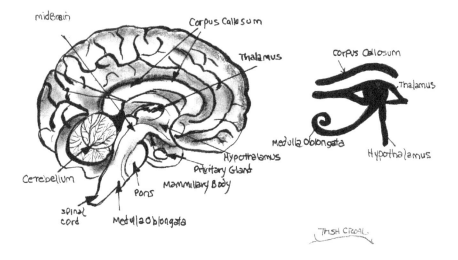

A very important symbol to the Egyptians was the ***All-Seeing Eye****, shown above. The "Eye" of the All-Seeing Eye corresponds with the pineal gland, found in the brain stem. This image stands for their beliefs in power and spiritual awareness. The Egyptian people frequently wore their make-up in a fashion resembling this All-Seeing Eye. This was a secret code that said you were "in the know" or part of a secret society. The other image next to the All-Seeing Eye, is a cross-section of the human brain including a diagram of the brain stem. The Egyptian All-Seeing Eye is, quite obviously, referring to the brain stem cross-section portrayed here. For centuries, it was a secret symbol known only to priests, Pharaohs and initiates until the great Masters brought this information forward to their students.

When the pineal gland and the pituitary body vibrate in unison completely, activation of the third eye begins. Daily meditation gradually over time will increase the power of the awakened third eye. Your consciousness will begin to rise. Eventually you will reach a permanent state of samadhi, or awakening. It works when a relationship is established between the soul and the pituitary body, and the photons operating through the pineal gland. This then creates a magnetic field that can host the "light". The negative and positive forces interact and become strong enough to create the 'light in the head.' Science verifies that vibrating electrons can absorb photons. This concept is further proof of the yin/yang theory whereby there needs to be an equal balance in the energy field for unified consciousness to manifest. The spiritual explanation would be that external photons are the same as spirit, only in the form of light matter.

As your technique and practice grow, you will simply concentrate on a point inbetween your eyebrows in the middle of your forehead. You are thinking of the pineal gland when you are doing this so the energy is being directed towards it. It activates. As you continue to withdraw the senses from your surroundings and focus on the pineal, the consciousness begins to awaken and grow. Your awareness should be centralized in the area between the middle of the forehead and the pineal gland. Concentrating at the middle of the forehead stimulates electrons in the pineal gland, which can absorb external photons during their vibratory experience in meditation. This then activates the "movie screen" of higher consciousness and your spiritual vision awakens. One day you will find yourself in the presence of the Holy Spirit and all truth will be revealed to you. Then the split in your consciousness will be healed and you will merge with the **One Mind***.

And Jacob called the name of the place Peniel: for I have seen God face to face and my life is preserved.
~ *Genesis 32:30*

Let's look at the healing of consciousness from the Vedic standpoint. Many of you have seen the distinctive image of Lord Ganesha. Ganesha is a Hindu deity and revered as the remover of obstacles. His large rotund elephant head makes him easy to identify. Ganesha is also the patron of arts and sciences and the deva of intellect and wisdom. He is sometimes referred to as the God of beginnings for which he is honored at the start of rituals and ceremonies. Ganesha is also invoked as patron of letters and learning during writing sessions. Ganesh's image is said to represent many spiritual principles. Among them are his large ears which stand for listening well. His rotund belly is said to mean digesting life peacefully. His huge head is said to mean that he surrendered the small ego self and took on the vast universal consciousness. And the mouse at his feet that he controls stands for the desires that he must always control to be in balance. But in deep meditation, I saw this image then came upon it. It spoke to me from within my soul. What I knew that it meant was the unification of consciousness and how that leads to awakening.

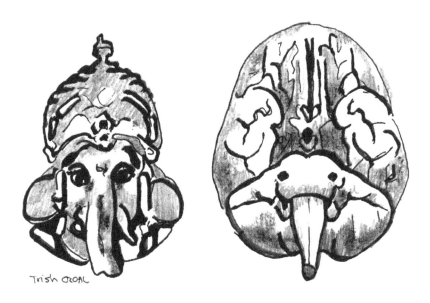

Trish CROAL

When the mind is split, as it is in our world today, you cannot see God, no matter what your conception of God is. You've been deluded by the spell placed upon us and the traumatic trance you are living in. It's like you are looking out through only one hemisphere of the brain or one eye. The view is distorted leading to distorted perceptions of life. Not until the unification of the fragmented parts of the mind and soul into the One Mind, with all barriers dissolved, do you reach awakening and see God. If you look at Ganesh's elephant head, you see how closely it resembles the bottom view of the brain with the brain stem. His elephant trunk is the actual stem of the brain, his ears the side lower lobes and the third eye in Ganesh's forehead coincides with the pineal in the base of the brain in the picture. During meditation it was revealed to me that this stands for the **Awakened Unified Mind of God***. When the mind unifies like this, duality has ended and the truth of our interconnectivity is revealed. When enough people reach this state, the world awakens, we are healed and all trapped energy is freed. Take some time in your meditation to contemplate this image and allow its truth to settle into your consciousness.

Ganesh is highly revered in Hindu tradition for his many talents and gifts he can give aspirants. Not only does he represent the unified mind, but he carries wisdom for life with him wherever he goes. Ganesh's trunk symbolizes the fact that the wise person has both immense strength and fine discrimination. He has four hands. In one hand he holds a lotus, the symbol of enlightenment. In the other hand he holds a hatchet. That is, the old karma, all your sanskars, the accumulated good and bad of past deeds, get cut when enlightenment comes. The third hand holds round sweet-meats. They are the rewards of a wise life. Ganesh never actually eats the sweet meats and is not shown this way. The wise man never partakes of the rewards of his deeds. He is not attached to them. The fourth hand is shown blessing the people. The wise man wishes the best for everyone. Ganesha has only one tusk; the other is shown broken. The symbolism of the broken tusk is that the wise person is beyond duality.

Each religion has similarly symbology but Ganesh's elephant head is a fantastic example of how esoteric wisdom is buried in images and symbology for the initiate to recognize. Realize that this is all around you in both dark and light traditions, including Christianity. Jesus Christ's images are filled with power and symbolism if you but look and ponder them, such as the fish, the halo and the Great Compassionate Heart.

The Bible is filled with references to the One Mind and spiritual sight as I've mentioned. Additional references are: Matthew 21.42: *'The stone the builders rejected has become the cornerstone; the Lord has done this, and it is marvelous in our eyes'.* Again the eye reference and the cornerstone are referring to the pineal gland, often called a stone, which is the cornerstone of higher consciousness. And a different version of Matthew 6:22: *"The lamp of the body is the eye. If, then your eye is SIMPLE, your whole body will be bright. But if your eye is wicked, your whole body will be dark."* Krishna referred to this in the Bhagavad Gita when he said, *"When meditation is mastered, the mind is unwavering, like the flame of a lamp in a windless place."* The "lamp in a windless place" Krishna refers to is the pineal gland inside the brain. All spiritual Masters, including Jesus, referred to the importance of unifying the mind through meditation on the pineal gland.

This is a major cornerstone (that word is even used by Jesus) in your own spiritual awakening. Your trauma may have shattered you, but it set the stage for your True Self and your spiritual power to emerge. So you see, even that is part of the unified mind, and the Unified Field. The dark unconsciously pushes the light to awaken who in turn then pushes the dark to fully awaken, thus triggering the **Ouroboros***(coming full circle), the eternal circle, the Yin/Yang of the circle of life. Yes, after all is said and done, everything is connected after all.

Chapter 13

Sacred Alchemy, Reiki & The Truth About Healing

Every cell in our body contains God's healing force. All that is required is to call upon it and healing begins.

~ Salini

Finally we arrive at the truth…..the truth that you can heal your-self…the truth that God gave us this birthright…..the truth that the body is designed from birth to be balanced and healthy with the ability to self-heal…..the truth that it's all energy…..the truth that we are all energy…..the truth that love is all there is……the truth that the higher your vibration is raised, the less likely you are to ever get sick…...the truth that it's all about the **Sacred Alchemy*** and how to use it to heal yourself and awaken spiritually…….the truth that **E** really does equal **mc^2**…..the truth that half the population does not have to get cancer and die of it. ….the truth that it's not all in your genes…...the truth that you are a holistic, spiritual being inside a physical body and not just a body with symptoms……the truth that we don't all have to die of viruses and plagues…….the truth that this wisdom has always been known and intentionally kept from us to keep us from healing and empowering ourselves……..the truth that the DNA-altering substances we are being sold are designed to keep us down, keep us from our health and keep us dependent on the lucrative medical and pharmaceutical industries…..the truth that we are here to awaken to the truth and be done with the lies…….the truth that you are divine and have always been divine….and that when you realize it, the charade here is over.

I learned this lesson over and over during my own recovery from several illnesses. Every time I activated the healing process and called forth the energy, I would pass through a healing crisis. And that healing crisis contained within it the seeds of sacred alchemy. This is something everyone needs to know and a skill everyone needs to have. And it isn't that mysterious.

The divine energy that heals is called Reiki, or **Universal Life Force*** in Japanese. Other cultures have a different name for it, but it's the same divine energy. The Hindus call it prana. The Chinese call it chi. The Christians call it the Holy Spirit. How does it work? It's simpler than you might realize. It's love in action. Love that is present in every single cell in your body…love that fills the seemingly "empty space" within your cellular structure….love that is actually a force of energy. Yoda called it **The Force***. And Yoda was speaking the truth when he said The Force is all around you and you have to learn to access it. This divine energy empowers all cells and is distributed evenly throughout your aura for your usage. But first you must master how to do that. And mastering the art of moving divine energy from the outer to the inner being is what the alchemy of enlightenment is all about.

Your divine energy rises and falls according to how you live your life. But what most people don't realize is they have the power to call upon this divine energy to heal themselves. Your cells contain individual particles that each have a function. Your divine energy keeps these cells operating and completing their functions. If you don't supply your body with the needed energy through food, exercise, nature, meditation or rest, the cell becomes depleted and dies. So you must learn how to keep your energy levels stable. If cells do die off, the human body will replace the dead cells with new ones that contain more divine energy. But we don't want to think of human cells as disposable like paper cups. We want to learn to hold our divine energy and utilize it powerfully, thus keeping our cells alive and vital. That is a process of learning about energy, your energy. And that energy awaits your command.

Your body is like a microcosm of the Universe. It's made up of chemical molecules which must interact with each other properly to keep order. These molecules are suspended in what doctors would call "bodily fluids". These bodily fluids are actually made of pure love. And it is actually this love which carries out all chemical processes. Love is the invisible healing agent which carries each molecule into its function throughout the body. Because the love requires a request to be activated, you must call for it while you are concentrating on healing your body. That is how the healing energy is called into action to work to restore balance in your body. That, and learning Reiki. We'll get to that.

> *When love enters the wounded place, the pain is violently ejected as it purifies and heals the wound. Whoever is the catalyst for the healing becomes the target.*
> ~ *Salini*

As I mentioned in Chapter 7, another way to describe this process of movement of divine energy is through electric frequency or vibration. The electric frequency or vibration of love is 528 kHz. Your heart chakra vibrates peacefully to this frequency, your body hums in harmony when attuned to this. Music played at 528 kHz will open and heal your heart chakra sending the love vibration throughout your body. It is this very powerful energy thrust which sends your molecules down their individual paths. When you activate the love energy through prayer or a Reiki treatment, you start the process of chemical changes. This causes the love frequency to radiate along the paths of the neurons as the electrical impulse is sent to the brain and the rest of the body. The chemical elements in your body then begin to return to normal status according to their divine blueprint. When I work on people, I can feel this occurring. I can feel the current of powerful energy passing through my body and into theirs, activating the person's healing potential. When their energetic body reaches a healthy homeostasis, the pulsation of the vibration of love and healing begins to die down and I know I have completed working on that area.

The person receiving Reiki will feel either a pulsation, tingling, heat or a combination of the three. They may also see images of past lives, the true causes of their condition such as hatred, anger or other damaging emotions, or remember significant life events such as a car accident or violent episode that froze the condition in their bodies. They tell me they feel the energy moving through their body, removing the pain, and lifting them to a higher plane. They often tell me they feel very relaxed and they sometimes fall asleep only to awaken refreshed and more energetic.

But the process of healing is much deeper and more transformative. You began as a caterpillar and are becoming the butterfly. What do you think goes on inside the chrysalis of transformation? How does a slow-moving, soft, squishy bug become an angelic, light as a feather, winged beauty? The answer to that is sacred alchemy, the same alchemy that is true for all forms of life. Including you.

We delight in the beauty of the butterfly, but rarely admit the changes it has gone through to achieve that beauty.

~ *Maya Angelou*

So how do we get there? How do we become the butterflies that lay sleeping inside our souls? It begins by waking up. Like the slow caterpillar sliding along unaware of its potential but builds its cocoon nonetheless, we must allow our soul to guide us to its inner butterfly. The caterpillar doesn't know it will be a butterfly one day, but it knows it has to create a cocoon. That is instinctual to a caterpillar. The same is true of humans. We know we must continue to evolve and improve ourselves but we may not know where we are going. That awareness comes when we grow as a culture, wake up and allow true healing into our lives. The healing wave of the future will be about healing deep trauma, pain, grief and karma, which are the true causes of disease. As our consciousness rises, we will begin to see beyond the physical realm and realize our illnesses go deeper, deep into our mind, deep into our emotions, deep into our souls. And when we realize that, we will realize that these conditions are suspended in our energy fields as trapped energy waiting to be freed. And what frees this energy is love.

And so we begin the great collective healing journey as a people, as nations, and as an international family of wounded souls, injured by our sick cultures, endless war, elite vampires and an illusion of lies. As we emerge out of the matrix they have spun for us, as we break the spells long held in place by dark magicians, we loosen our chains of ignorance and enslavement and begin to feel humanity's long-held, long-denied pain. And then our healing crisis has begun. We must allow ourselves to walk through the pain of transformation to emerge as butterflies in the end.

Let's talk about sacred alchemy. What is it and how does it work? Obviously something is happening inside the cocoon that transforms the body of a caterpillar into the majesty of a butterfly. That process is known as alchemy. Most people have heard of the alchemy of metals. People who tried to turn the metal lead into gold or silver through purification techniques practiced traditional alchemy. It was common in days of old when metals were very valuable commodities. An alchemist was a highly respected trade. But throughout history there has been another kind of alchemy. That kind of alchemy is spiritual alchemy. Spiritual alchemy is also a form of physical alchemy. What we see occurring with a caterpillar and a butterfly is physical alchemy but also a spiritual experience for the caterpillar as it evolves into its higher self. The slow, dull caterpillar undergoes an amazing internal alchemy to become a brilliant butterfly. Butterflies don't live long but live to pollinate and reproduce primarily. Their lives have transformed completely. As a caterpillar they cannot fly or move quickly. As a butterfly they fly freely everywhere, landing on flowers to pollinate and mate. Their transformation is complete. But you can see by their drastically altered appearance from a caterpillar to a butterfly that something dramatic occurred within the cocoon. The same is true for a person. When you enter a crucible of transformation, you will begin a powerful inner alchemical change. It will change you physically, mentally, emotionally and spiritually.

Alchemy works like a hot furnace. Some kind of heat is needed to fire up the process. All basic elements in nature are utilized – air, earth, fire and water plus metal. It's the percentage of the element plus the degree of heat that determines the substance achieved. This is true within a person's soul as well. A very simple explanation is this: three basic elements are required for alchemy to occur. You need a container of some kind to contain the reaction. In the case of caterpillar alchemy, the cocoon is the container for the caterpillar to become a butterfly. In the case of humans, the human body itself is the container of the consciousness to be transformed. Then you will need a substance to be transformed. Using the caterpillar example again, the substance is the body of the caterpillar itself which transforms. In humans, it is primarily the consciousness that transforms, but physical changes do occur. Finally, you require some form of energy or heat to spark the transformation. For a piece of paper to transform into ash, you require fire. For lead to transform into gold, you need a hot furnace inside a foundry designed for transforming metals. For a caterpillar to transform into a butterfly, there is a chemical reaction that takes place within the body of the caterpillar while in the cocoon that creates heat and changes the form of the body. For a human, there must be an internal fire that sparks the change in consciousness. This is not a literal fire, but it can be a high temperature or spiritual fire.

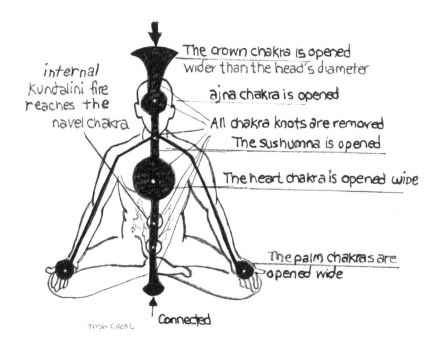

The heat required to transform consciousness alchemically can occur within the daily practice of meditation. The process of meditation creates an internal fire that heats up the life force, or **Reiki**, and sends it up the **Sushumna***, the central energy channel, or primary nadi, in the human body. The other primary channels, the **Ida*** and **Pingala*** also experience this rising heat according to the steadiness and perfection of the meditation practice. When this heat rises, it passes through the chakras and your soul's life force energy. That energy is heated and purified as it travels upward along the Ida, Pingala and Sushumna in a process known as **Kundalini Rising***. This then becomes the fire element needed for the consciousness to transform alchemically within the container, the human body.

As the consciousness energy experiences heat and rises, it begins to purify and lighten up. It passes through each chakra; the chakra knots of bondage at different levels will eventually break open with sustained practice. When that happens, an awakening occurs. However, if there is too much "dirty" energy in your chakras, it will carry that energy up to the crown chakra and a Kundalini psychosis episode can occur. That is a psychosis from a rush of chaotic, unhealed energy into the brain, overwhelming the person's ability to mentally cope. A period of acclimation to the new energy and energy healing treatments for stabilization are required to recover from such an episode. I have had to clear many people who had learned yoga from untrained or unscrupulous teachers who rushed them through Kundalini experiences in their yoga training and the person went into Kundalini psychosis. Additionally, Reiki training taught incorrectly, such as Reiki 1,2 and 3 in a single weekend, can trigger a Kundalini rising episode and throw someone into Kundalini psychosis. Reiki 1, 2 and 3 should never be taught in a single weekend. If taught and attuned properly, the energy passed is far too much for anyone just starting out to handle. A responsible ReikiMaster will teach you over time assessing your ability and readiness for higher levels of energy. Reiki alone is enough to trigger an alchemical spiritual awakening when taught and done properly.

Finally, an illness can be the genesis for an alchemical transformation. Illnesses are characterized by profound soul changes, especially if they are long and cause much suffering. They are your soul calling for attention to something, to an issue, to karma, or to begin your journey of transformation and awakening. No one wants to go through a serious illness, but often they are the beginning of a truly spiritualized life, instead of an ego-driven life. They were likely a course decided upon by the soul long before entering the body. The soul knew what it needed to awaken and set this course in action. Try to surrender to this. Resistance to this truth lengthens the suffering.

Below is a flow diagram of the process of alchemy in the declining phase. These are the missing puzzle pieces to disease you never hear about. The energy has begun to stagnate. But it can be turned around at any stage with solid healing energy work and spiritual practices.

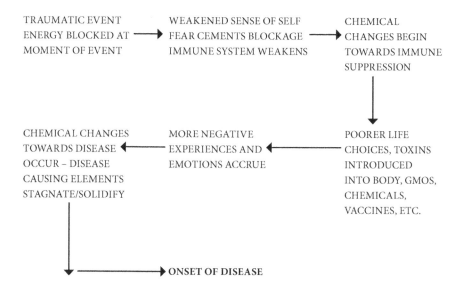

TRAUMATIC EVENT
ENERGY BLOCKED AT ⟶
MOMENT OF EVENT

WEAKENED SENSE OF SELF
FEAR CEMENTS BLOCKAGE ⟶
IMMUNE SYSTEM WEAKENS

CHEMICAL
CHANGES BEGIN
TOWARDS IMMUNE
SUPPRESSION

CHEMICAL CHANGES
TOWARDS DISEASE ⟵
OCCUR – DISEASE
CAUSING ELEMENTS
STAGNATE/SOLIDIFY

MORE NEGATIVE
EXPERIENCES AND ⟵
EMOTIONS ACCRUE

POORER LIFE
CHOICES, TOXINS
INTRODUCED
INTO BODY, GMOS,
CHEMICALS,
VACCINES, ETC.

⟶ ONSET OF DISEASE

Negative emotions create disease-causing chemicals to stream through your body, cells and organs, weakening them and your immune system. Traumatic events do the same thing, and add your brain into the mix. If toxins are also introduced, the balance of the scale is tipped towards disease. That doesn't even factor in karma or genealogy. You must address all of the above to correct this downward slide towards illness.

A human virus, much like a virus in your computer system, is like a faulty program inserted into your energy mainframe. It corrupts the system. And like a computer virus, it can be cleaned out, purified. Many of these current human viruses have been inserted with programming us much like a computer. We need to debug our systems with anti-virus software. Reiki is your full-time, big-time hitman anti-virus software for life. You can heal anything with it as long as it isn't karmic. In the course of my healing journey, I experienced several serious life-threatening illnesses. Often these illnesses were viruses, another time it was cancer. They required a purification process to restore balance to my energy body. I utilized Reiki and sincere prayer. This activated a powerful alchemical change, a healing process, which resulted in my recovery and awakening. The alchemical process in the human body of turning lead - a dull consciousness, into gold - an awakened consciousness, requires heat. If you are not involved in spiritual practices such as yoga, meditation and/or prayer, the consciousness does not rise spontaneously. There has to be intent, discipline and a request for spiritual awakening. In my case, I have been meditating, praying and doing Reiki since I was very small. I asked for, intended, and performed regular spiritual practices for the purpose of awakening. Reiki itself creates heat in the body. If you receive regular Reiki treatments, or even better, become attuned to higher levels of Reiki, your divine energy will begin to transform, purify and eventually awaken. Reiki is, all by itself, a path to spiritual awakening. Reiki is, as are all divine energy concepts, simply God's divine love in action. All toxic wounds, whether they be physical, mental or emotional, are healed with God's love. This is the essential principle of healing everything.

In the case of the viruses, my body produced a fever to fight off the infection. My fever went up to 105°, heating my body up tremendously. The process of purifying my soul's energy was underway. I experienced dramatic internal shifts and a Kundalini rising out my crown chakra. My soul left my body. The outcome was a healing and a profound spiritual awakening. My body was the container, my soul the substance and the fever was the heat. It changed me forever. And that was just one of such episodes in my life that triggered massive healing. The result was deep internal transformation, re-unification of the parts of my broken self and spiritual awakening. And I have seen this on many of my students and clients during the course of my healing career as well.

So, to awaken through sacred alchemy, you may choose between several approaches. There are solitary spiritual practices such as yoga, deep meditation, Tibetan tummo, Hindu spiritual practice and meditation, Reiki, or other Eastern practices. People who have awakened this way are Paramahansa Yogananda, the Dalai Lama, and Dr. Mikao Usui – the original Reiki Grandmaster. There are also Christian mystical practices of spiritual awakening such as prayer, fasting and contemplation on Jesus of Nazareth and the Saints. Those who have awakened this way are Therese Neumann – the German Saint, Padre Pio – the famous Catholic Priest and Father Arseny – the Russian Priest who prayed through his harsh years in a Siberian prison camp. These people were able to create internal fire through prayer, faith and fasting which resulted in profound spiritual awakening, or purification of their energy field resulting in mental, emotional and spiritual healing.

Still another path of sacred alchemy is through sacred sexual union known as Tantric Alchemy, or Tantric Yoga. In sexual alchemy, the result is the same. The energy travels up the spine and the nadis towards the crown chakra when the process is initiated and fire generated. What's unique about this approach is that it is done in sexual union with another person. These sexual techniques were perfected thousands of years ago in the Egyptian temples of Isis where the High Priestesses were trained in the practices of Tantric sexuality. The partners may have sexual union to initiate the rising Kundalini, but the goal is not orgasm or pleasure. The goal is spiritual awakening. This necessitates conscious sexuality, not just lust and thrusting wildly to get to the end result. Conscious sexuality entails holding back orgasm for the male and being conscious when the Kundalini begins to rise up the Ida, Pingala and Sushumna towards the crown chakra. That can take a while to master. Ultimately the idea is to bring both people to spiritual union at the crown chakra where a mutual awakening occurs. Both parties must be very committed to these practices as they are difficult and lengthy. Many believe this is what occurred between Jesus Christ and Mary Magdalene.

Finally, spiritual alchemy and awakening can occur with a spontaneous event or illness or by some divine incident occurring. For example, Dannion Brinkley, the author of <u>Saved By the Light</u>, described his awakening as a result of being struck by lightning and having a near-death experience. He experienced a meeting with beings who gave him a life review and asked him to return and teach others about spirituality. His sacred alchemy occurred while he was passing through near-death. I had other such experiences beyond just the illnesses. One is recounted below.

Here is a personal story of sacred alchemy that altered me completely.

*In January of 2001, I visited a friend of mine one day for a spiritual gathering. He had a group of friends from India visiting and we got together for a spiritual conversation. Out of the blue without any prompting, one of his friends said to me, "I'm returning to India for the **Khumba Mela*** spiritual gathering in two weeks. I'm going to bring you back something." I had no idea what he was referring to but thanked him. About six months later, there was a knock on my door. When I opened it, standing there was this friend from India. He had a jar in his hand. I welcomed him inside. "I kept my promise to you. Here is the gift I brought you from India." He said to me as he held up the jar proudly for me to see. The jar was filled with something that looked* *like water. "What is it?" I asked him. "It's water from the River Ganges that I scooped up for you during the Khumba Mela gathering. 40,000 monks, sadhus, yogis, lamas, and other spiritual masters chanted into the great river for 7 days straight. It holds the power of all those sacred chants by all those monks and thousands of years of spiritual power. It can heal your karmic path. Use it as you see fit." He handed it to me. I stared at the jar. It was hard to believe this small jar of cloudy liquid contained the power to change my spiritual path. I thanked him. We talked a while and he went on his way.*

Over the next few days I meditated on the jar and its contents. I got the distinct impression I was to take the jar with me to see the Holy Mother Ammachi when she visited next. I made up my mind to drink the water while in her presence. If something was going to happen to me, I would be within her divine presence. I brought a friend along to help drive. We arrived there and I brought the jar of Ganges River water in with us. We found some seats and got settled. I took the plunge and drank the holy water, all of it, then and there. Within a half-hour I began having an out-of-body experience. I could feel my body become leaden and unmovable. Slowly, my spirit left my body and rose up. I looked down and saw my body lying on the seats. But unlike the previous experience when I had viral meningitis and was dying, there was no feeling of an individual spirit rising up, no sorrow, anguish or suffering. I felt great peace instead. In fact, I no longer had a separate spirit at all; I was pure spirit. Suddenly, my consciousness merged with the One Mind. A cacophony of noises filled my consciousness.

What was I hearing? What was going on? Was I dying? Straining to focus, I heard many voices speaking in many languages. Not voices in the room, but from somewhere else. Some were singing, some were praying, some were Angels floating. I still didn't understand what I was hearing or experiencing. I turned my attention to individuals in the room where we were all gathered to see Ammachi. I looked at the cashier selling books. As I focused on him, I could hear his thoughts. He was calculating the cost of the books he was ringing up, silently to himself, no words spoken. I focused my attention on someone else in the room. She was meditating but I heard her thoughts expressing how sad she was about her marriage, her family and her life situation. No words came from her mouth and her eyes were closed, but I heard her thoughts clearly. I continued this with several other people in the room, always hearing their thoughts without them speaking as they were meditating. It was astonishing to realize I was hearing everyone's thoughts as though they were my own. Is this the One Mind they speak of in spiritual circles was my thought?

*As I pondered that question my attention fell upon the Holy Mother Ammachi as she sat at the front of the hall giving thousands of **Darshans*** to the people lined up to receive her great divine blessing. As I focused my attention upon her, I connected with her consciousness. I began to hear Amma's thoughts as she was giving Darshan. I heard her sacred prayers going over and over in her head. I felt the stream of divine consciousness connect between her mind and mine. I was overwhelmed with a feeling of divine love. And then I heard it…..the answer to your question is yes darling daughter…..*

wait a minute my consciousness asked itself......what am I hearing......and I heard it again.....the answer to your question is yes darling daughter.....I continued to focus my attention on Amma.....I could still hear her thoughts........then I got very specific.......Amma, can you hear me? Am I experiencing the One Mind?......I saw Amma glance up towards me for an instant......and then it came loud and clear......I told you, the answer to your question is yes, darling daughter. We are always connected in the One Mind. I am always with you........I felt the shock of recognition of my Oneness with all of life......I turned my consciousness around the room to test it again.....and again I heard the thoughts of those deep in meditation as though they were my own....... then I asked permission to hear the thoughts of people in other lands, other places.........and a roar of a foreign language came through, like an African tongue perhaps...then I asked to hear the voices of nature......and I found my consciousness in a rainforest in South America where insects clicked and buzzed and whirred around, where hissing snakes and frothing waterfalls swooshed by my hearing....then I could hear the sounds of animals interacting with one another, some communicating their concerns to each other, some of them quarrelling over food, others fighting for their lives.....next I heard the plants and bushes communicating clearly.....they spoke of their fear of encroaching deforestation, of poisons touching their roots, of the disrespect of nature..... then the trees spoke......they had begun to grieve for one another for many of their clan had been cut down. They are all connected by their roots that stretch far into the Earth like tiny wires of communication grown hundreds of feet to the next root ball and sharing infor-mation…….they spoke of their brothers and sisters who had fallen miles away as though they were right there in front of them…..they spoke of the danger the world faces if they are allowed to be destroyed…..without us they will be starved of oxygen, they said, and all life will end……will they understand in time the trees asked…… other trees answered that humans will not understand in time ……and the discussion continued with the plants chiming in and asking for protection from the trees…… then suddenly I had traveled to India and was witnessing the saints there praying and blessing millions of people, their prayers echoing in my consciousness, their poetry lilting through my soul…….and then my consciousness returned to the room and its people……I saw Amma still giving Darshan and had no conception of time or how many hours had passed……I still heard her beautiful sacred prayers chanting in my head as I slowly returned to my body….

After a while I realized I was back in my human body. But it felt very different, very strange and slow. My friend and I tried to get up and walk around but I couldn't walk far. He told me I had been "asleep" for 3 or 4 hours at least. I told him I wasn't sleeping but oh well. I told him now I really needed to rest and lay down right on the floor. Soon I was sound asleep. And I slept there right on the floor for several hours. After awaking, we went up to get our Darshan. When I got to Amma's lap, she winked at me and smiled. I smiled back.

I would never be the same after that night of the holy River Ganges water. And neither will my consciousness.

The Divine is always available to us if we but ask for its presence. You are never alone, but connected one with another eternally.

So why isn't everyone reaching for divinity you may be asking? This is the eternal question philosophers and holy men have been asking for ages. The journey to an awakened consciousness always begins with an unawakened one. We all begin leaden and dull in our thinking. Think of what it was to be a caveman millions of years ago. Were they pondering philosophical questions such as why am I here? Is there a God? I seriously doubt humans of that era had the capacity to think through these issues. And science has confirmed that. The cavemen of that time thought nothing of killing another caveman if it meant taking his meat for his own family. There were no laws or morals preventing such actions. They were like animals then, doing what they could to survive. These were the days of leaden consciousness, with only the earliest murmurs of thinking. One of those days one of them discovered fire and changed the world. A step forward happened. Then another invented the wheel and civilization began. Slowly, there was a spark of knowledge. This spark led to a painfully slow rise in consciousness that took billions of years to arrive at where we are today. We've only been industrialized a little more than 100 years. Having a survival-oriented consciousness was the norm for millions of years. The earliest laws didn't even come into play until humans formed communities and tried to work together in harmony to hunt, grow food and live together in rudimentary dwellings. We were still at the first, or root chakra, where survival, sex, fear and reproduction ruled the day. For many, the evolution of their consciousness hasn't progressed far beyond that point even today.

The lead alchemy of early consciousness lasted a long time with only an enlightened being arising here and there and struggling to survive in such circumstances. But with the arrival of the holy men and women to Earth, little by little they dropped the seeds of awakening into darkened minds. And gradually, humankind began to awaken to higher consciousness. Today, we have the possibility to fully awaken and transcend this realm. Many are doing so. Once you accomplish that, your soul merges with the Divine.

The natural force within us is the greatest healer of all.
~ Hippocrates, father of modern medicine

And as you awaken, your divine energy rises within you, liberating your soul, reviving your cellular structure and strengthening your immune system. The real solution to a health crisis is pursuing your spiritual awakening and welcoming the Holy Spirit into your life. As your body, mind and spirit stabilize and balance, and your divine energy flows freely again, you return to homeostasis. Your healing has begun.

But there is another vital issue that must be addressed. And that is the problem of ***Magnetic Deficiency Syndrome****, which I discuss in greater length in the next chapter. Magnetic deficiency syndrome is a condition of a depletion of the magnetic energy in one's energy system. The earth is a giant magnet made up of yin energy. Yin energy is the feminine energy and is magnetic. It's where the feeling energy is stored. Yang is masculine energy, comes from the sun and is electric in nature. It's where action energy is stored. They must work as a team. Few know that a balanced electro-magnetic frequency plus feeling equals manifestation. These secrets have been kept from us for the elite. It's time to claim them back. Together yin and yang energy make up an electro-magnetic field, similar to a battery. When the field is properly connected and the poles are aligned, a powerful, balanced current of energy flows through evenly and a spark is generated. But because we have created blockages in the electro-magnetic field, primarily in the Earth's magnetic field, it has impaired our ability to receive enough magnetic energy. As a result, more and more people are becoming depleted and their immune systems are failing. These blockages are things like power poles, computers, roads and cement covering the Earth, microwaves, televisions, nuclear energy and other unnatural forms of energy that interfere with Earth's magnetic field and prevent it from coming into our chakras. When this happens, our sacred alchemy is also impacted and impaired. It's difficult to transform and awaken when your divine energy is completely depleted. And it's difficult to heal from an illness for the same reason. So, it becomes vital for many reasons to undertake the restoration of your energy system. It isn't the only reason you have an immune-related illness, but it is one of the main reasons. Find the right healer and/or teacher and begin the process. Yoga, meditation and Reiki are some of the ways to achieve this. When you begin, you will naturally begin a process of sacred alchemy. It will become clearer to you that you are transforming for the better as you stay the course of your spiritual practices.

Reiki

I was blessed to be introduced to Reiki as a small child. From the beginning I saw how the energy of the planet could be called upon to heal and that I also carried this divine power within me. I never had to overcome the dogma, fear, skepticism and suppression that most people were raised with regarding healing with divine energy. It's God's sacred gift to all of us. I've always known it works. And that faith strengthens Reiki's ability to heal. The more faith you have, the wider the channels open to receive the divine pulse. And that includes all faiths; we are not separate but are all one within our Creator's heart.

Disbelief immobilizes the life energy and prevents
the perfect working of The Divine Doctor.
~ Paramahansa Yogananda

I was doubly blessed to be mentored by the GrandMaster of Reiki Hawayo Takata. Mrs. Takata became both my spiritual and personal mentor, guiding me in the sacred use of Reiki and in living my life. Not only does Reiki heal people of illness, but it awakens and transforms them all the way to their soul. Whatever karma you've brought in, whatever illness you carried from a past life, whatever people you are working issues out with, Reiki heals them all. It is a code, a path and a discipline to live by leading you straight to the Holy Spirit and to Oneness.

Reiki has several basic principles, created by Dr. Mikao Usui. And they are:

Just for today, I will not be angry.
Just for today, I will not worry.
Just for today, I will be grateful.
Just for today, I will do my work honestly.
Just for today, I will be kind to every living thing.

These basic principles can be expanded upon to include developing your spirituality, learning to trust that the Universe supports you and how to use the energy in your life on a daily basis. Those are some of the things you'll learn in First, Second and Third Degree Reiki. In **First Degree Reiki***, you learn the basics of healing with energy. The body's energy system, chakras and the etheric layers of energy around the body are part of the curriculum. You get the opportunity to practice on yourself and others and become familiar with the energy field of the human body. Learning Reiki includes being attuned, or calibrated, to a higher energy vibration in your body. Each level of Reiki raises your vibration to a higher and faster level. Whenever that occurs, you will begin to transform as the energy sweeps through your body, chakras and nadis to awaken, vitalize and empower you. You will also experience an alignment within yourself of your chakras, your energy and your soul's purpose. Many of my students have told me that after learning First Degree Reiki they found the job of their dreams and their true soul purpose. Other students began a massive healing and transformation. Some people begin to experience internal cleansing, either mentally, emotionally or physically. Whatever barriers there are to healing and awakening will be dissolved.

With **Second Degree Reiki*** you will begin to experience massive emotional and mental healing in conjunction with your physical healing. The consciousness is deeply touched by the attunements at the Second Level of Reiki. This triggers a massive release of stored toxic emotional energy from whatever negative and traumatic experiences you may have had. Releasing these blocked energies can sometimes be traumatic. For this reason, different Reiki levels should ALWAYS be taught spaced apart and NEVER in one weekend. It's risky to attune someone to all levels within a few days as they may not be able to acclimate to the energy. A wise and honorable ReikiMaster will observe your progress and attune according to what you can handle, allowing your body, mind and spirit to acclimate to the new energies. After a 21-day period of acclimation after each level of Reiki, you can begin practicing on family and friends. Later you can begin on clients, after you have mastered the energy coming into your hands.

As a practitioner of Reiki, you will come across many people with buried trauma which has been repressed. It's a silent epidemic causing many different types of illness, including cancer, Multiple Sclerosis, Lupus, Rheumatoid Arthritis and many more. In my practice, all types of illness have presented themselves at my door. Even though toxins and lifestyle played a part in their illnesses, most of them had an underlying emotional root issue that locked the illness in place. Once I began giving them Second Degree Reiki treatments, it unlocked the trauma for release. Your ability to give them a Mental/Emotional Reiki treatment will go a very long ways towards healing these issues and their illness. You will find the trauma to be frozen and stagnant within certain areas of the body. These areas become hosts for disease. You will have learned how to find these hot spots on the body. As soon as you activate the Reiki, say your prayers and call for the healing to enter the body of the person, the stuck energy will begin to be dislodged, released and brought to the surface for transmutation. Reiki will find the energy patterns of the trauma and the mental and emotional stagnation connected to it and begin to dissolve it. When this happens, the person may feel emotionally or mentally uncomfortable as the energy of the trauma begins to move out of their cellular memory and body, where the mind/body stored it to protect itself from the experience. Practice extensively before going public with your work. It can be difficult to walk someone through this process and you need to be ready and professional. But Reiki is gentle enough to make this experience easier to handle than other forms of treatment. With Second Degree Reiki, the mind and body balance and stabilize, and learn to cope with this threatening event over time.

As I mentioned, the energy of suppressed trauma becomes a host area for the development of disease. It must be dispersed and transmuted with Reiki to heal the whole being. The stage of illness at which someone comes to you and their commitment to their healing determine the outcome. You are not responsible for their recovery, only the treatment process. You are the facilitator of the process, God is the healer. The better you become at surrendering your body and soul as a channel for the Holy Spirit is a factor in the healing process, but not the determining one. Their recovery is between their soul and the Holy Spirit. They must make the choice to live and do the work required to achieve that. You become the vessel of God's healing power.

When a traumatized person begins to heal, they may experience the dissociation again while remembering and begin to re-enter the body. After dissociation, they feel more connected to themselves and to the world. These experiences were never completely felt when they happened due to the distancing, or disassociation. Suddenly, they rush in and the shock of feeling them is very distinct and painful. The body and mind react to that feeling, and to the feeling of releasing it from stored cellular memory. Much Reiki is needed at this time, especially Second Degree Reiki. It's important for them to eat right, be supported, rest, and receive bodywork and the like at this time. Self-care is mandatory during healing crises to be able to integrate the material.

What most individuals healing from trauma experience over many years is a slow release of the abuse experience through memories and illnesses that gradually prepare the mind to accept the truth. Seeing it all at once would be too traumatic. Or some never see it at all. Many people suppress the truth of their trauma for life. This often results in an illness. Not everyone gets ill, but many do. During the course of my illnesses, I experienced prolonged episodes of remembering the trauma. At the end of each episode of memory, I would get sicker temporarily, then much better. As the energy of the abuse was leaving my body, it made me feel sicker for a time, which is again the healing crisis, then I experienced the purging of the energy. After a while, I was better all the time. Exercise is not an option when you are in a memory/healing episode as it uses precious energy needed for expelling the abuse energy and integrating the event. Most people get sicker if they exercise at this time.

So, the energy becomes caught up in the illness and managing the illness and all such distractions. The energy of the episode stays in the body and causes the tissue to deteriorate if not broken down and transmuted. Energy needed to function powerfully in life is trapped in the episode of abuse and in holding down the memory of the abuse from the conscious mind. It is very exhausting to be holding all of this in for years. In recovery from energy or immune disorders, one must temporarily give up exercise as the all the body's available energy is desperately needed for healing. Something like Tai Chi, or light floor exercises and stretching is good. All forces are mustered to face this "perceived threat" from the past and cannot be used for anything else. Much fear is attached which also drains energy. And anyone carrying trauma has damaged chakras and a damaged aura thus causing constant energy leakages. All this must be addressed and healed by the skilled emotional energy healer. Developing an ability to do **shamanic dialogue*** is necessary to fully assist the healing person because you will access their higher self where the Higher Self dwells. The Higher Self is free of illness and awake; it can assist with the healing process.

If you or your client are not someone who has had obvious deep trauma this process still applies. In those cases, the trauma can take ever more subtle forms of pain within the psyche and body. For example, a child witnesses his father abusing his mother when he is small. The child internalizes this violence against a beloved figure – his mother – and it turns toxic within him. Sometimes a child will blame themselves for this kind of behavior. Other times, the boy will grow up to emulate it. Or in some cases, a related illness will develop as in the case history I told earlier. This emotional wound will not heal until its felt and grieved out. If that doesn't happen, illness could develop.

One client I treated was having different physical symptoms and complaints that seemed unrelated, nothing life threatening. She had been single for many years also. She had tried many doctors and techniques but felt something was being overlooked. I began doing Reiki treatments, including emotional/mental healing treatments, on her. She began from the first session to have deep moaning and crying jags that would peak in howling at some points. She experienced memories of her father ignoring her and preferring to pay attention to her brother throughout her childhood. She tried to get his attention throughout life by being a successful stage actress to no avail and had frequent bouts of unresolved illness. She had no realization of how deep this longing was until receiving Reiki. After three treatments she left saying she felt much better. About six months later, I saw two of her friends who said they could not believe the change in her health and life since coming to see me. Then she called to say she was completely healed and happy and dating again.

You must never try to talk anyone who is going through a healing episode, <u>including yourself</u>, out of their feelings. Feelings are feelings, not sins or faults. They are the emotional body's response to an event. They are the language of the soul and describe how the soul interprets its surrounding experiences and how it will process them. To discount someone's feelings is to continue the suppression of the event they are trying to heal. Strong feelings are a signal something traumatic has happened. Never judge them. Empathetic listening and staying present emotionally are the greatest tools you can offer, other than Reiki.

Reiki has Divine Intelligence and will go where the healing is most needed. There may be after-effects, especially if they have been sick awhile. Let your clients know that a healing crisis is underway and not to expect to feel perfect the moment you finish a treatment. Eventually they will feel better than before because something has been released and integrated forever. The cells will then rejuvenate themselves and be stronger than before. The brain will integrate and accept the truth, freeing up more power and energy for life.

> *A true wizard is not bound by the spell of time. We live in the past, present and future all at once. Return to another time, when you had power and save yourself now.*
>
> ~ Salini

People will sometimes say to me, but I was damaged so early, it's too late for me. Not so, I tell them. With Reiki you have the power to heal through time to the past when you were originally wounded.

Realize you have the power to do this, to reclaim your powerful self and reintegrate yourself. With **Long Distance Reiki*** you can access the child at the moment of wounding, speak to their Higher Self and discover the cause of the incident (probably a past life), then travel to the original issue that created it. Then you can commence the healing. Reach far into your past, all the way into your Akashic Records where you made your first missteps and seize your power. You need to heal yourself in the past so you can live in the present; otherwise you have no present or future. Realize that your task is to remove all that blocks you from love, truth, power, wholeness and living in the present moment. You must walk towards your awakening. When you do that, your life will fall in alignment with the Universe's divine order and your future will be bright.

And then there is the matter of your family. You were born into a dysfunctional family. Everyone has issues. Everyone needs healing. Where do you begin? If you are a healer, your work is cut out for you from day one. You will be able to bring much healing to your family with Reiki. Even if your family isn't interested in healing, with Second Degree Reiki you can reach their soul for healing. In all cases with Soul Healing, you must ask the person's soul for permission to commence healing. But with Long Distance Reiki, you can have that conversation with the person's soul. You may meet their soul in the inner planes and ask permission to bring healing to them. You will be surprised to find out many souls who may be angry, reluctant, drug-addicted, diseased and comatose, etc., will be there to meet you in the Unified Field, where Higher Selves meet in understanding. Let your heart lead you and always respect the process your loved ones are going through.

Finally, there is **Third Degree Reiki***, the Master level. There you will learn to heal the soul and in turn the rest of the body/mind/emotions will follow. ReikiMastership is not for everyone. Only those with a deep commitment to awakening and healing will feel drawn to this path. It is a path of profound spiritual awakening. And only those with the proper respect for the Master teacher, the lineage, the teachings and Reiki itself should be admitted for training. There are just three levels of Reiki. There are no additional names that need to be added to Reiki. Everything you need is contained within the simplicity of the original, Authentic Reiki teachings of Dr. Mikao Usui. All else is superfluous or false. Find a teacher of integrity, wisdom and love who knows Authentic Usui Reiki and who resonates with you. Let them guide you. Reiki is an egoless path and the student surrenders to the Master Teacher's guidance. That is how the student gains the most power, in humility. It's about the divine energy, what it is, what it can do and where it originates from. Reiki is God's divine energy and thus requires nothing else. It is changeless, formless and eternal. It does not evolve, it exists eternally. So don't be fooled by false paths or teachers. It's your task to discover it and use it to awaken yourself. I bless you on your journey. Namaste.

Chapter 14

Soul Transformation & Reiki Healing Miracles

We only need one small shard to reconstruct the whole...
~ Clarissa Pinkola Estes
Women Who Run With The Wolves

And now we arrive at the point where the healing begins. Up until now, we walked through first the innocence that we brought with us to Earth. Our beautiful souls, full of Dharmic purpose, God's grace, hearts alive with love, and a joyous anticipation of the journey ahead. We also brought with us to this plane whatever karma we contracted to work out. Our karma is what shapes our path and our Dharmic purpose. We will be born into the situation we need to be in to complete karma, accomplish our contracted soul goals and move towards awakening. Every person on Earth is here to awaken, nothing else. All other activities are secondary to that. And each of us has a part in the collective global awakening taking place. The world lives in duality which fosters delusion, hatred, judgment, war, greed and oppression. When people awaken, they end duality and enter Oneness which brings everyone a step closer to it. Therefore all of us are here to do that whether we realize it or not. There will be many experiences that will stimulate that awakening.

At some point in our journey, either in childhood or later, we will experience the wounding. This wound can be physical, emotional, mental or spiritual. It can be small, large, huge or invisible. It can be a car accident, a childhood tormentor like a neighbor bully, a physical deformity, sexual abuse, the loss of a parent, or the death of a sibling and more. There are so many ways to be wounded but each is the catalyst that sets our soul on its journey towards transformation. The wound is like a ticking time bomb inside our being. It can even be brought from another life. It's as though it has a timer set on it. It often sits there percolating, bubbling inside, until the moment when your soul transformation is scheduled to begin. We go along believing we are going to follow a "normal" path, go to school, marry, have a family and so on, but as John Lennon said, *"Life is what happens when you're making other plans."* The wound is the point of happening where the other parts of your soul's journey can flower and open. But for some, the wound happens so early and so traumatically that it is not remembered. If you have experienced early childhood trauma of any kind prior to the age of five years old, it's likely you will not know, remember or understand your wound. It may take a lifetime of unfolding and understanding to realize the lesson. And it may take a lifetime to realize the gift inside the wound.

Your wound will cause you to seek healing of some kind depending on its nature. In doing so, you encounter healers, teachers, sages and other spiritual guides along the way that will guide you to the awakening your wound has triggered. You will also encounter those who wish to wound you further because they see your wound. You must learn discernment and develop your spiritual vision to survive. This can be an ever-unfolding process, like a lotus opening to the sun, where one experience leads to another, then to another teacher, then to another piece of awakening. It's a cascade of magical happenings that are divinely guided every single step of the way for your highest good. *But*…..it may not feel like that. Since my wound started at birth and I was mentally conditioned to believe it was normal to live that way, to be in physical and emotional pain every day, to live in terror and to constantly strive for the love and acceptance that never came from my family, it took many years to reach the spark of divine realization that I was moving into deepening awareness and away from the wound. But it was the original wound that triggered it all.

Once you've experienced the wound that divides your body, mind or spirit somehow, you begin to live in the separation. You begin to view life from the perspective of how your mind and emotions were warped by the wound. In the case of trauma-based mind control from secret societies, your mind will be shaped to serve the Master, to be the good slave and to fill a role designated for you by your gifts and strengths. They will attempt to wipe your free will, your individual spirit and your memories and shape you into a very divided mindset, a permanent state of separation from God's grace, and someone easily controlled. Every wound shapes a mind differently. If it's alcoholic parents, you experience abandonment and from then on, that is what you fear and will likely experience. If you experience extreme bullying in childhood, fear and low self-esteem separating you from your True Self will dominate your mind until the day it triggers your healing and soul transformation. And so on.

Most people bring their separation consciousness with them into the current incarnation or they wouldn't be reincarnating. Awakened souls do not reincarnate unless they come to assist others to awaken. And yes, Jesus taught reincarnation to his followers. It was during the 3rd century, around the time of the Council of Nicaea, that the Orthodox Christians removed the reincarnation teachings, and all references to Jesus' Eastern mysticism teachings from the Bible. Much of the missing pieces of Jesus' teachings can be found in the Apocrypha and Gnostic Gospels and Dead Sea Scrolls. So, when you are reincarnated, you have a set of experiences that are designed to finish your karma as expeditiously as possible so you can awaken to your True Self. And even if you have no faith or damaged faith, you are guided to your spiritual awakening.

I helped a man to awaken to his true spirituality when I lived in Mexico years ago.

__Jeff's Story__ – I lived in Mexico for a time while I was recovering from my sister's death. I have found it's not unusual for people to find me wherever I go and ask for help. I've come to trust that God has sent them to me for healing. One day when I was at a restaurant having lunch, a man came over and sat down at my table. He said he was desperate and could I help him. I asked him what was wrong. He began to cry and said that he had come to Mexico to kill himself from his home state of Washington. I asked him why. He told me he had committed a great sin.

"What sin is that?" I asked him. He said through tears, "I'm married but I had an affair. In my church, it's a mortal sin. The minister tells me I'm going to Hell. All the parishioners have judged and exiled me. I'll probably be excommunicated. I can't leave because of my family and can't redeem myself because my soul is eternally damned. My only way out is suicide." He said he was contemplating that very day whether or not to kill himself when he saw me and felt compelled to come over and speak with me. "I'm glad you did." I said to him. He said there was a blackness on his heart. "Why did you choose to have an affair?" I asked him. He told me that he was in a loveless, empty marriage with another church member who was very judgmental and full of fire and brimstone. He said he felt like a sinner when he was with his wife anyway because of

the way she treated him. He told me that the woman he was having an affair with was kind and loving and he wanted to marry her but his church said it was too late and he was condemned to Hell.

Jeff was from a very strict fundamentalist church that even believed it was a sin to dance or sing. He wasn't allowed to have fun at all or was told he was going to Hell ever since he was a boy. He wasn't even allowed to play with other boys when he was a child. His joy was stifled. Jeff told me he loved God and Jesus but that he was dying in the marriage and in his church. He said it was affecting his belief in God and wasn't sure he wanted a relationship with a God who condemns people. He wanted to end his life rather than return home to his marriage and church.

"We all commit sins of one kind or another Jeff, but we aren't all going to Hell." I told Jeff. "What do you mean?" he asked me, surprised. "God loves us all unconditionally and forgives us as we all make many mistakes throughout our lives. It's God's forgiveness and mercy that make it possible for us to start again after we've realized our mistakes. Otherwise, we would all be in Hell. I'm sure your minister has made a few himself. Too much judgment kills life. It's the opposite of God's love." Jeff was quiet a few moments. "I've never heard anyone say that." He told me. "What would you do if you could do anything besides committing suicide?" I asked him. He pondered that for a moment. "I would marry my girlfriend. She really loves me. But I can't, something has a grip on my heart and I feel it squeezing the life out of me. I hear a voice telling me to die all the time. That's why I'm here. I'm fighting it right now."

He told me. I thought about it and then offered to take him home for a Reiki treatment. I knew my roommate would be there. He agreed.

At home, I got Jeff on the table and we talked some more about his church history. He said that he felt a dark fear and something gripping and squeezing his heart all the time, especially when he went into the church. He said they used to pray very dark prayers over him, telling him he was evil, even when he was a child. It became clear to me that some of his church members were less than pure in their motives with Jeff. He wasn't learning anything about Jesus' true teachings of mercy, forgiveness and unconditional love. It's likely he had a spell of some kind cast over him, maybe a spirit attachment. From what he told me, it sounded like he had been taken to a black magic ceremony when he was very small. I asked him if he wanted the energy out. He said yes, please go ahead.

I began giving him a special treatment to draw out any negative energies from him. I said some prayers to bring in divine assistance for protection and to draw out whatever energy was there. These prayers always include Jesus, Mother Mary and all the Masters and Archangels who assist us from the other side, a universal approach that includes everyone. I started a Reiki Mental/Emotional treatment on Jeff and created a boundary of safety around his aura where only pure spirits could enter. After completing that, I went to his heart and began sending unconditional love in the form of Reiki there. Jeff began sweating intensely and shaking all over. He told me he could feel something holding onto his heart. He could hear a voice threatening him as well. He looked at me frightened and said, "It's going to kill you when it comes out. And then it will kill me." I replied, "No it won't. We are protected by the Holy Spirit." Jeff thrashed around while I kept just a few fingers on his heart chakra and sent unconditional love as Reiki into his heart. I prayed continuously. As big as Jeff was, he told me he was unable to rise from the table, he felt he was being held down by something. Jeff was probably 6 feet 5 inches at least and around 250 lbs. of solid muscle, maybe early 40's. I only had three fingers on his heart. I could never have held him down on my own.

Suddenly, Jeff jerked violently and lunged upward momentarily, then lay back, taking in a deep breath. Then he heaved a big sigh of relief. I felt a cold energy pass by me. I had opened the doors and windows. I commanded the energy to leave with the Angels. Something brushed by me. I then prayed another prayer over Jeff and asked the Angels to heal, love and protect him. I kept my hands on his heart awhile, then went back to his head. I said a prayer of protection and sealed his aura from intrusion. I asked him how he felt. He was sweating and breathing heavily but he sat up. "That was amazing." He said. We talked about the experience. He told me he could see a dark entity inside his inner vision. It had a hold of his heart and was whispering hateful things to him. It told him that he was unlovable and evil, and that it was protecting him. It said that if I removed it, he would die and then I would die. He said he was terrified during the treatment and heard many threats, but then suddenly he saw it leaving him. After that, he said, peace settled over him.

He said for the first time in his life he could feel love entering his heart. He said he felt God's presence and a new sense of peace. He thanked me, gave me a huge bear hug and went on his way.

Jeff called me months later to tell me he decided not to kill himself. He returned home to Washington state and filed for divorce. He moved in with his girlfriend and left the church. He began to develop his own relationship with God that was without constant reminders of hatred, judgment, evil and sin. Eventually, he found a different church that was peaceful, loving and forgiving. He felt he could be himself there. He never left God and God never left him, he simply met God for the first time in his life…..finally.

God's power is infinite to dispel darkness. Remember always that you are filled with light.

The separation between God and self can go on a long time, even many lifetimes before a person has the divine spark of awakening. This is why even a terrible experience of trauma can quicken the process of awakening and cut many lifetimes off a soul's journey to wholeness. There is a gift inside the trauma after all.

After living a while in separation and experiencing a shock of awakening, you begin the integration process. The healing crisis. You understand your wound must be healed and you've started down the path of finding the broken pieces of your soul. This can be a year, 2 years or 20 years, or even longer. The deeper the wound the greater the potential for awakening and the greater the spiritual power at the end. You may need many teachers, healers and angels along the way before you reach the end of the integration. But once you've started the work, you are on the journey homeward. During this process you will have many spiritual awakenings and experience many miracles.

Few there be who solve Kali's mystery! Good & evil is the challenging riddle which life places sphinx-like before every intelligence. Attempting no solution, most men pay forfeit with their lives, penalty now even as in the days of Thebes. Here and there a towering lonely figure never cries defeat. From the Maya of duality she plucks the cleaveless truth of unity.

~ *Paramahansa Yogananda*

Finally, you've arrived at your destination. It may have snuck up on you because you've walked it so long. But peace and clarity have arrived once again. You have resurrected yourself. The final stop is **At-One-Ment***, or atonement. You've made your amends to yourself and to God. You've reconciled your separation, your wound, your journey and with those who hurt you and those who you have hurt. It's time to settle into Oneness and remain eternally in the presence of God.

But there is one final step, a big one. Currently throughout the world, there is a massive dismemberment ceremony taking place. Remember what I said about dismemberment and how we are broken apart? We are being torn down to be rebuilt into a bigger and better world. The process is painful, but very necessary to overcome our global shadow. And we are smack dab in the middle of it right now.

So let the grieving begin. Let's cry for what the lie has done to America and to the rest of the world. Cry for what this life of oppression, surveillance, medical mafia and big pharma, chemtrails, war, banksters and bailout crimes, government full of criminals and corporations, environmental disasters and so on has done to you. Let's do our global grieving and awaken from the collective nightmare of mind control, fascism and enslavement that we have all been subjected to for so long. Let's release the pain and sorrow of it all and detach from those who have harmed our souls so deeply. They have no power over your soul, it's time to take it back.

*It is our grief that will lead us to resurrection
as a healed and loving species. Our tears are
the healing oil that recaptures our humanity,
unconditional love and wholeness.*

~ *Salini*

Take back your power from the lie that you can't heal. The body can restore itself if given the chance. Take back your power from the lie, like when they tell us that we have to do the bailout to save America or our economy will collapse, or that we need another war, or more taxes for the rich. Take back your power from these people who care NOTHING for your life and your future. On the contrary, they are scheming to destroy your life, take your money and property and steal your soul. Take back your souls from the secret societies that practice Satanism and use your souls as collateral to purchase sanctuary for themselves. Take back our children from the hands of the traffickers who use them for pleasure and profit and have long since sold their souls to the dark path. Take back your minds from any false teachers in any religions or paths that deceive you into sacrificing yourself and your power. Your soul is yours to have forever. Your energy is yours to use to survive in this life, not to fuel their greedy dreams.

Rosalind Franklin, the forgotten female chemist whose work was stolen, cracked the source code of the human DNA strand long ago. She mapped it for science and the world. But she never realized how they would abuse her discovery. Once they got that information, the elite scientists of the dark began creating viruses and substances to kill, disrupt, modify and control our DNA. This is what GMOs are all about. This is what they are putting in vaccinations to weaken our immunity. This is what the chemtrails dropping poisons down upon us daily are doing. These are the diseases they are unleashing upon humanity. Death is what they seek for us. We are in the midst of a timed period for depopulation devised by the global elite. ***But there*** *is a solution to this. There is a way to save yourself. If you match your frequency to the Divine Source Code of Life, you can stave these inevitabilities off.* You *can* strengthen your vital energy/divine life force and increase immunity. This is done by raising your vibration. And that can be done a number of ways. Let's find out how.

We've been blocked from having access to most of the alternative healing and energy methods for a century now. Some of these tried and tested successful methods are Max Gerson's juicing therapy, Dr. Royal Rife's cancer healing machine, Laetrile, Nikola Tesla's work, Dr. Gaston Naesson's 714X cancer cure and many, many more. By blocking true healing, which permanently raises your body's healing frequency; they are suppressing your ability to heal. Instead they focus on disease maintenance instead of prevention and holistic re-juvenation. This approach has a ripple effect throughout the universe since we are one interconnected energy field. The energy must be allowed to flow unhindered through the body and the surrounding environment. The body has always had the ability to heal itself. It's simply a matter of removing toxins and energy blockages, addressing all four quadrants of health, and allowing the divine energy to flow in again. The divine healing energy has an innate spiritual intelligence that knows where the body, mind or spirit needs healing. It simply needs to be able to flow freely to do so.

There is not one, but many cures for cancer available; they are all being systematically suppressed by the American Cancer Society, the National Cancer Institute and the major oncology centers. They have too much of an interest in the status quo.
~ Dr. Robert Atkins, M.D.

All treatments that worked to heal cancer and other diseases were available 70-90 years ago but were suppressed. The cancer industry is the most blatant example of the control over our health. There was a time when doctors believed that "bleeding" someone would allow the infection to leave the body. Today everyone knows how ridiculous that kind of treatment is. Now we have the same issue with chemotherapy, widely accepted but hugely toxic. Today, 80% of all doctors and scientists refuse chemotherapy for themselves and their families because they know it doesn't work and destroys the immune system. The success rate for chemotherapy is extremely low. But the big business of cancer means the truth is hushed up.

Besides spreading cancer cells, chemotherapy inflicts serious damage to the immune system, the body's natural first line of defense against cancer and other illness. This sets the immune system up for the remaining cancer cells or future cancers to overwhelm a body that is even less able to beat the cancer that got past the immune system in the first place. Chemotherapy also results in serious and even fatal damage to major organs, particularly the liver. Max Gerson, raw foodist and cancer pioneer, stated the liver is already impaired in cancer sufferers so to add chemotherapy to the mix is deadly. The heart is also frequently seriously damaged by chemotherapy. *There is a better way.*

Instead, begin your **Soul Transformation**. Start the process of restructuring the matrix of your soul towards divinity and wholeness. Bring your frequency back to the Divine Source Code. It is then you rise above it all and become *spiritually immune**. Our original DNA was perfect. Yes, some people are born with genetic issues, and sometimes doctors can really help in these cases. Some of them are irreversible. But others are repairable. DNA not only remembers its deficiencies from earlier generations, it remembers its state of perfection. Since DNA is passed from generation to generation from the beginning of time, it isn't just the flaws that are passed. The presence of the original perfect DNA and the possibility of reviving and restoring it to perfection is also ever-present. It lies dormant, but can be reawakened in many cases. Divine healing energy, which God has given us as our birthright, is what restores everything to perfection. No virus can affect the innate perfection of your DNA code when God is allowed to enter and restore it. Trusting and allowing this to take place is the necessary step to open the pathways to total healing and restoration of the body. But with the current ecological disasters taking place, your DNA has been altered by chemicals, pollutants, vaccinations filled with poisons and GMOs, among many toxic substances. They don't want you to know you can heal yourselves. Once they have accomplished altering your DNA structure, they can enslave you. It's up to you to reclaim your body's state of perfection. It may take some hard work but yes, it can be done.

I learned a huge lesson when I experienced my near death experiences as an adult. Over and over I was told by doctors that I was going to die.....my body wasn't strong enough......I had a fatal disease...I had 6 months to live....I had to take their medicine or risk death, or some other similar statement. I could never afford health insurance nor had the cash to pay for expensive medical treatments. So, in each case I had to undertake self-healing. Between my illnesses, the illnesses of family and friends, my work and my upbringing as a healer, I learned a lot about what causes illness and how the energy of healing works. I also went on to master Reiki, massage, counseling and many other healing modalities. I learned that the divine energy of our bodies is perfectly designed to restore us to health if it is allowed to flow freely in a balanced fashion throughout our system. When I healed myself of viral meningitis and cancer with Reiki and God's grace, after being told both times I was going to die, I knew anything was healable. I witnessed and experienced my body restoring itself. It was a miracle to behold.

The same thing happened with my child. Here are two stories about her that illustrate this.

A Reiki Miracle - *When my daughter was four years old, she fell one day and tore a huge chunk of skin and muscle off her ankle all the way to the bone. We took her to the emergency room and the doctor there told me it was too serious and would not heal because there was no skin left on such a large area over her ankle bone. He said she would need plastic surgery and a skin graft. He showed me how to change the dressing twice a day and told me to bring her back for a skin graft in two weeks. I said ok, but I didn't tell him about Reiki.*

I changed her dressing daily but also gave her Reiki treatments every day several times a day right on the injured spot. When I changed her dressing, I noticed a white spot on her ankle bone but I didn't know what it was. We returned to see the doctor in two weeks and he took a look at the wound. When he looked at it, his eyes widened. He said something like, "This is amazing. I've never seen anything like it. An island of skin is growing right on top of her bare ankle bone where there is no skin. This is impossible because there is no skin connecting this little patch to the edges of the wound. It's growing spontaneously over bone, something I never thought possible. It looks like this lone patch of skin is going to grow all the way to the edges of her wound and join the other skin. She won't need a skin graft after all." The white spot I had seen was her skin growing but it was so white and pure looking that I didn't realize it was skin. The patch of new skin was growing directly on the spot where I had placed the center of my hand chakra. This is the place where the most concentrated Reiki comes out of the hand. I continued giving her

Reiki daily and sure enough, the little island of skin grew to the edges of her wound and covered the raw open sore completely and healed over.

She recovered completely without surgery from that incident. This next story was more serious, but Reiki saved the day.

Another Reiki Miracle *- When my baby daughter became ill at 5 months old, began vomiting and had intestinal issues constantly, her doctor told me she had Cystic Fibrosis or Leukemia and might die soon. I suggested she may have food allergies since it began as soon as she stopped nursing and started on a cow's milk formula. The doctor laughed this off and ordered her into the hospital for testing declaring her a "failure to thrive" baby. I was yet to be empowered about my health and my family's health. Despite testing negative for Cystic Fibrosis, Celiac Disease or Leukemia numerous times, she was sent to Los Angeles Children's Hospital under the care of two of the most famous doctors in the world. They ordered more painful tests done on her tiny body but were still unable to identify any disease condition.*

My daughter continued to decline and lose weight under their care until she weighed only 9 and ½ lbs. Her thin, bony arms and legs and engorged belly made her look like an African child from the deserts of Somalia during a famine. She was starving to death. One day, when they didn't know what else to do, they decided to give her a particularly invasive kidney IVP to determine her "disease". Because she was too small and no other vein was available, they accessed her jugular vein *on her neck to inject the fluid for the X-ray. I could hear her screaming for one solid hour and they wouldn't let me in to comfort her. When she came out, her neck had swelled to triple its size overshadowing her head in a monstrous way and she had a terrible vomiting episode. That was the last straw. It was obvious they didn't know what they were doing. So, I fired the famous, expensive doctors who didn't have a clue and took over her care myself. They charged us $100,000 anyway. Fortunately, we had health insurance then; otherwise we would have lost our home. That would happen later as doctors continued to empty our bank account without helping us.*

My baby daughter was now 10 months old and very thin thanks to listening to doctors instead of my intuition. Now I trusted myself with what I observed and felt was wrong. I began giving her daily Reiki treatments. I studied food allergies and fasting and found a safe cleansing fast for her made from brown rice. I made batches of brown rice milk for her myself and put her on a week-long fast with only the rice milk. I gave her Reiki morning, noon and night. After months of vomiting and diarrhea, she stopped both immediately. Once her digestion was calmed down, I began a food rotation diet where I gave her only one kind of food every 6 hours. If she was allergic to it, she would begin the vomiting cycle and I knew to eliminate it from her diet. If she wasn't allergic to it, she had no reaction and I could safely include it in her diet. In this way I was able to identify 10 foods she was highly allergic to and eliminated them from her diet. Among them were corn, wheat, cow's milk, sugar, corn sugar/syrup, oranges and dairy products. These foods are common to many processed foods today and cause hyperactivity, runny noses and ears, and loss of focus in children. Today a fifth of all children have ADD/ADHD, when it was unheard of when I grew up. Toxic, processed, chemical-filled foods have a lot to do with that. After dozens of Reiki treatments stabilizing her energy and immunity and eliminating these foods from her diet, she made a speedy recovery and gained weight. Who knows if some of those foods were also early GMO foods which ALL people are allergic to?

I continued the Reiki treatments daily. I then planted a vegetable garden in the backyard and from that day forth fed her only homemade organic foods which have a higher vibratory rate than processed foods. Her immune system strengthened. She recovered completely. When she avoids these foods, she doesn't get sick. The doctors never called to check on her and didn't even want to hear about it when I called to tell them it was food allergies after all. What took them 5 months and $100,000 with no results, took me 21 days with Reiki, a cleansing fast and the removal of foods she was allergic to. And it was free.

In China, doctors are not paid until AFTER and only WHEN a person recovers. If the person does not recover, the doctor receives nothing. Think about it. Would you pay your car mechanic up front if he said, "Maybe your car will be repaired and maybe it won't but you still have to pay up front"? Our allopathic medical system of health care is itself seriously diseased, co-opted and out of balance. Doctors have no incentive to provide health care that is effective and health-ful because they are paid high sums regardless and are compensated through a skewed health insurance system. Additionally, never did anyone tell me there was a possibility of total recovery, alternative healing, natural methods, healthy foods, spontaneous healing or energetic restoration. At least not any doctors. I was fortunate enough though to learn and observe as a child how healing works and witnessed many spontaneous healings and divine energy entering and healing people. I drew on those experiences, and those of mothers who shared information with me, to trust my intuition and healing powers to undertake healing my children.

These early life experiences catalyzed my desire to become a healer. Over the years I worked on dozens of people with various problems from broken bones to diseases to brain tumors to cancer. I also worked on many animals. I remember one time I came across a waiter in Mexico grasping a beautiful white heron by the neck, choking it and throwing it out the door of the restaurant. He threw it into a nearby pond and it immediately slumped onto its side in shock. It looked dangerously weak. I rushed and picked it up and held it to my chest, giving it Reiki and praying for its recovery. Suddenly, I felt a rush of very cold energy leave the bird and come into my hands. I shook off the cold energy and returned to giving the bird Reiki. Immediately afterwards, a rush of very hot energy left my hands and went into the bird. After about 15 minutes of this, the bird revived and flew away. Otherwise, I'm certain it would have died.

Reiki heals most anything if you get to the source of the problem, but you have to take karma into consideration. Like in Rina's story, coming up ahead, of her past life as a Scottish soldier, it's vital to understand that if you have brought karma with you to this lifetime in the form of an illness, the karma must be completed for you to heal. All Ayurvedic doctors know this and check a patient's Vedic birth chart for karma before undertaking healing on their patient. The severity of the karma and the person's commitment to growth and service will determine the length of the illness but there is no scale to measure the time by. Some illnesses are for learning spiritual lessons as well. It's the person's soul journey or contract they came here to work through. Illness never seems fair and is not an easy subject to discuss, especially where children are involved.

As someone who has been very ill, I was in no mood to talk about my spiritual lessons at first, or if I had any karma. I was just sick and frustrated that I was going through it. But I continued to work on my recovery in all four quadrants of my being – physical, mental, emotional and spiritual. And I gave myself Reiki every day of my life, which I still do. I have learned to ask the divine energy to come into my body and heal me. I call forth the healing. I ask for God's help. As I slowly healed my mind and emotions, my body followed. As I added in my spiritual practices, my health and life improved even more. Every illness and challenge became more information and knowledge to use when healing others. It was all a gift of acquiring healing power and spiritual wisdom. It was all in my perspective. I could condemn the experience or embrace it. At first I was hurt and angry. But eventually, I embraced it and gained even more skills along the way. And now I'm healthy, awake and free of illness.

Eventually I began to see a pattern emerge. People were coming with illnesses, injuries, rashes, back problems, intestinal blockages and many other conditions. But when I started to work on them, deep emotional pain would surface for release. Often they would begin to sob deep, wracking sobs. Over the course of a few treatments, much long-stored emotional trauma would come to the surface to be cleansed out. As we did this work, they would recover. It didn't matter what the illness was. It was their feelings and perception of their situation, their pain and their lives that created tremendous suppressed and stagnant energy pools within their bodies. These stagnant pools, where the energy had been held, sometimes for their whole lives, became the host and genesis for illness. And quite often, they would remember a past life or two. When these memories surfaced, a lot of long-stuck energy would pass out of their bodies. This was energy they brought with them to heal in this lifetime. We have to stop looking at disease monodimensionally as only a physical manifestation. Disease always begins in the mind, where faulty thinking takes root and creates imbalances that become the hosts for disease. Therefore, we must always treat every ill person holistically, and address all four quadrants of the person – mental, emotional, physical and spiritual.

Here is another amazing story of healing with Reiki that defies medical reason.

Leonard's Reiki healing story – *Leonard came to me at the request of a family member. He was 42 and had suffered from severe depression for 25 years. He had a long-standing back condition that dated back to his teenage years. Leonard said he did not have a significant injury that caused his back to begin to be twisted and painful. He told me it just started spontaneously. And that he had become debilitated as a result. He went to a chiropractor every week for years who told him he wasn't going to improve any time soon because his back had seized up and would not respond to treatment. The chiropractor put Leonard on a series of exercises designed to heal his back and herbs for depression but Leonard hadn't seen much improvement for many years. He had stopped working years earlier and was very involved in dealing with his back and depression constantly. It was taking over his life and he was giving up. He was afraid he would never work again and had become withdrawn and shy. His family member told me that Leonard was having a hard time transitioning from dependency upon his parents to self-responsibility. So, Leonard agreed to come and*

try Reiki. We agreed we would work together for two months on a weekly or bi-weekly basis to move through his pain and debilitation.

When I began working on Leonard, I immediately had the distinct feeling his condition was temporary and he was going to recover. It was as though a cloud, a malaise, had settled over him and was sapping his energy and peace. I went through the treatment and arrived at the point of the Mental and Emotional healing. During the Mental Treatment, I asked the energy of depression and pain to leave him immediately and the energy of healing and rejuvenation to take over healing and dispelling his suffering. After completing the first part of the treatment on the front of Leonard's body, I asked him to turn over to finish treating him. As soon as I began working on Leonard's back, something amazing happened. I could feel tons and tons of pain leaving Leonard's back and coming into my hands and forearms. My arms ached with the pain leaving Leonard's body. I had to stop several times to cleanse off my arms with salt water and shake out the painful energy before returning to work on him. Each time my arms would fill up with excruciating pain. Since there was non-stop pain coming out of Leonard's back that day, I decided to work extra-long on him.

After about two hours, I felt an easing of the pain coming out of Leonard. It was beginning to dwindle down. So I completed the treatment, cleansed off my hands and had him sit up. He was very relaxed and told me he felt great. We agreed he would return next week for more to keep the healing going. [It's advisable to always receive 3 Reiki Foundation treatments to anchor the Reiki in the body and keep the healing going.] I asked him to give me a call to let me know how he was doing. I didn't hear from him for a few days. I decided to call and check on Leonard.

When he answered I asked how he was doing and what day he wanted to return for his next treatment. Leonard replied that he wouldn't be coming back for another treatment. I asked him why. He said, "Because you healed my back in one session." He said he went to his chiropractor as usual for his weekly adjustment and the chiropractor said "Your back has healed completely. You won't require any more adjustments." Leonard told me that his back adjusted continuously for several days after our treatment and that he felt the misaligned vertebrae go into place and stay in place for the first time. He said the muscles that had been holding the vertebrae in those positions for so long had shifted but were spasming. He needed to get some massages to get them to relax and realize everything was ok. He also said that he felt a huge lifting of his depression and felt overwhelmed by the shift in his health. He said he wanted to take time to assimilate to the changes and learn to live without depression and be pain-free. He thanked me and said, "You changed my life. Now I'm going to go live it."

Sometimes when I work with someone there is no clear origin or blinding light of understanding as to how and why a person is ill. In Leonard's case, I sensed a cloudy presence, possibly a spirit that had latched onto him and was sapping his energy and joy. Leonard had shared that at one point in his life he had used drugs and marijuana regularly. I have been an Addictions Counselor for 30 years and know that when people use those substances continuously, they open portals to spirit attachment. I have had to remove many spirits from clients who were addicted. The spirits are often of departed alcoholics and drug addicts who want the human being to continue using for them. Their addiction continues in the spirit world. I had many such clients when I created my program for street addicts and alcoholics. Many of these spirits would lash out at me as they left the person's body but I always say my prayers at the beginning of a treatment for protection. Leonard had clearly picked up some entities from years of smoking pot and using drugs. His life force was being sapped and vampired by these spirits.

And so as you begin your **Soul Transformation**, you must look at all quadrants of your being. Illness is never just physical. In fact, all disease begins in the mind, where the ego is seated, when false beliefs about life and about you are formed. The process of self-healing begins with an examination of each of the four quadrants that make up your holistic self. Once you have made such an examination, you must begin a massive cleanse of each quadrant and restore yourself to *homeostasis*,* or internal balance. So, let's go into what that means.

> *All healing, mental or material, is attuning each atom of the body, each reflex of the brain forces, to the awareness of the divine that lies within each atom and each cell of the body.*
> ~ *Edgar Cayce*

I mentioned earlier that the vibration of love is 528 kHz. This is the vibration we must all aspire towards. It heals and repairs the body, and restores DNA. There is a little more to that story I didn't tell you. While geniuses like Tesla, Mileva Maric Einstein and Rosalind Franklin were cracking the codes of energy, relativity and DNA, Nazi scientists were also figuring out the secrets of math and its universal patterns that run the Universe. After extensive research, they discovered that music keyed at the dissonant frequency of 440 kHz, known as the Devil's Tone, would create an atmosphere of chaos, fear and distress and make it easier to control people. This is what prompted the global elite to standardize all music to 440 kHz before WWII, especially rock and roll. Musicians weren't too keen on this arrangement knowing full well that this key caused fear, not joy or love in their musical compositions. Nevertheless, 440 kHz became the norm.

Enter the Beatles and John Lennon. John Lennon knew that this was occurring and that the elite were trying to use music to negatively influence the next generation. They weren't even allowed to record their own music in anything but 440 kHz. So they made their famous movie *Yellow Submarine**, which is the story of the suppression of music told in cartoon-style. In the movie, the Blue Meanies covered the vibrational love tone of 528 kHz, the C note on the musical scale, with the fog so they couldn't play it anymore. It was the Beatles' parable about musical tyranny to the world. Few people knew that this was a message to humanity. Musical suppression continued on. To combat this, John wrote *Imagine**, and *Working Class Hero** in the key of love, 528 kHz, the first major songs written by a major star in the key of love. They became monster hits. John and Yoko made it clear they were standing up to the elite by promoting peace and love. It wasn't long after that he was killed. He sacrificed his life to try to bring love and peace and truth to us all. He remains a hero for humanity.

But John's legacy remains strong. Today, musicians everywhere are beginning to write in the key of 528 kHz. Everywhere the world is opening up to love and their grip is loosening. 528 kHz is also the key to DNA repair. Dozens of songs and videos can be found that play the 528 tone for healing. As I mentioned earlier, DNA can be rejuvenated. Listening to the 528 tone is one of the ways to do it. Receiving or becoming attuned to Reiki is another. Learn Reiki. Once your vibration is raised and your DNA repaired, you become increasingly immune to illness, as long as you take care of yourself otherwise. Additionally, the more Reiki you practice, the higher your vibration climbs.

> *If you wish to understand the Universe,*
> *think of energy, frequency and vibration.*
> ~ *Nikola Tesla*

And so we arrive at the point where we begin to do our holistic healing. To do this means to cultivate an understanding of the holistic nature of the body and each quadrant of health. It starts with the four quadrants below.

Four Quadrants of Holistic Health

A human being is a complex structure with multiple systems like the brain, the nervous system, the cardiovascular system, the lymphatic systemic and so on. But humans are much more than blood, brain and tissue. They are also made up of energy in strands, layers and something akin to air and fluid. Like the planet's four directions - North, South, East and West - and Earth's four elements - Air, Earth, Fire and Water – a human being has four distinct energetic quadrants. These quadrants are - the body, the mind, the emotions and the Spirit (or Soul). These quadrants function as one unit, and are inextricably linked. They are not divided in fours like a pie, but work together woven like a fabric throughout the body and cannot ever be separated. In order to be a healthy, functioning human being, all four quadrants must be balanced, nourished, and supported equally.

Similarly, the energy field of the Earth - its life force - is comprised of Yin (female) or Yang (male) energy. One energy cannot exist or function properly without the other; they are parts of a whole. If either the Yin or Yang energy is lacking or excessive, the Earth will become imbalanced. This, in turn, then affects the whole of systems and people. As the life force moves around the cycle of life and through the human system, it must be equally distributed within each soul quadrant. If it becomes stuck or engorged in any one quadrant of life, an imbalance can occur that can have consequences to one's health or well-being. Earlier cultures understood the holistic nature of life and the energy that empowers it. Their shamans and healers treated the whole being, not isolated parts, successfully. And their holy men and women performed rituals to keep the Earth's energy in balance, such as the Hopi ceremonies I witnessed.

In every culture and in every medical tradition before ours, healing was accomplished by moving energy.
~ *Albert Szent-Gyorgy*
Nobel Prize-Winning Biochemist.

What are commonly acknowledged today are physical and mental imbalances. Sometimes, emotional imbalances are recognized, but not as comprehensively as they need to be for overall health. No discussion of emotional energies that have penetrated the person's field are mentioned when people go to doctors or counselors, yet most people who are emotionally troubled are experiencing emotional penetration by energies around them, or soul wounds. It could be from a family member, it could be from a spirit, it could be from a past life or it could an emotional wound. These energies must be addressed and released depending on their origin. Rarely is the whole being treated in a holistic fashion, or in a deep enough manner. Instead, people are farmed out to separate practitioners of various types who do not communicate with one another. The person is treated fragmentally. The results are often less than satisfactory because the split in human consciousness is still being supported, and the wholeness of our beings are still being denied.

The cure of a part should not be attempted without treatment of the whole.

~ *Plato*

The foot doctor treats the foot, the counselor the emotions, the minister the spirit, and the psychiatrist the mind, but do they consult on the interconnectedness of the conditions their patients suffer? Do they address the cause holistically? No, they do not. Every body part is treated separately as if they have no interrelation. These are the critical questions we must ask today as we enter into new forms of health care.

Healing Holistically

When we enter a crisis of some kind, it is likely that the spiritual aspect will be the one continuously neglected, and the last considered. Yet, when a crisis begins in our lives, it is the spiritual aspect of ourselves that has triggered it. When the soul is not being acknowledged, and its purpose is denied, a "soul crisis" will begin. It could manifest as a physical problem, a mental problem, an emotional problem or a life problem. So, it becomes necessary to begin there, at the spiritual level, and determine what the soul is asking for, however difficult that may be. **Soul Transformation Therapy*** brings together the fragmented portions of the soul in a diverse form of therapy. All four quadrants of the soul are addressed, and through a consultation process, an individualized treatment plan is created. Soul Transformation Therapy is for anyone who hears the call. The basics of this approach are simple to understand and can be fundamentally described as follows:

Quadrant #1 - THE BODY - Our bodies should be kept fit and healthy as much as possible. Continue to eat right, exercise regularly, get out into nature, and get enough sleep. If addictions are present this must be addressed. If the body is unhealthy and unbalanced, it will tip the balance against other quadrants. These are the basics of self-care to set the foundation for addressing the other three quadrants. Some people have greater physical limitations. Don't let that stop you from transforming. Find simpler exercises to do. Keep working at it, perfection is not required. Further suggestions individually designed for your personal transformation may be offered. After doing the basics for your body, go a step further and ask yourself... is there something deeper troubling me? Is something nagging at my heart, mind or soul that I've ignored? Could that be affecting my health, my serenity or my sanity? If so, keep going....

Quadrant #2 - THE MIND - Our mind is the creator of our circumstances, so it is imperative to gain mastery over thoughts, beliefs, fears and other objects of our attention that may take us places we do not wish to go, and shape our lives unconsciously. Beyond the obvious suggestions of think positively, let things go, etc., there are the deep issues of ancient beliefs, family myths, mind-control and buried trauma that can short circuit mental health and affect other quadrants. Thought forms are thoughts that become deeply embedded in our brain and repeat themselves constantly in our mind as I explained in previous chapters. For example, someone with Obsessive Compulsive Disorder who never stops cleaning for fear of contamination. When this happens, those thoughts begin to create our reality. If those thoughts happen to be consistently negative, they will magnetize negative experiences towards you. Now this differs from the earlier discussion on acknowledging your darkness. Owning your darkness is for the purpose of transforming it, not hanging on to it and letting it run rampant in your life. A distinction must be drawn between denying dark thought forms and allowing them to rule through your subconscious, and owning them and transforming them through sacred alchemy. To deny you have darkness is to be half-awake. To own the dark thought forms is to regain power over them and over yourself. That's the difference between positive thinking and powerful thinking and between being half-awake or fully awake. Positive thinking is just being half-awake and ignoring your shadow. Powerful thinking is owning both your dark and light consciousness and transforming the dark part to a force that works positively in your life. And it's denial that bridges the gap. Recognition of your own denial and having the willingness to remove it will open the pathway to the reclamation of your power.

Quadrant #3 - <u>THE EMOTIONS</u> - Emotions are the language of the soul. And like our minds, our emotions can enrich, or enslave us. Some people have a richer palette of emotions than others and need more help managing this quadrant. Within our culture, many emotions are judged and suppressed, causing soul imbalances. What is most harmful to the emotional body and ultimately human health is the suppression and denial of your feelings. For men, most all emotions are taboo except anger and passion which exacerbates their addiction to lust and the suppression of valuable yin emotions like tenderness and compassion. For women, anger is denied us and passivity is encouraged. If we show too much anger or power, we are ridiculed and often called crazy. The more powerful a woman is, the more likely she will be labeled crazy. Take it as a badge of honor ladies if you are called crazy or a bitch. For men, if you are too loving or sensitive, you might be labeled gay. Take that gents as a sign of your courage to be willing to show your vulnerability to a harsh world. It's now becoming more universal that both men and women are suppressed as we move through this period of global domination and abuse of power.

The emotional body must be healed because it is the magnetic energy field of the human body, and it is that magnetic energy that draws in the Holy Spirit, holds God's presence and maintains the person's spirit in steady manifestation and wholeness. A person simply will not heal or fully manifest without a full expression of their deepest feelings and magnetic energy.

When you deny your feelings, your pain and your truth... your shame core begins to form. The longer it is denied the bigger and more powerful it becomes...and the more it rules your life.
~ *Salini*

The two Yin/Yang aspects are intermeshed and each hold vital components of the soul's overall experience, including emotions. Throughout recent history, the Yin energy within us all has largely been suppressed, ignored and sidelined. This causes imbalances in everyone, male or female, and is a primary change that must occur for health to be restored. Learning to honor and process difficult emotional states is a primary function of transformational work.

Quadrant #4 - THE SOUL, SPIRIT - And last, but definitely not least, we look into our souls, our spiritual lives, a place often neglected, for a deeper look at where we have arrived, what's going on, why we are here, and what we can do about it. In this quadrant we will begin the deep soul work of **Soul Transformation Therapy**. When this quadrant is properly nourished, the other three will follow effortlessly. If it has long been denied, pain is inevitable somewhere in your life. That pain can translate into much greater life problems, even illnesses, and can be approached through **Soul Transformation Therapy**.

Throughout my many years of working with people, I've discovered that deep trauma can cause seemingly incurable diseases, when in reality it's nothing more than trapped energy. I've worked on many cancer patients who were severely traumatized or emotionally wounded in a way that prevented their healing. That is until they came for **Soul Transformation Therapy**. Once the original wound or the karma is identified, the process can begin to work on moving it out of the soul. With trauma, there is usually a massive shame core that must be healed. Your True Self doesn't fully emerge until you have first dealt with your shame core. The shame core is filled with traumatic experiences which created negative beliefs about you. They must be addressed and healed so your beautiful True Self can come to life. This can only be accomplished with a spiritual healing. If you try alone, you will face the scorching heat of your own self-hatred which resides inside the shame core, and the pain of that will kill you. Only God's love is powerful enough to heal our core. So you absolutely must practice a spiritual path of healing to fully heal. Otherwise, it's only a partial healing.

And if it's sexual trauma, the shame core will be the most pronounced and deeply buried, hidden away from the conscious mind, but still directing one's actions. The secrets will be buried deeply in the brain. They are a psychic poison that has an energy of its own which is highly toxic. The place where this toxic psychic poison is stored will become a host for disease. The longer it's held there, the more likely disease can occur. I suggest that neurosurgeons pay attention to tumors of the brain stem especially as evidence of serious trauma. Additionally, I have found that people who carry deep secrets have a segmented or compartmentalized consciousness which alienates them from God, from life and from their healing. This has to be healed in the mental, emotional and soul components of therapy and a spiritual practice undertaken.

Lou Gehrig, the famous baseball slugger, is a case in point. Doctors at the Veterans Affairs Medical Center, and the Boston University School of Medicine, primary researchers of brain damage among deceased National Football League players, said that markings in the spinal cords of players who received a diagnosis of A.L.S., Lou

Gehrig's Disease, indicated the men did not have A.L.S. They were suffering from the effects of concussion trauma that erodes the central nervous system in similar ways. They suggest that the deterioration of athletes like Gehrig, as well as soldiers from battlefields, given a diagnosis of amyotrophic lateral sclerosis might have been caused by injuries such as concussions and other brain trauma sustained on the playing field. Gehrig had a well-documented history of significant concussions on the baseball field. It's possible that Gehrig's commitment to playing through injuries like concussions, which resulted in his legendary streak of playing in 2,130 consecutive games over 14 years, could have led to his condition. *Doctors need to take note of the trauma connection to the development of all disease.*

Part of what's wrong with modern *allopathic** medicine is that the focus is on the suppression of symptoms rather than on allowing the symptoms to fully express themselves. When you suppress the body's natural symptomatic response to illness, you are blocking the body from self-healing. The body will express its full array of symptoms as well as its ability to heal those symptoms but it has to be allowed to run its course. The body knows how to heal itself. What's happening is a purification of the body and that needs to continue, unless it's more serious of course. Use common sense when making health decisions in these cases. Sometimes we need to see a doctor.

But in the case of karma, some illnesses heal and some do not. What Western doctors don't understand is that many diseases are karmic. Time is wasted looking for pathogens when a pathogen is nothing more than a congealed thought form, traumatic event, karma, energy blockage or an accumulation of toxins. Ayurvedic doctors understand this and every patient must first have a Vedic reading before proceeding with the doctor. Ayurvedic physicians understand the soul component of illness and realize that many people have come to work out their karma through serious illness. Once the karmic cause has been identified, it's clearer how to proceed.

There are three distinct types of karma – light, moderate and severe. Light karma is karma that is easy to overcome, perhaps a minor violation in another life. Doing humanitarian service usually wipes this type of karma off the book of your Akashic Record. The next level of karma is moderate. This may or may not be removed but you must undertake *selfless seva**, or service, immediately to pay back for this karma or it will cause difficulties for you. The third and final type of karma is severe karma. This type of karma often appears in the form of serious illness. Sometimes it can be eradicated by the person just living through the karma and repaying the karmic debt. Most likely it will not. If that type of karma is present, it's advisable to adopt a spiritual path and stick with it, doing as much service as possible along the way. These efforts will lessen the karma but not eradicate it if it's a very serious offense from another life.

Here is one of my case histories that illustrates soul healing. The case is both fascinating and amazing, and was to both doctors and healers alike who worked with her –

Rina's Reiki healing story - *I met Rina when she attended my weekly Reiki healing and meditation circles that I had in my home for many years. We became friends. Rina was very spiritual and studied a number of religions. She was a Buddhist but had been a Christian at one time. She prayed and chanted daily. She was a seeker of truth and of God and we spoke of it often. Rina was born with Situs inversus, a condition where the internal organs are reversed in the body and face the other direction. The liver is on the left side, the heart is on the right side, and they are usually facing backwards. She was also born with scoliosis, a condition where the spine is curved like an S. She had been under lifetime care of doctors and chiropractors but no*

improvement in her health had occurred. Additionally, her lungs were weak upon birth and one was removed soon after she was born, leaving her with one lung for life. The doctor commented at the time that he thought it so odd to find sand inside the lung they removed although she was only a few months old at the time. At this point in her life, Rina was on the waiting list for a lung transplant since her only lung had been over-worked and was weakening further. She wore a beeper at all times in the event a lung became available.

Rina decided to take First Degree Reiki. She was worried about her life span shortening and time running out for her. She wanted as much healing as possible. Prior to class, she saw me for a few sessions. As I worked on her, I received a distinct message, as I sometimes do when working on people, that she would receive a lung after she took Second Degree Reiki. I heard that her body would not be strong enough to endure the operation without Second Degree Reiki. Rina proceeded with her First Degree Reiki class which she thoroughly enjoyed. She was a natural and her hands were hot and energized after the first attunement. She completed the class and went back to work.

The first day back to work for Rina after the class, I received a phone call from her. She sounded a bit scared. "Help Sensei." She said to me. "What's wrong Rina?" I asked. "Well, I'm not sure. My spine is popping and adjusting by itself and making loud cracking noises. What should I do?" "Does it hurt?" I asked her. "No. It's just that my entire spine is adjusting and straightening right here at work. It's a bit distracting to say the least." She said. "That's fine. You've just received your attunements up your chakras releasing your Kundalini. Your spine is responding naturally by straightening. As long as it doesn't hurt or is uncomfortable, just let it continue. Go see your chiropractor and have him take a look as well." I suggested to her. "Ok, I will. I'll call you as soon as I get back."

Rina went to see her chiropractor that day. She called me later to tell me what he said. "You're not going to believe this." Rina told me. "Yes, I will. I've seen what Reiki can do." I replied. "Well, my chiropractor was blown away. He said my spine, which has had scoliosis since birth, has completely straightened in one day after 45 years of being curved. He asked me what I did differently and I told him I took Reiki. He was shocked and said where can I learn?" she told me. "No surprise Rina. Your Kundalini has been unleashed and is traveling up your spine. Your spinal condition is being healed. That's what happens with Reiki. Many mysterious things happen to people. Sometimes it's a physical healing like this, other times it's a huge emotional healing, still other times it can be a life event like a new job comes along, or other times a spiritual awakening occurs. It can even be an ending of something that needs to end, like a marriage, a job or a living situation. Reiki brings healing and change whenever it comes into our lives. For you, your spine is healing. Congratulations, I am so happy for you." Her spine straightened completely over the next few days and she was free of discomfort for the first time in her life.

After the required waiting period between classes so Rina could acclimate to the Reiki energy now coursing through her body, it was time for her to take Second

Degree Reiki. I knew things would really shift for her after that. But first we did some treatments to strengthen her organs, especially her one lung. Her body was going to be split open at the chest bone. She needed all the energetic support possible. We were working together one day when Rina began experiencing a soul retrieval. She saw a past life as a Captain in the Scottish Royal Army several hundred years ago. In this position she commanded a large troop of men. She observed herself as the Captain overhearing the men plotting to kill the King of Scotland. She was out of their sight so she thought they didn't see her. She was pondering this for a couple of days, trying to decide what action to take. Suddenly, as she watched this lifetime pass by her view, she saw the Captain be overtaken by his troop of men. They knew he had overheard them and had to kill him. They grabbed the Captain and carried him to a cliff and threw him down the rocks to the seashore. She saw herself in that life bouncing down the cliffside over rocks, striking her back and bones all over the rocks and breaking them. She saw her back break and twist as she rolled over and over, landing on the sand. Yet she was still alive but broken as she lay on the sandy beach. Her men climbed down the hillside to see if she was alive. When they saw she was, they grabbed fistfuls of sand and stuffed them into her mouth to suffocate her. And this is what finally killed her. As she told me this story, I remembered what the doctor had said when she was born into this life, that her lung was filled with sand!! Where would a small baby get a lung full of sand at one month old? From another life, that's where.

"I'm dying," she said to me as she watched this

lifetime. "What are your final thoughts as you left this world then Rina?" I asked her. "I felt so guilty for not saying something to the King in time. Now they will kill him and I could have prevented it. I was trying to figure out a way to save my men. Instead they turned on me. I felt responsible for the King's death. I'm feeling extreme guilt as I die, like I failed my duty as a Captain to my King." She replied, her face distorted in grief. "Then that is the guilt you brought to this life to heal, and that is why your lungs were filled with sand at birth, the sand your men put down your throat. It's why your spine curved and broke and your organs were twisted backward, just as they were when you were thrown down the rocks." I told her. She gasped. "You're right! O my God! I'm injured in this life the way I was injured in that life! What can we do?" she asked me. "You must forgive yourself for your actions then. You made a decision that cost your life, but you didn't know your men knew and would turn on you. You simply made a mistake, a judgment call. It was never intentional to hurt your King. Forgiving yourself unlocks the healing. Let it happen Rina." I moved to give her a deep Soul Reiki treatment and release the past life memory. I asked her to repeat to herself I love myself unconditionally, I forgive myself completely over and over until she felt the guilt, the pain and the memory leave her. She did that a long time, crying as she did it. After a while, she heaved a big sigh and the process seemed to complete itself. She said she felt much better. Her lung was getting stronger.

Rina took Second Degree Reiki. Ten days after the class, after waiting years for a lung, she received the call. A lung was waiting for her. A young man had died *and left his organs. She would be getting the lung from a healthy, young male who had died in a motorcycle accident. She sailed through the operation and completed her karma and had a very peaceful life after that. It was a happy ending.*

Reiki can heal past life karma because it's connected to the Akashic Records and the Universal Energy field that connects us all. All life experience is held in the field as trapped energy until we free it with love and forgiveness. Reiki frees all forms of trapped energy. We come back to finish things we couldn't in our old bodies when they give out. Whatever is left over to work on we bring to the next life to finish.

At this point in human evolution, we have the greatest possible opportunity to release trapped energy, cleanse out karma and awaken more rapidly than any other time in Earth's history. The Universe has aligned itself to support spiritual awakening, to end the dark age of materialism (Kali Yuga) and move us into the golden age of Aquarius, bringing back the Sacred Feminine energies. Everything is in alignment for the balancing, healing and awakening of the human soul. All you must do is allow it to happen. And when you do, you move into the Fifth Quadrant.

After you have completed the Fourth Soul quadrant of healing, you are introduced to the Fifth Quadrant, an expanded state of being now emerging everywhere on Earth. This is the dimension of your spiritual awakening. Once you have arrived there, your life will never be the same. You will begin to experience magical events around you. The boundaries of conditioned thought will begin to fall away and you will merge with universal consciousness. More and more miracles will happen. You will find that the laws of nature often are bypassed as things are manifested for you. You find synchronicities, serendipities and unexplained events begin to happen with regularity in your life. Your needs are fulfilled with only a thought. Your inner vision increases and you begin to know what's coming ahead for you. Not too far ahead, but just far enough to make the proper decisions. You have entered the Fifth Quadrant, this is where you will awaken to the Oneness of the Universe.

From the smallest particle to the largest galactic formation, a web of electrical circuitry connects and unifies all of nature and the Universe. There are no isolated islands in an Electric Universe.
~ *Thunderbolts of the Gods*

But before you can do that, you must release your ego. That ego takes form to show itself in the illusion you were living in before the Fifth Quadrant. To survive in a world of constricted, reduced consciousness, you have created a mask over the power of your True Self. We all have. As our divinity bursts out of the confines of suppressed consciousness, our old masks cannot contain it; they become outworn and must be discarded. I'm sure you can remember who you were at 16 years old. Then later when you were 25 you thought yourself so silly and immature at 16. Then you become 35 and laugh at the mistakes and ignorance you displayed at 25. And on through your life until at 55 you are looking back at the person that seemed so important to be at 30 or 40 years of age. But now, you are not even that person anymore. You have begun to shed your **Narcissistic Mask***, the mask of the ego we wear in life until we are ready to stand in our True Self.

The Narcissistic Mask is a false persona representing your ego that we create to make our way through the world that is still in denial and illusion. It's made up of charm, personality, coping mechanisms, fear, survival behaviors, humor, wittiness and whatever else the ego can come up with to avoid being exposed. For example, I knew a person who was extremely charming on the outside – attractive, funny, talented and intelligent and accomplished in many ways. But much of this was a show. When I got to know him a little better, privately he was child-like, terrified, selfish, demanding and irresponsible. The difference between his outer Narcissistic Mask and his wounded ego self was startling to behold. His Higher Self was nowhere to be found. He had a tremendous amount of personal work to do, but was completely attached to and identified with his Narcissistic Self instead of the beautiful, gifted person he really was. He bragged and flaunted this false persona proudly. His ego was ruling the day and he didn't even realize it. Inside he was still a scared little boy not fully in his power. Many of us are still scared children holding our early traumas close to our chests without knowing it. The traumas block us from fully self-actualizing. But the terror of facing our pain and fear is a strong motivator for hanging on to the Narcissistic Mask. This is why a later trauma can be a much needed wake-up call.

Your Narcissistic Mask cannot exist without the traumatic trance in place. When you begin to leave the trance and awaken to your True Self, your mask begins to dissolve. Your mask is an integral part of your personal traumatic trance, attached to it and codependent upon it. Until your trauma is healed, the mask serves the function of protecting you from your pain, your truth and your trauma. It has a very important purpose for a time, much like a scab over a wound. Without the scab, your wound can get infected. While the wound heals, the scab protects it from intrusion from germs. The same with your Narcissistic Mask. It's protecting you from feeling the scorching pain of your flaws and shame core which you are not ready to face. Enough healing must occur, and enough forgiveness and self-love must be present for you to drop the mask. Otherwise, you might become self-destructive, even suicidal. The average person does not carry enough self-love to face the truth of both their shame and their divinity without self-destructing. Our self-hatred is in the way. When you have acquired divine love, you will be comfortable in your True Self and not need the mask. But this is something that must be cultivated through spiritual practices. We are rarely born with enough love to love ourselves through life. This is why we become dependent on the love of others. But that moment when we are faced with the brilliance of our true divinity is the moment when we know if we've done our spiritual homework. We are strong enough to stand in our true spiritual power finally.

As I stated before, the traumatic trance is the unconscious state of living in the trance created by the traumatic trancebond. The traumatic trancebond, or traumatic bond, is the toxic bond that exists between one person and another person, or a group of persons, or a traumatic event that remains in place unconsciously and dictates the actions, reactions and feelings of that person for life, or until it becomes conscious. The traumatic trance is frequently accompanied by one or more addictions. Any forced attempt to break a traumatic trance will result in fiercely defensive behaviors by the entranced individual who is protecting the possibility of having to re-experience the original wound. They are not yet ready to surrender their ego, remove the Narcissistic Mask, and feel the pain.

The Trance victim's ego has created an entire world around the false self. The ego is deeply entrenched in this false self, which can often include an individual's long-time career and talents. Everything is riding on this person's investment into the False Self/Narcissistic Mask. When the Narcissistic Mask attaches itself to a person's life gifts and special talents, it can use these for personal gain and aggrandizement, wasting its divine potential. In contrast, when the True Self is attached to someone's gifts and talents, this is the authentic purpose of the Divine Self in action. It is acting from your dharma, your true soul purpose.

So, the goal is to detach the Narcissistic Mask from the ego, dissolve it along with the ego, and allow the soul's true gifts and purpose to regain their proper placement within the True Self. However, it is the Traumatic Trance's existence that blocks this from happening. As long as the trauma remains buried and unconscious, the individual remains entranced. This trauma then acts as the driving force of the ego, protecting the "wounded" ego from realizing the truth of the trauma, and healing into the True Self. This is where we begin the work of healing the trauma, the ego and the mask to reveal the jewel of the healed True Self within.

The Narcissistic Mask is tethered in place to the ego through a number of personality and behavior characteristics and beliefs, most of them created by the ego. These features act as a rudimentary scaffolding, if you will, that attaches to the false self. The more one practices these artificial, and often addictive, patterns of thought, action and belief, the stronger the false ego self becomes and the deeper the True Self is hidden from consciousness. The first steps to dissolving the Narcissistic Mask, and in turn, releasing the Traumatic Trance and becoming the True Self, are to begin to identify the patterns, behaviors and beliefs that tether the Narcissistic Mask in place to the false ego self. If you do this personal work diligently, the True Self can safely emerge and your True Dharmic Path be resumed wholeheartedly and successfully.

~~~~~~~~~~~~

The Stepping Stones
to
Soul Transformation

A Soul Transformation is always holistic. This is because all dis-ease, whatever form it takes, is also holistic. Until the deep soul issue is addressed, the condition won't go away. You must not overlook any aspect of your being. It will simply appear in another form somewhere in your life. Steps must be taken in every one of the four quadrants to fully heal. Below is a ***Basic Soul Transformation Blueprint****. This is the beginner's program. There is a more advanced version if you choose to go more deeply or work with me individually. You are entering a spiritual path. You will be laying down your illusions and exposing the lies. You will experience massive mental and emotional healing. Don't expect this to happen quickly. Realize that this is a lifelong journey. Start with the Basic Blueprint and move up when you've mastered each step.

Don't try to do everything at once, but make a good start. Go as slowly as you need to for your nature. Know that it takes 21 days to establish a habit, good or bad. And it takes 21 days to break it. You will be most tempted to stop your program in the first 21 days. This is when you must fight your demons off and make new, life-affirming choices. If you feel tempted to go back to old habits, go into prayer and meditation immediately and ask for help maintaining your new program. Then make those 21 days count, however, large or small your beginning is. For example, if you are giving up smoking and can't do it all at once, start by reducing your smoking habit. If you smoke two packs a day, go down to one pack. If you smoke three cigarettes a day, go down to one a day. Just taking a small step has power. After the first successful 21 days, start a new round and quit completely. When you have taken the plunge and are trying to improve yourself, pick smaller habits to break at first. When you succeed at those, it will give you strength and confidence to tackle the harder ones. Don't expect perfection from yourself because no one is perfect. There is always room for improvement. And don't beat yourself up, just keep going. Small victories will appear along the way. Savor them for the dry desert of the rest of the journey. There is ALWAYS an end to the process and victory at the end if you don't give up.

~~~~~~~~

Healing Trauma Meditation

Before beginning the Stepping Stones to Soul Transformation, take time to do some meditation designed to create space for healing trauma. Find a quiet place, somewhere private and alone. Shut down any distractions. If you like to meditate with music, put something on that's peaceful. A 528 Hz tone would be helpful. Sit comfortably and close your eyes. Go inward deeply and picture yourself inside your inner core self. Search around until you find your inner child. When you find him/her, approach slowly with gentleness and respect because she may be the traumatized child. Sit with her awhile in a peaceful, safe location and just be with her. After a few moments of quiet, tell her you would like to show her a place of safety. Ask if she wishes to go with you. Stay there until she is ready to go. Do not force her. You are redeveloping trust with your inner child who may fear you due to your unconsciousness and how that has hurt her. Take time to know her and respect her feelings. Do this as many times as you need to until the child trusts you and is willing to go with you. When she's ready, take her hand and walk her towards the "vault". The vault is the safe locked place where all memories, pleasant or unpleasant, are held. Show her to the door. Let her know that she only has to see whatever memories she is ready to see, nothing more. Let her know that the vault keeps the memories safe and away from her. She can put them back in and lock them up any time she wishes. Hand her the key to the huge steel door and tell her she can take a look now. Let her walk to the vault door and open it on her own. Ask her to take out whatever memories she wishes to work with right now. Watch as she reaches in and pulls out some scenes. Tell her to lock the vault securely again and walk back with her to the peaceful safe place you found her. Go over her memories with her, whatever they may be. If they are unpleasant, help her work through them. Tell her you will return regularly to help her work through these memories until she's feels she has processed them and is safe with them. Let her know she can take them back to the vault whenever she wants. Listen to her feelings and thoughts about these memories while you are meditating with her. When she is finished processing, walk her back to the vault and return the memories inside. Let her know that these memories can never come out and hurt her again because they are locked inside the vault and she holds the key. Leave the key with her and let her be in control of what, when and where she accesses the memories. Walk back to the peaceful place where you were sitting and sit down with her a while. Make sure she feels peaceful, then tell her you have to return to the world now. Tell her you will return to check on her regularly to see how she is doing. Let her know that when she is ready, you will return to help her access more memories. In doing this, you are re-establishing contact with your split-off traumatized child that does not trust the outer world, including you, her adult self. You must reconnect with these broken, hurt parts and create rapport and trust again to repair your inner damage. Do this regularly and you will see many pieces of fragmented soul parts begin returning to you. The process of integration can be safely undertaken this way. End the meditation by saying goodbye to her for now and slowly return to the conscious world. Sit still for a while to make sure you feel alright. Then move slowly out of the meditation. Do this meditation throughout your Steps to Soul Transformation whenever you need to. Keep contact with the inner child strong and healing throughout this process.

~~~~~~~~~

Action Step One ~ Physical, Mental, Emotional & Spiritual
Gather Your Healers

First choice would be to seek out an authentically trained Usui ReikiMaster with correct training in the original Reiki form. Find someone who understands how to move energy and heal the energy systems in the body. Find someone intuitive, awakened, light-based, dynamic, talented and unafraid to take you into the depths of your soul healing. Often a shaman can be that person since they are trained in soul healing. If they are not trained in energy healing, they cannot fully take you through the process, which is alchemical in nature. A skilled, trained energy practitioner will trigger the healing alchemy and move you more quickly through the process. Depending on the abilities of the person working with you, you may also need a counselor to help you work through the issues that surface, especially if trauma is present. Each practitioner is different. Some can work with trauma recovery; others do not include that in their work. Make sure your support system is in place as you begin the journey of your healing and awakening. Keep asking for help, God will send the right people to you.

Action Step Two ~ Spiritual
Build Sacred Space

Create an altar. Make it reflective of your soul and beliefs. Put items that are sacred to you on it. Sacred items have healing power and the ability to draw in protection and positive energy. Never put anything negative, dark or angry on an altar as it negates all the work you will be doing. Put things that bring you joy, love, peace and healing such as a rose quartz, a picture of a loved one, a crucifix, a holy symbol, a candle, a picture of a Saint, or a flower. Keep it clean. Sage it, put holy water on it, pray over it, or whatever else cleanses it from time to time. Place it somewhere safe and quiet, a central point of your home that brings you blessings. You will be using it daily from now on so make it holy. Get the spiritual ball rolling. Begin with a simple spiritual practice like asking for the healing of a loved one, or a blessing on your home. Ask for help from the Universe in healing your issues. Do this every day. That's a good start, but feel free to do more prayers, blessings, chants or meditations as suits you.

Action Step Three ~ Mental
Weed Your Garden

Continue your spiritual practice. Now it's time to clear your mind of any persistent negative thoughts or beliefs. Anything you are clinging to that is about doubt, shame, negativity, illness, self-loathing, fear, rage, etc. needs to be gone for a full Soul Transformation. I realize this is a tall order. It could take many years. However long it takes, just begin. Just imagine you own a large meadow. This meadow is filled with wildflowers. They look beautiful. But the meadow is also filled with weeds that choke out the wildflowers and cause them to die out. The same is true of your mind. Until you weed out the mental weeds of despair, doubt and self-destruction, the flowers of your soul cannot fully grow and bloom. Persistent thoughts create grooves in your brain and lead you to self-defeating thinking. They create what is known as thought forms, or thoughts that have solidified and are now running the show. They need to be broken up like a piece of calcified bone growing twistedly out of the side of your toe. The bone blocks you taking steps, so do thought forms. Persistent thought forms of hatred, anger, illness, death, or greed are like secret poisons in the body. They will eventually create disease. Love and truth will heal them. Bring them out into the light of day. They can be weeded just like a garden and new seeds of hope planted. Get a sheet of paper. Make two columns. In the left column, write down thoughts you repeatedly have that are not hope-filled, are negative, are filled with self-loathing and the like. For example, you may think about yourself, "I'm too fat." Or, "I'll never get a job." Or, "I don't have skills or talents to offer in the workplace." Or, "I'm not lovable." Or, "I'll always be sick." And so on. If these are deeply ingrained beliefs, especially ones that came from our parents, they sink into our subconscious mind. And it's our subconscious mind that directs our lives and creates our opportunities as it connects to the Universe of unlimited possibilities. And limiting beliefs will act as barriers to the realization of your dreams. So, weed your mental garden. In the right column, directly across from the limiting statements, write a new statement. Create a positive statement that completely wipes out the original negative statement. For example, if your negative statement was "I am unlovable", on the right column write "I am loved unconditionally and eternally at all times by the Holy Spirit." Or perhaps, "I love myself unconditionally." If your negative statement is, "I have no talents and can't ever find a job." Write, "I have unlimited skills available to me and will find the right position for me." And so on down your list until you have changed ALL of your negative beliefs into positive statements about yourself. There can be no hint of negativity or doubt in your new statements. After you have completed re-writing your statements, begin meditating and repeating the new statements for a minimum of 21 minutes. Also, if you know Second Degree Reiki, give yourself a mental treatment….every day from now on. Weeding your garden can be a long process. Do it as often as it needs to be done, especially if you find yourself dwelling on negativity again. Get right in and meditate on these if you find yourself doing that. Eventually, with discipline and consistency, you will find that you no longer think that way or stay stuck in those thoughts. And when the mind begins to change, so does your outer circumstances. When your mind changes about yourself, your body also begins to heal. If you can get regular Reiki mental treatments, do so. Keep your affirmations on your altar. Put a sacred object on them. Ask the Universe to help you with weeding your mental garden.

Action Step Four ~ Mental
Meet Your False Self

Continue your spiritual practices. Make a list of beliefs, actions, habits, behaviors, and characteristics that you believe tether you to your Narcissistic Mask/Ego as explained earlier in this chapter. After doing this, list steps you can take to dissolve these attachments to the Narcissistic Mask and its destructive patterns, such as ending an entrenched habit of lying, bragging or overspending to comfort yourself. Begin to take these steps and in doing so, cease any behaviors from your list that are keeping your Narcissistic Mask in place, and preventing you from realizing your True Self and potential. If you know Second Degree Reiki, give yourself a Mental & Emotional treatments emphasizing separating from your Mask/Egoic self. Or have your Reiki healer work on you. Work on dissolving the attachments to them during the treatment. Then put your list on your altar inbetween times you are working on these issues. Place sacred items on top of the list such as a quartz crystal, a cross, a photo of a loved one, an Om symbol, a heart, or a photo of someone holy to you. Whatever is sacred to you will have power to heal and bless your life. Ask for help from the Universe in healing your issues. Do this for 21 days. Then rest for 7 days but continue your spiritual practices.

Action Step Five ~ Spiritual
Find Your True Self

Continue your spiritual practice. Don't restart the bad habit; just let your progress sink in. Give yourself credit for a step taken and accomplished. Then begin meditating on your True Self. During meditation, ask it to step forward. Allow your True Self to identify itself and its true characteristics. Pay attention to your inner voice, listen to the answers and do not judge with your rational, egoic mind. Just allow your inner truth to surface slowly like bubbles to the surface of a pond. Eventually, their truth will become evident to you. Write down what comes up as the aspects of the True Self. Then later, after making regular, strong contact with your True Self where you feel the connection clearly, ask your True Self to identify the Traumatic Trance and the Traumatic Trancebond's origins within yourself. Write down what your True Self tells you in meditation. During the subsequent meditations, when you have established a strong, safe connection with your True Self, ask your True Self to begin safely dissolving the Traumatic Trance and Trancebond. Write down what happens during this process. Seek help. Don't try to do this alone. This is where you may need the most help. Discuss it with your healer, counselor or shaman or whoever is guiding you through this process. Do this for 21 days. Place this list on your altar inbetween times you are working on it. Put a sacred object on top of the list. Ask for help from the Universe in healing your issues. Rest the process for 7 days.

Do your Healing Trauma Meditation here and from now on for much suppressed energy will rise from this point.

Action Step Six ~ Spiritual
Connect in Sacred Dialogue

You must learn to create a dialogue with your True Self, (also known as your Higher Self) a *Sacred Dialogue** that reaches deep into your soul and awakens long dormant parts of yourself. You may need to go somewhere far away, be alone for a while, or follow your passion to be able to do this. The suppressed, false illusory world we live in blocks your soul's emergence. It remains asleep until you bring it to the surface. You must speak to your sleeping soul as if you are the teacher, the parent, the guru, the coach, the loved one, the personal trainer and the Buddha. There won't always be someone to do this for you. Become your own personal Yoda. You might be the only one in your corner. So, when no one else is there, you must undertake the resuscitation of your lost, stolen or broken spirit. You must learn to dialogue with your inner self. Shamans know how to do this, as do spiritual teachers, mystics, monks and other sages of the soul. Become one. Develop your spiritual strengths by entering into the secret labyrinth of your soul to find yourself again. Use Reiki creatively here by sending healing to your Higher Self. This opens the channels of connection for dialogue.

Sacred Dialogue with your Higher Self

I am now speaking to your Higher Self, the True Self, present eternally. By the power vested in me, I command the ego to step aside to allow healing and love in. Here is the truth you must grasp ~

You are living imprisoned behind the Narcissistic Mask. It is safe to step free now. You will be loved and cared for when you release this Mask. It does not serve you, but cages your spirit, your love and your power, and sabotages your life, your dreams and your destiny. Your Mask came into being within your Mother's womb, in other lifetimes and experiences there, and during current trauma to serve your Soul in this sojourn until you were ready. It came into being because you were afraid and believed you were separate from the Holy Spirit. The many shocks you received stunned your Divine Soul, causing it to retreat into a safer place, many moons away behind your Mask, until it felt safe enough to return & emerge. You did not know then that you were Divine, eternal and that it was impossible to hurt you. The Mask came into being to hold the shocks until you could process them effectively, to hold them apart from your Divinity until your body, mind and spirit could unify sufficiently to experience the pain of the truth. Your Mask held them there until you realized Who You Were, the Divine I AM, the One who dissolves all untruth for truth and emerges as pure love.

Your Mask has served as the skeleton of your personality, giving structure to the ego face you choose to give the world. It is only one phase of emergence. It acts as a clumsy apparatus around your soul body through which your person speaks, works, creates, lives and functions as the false self. It is a poor substitute for Who You Really Are. Behind it resides the True Self waiting to emerge. You have asked to come forth, I respond with healing. Let it happen.

Your Narcissistic Mask is one of the last stage ego structures to form to protect and block the Divine Self. Just before fully emerging, the Divine Self begins to penetrate the ego structure and personality. When the True Self begins diluting Your Mask, a highly inflated sense of ego develops. The ego is beginning to know who the True Self is and does not want it to emerge and replace it. As devious as the ego always is, it uses the knowledge of the True Self's presence for its own purpose, instead of stepping aside and letting it emerge. This Mask persona, although very powerful and at times highly beneficial to humanity, is tainted by remaining ego structures, trauma, lies, brainwashing, contracts, vows, karma, cultural beliefs, theological beliefs, biochemistry, addiction, lust, extreme selfishness and other functions of the imperfect ego as it attempts to survive it's coming destruction. This can, at times, be the most selfish, destructive stage of the ego, hence its name – the Narcissistic Mask. Much damage can be done to the soul and to others at this stage.

Your Narcissistic Mask is characterized by extreme narcissism. It is intensely focused on the self, its goals, its pleasures & comforts, its addictions, its desires, its belief in its invincibility, grandeur, and importance over others, specialness, superiority and even its existence…which is blatantly false. Nowhere are the virtues of charity, compassion, service, simplicity, selflessness or humility present in the Narcissistic Mask. At this stage, your Narcissistic Mask has inflated to its greatest point and height, with the most pride available. At this point, at its height, your Narcissistic Mask begins to implode, dissolve and melt away, like an over-inflated balloon that cannot contain anymore hot air of falseness. The air begins to sputter out and it spins around in violent bursts as it dies out. In short, pride goeth before a fall. But the fall is into the arms of the Divine…

The Sacred Dialogue continues….

Your Narcissistic Mask can survive a long time, and will divert its attention to other projects to keep itself alive a long time, give itself a new shot in the arm for another go-round as a function of the dying ego. Some people live there whole lifetimes. But…the moment you asked for Divinity, for your True Self to emerge…you set in motion the dissolution of the Narcissistic Mask. In other words, you have asked for this and it has begun. The journey is underway and may be rocky, sudden, unstable, even violent, but always, always leads you to your True Self.

Your Narcissistic Mask is obvious for others to see, but not for you to see. You are always the last person to recognize its presence and will often deny its existence long into the process of its dissolution. That is the voice of ego trying to convince you to hang onto its false persona as long as possible, fearing its own demise. Don't listen to the Ultimate Liar. I have seen it a long time, I am happy you wish it to go so your True Self can finally emerge. We all see your true beauty.

The Narcissistic Mask is only present where there has been trauma to the Divine Self-Image of great enough strength to block you from seeing your Divinity. Because of this trauma, fear and separation are generated, which in turn signal your ego to create a false self to stand in place until You show up. But the ego places a high value on its position in that place and will not relinquish it easily. Prepare for a struggle. The process of dissolution of the Narcissistic Mask isn't always pleasant.

In short, your Mask covers your pain and your trauma as well as your True Self. In order to get to your True Self, you must run the gauntlet through the pain and trauma and face it down, stripping it of its power over you. There are no shortcuts, no quickie treatments, no shots, no pills or fake doctors or gurus to breeze you through this. They will say it's going to be easy; this is a lie. The true path is this......You must become a Warrior of Truth and Power. You must defeat the false truths your Mask has come to represent for you. You must believe more strongly in your True Self than your Narcissistic Mask self. And you must recognize the difference. This is the only way you can help others. Otherwise, you will be teaching narcissism and ego. You must strip yourself down to the truth. This process has now begun for you. Your power, your dharma and your joy begin at the end of your comfort zone.

One of the aspects of your Narcissistic Mask is addictions. One of Your Mask's addictions is comfort. This path is about humility, renunciation, simplicity and no ostentatiousness. You are being stripped of your worldliness to serve Spirit, but ONLY EXACTLY AS YOU HAVE REQUESTED WE DO SO TO YOU. NOTHING IS DONE TO YOU WITHOUT YOUR CONSENT AND REQUEST.

The final part of this lesson is this...prepare to be destroyed.

As you embark on this path of ego death and renunciation, when you begin to look at the True Self square on, it will annihilate you...the false you....unless....you can embrace and absorb enough unconditional love deep into your soul to love and preserve the Glorious True Self you see. As God said to Moses on Mt. Sinai in the form of the Burning Bush, "You cannot look fully upon me now for it would destroy you." The Divinity you truly are is greater than the Narcissistic Mask can bear. Your Mask will be destroyed, and with it, your ego. There may be pain. I'll be there to hold you through it. On the other side is your Divinity...I await you there.

Take it one day at a time, one moment at a time, one atom at a time and always, always, always, take refuge in the Holy Spirit at every moment, as Amma, Jesus, Mohammed, Krishna, Mary, Quan Yin, Buddha, and all forms I take to hold and love you. I am always there... .....bless you on your journey Beloved Child.

Continue your spiritual practices. Ask the Universe for help and guidance throughout this process.

~~~~~~~

Then we come to the advanced action steps. You will need time to do all this. It should never be undertaken in a short period of time. The unraveling of the Narcissistic Mask may take months, even years, because this is your ego self you are challenging. It's going to fight back. So don't rush it. But if you are feeling ready, the next steps are very important to fully detaching from your Narcissistic Mask. You can't fully let the ego and its mask go if you are still full of addictions. So, your recovery from the ego attachments will include the next steps. These steps are major and will likely require professional assistance to get through, especially if it's drug or alcohol addiction you are dealing with. You will need a skilled addictions specialist to assist you with these. Never detox from a serious addiction without professional addictions help. It can be life-threatening. This is one of those times when you should consult a medical doctor for a physical as well before undertaking a comprehensive physical program of detoxing. Also consult a naturopath for an assessment of nutritional deficiencies within your body that might affect your overall recovery.

~~~~~~~~

Action Step Seven ~ Physical
Purify Yourself

Continue your spiritual practice daily. As much as possible, begin a purified diet. Health begins with what you eat, or don't eat. Begin to eat an organic diet free of adulterated foods, sugars, toxins, GMOs, chemicals, pesticides, hormones, steroids and similar poisons. If you can give up meat, do so. At the very least eat organic meat. Factory farmed meat is the source of more disease than almost any single food on Earth. It creates heart disease, obesity, and many other illnesses. Take a hard look at your eating habits and begin a detox program. If there has been trauma, there will be food addictions used to mask it. Perhaps other addictions as well. But with sexual trauma, there is always an eating disorder lurking somewhere. Are you binging on carbohydrates? Are you addicted to sugar in everything? Sugary drinks, candy, gooey desserts? Do you gravitate towards foods that are starchy? These are signs of white flour/sugar addiction and that addiction is the addiction of the sexually abused. It's the first addiction we develop because we can eat these things as a child. If you were sexually abused very early in childhood, we get hooked early on to sugar to endure the violation to our bodies. This one can last a lifetime because no one will arrest you for eating a doughnut. Unless you are robbing a doughnut shop while the police are there having their doughnuts. As soon as you stop eating white flour, sugar and most carbohydrates, you will begin to have a withdrawal and may begin remembering your trauma. At the very least, you will feel the feelings of your trauma. You will need support during this period as it can be very difficult. Seek a healer, counselor, shaman or other individual skilled in trauma recovery. Reiki is extremely powerful in releasing and healing trauma gently and swiftly, so receive Reiki treatments as often as possible. Ask the Universe to help you with your issues.

~~~~~~~~~

Without abstinence from these foods, you will not heal the trauma completely. And then, if your food addiction is more advanced, you may have taken it a step too far into this territory. Are you obese? Is it hard for you to stop eating? Do you go for huge meals like fast food burgers, fries and milkshakes every day? Are you the big guy on your block? Does everyone gravitate around you because of your size and it makes you feel important? These are some of the symptoms of early trauma that have created your Narcissistic Mask. You use the "Big Guy" persona to mask your inner pain. If you were to stop your food addiction and lose weight, you may not feel powerful anymore. The guys may not hang around you as they once did. You will have to learn to love yourself. Or if you are a young, overweight woman, you've come to believe that if you lose weight, you will become the target of sexual predators like you were as a child. Sometimes there are other addictions covering your trauma too. Maybe you are the "hot guy" on the block with a steroid and sex addiction to feed your empty soul…big Narcissistic Mask attachment there. Or are you the life of the party person who brings the booze and fun wherever you go in an attempt to buy friendship? But when the booze is gone, the party's over and the hot girls and guys have disappeared, will they stay to love you for who you really are? These are all deeply buried feelings and fears that hide under layers of fat, addictions and other behaviors. And perhaps being overweight has become your safety shield, your power mechanism or your hiding place. But your trauma is showing through. Your health is being affected. And your power is not in your own hands. Your addiction has you.

~~~~~~~~~

Action Step Eight ~ Physical
Achieve Holistic Sobriety

Keep doing your spiritual practices. If you have other serious addictions, such as drugs and alcohol, now is the time to let them go. Give up alcohol, cigarettes and any other addictions. These addictions may also be masking trauma. It's impossible to progress holistically and spiritually while in the grip of addictions. The alternative is illness and possible overdose. As I said before, get professional help with the addiction healing process but you must begin it. Cold turkey rarely works for hardened addictions. Much more is required for addiction recovery. The first step is sobriety. **A Soul Transformation will not occur if you are actively engaged in an addiction.** Addiction is a holistic illness - the mind, body, emotions and spirit are all sick and out of balance. They require comprehensive care. Learning Reiki assists with sobriety like nothing else I have seen. It reconnects the addict with their spirituality which in turn begins to heal the addiction and end cravings. As an Addictions Counselor, I created an advanced program of recovery for addicts and alcoholics which I recommend for people attempting to heal holistically. The program is my **Reiki Recovery Project**. For now, do this for 90 days continuously before resting. You will not be picking up your addictions again, but you can rest from all the other exercises at 90 days. Do not stop your spiritual program. Do not stop your meditation or prayers. Continue your program of healing and transformation. Don't drift from your goals and practices, just rest a bit when you need it. Resume your exercises, keeping your lists and putting them on the altar. Ask the universe to help you every day.

Action Step Nine ~ Physical
Strengthen Your Temple

Keep doing your spiritual practices. Begin an exercise regimen. You don't have to become the next Arnold Schwarzenegger. There are many simple possibilities. Start with walking and stretching every day. Find a yoga routine that works and do it at home. Practice Tai Chi in your living room. Take a dance class. Do some Jazzercise. Or join a gym and learn a routine that includes weight-bearing exercises. But get a professional trainer to start you off. Never try to lift weights or do too much if you are out of shape. Use your common sense. If you can't afford a gym and want to keep it simple, walk an hour a day and do floor exercises at home. There are many exercise programs available. The increased blood flow and oxygen will begin to heal your body, mind and spirit even if your movement is limited. If all these options are too difficult for you, sit in a chair and exercise if you can. Once you've started, you will gain energy and strength. The health of the body will stimulate the mind to heal and vice versa. Ask the Universe to help you along the way. Make sure your body is ready for exercise so getting a medical physical is wise.

Action Step Ten ~ Physical & Emotional
Release Toxic Energy

Keep doing your spiritual practices. Along with Reiki, start getting different types of bodywork to complement your energy and soul work. Your body will begin to release the toxic energy in the form of emotional release, sometimes expelling toxins through vomiting, rashes, colds, etc. Bodywork helps to move the energy out of the body safely and more quickly. Because I had received so much violence into my bodily tissues, I required many years of bodywork to extricate it. Reiki and bodywork together go a very long way to healing stored trauma. My sacrum was still fractured, swollen and bruised 40 years after the sexual abuse ended but bodyworkers and healers healed it. Reiki healed my emotions, mind and broken heart as well as my body. Chiropractic is a valuable tool for keeping the flow of energy balanced in your body's system. There are many excellent forms of bodywork, but for trauma I found that *Myo-Fascial Release Work**, and *Cranial-Sacral Therapy** were the most helpful in moving the pain energy out of the body. However, it's important to understand that bodywork is far more traumatic and forceful than Reiki. When the trapped energy is released, it can sometimes hurt as it comes out because it contains long-held pain. Some people will not be able to handle the sudden release of trauma that can accompany these two forms of therapy. Additionally, if there is severe trauma, the client will need immediate counseling upon releasing the trauma through bodywork. Be sure you have your support system in place before doing deep bodywork. For the more seriously traumatized individuals, Reiki will be the best healing tool available as it is pain-free and without body manipulations of any kind. In the case of Cranial-Sacral Therapy, I have found that it will release trauma stored in the brain, brain stem, spine, and sacrum, including bringing up suppressed memories. But it can be very traumatic to someone with chronic pain. A skilled practitioner is required to release the pain more gently. Monitor your sensitivity carefully. Don't push yourself before you are ready.

Action Step Eleven ~ Physical
Live Naturally

Keep doing your spiritual practices. Live as much off the grid as possible. The earth's electro-magnetic field has been compromised by electricity and power poles, nuclear power, computers, TV, Radio, satellites, driving in cars, pollution, chemicals, cement, and many other pollutants that interfere with the Earth's natural magnetic field. The more electricity, computers, TV, etc. that you use, the more your electro-magnetic field is impacted negatively. This, in turn, can impact your health and halt your spiritual progress. When the field is interfered with, your own energy field is compromised and your yin/ yang energy will be out of balance. Additionally, your intuition and awareness are dulled. Install solar and learn to charge your phones and other technological products with solar. Stay away from processed foods as much as possible for they are contaminated with GMOs, steroids, antibiotics, food dyes, preservatives, formaldehyde, aspartame and other toxic chemicals. Grow a garden and eat as much organic, natural food as possible. Walk in nature whenever possible. Put your feet in the soil, the sand and the sea, and let the Earth's energy come into your feet and root chakras and empower you. Purchase and sleep on a magnet pad to restore your electro-magnetic field. Drink alkalized, magnetized water. Cleanse the energy field of your home with Reiki, sage and prayers and chanting.

Action Step Twelve ~ Physical & Mental
Exit the Matrix of Mind Control

Stop watching TV and listening to the radio as much as possible. Don't overuse social media. There are mind control programs in place in all forms of media, including social media. You are being brainwashed by the Lilly Wave brainwashing program whenever you turn on your cellphone, radio or TV. In the case of your phones, they emit radiation as well that can cause cancer when held next your head too long. There are other frequencies being tested on us through these devices. When you listen to music through your radio or these technologies, your brain is receiving massive amounts of 440 kHz Devil's Tone frequency which is impacting your pineal gland, your brain, your emotions, your stress level and your ability to grow in consciousness and be self-aware. Your mind is being segmented, portioned and compartmentalized. Strive for unity within your being at all levels. You can begin listening to music that is created in the key of love, 528 kHz, which can be found on the internet or ordered on-line. There is an online radio station devoted only to 528 kHz music where all the music has been rekeyed into the key of love. Most all of your favorite songs are available there. Abstain from all media that contains these dissonant frequencies designed to harm your brain, health and spiritual growth. Avoid excessively violent or sexual media content as it lowers your vibration and spiritual frequency, making your immunity weaker and your mind open to negative suggestion. Meditate daily and it will mitigate the energies filtering into your consciousness. Ask the Universe to help you with your healing.

~~~~~~~~

Here is where you will have to begin another aspect of healing your ego/mask. The time has come to face your shadow self. I spoke earlier of facing and acknowledging the shadow. I also discussed the problem with wetiko, or denial of the shadow altogether. As I said, there is a distinct difference from being a positive person in life and from denying you have a shadow at all. Apples and oranges. I encourage you to take a positive stance on life, believe in your future and work towards your goals. But you will be totally unable to do this if you are in denial of your shadow. If you wish to progress in life, turn and face your shadow and begin to heal it.

The shadow self differs from the Narcissistic Mask in that it's usually more hidden and unconscious to us, and usually less dramatic. That is unless you are a full-scale criminal or sociopath, and we have a lot of those running the world today. The Narcissistic Mask is most prevalent in people with serious trauma. They have created a huge outer persona to hide the inner shame and wound. It's more obvious to others who see the grandstanding and braggadocio that often accompany it. Their mask isn't really hidden from others, only from them. But for the average person who has had a fairly stable upbringing and life, the shadow is harder to see and more likely to be deep in the background. Your shadow self will motivate you to do things like steal from your business partner secretly or cheat on your spouse. Or even more minor things like procrastination, laziness, overeating, cheating on tests at school, or lying to family members. The shadow self emerges from a belief system that diligence, integrity and truth are not enough to make it in the world and that shady behavior is the only way to survive. Faith in divine order and the support of the Universe is missing. For this reason, the shadow of this planet is huge since most everyone has some aspects of shadow. The range is vast of course from minor to serious.

The person who has the character to always be honest and behave with integrity is less common. And it's likely that whoever behaves this way believes in themselves and has a relationship with God in some form. Because once you have a strong relationship with God, whatever your faith, you know you will be provided for. All you need to do it is live sacredly and in integrity. Life becomes much simpler then. You live to meet your obligations, give service and respect God and others. All this striving and ego strategizing falls away. You see the truth in a glaring and clear light. You are connected to everyone else and everything you do impacts everyone else. Suddenly you see it's your responsibility to be accountable and respectful, as it is everyone's.

Are you ready to do this work and discover your True Self and the potential held captive there? Can you face your shadow? If you can make your shadow patterns conscious, they will naturally decay and dissipate in the light of day. If you keep them hidden, they will continue to rule your life and your accomplishments, limiting them. This is akin to the compartmentalizing of the mind that I explained in earlier chapters. The main purpose behind the elite doing this to us is to prevent us from accessing our power held within our shadows. If they can make our divinity invisible to us by segmenting it into a forgotten corner of our minds, we never rise to our real power and throw off their dominance. It is the recognition and removal of the denied shadow that opens the door to reclamation of your personal power. It's time to reclaim ourselves and this planet for good.

Action Step Thirteen ~ Emotional
Heal Your Shadow

Continue your spiritual practice daily. It's time to withdraw your projection of your faults, lies and fear onto others and return home to your heart for healing. Get honest with yourself. This time, write down shadow behaviors, even the most minor of them such as procrastination, and begin to examine how those are linked to your lack of faith in yourself to accomplish any task at hand. You were born with the tools to complete the jobs placed in front of you. Why don't you believe you can do it? People may have interfered with your gifts, whether they were parents, teachers or others who may not have had faith in you. They may have projected their fears, shortcomings and pain onto you. This may have caused you to develop similar doubts and fears about yourself and your ability to survive in the world. As a result, you may have created and hidden your shadow behaviors from yourself so you could survive. This is different than weeding your mental garden or removing the mask. This has more to do with shadow behaviors, your dark side, that you may be hiding from the world but engage in when no one is looking. Bring them up to the surface. Meditate on them. Make them conscious and write them down. Look at them, own them. Place your list on the altar. Put a sacred object on top of it. Ask for help from the Universe in healing your issues.

Action Step Fourteen ~ Emotional & Spiritual
Create Your Web of Power

Continue with your spiritual practice daily. After you have written down the shadow behaviors, begin to connect them to their origins. Maybe you began cheating at math because your Dad was a math genius and ridiculed your math skills. Maybe you were abused when small so you began choosing unhealthy partners in life. Perhaps a role model told you that you would never amount to anything so you developed bad habits of self-sabotage. Maybe you watch too much TV to escape your responsibilities in life. Make a large inter-connected web on a big sheet of paper. Write down each shadow behavior, where you think it may have originated from, and the name (if there is one) of the person who catalyzed the beginning of this behavior. If it caused a cascade of behaviors, connect them like a spider web one to the other so the pattern becomes clear to you. Be honest. If you started it by yourself out of selfishness, laziness, greed or whatever, own it. Write it down and put your own name next to it. Connect the dots. See the pattern emerge and how one thing led to another. See what shape and direction it takes. It will help you follow the thread back to wholeness when returning to your healed self. Then color it in lightly with colors so you can still read the behavior and the names connected to them. You can make it look like something if you want, an animal, a monster, a plant, or a scary person. You've just identified your shadow self. Now end your denial, own your shadow and make the necessary changes in your behavior. Forgive yourself along the way whether anyone else does or not. You won't awaken or progress into the Fifth Quadrant if you haven't brought in enough self-love. Place your shadow web on the altar. Put sacred objects on top of it. Ask for help from the Universe in healing your issues. Voila. You've begun your Soul Transformation.

Action Step Fifteen ~ Mental
Finding Your Truth

Continue your spiritual practice daily. Make a list of beliefs you were taught as a child by your family, your school, your church or anywhere else that was significant to you. They can be beliefs about the world, about life, about your family, your school, your abilities, your appearance, or anything else about yourself or another. For example, I was taught in school that Indians attacked the settlers for no reason and killed many of them. Later I learned it was the other way around. Maybe you were taught that you were ugly or stupid and believed that your whole life. Write it down. Maybe you were taught that a certain race of people were bad. Write it down. Maybe you were taught that women were inferior and should stay home, or vice versa, that all men were bad. Maybe you were taught that you should always be afraid. Perhaps you were even taught one of your parents was honest when in reality they were committing fraud and thievery. Write down whatever your early beliefs and myths were. Now that you are an adult, examine these teachings. Are they still correct? Or did you learn that some of them were false? Make a new list. At the top of the list put two columns, one that is headed by the word TRUE, and the other that is headed by the word, MYTH. After you've decided which of your beliefs are still true, put them under the column headed TRUE. Those that you now realize are myths, put those under the heading MYTH. Spend some time meditating on this list. Ask your soul to discard any beliefs that aren't true. Spend some time letting your mind release the falsehoods. See them go. Then ask your soul to bring the truth to you. For this part you will meditate many, many times, listening for the still, small voice of your soul speaking. Cultivate the voice of truth within you. Soon it will be easy to hear. Place your list upon your altar. Put a sacred object on it. Ask the Universe to help you heal your issues.

Action Step Sixteen ~ Mental, Emotional & Spiritual
Establishing Your Power

<u>Continue your spiritual practice daily</u>. Then one by one, write a statement of personal empowerment to the person who hurt you or triggered your shadow behavior. Write down how you feel about what they did to you and how it affected your life. Write that you are done with the damage they caused in your life and you ready to be whole. Inform them you are reclaiming your power. Then bring this statement into ceremony. Create a sacred space in the form of a ceremony. Make it a circle with a candle, or other things that feel sacred to you. Be sure you aren't disturbed. Meditate or pray for your Angels or guides or Holy Ones to join you in your sacred space. Surround it with the Violet Flame of purification and protection. After the space has been established and it's safe, pure and closed, call the offender's soul into the circle as though he/she were in the room. Tell them to step through the light of Christ for purification as well. Imagine their soul is seated before you. Greet them respectfully and tell them you have something to say to them. Read the statement out loud to them. It's rare, but if it's possible to read the statement directly to the person who caused the problem without harming someone, do so. Don't have any expectations of apologies or amends. You are doing this for yourself and your healing. It helps if they apologize but don't count on it. Their reaction is immaterial to your healing. This process will work to heal you anyway. You can then walk past that person with your power reclaimed forever. Read your statement and claim your power. It's not a discussion or a debate; if the offender is present, he/she is not allowed to speak unless it's an apology or unless you wish them to. It's your healing ceremony. After you have spoken, if you are ready, let the offender know you forgive them and thank them for the lesson. The longer you hold onto the hurt, the longer they have your power. Let them go right away if possible. Dismiss their spirit from your ceremony. Send the person out of the room if they are physically present. Then release the energy of the offense. Close your eyes and visualize yourself cutting the strands of the web that connected you to that person. Visualize fresh air and water and the Violet Flame washing those connecting points clean. In your vision, weave some new fresh strands where that person once was, free of any toxic connections. Tie those strands to a new, energetic web that you are weaving. Do this with each behavior and person. Create a new, balanced, healed energetic web of life and love for yourself free of toxic behaviors. Like a spider would care for its own web, keep repairing and rebuilding your new web whenever necessary. If it's your own self who caused the behavior, you will be encountering and challenging your own shadow self in your sacred circle. You will have to work at disciplining the lower part of you that wants to hurt yourself or others. This is likely to be the hardest behavior to change as your shadow self will be tempted to return to the bad behavior. After each ceremony of healing, burn the statements so you aren't tempted to take up resentments and revenge against these offenders again. Be done with it completely. Take the ashes and wash them away symbolically in water somewhere. Try to abstain from the old behaviors no matter what. After 21 days, the grip of the habit is broken. After that, it's up to you to enforce the changes and not slip back into the damaging behaviors. The longer you go without the behavior, the stronger your higher self will become and the easier it will be to grow, change and awaken. Give yourself Reiki mental & emotional treatments whenever possible. Place your new web of energy and support on the altar. Put a sacred object on it. Do this for 21 days. Rest for 7 days. Ask for help from the Universe in healing your issues.

Action Step Seventeen ~ Spiritual & Emotional
Healing Your Past

Keep doing your spiritual practices. Now make a list of wrongs and bad behaviors you have committed against others. Perhaps you are the one who has created a shadow in someone else. Your own shadow will not want to acknowledge this. Do it anyway. Then make amends to those you have offended whenever possible. The bravest and most likely to awaken are those who acknowledge their shadow behaviors towards another. Facing those, and the damage you may have caused, and making amends is the most powerful step towards spiritual awakening and total healing. The rewards for this step are enormous. Your shame core will wither up and die. Self-love will enter your heart. You will learn to forgive yourself. As you forgive yourself, even more love enters your being. As that happens, you will be able to share even more love with others. At this point, a peace that surpasses all understanding will begin to arrive. You will learn that to be forgiven, you must forgive, and that forgiveness opens all other doors to love.....God's love and the love of others. If you are attuned to Reiki, use a Long Distance treatment and access your past self, then give your past self a Reiki Mental & Emotional treatment. Place your list on the altar and put a sacred object on top of it. Ask for help from the Universe in healing your issues.

Action Steps Eighteen ~ Spirituality
Anchoring Your Spirituality

Find a spiritual path and begin a daily spiritual practice. To completely heal holistically, the final step is to make the spiritual connection with the energy that empowers the Universe we all live in and are connected to. Then you are never empty again. Every person has a different orientation to life, to their culture and to God. Choose that which appeals to your soul's innermost belief. This is your decision…. not your parents, your spouse, or your church/synagogue/mosque/ temple leader's. What is spiritual for a Native American will not be the same for a Christian or Buddhist. What is Allah to a Muslim will not be the same to a Hindu or Jew. No one can make this decision for you. Make sure you honor the Goddess who created us all in your practice. She has been long forgotten. Her time has come. We now include her in all our power ceremonies, and in doing so you awaken your own inner Goddess and reclaim that divine loving energy to heal your soul. During the course of your meditations and contemplations as you do the other steps, listen for the still, quiet inner voice that is your soul speaking to you. Take direction from yourself. Find the spiritual practice that suits you but that will connect you to the energy that empowers us all, and to all other life forms on Earth and in the cosmos. We are never separate from one another; be sure to choose a path that unites you with humanity and the Universe. Once you find this inner direction, follow it diligently. Create a spiritual practice that honors this voice, your soul and your heart. As you practice all these steps, and cement them with your spiritual practices, your soul will begin to heal, grow and awaken. Many problems will fall away and a new peace will arrive.

Action Step Nineteen ~ Spiritual & Emotional
Ceremony of Forgiveness & Healing

Create a ceremonial circle for forgiveness and healing. Visualize the Violet Flame circling it. Nothing but those filled with love can enter your sacred circle, all are purified by the Violet Flame. Place sacred objects in your circle. Have music playing such as the Om, or the Heart Sutra. Place white candles around and light them. Scent the circle with Frankincense, Sandalwood or Rose oil. Bring the lists of things you have discovered about yourself that may be negative or hurtful. Prepare to read it aloud and be ready to release these behaviors for good. Also be ready to apologize to the souls of anyone you may have hurt. Begin your ceremony. Call those souls you've hurt into the circle and make your amends to them. Read the Prayers of Detachment and Release and Prayer of Forgiveness below to them. Release them. Continue on making your statements and prayers to those who harmed you in any way. Be ready to release them. Say your two prayers below with each person. Then release the energies of darkness from your past to the universe for healing. Surround them with Angels and Angelic light and let them go. Do not try to stay attached to them. See them leaving. See the connections dissolving and the energy transforming into light. Then visualize yourself going into a deep sacred pool prepared for you. This pool is tended by Angels who have prepared it with sacred oils and flowers for your purification. Step down into the pool. Dip yourself fully under the water before coming up and floating on the surface. Float there a while. Meditate on your new liberated, purified soul and its divine purpose. Repeat the prayers as often as necessary until you feel fully released and purified. Remain there until peace has entered your spirit.

Prayer of Detachment and Release

I sever permanently all bonds, ties, vows, contracts, promises, oaths and forms of bondage made to the servants of the Underworld, the secret societies, entities or beings, satanic forces and other Lords and Ladies of Darkness at any point in my soul's sojourn, this life or past lives. I burn those connections with the Violet Flame. I take back my soul, energy, power, truth, dharma, light and love from you now to be cleansed and utilized for my Divine Purpose. You have no more power, influence or control over any aspect of my life or the lives of any human on Earth. All past hurtful or negative connections to me and other humans are permanently broken and dissolved. I release all ties to you and your beliefs and actions. I take my soul, energy, light and love for healing and purification to those Angels, Goddesses and Masters assigned to heal and love me. I am surrounded by the Violet Flame of purification and God's love. I seek my divinity and divine purpose with God only. I am safe there where only unconditional love, sacred interaction and light reside. I rejoin the Oneness that we are all a part of. Thank you for the lesson in power, control, hatred and bondage. I have learned it and reject it in favor of love, sacredness and forgiveness. I release all of you to your healing and divine purpose. May your darkness be healed and return as divine energies to assist Earth and her people. I release this completed karma for all time to the Holy Spirit to be burnt in the fires of the Holy Flame of the Compassionate Heart and dissolved for all eternity. We step into the healed Earth.

Prayer of Forgiveness

I extend forgiveness to all those who participated in the torture, rape, extortion, delusion, trickery, magic, sorcery, hatred, stealth, lying, sacrifice and other forms of suffering you inflicted upon my soul and the souls of humanity in this and all other lifetimes while in your unconsciousness. I extend my gratitude to you for helping me complete my karma and fully awaken. I apologize to any souls I have hurt in my lifetimes of unconsciousness and ask your forgiveness. I extend forgiveness to myself for any lifetimes where I participated in these activities out of unconsciousness, fear or enforced capture or imprisonment through vows or bondage. I release any attachment or resentment to all of you for these actions and dissolve all false connections with you for all eternity. I bathe all previous connections in the Violet Flame of purification. I release all attachment to pain, judgment and resentment towards myself for participating in these false and hurtful actions in other lives and dissolve all connections to those beliefs, thoughts and actions. I release these actions and thoughts to the Holy Flame of the Compassionate Heart for healing and purification. I step into my Divinity, Divine Self and Sacred Dharma healed, whole and free.

Action Step Twenty ~Spiritual Soul Power
Create your Statement of Intention

Write a **Statement of Intention*** of how you plan to claim, live and hold your power, truth, sovereignty and divine purpose from now on. In the beginning of this statement, inform your former adversaries or others in your life that you intend to hold them accountable and expect to be treated fairly, equally, respectfully, sacredly and lovingly. State that you will not tolerate any future abuse, disrespect, bondage, lies, suffering or threats leveled towards you from them. Visualize them surrounded in the Violet Flame cleansed of all negativity. Let them know you now live within your circle of authentic power and protection and they are not welcome there unless they have made amends and surrendered their darkness. You will be taking this statement into your circle of power that you will soon create. You may forgive them if you wish there, but not without a boundary. After trauma, black magic, lies and other torture, the only forgiveness possible is **Boundaried Forgiveness***. This is a method of forgiving whereby you offer forgiveness to the perpetrator either within yourself alone, or to them in person if you feel safe enough to so, but only if they honor specific boundaries that you set. You are creating your circle of power and safety for yourself. Create it on your terms so you can heal safely within it. After that part of the statement of intention, tell how you plan to move into your power and create with it. How will you utilize the long withheld divine energy that was always yours? What empowering steps will you take now that you are healed to create a more whole, healed life? Write whatever suits you. There is no required length or style, just let your soul fly free. Finally, welcome your shadow self home. Tell it you are embracing and healing the long neglected parts of yourself that have become suppressed, unloved, dark and diseased. Let it know that you love these parts of yourself and extend healing and forgiveness to them for whatever mistakes and sabotaging actions they took in your life. Tell it you will be making all the decisions now and that it doesn't run the show from your unconscious mind anymore. You will love it, stay in touch with it, but it will no longer sabotage your dreams, hopes and relationships. Invite it to speak, sit with you or anything else to start the healing and integration process. Remember it's there and check in often so it remains conscious. Finish off your statement of intention. Bring it with you to Step Thirteen. Give yourself Reiki whenever possible, or receive a Reiki treatment whenever possible. Place the statement on your altar until you are ready to declare it. Put a sacred object upon it. Continue your spiritual practices. Ask the Universe to help you hold your power in place.

Action Step Twenty-One ~ Physical & Spiritual
Grounding Your Power

Create a grounding circle somewhere in Nature where you won't be disturbed. Bring sacred objects that have meaning to you and that are related to Nature. Have an object that represents each of the four directions East, West, North and South. Bring and place an item that represents the element of Air at the North point, an item that represents Water at the South point, an item that represents Fire at the East point, and an item that represents Earth at the West point. Wear a grounding necklace of crystals, organite, a cross, mala beads, feathers or something significant to you. Bring an offering to Nature with you such as a prayer tie, a leaf dipped in frankincense, a small piece of your clothing, something to leave in the circle that is of you. You may bring your Angel guides with you into the circle if you wish; they are there to protect you. Bring crystals and any other items that have meaning and power to you and place them in the circle. Begin a shamanic grounding ceremony with the Earth. Take off your shoes and place your feet in the Earth. Ask for and receive the love of Mother Earth and honor the Goddess within Her. Stand there awhile and feel the Earth's magnetic energy come up through your feet chakras and into your energy field. Say a prayer of gratitude and respect for the Earth before entering the circle, asking for permission to enter. Enter the circle from the South and walk towards the North on the West side. Sit at the North point first and meditate. Ask for direction from the North/Air energy, listen for direction, remember or write down what was given to you. After a period of time when you feel done there, move to the West point and sit there. Ask for direction from the West/Earth energy. Repeat the process. Move to the South/Water energy and repeat the process. When ready, move to the East/Fire energy and ask for direction. Repeat the process. When you feel complete with that, go to the center of the circle. Sit down there and get comfortable. Ask for your guides, whoever they may be, to approach with guidance and protection. Prepare to meet your guides who may be animals, spirits, shapeshifters, insects, or even the wind. Listen for the voices of Nature, perhaps the wind, a whippoorwill, maybe a tree. Each voice will have a message for you. Listen closely; write it down if you need to. You may be asked to complete a task or challenge of some kind. If so, bring it back to your home later, or to the group if you are in class with me, and we will discuss it. Or keep it to yourself if it's meant to stay private. After hearing the messages of your guides, ask for their protection in your life from now on. Tell them you have claimed your power and need their support. Ask them to join your other protectors such as the Angels or whoever they may be to make a complete impenetrable circle of power around you. Visualize that fortress of power around you now in your mind's eye. Claim your place in the center of that power circle. You belong there; it's your sacred space. <u>Then make your statement of power and intent out loud</u>. Announce to those who hurt you, and may wish to return to your life, that you now stand in the center of your circle of authentic power. Tell them there is a boundary of protection around you and that they may not enter unless they have made their amends and are sincere. Order your protectors to take whatever protective action is necessary. You may need to do this ceremony several times to create a powerful circle of protection that you feel comfortable with around you before announcing this. If someone does approach from your past and attempts to trick you, your circle will burn off their energy and repel their approach. Visualize this a while. You are within your power circle; no one can harm you there. Finish your prayers and meditation. As you prepare to close your power and grounding ceremony, Say a prayer of respect for what the Earth has given you in this life. Leave your offering. Close the ceremony. When you feel complete, rise and go around the circle again leaving at the South point. Gather your things and go respectfully and silently. Do this whenever you feel disconnected from Nature and life to re-ground yourself to the Earth you were born to walk on. This is your birthright. You have a right to be here in your power. Claim it.

~~~~~~~~

The number 21 represents a sacred cycle. As I mentioned, it takes 21 days to start or end a habit. Then there is a rest period of acclimation of 7 days, also a sacred number. Think of nature's cycles, like a woman's menstrual cycle which is 21 days off and 7 days on. These numbers are embedded throughout nature, science and math and represent sacred geometry. Do a minimum of 3 cycles of 21 days of these exercises plus the 7 days off inbetween. It's going to take more than 84 days. But you will have established a strong foundation of personal and spiritual practices that likely have broken the bad habits. Of course, it's going to take much longer to completely transform. And it's entirely dependent upon your personal situation and condition. It's up to you to stay the course of your total transformation. It may be a while. But emerging on the other side is worth it.

> *If you only knew the magnificence of the 3, 6 and 9, then you would have a key to the universe.*
> ~ Nikola Tesla

We've been programmed scientifically and mathematically by brilliant forces who understand sacred geometry and the forces of the Universe. They know how to manipulate us through precise figures and actions. But we have the power to do the same thing to reverse the damage. We can break the programming if we practice our own program of precise de-programming and re-building our consciousness towards divinity, wholeness, health and love. It starts here, with you undertaking a Soul Transformation. What have you got to lose? Only all that is false and harmful in favor of all that is true, loving and whole.

Action Step Twenty-Two ~ Spiritual
Give Selfless Service

After you have passed through the initial 21 stages of your Soul Transformation, seek somewhere to begin giving back the gifts of healing God has given you to humanity. There are so many places that need assistance you should have no difficulty finding places to serve. Share if you can afford it. If you have spare time, find a charity and pitch in to help. If you have extra food, give to the homeless and jobless. And so on. The final stage on the path to spiritual awakening is the arrival of the soul at a state of egolessness. There it joins with all of Creation and lives only to love and to serve others. I hope to meet you there one day.

~~~~~~~~~

As you do the steps above, you will begin to untie and unravel the knots of twisted energy, trauma and pain that keep you in bondage to your shadow self and ego. The suffering there will never end until you surrender the ego completely. As these barriers are removed and the energy released to flow freely, you will find yourself naturally waking up and healing. Many realizations will come to you. You will embark on a whole new life, with a whole healed soul. Eventually, all your striving for fame, fortune, possessions and sensory gratification will die off and your soul will merge with the One Mind, our Creator. When this occurs for you, you will see all of the Universe in the blink of your eye. I bless you on your journey there.

Chapter 15

The Great Awakening

When love is the bottom line,
Earth and Her people will heal...

~ Salini

Above the clamor of the naysayers,
Truth rings the highest.

~Salini

As I sat on my Maui lanai looking out on the palm trees swaying in the wind and the moon rising mystically behind them, I realized I had come full circle. I began life in Hell. I'm ending it in Heaven. A lot happened inbetween. The devastation of my childhood has given way to the peace of awakening. The rage, pain and sorrow I felt for so long are transmuting to forgiveness. And in the crucible of forgiveness, a million transformations take place. It's the place where the love enters the fear and dissipates it. It's where the wound is bathed in light and heals itself. It's where the hatred is transmuted to love and the doors to your heart and soul are flung wide open. The process is ongoing, like splinters emerging from the skin six months after going in. The skin needs time to be healed and become strong enough to eject the sharp pieces. Such is the process of our own healing; time and recovery are needed to complete the healing. Trauma needs time to assimilate and integrate before we can let it out in the sunlight to release it. The emotions need to mature to a point where they can be understood, felt and embraced. The mind needs to time develop a strong enough sense of self to do the deeper, more painful work.

I needed a lot of time, diligence, patience and healing to get here. I will continue to work on this until I am fully awakened and my ego is totally gone. If I hadn't had the harsh beginning, I would never have sought God so fervently. The shattering was so total that I had to rebuild every piece of my soul. In my painful, agonized surrender, God enveloped me in love. I didn't always know what was happening because the pain was so excruciating. But I knew that God was there, working on me somehow.

I reflected on the closing courtroom drama that played out with my father and saw God's hand at work. After our final court battle, I walked outside to ponder the journey. I just heard Dad repeat the same tired mantra I had heard since I was a small child as he continued to try to disenfranchise, disempower and discredit me, "She is a bad person. No one loves her. She is a loser." The judge had silenced and berated him saying, "How could you treat your own daughter this way?" I listened gratefully to this kind judge and knew the war was finally over. Regardless of the outcome of the case, the demons had lost. I was sad for Dad knowing he was still trapped in his illusion and pain and didn't realize the damage and suffering he had caused and the severe karma ahead for him. I was sad for his lost soul and prayed for his release from the lie. I also remembered the good things he had done for me. The human drama was completing itself. Only a powerful enemy can help you develop deep soul muscles of patience, strength, surrender and compassion. Dad was that enemy…he taught me the hardest lessons of life. The ones only the finest warriors learn. You can either let them teach you forgiveness…or hatred and revenge. The choice is yours. Mom taught me to love. But Dad prepared me for battle in so many ways. And life can be a great battle at times. I am prepared for both.

I took a moment to feel my true feelings deep inside. I had returned from the underworld of punishment and suffering, restored myself and re-entered my heart. I realized I loved him anyway. And I forgave him. It was then I realized I was really free. He never succeeded in killing off my ability to love. My heart remained intact. I brought back the Holy Grail of the healed soul for humanity. I completed the Heroine's Journey. I was now free to love everyone, including myself. I thanked him, and all my teachers, and the Universe silently for the lessons and walked out into my new life. I decided to take one last trip to see our old family home which was nearby. I knew I would never return, so this was it. Time to say goodbye to all the pain of my life there. During past visits, I was unable to walk even near the house because the pain in my body would accelerate to high proportions the closer I got to the house. It was the house of horrors. As I rounded the corner and pulled up in front of our old home, I saw a bulldozer there poised and ready to raze it to the ground. The engine was fired up and running loudly. I jumped out of my car and walked over to the foreman.

"What's going on here?" I asked him.

"We're about to bulldoze this house." He replied.

"My father built this house. I was born and raised here for 18 years." I told him.

"Well, do you want to watch us tear it down?" He asked me.

I looked over at my childhood home for a moment and paused in shock. Memories flooded in, both good and bad. I felt emotion well up in my chest and face. I was astonished that after all the suffering I endured there, all the adventures and all the healing I had done, this house was about to be history. It was symbolic of my journey. It had no foundation to stand on any longer because I had destroyed it with my love, faith and healing. It no longer existed in my consciousness even. The Universe was about to prove to me that I completed my homework.

I turned to the foreman. "What's going to be built here instead?"

He smiled a broad smile at me. "A church."

I stared back at him in awe and a tear began to form in the corner of my eye. It welled up and spilled over, rolling silently down my cheek. "Yes, I absolutely want to watch that happen." I said slowly. "Do it."

He laughed and turned to the bulldozer crew and gave the signal. I watched as the growling machine plowed into the side of our home like a wild animal. It ripped a big hole through the wall and kept going. When it got deeper inside, it ripped the guts of the house out. The roof came crashing down with a roar. I felt a small sense of justice as I saw the house be ripped apart. It was a place of secrets and suffering. No one was allowed to talk about the torture we endured there. But God had prevailed. A church would stand where demons once did. And God made sure it happened the one and only day that I decided to stop by, the very same day of my final court date with Dad. What an incredible miracle it was and proof of God's omnipotence and power. I silently thanked God that I was there to witness the falling of the power of such darkness. The next day I received word I had won the case. I knew then that darkness was beginning to fall everywhere. The Earth was awakening and God's light was now prevalent for all to see. I dedicated myself on the spot to helping the world see it. And so this book was born.

That day I turned on the news to hear the announcer talk of the new war, the new "enemy", world-wide terrorism, and that we all had to be ready to sacrifice everything to "protect freedom". Here we go again I sighed. New leaders, new nations, but the same old drumbeats of war. A brand new holocaust brewing. Only this time there was so much more at stake. We now have the capacity to destroy the planet. We are on the brink of doing just that with another war, a nuclear disaster and an ecological death. Who would start this war and who would die this time? And who would be enriched by it? That's where we need to look to see the truth behind the veil. And most critical of all, do we have to do this again or can we finally master this lesson? Something radical needed to alter that cycle or there was no hope for awakening.

I realized that night as I listened to the rain softly pelting the palm leaves outside that it wasn't a new enemy we faced; it was the same ancient one. The one plaguing mankind since the beginning of time. It was the illusion we are all taught...fear, hatred, separation and Godlessness, that we don't deserve love, that we should always be ashamed, and that we should give over our power to authorities to decide things for us. And who do these authorities answer to? Not to you and certainly not to God, as they should be. These forces answer to darkness in all its forms. This was already manifesting badly globally as we watched the global elites take us into deprivation and destruction. We were once again becoming serfs on our own land. As we held our shame and fear closely to our breasts, we were vulnerable to the abuse of power over our lives. We were losing our freedom.

In my unique upbringing, I was privileged to see the two wounded halves of human consciousness at play...the beauty, power, love and sacredness of the divine feminine as they were embodied by my mother and my sister, and the darkness that had overcome my father. He was so consumed by the lust for power, money and recognition that he fought, destroyed and lied for it in a desperate attempt to fill the hole in his heart and soul. On the opposite side, my mother and sister gave their love away freely without requiring a sacred partnership. It was a drastically unequal alliance that ensured too much for one and not enough for another. And that is where the two broken halves of consciousness merged chaotically. The eternal cry for love, the give and take of the power struggle over the energy of love. That same sick patriarchal alliance exists everywhere in the world today.

And it damages everyone involved. It was weakening our oneness, our souls and our communities.

This is the ancient curse we all live out as the sacred feminine is destroyed within us all. The time has come to bring together the wounded masculine in healing and partnership with the healed sacred feminine and truly love one another sacredly and equally. The Divine Mother has returned. Her love will heal us all. The time has come to honor the Goddess for all of eternity. In doing so, all men are blessed, loved and honored as well. In doing so we are all enriched and expanded. In doing so we are healed, whole and stronger. We can stand up to the abuse of power around us.

As I watched these elements merge together in the crucible of my transformation, I saw the truth of all the suffering that went back many generations and many eons, not just in my family, but in many religions, in many lands, and in many cultures. And as I did, in one blinding flash I felt the forgiveness rush in. It rushed in like a great breaking wave that overwhelmed me and churned me underneath it. I choked upon it and swallowed it deep in my lungs, gagging and coughing on the power of it. I didn't want to breathe it all in just yet. I wanted to hang on a bit longer to my resentments and righteous anger. They were so comfortable and known. My ego enjoyed those juicy moments. But to what end my soul cautioned me? How much longer shall we carry the raging torch of hatred around in our hearts burning a hole in our souls…it spoke to me? How many more lifetimes do you want to meet this lesson? Not one more I answered softly. Help me to forgive I prayed. Help us to unite and reclaim our power. Help me to heal them.

I loved my parents both so much I gave them all the love I could to heal their hearts for them. I took all their pain inside my heart. But it still didn't work and now my heart was hurting. And everywhere I looked for the rest of my life there were so many others suffering as well. Wherever I went they found me and cried out their stories on my shoulder. It was a tsunami of torture, suffering and abuse. I buried so many I loved. The sorrow was crushing me. So I had to strike out and begin the process of sacred alchemy. I had to take this sacred journey for those coming behind me who had no guideposts on this difficult path and looked to me. I didn't realize as I was doing it that it would transform into a love for of all humanity. But it has. I care so much about everyone that sometimes it breaks my heart.

I often wondered why I survived but others did not. Then I heard Elie Wiesel, Auschwitz holocaust survivor speaking. He said he shouldn't have survived, that others were stronger. But it was his eloquence on paper that told the story of so many others who didn't make it. He became the witness for the 6 million people who were not there to tell their stories. He was needed to cast light on great suffering so no one would ever deny it again. And as I listened over the years to the constant ridicule and denial of smug power brokers, sex traffickers, child abusers, pornographers, wife beaters, and other people who denied the suffering of rape and abuse survivors, ritual abuse survivors and mind-control survivors, I realized why I survived. I realized then that I survived to tell the tale of the secret global holocaust of sexual, physical, mental and spiritual abuse of millions, many who have died silently and secretly in back rooms, basements and forests without anyone knowing or caring. I was whole and alive to give testimony to the harsh facts that millions of children had been sacrificed for the sick pleasure of deranged adults the world over, and that I was one of the few who made it out. As painful as it was for me, I had to speak for them. It was time to silence the arrogance of those who abuse their power over others at the expense of the helpless, innocent, voiceless and powerless for their dark power rituals. I am here today to tell you that it's true, that it happened to me and so many others, and that it continues to happen right now somewhere every day.

Watching my sister, mother and best friend die in my arms

of abuse, and then soon after the hundreds of clients that passed through my office who also had been abused and had become addicted to hard drugs or alcohol and had lost themselves in pain and suffering, I knew I had to survive and more than that, triumph over what the soul stealers of death had tried to do to us. I wanted to rise up from the ashes and show them they hadn't destroyed us all. I had to emerge from the matrix of death they had constructed. It was the new and most secret holocaust of them all. There were no bodies to see and bury, no buildings filled with torture implements, because it was the rape and sacrifice of children and the stealing of minds and souls. And it was done in secret, hidden away. Someone needed to tell the truth of what was going on. And now you know.

But my heart was so shattered by this experience that only God could heal it. I prayed a long time for that healing. I worked at it diligently for many years. And one gentle day, I felt the worst of the pain lift off of me. And when that happened, I saw a huge sacred heart beating inside of my chest. It was an indestructible heart...like the one in the paintings of Mother Mary, yet open and always bleeding. It was big enough to hold everyone inside. I was awestruck. Where did this come from? Intuitively, I knew the answer. I had done my homework. I had graduated from the University of Soul Transformation. God had gifted it to me. But it came with an assignment; from now on I was here to love those who could not love themselves. And to that end, I have tried to honor God's request of me. *Love thy neighbor as thyself.*

> *Purify your heart, see God in everything and love all beings. You don't have to do anything else.*
> ~Holy Mother Ammachi

We are all born free, its remains your birthright no matter what happens to you. As you awaken to the astonishing beauty of the Holy

Spirit and your Oneness within it, you will realize the purpose behind your suffering. You will scarcely care anymore because the suffering will have died out with your ego. It's reminiscent of childbirth. While it's happening, you swear you'll never do it again. The pain is too great, you want it to end. But once the baby is in your arms, the beauty and love envelop you and you quickly forget the pain. You become so grateful to have the babe in your arms that you thank God for the whole experience. This is what awakening to your Higher Self is like. Soon, you have regained a sense of peace and purity. You become the innocent child again, looking out joyfully at the world and enjoying life again. I know because even after years of physical suffering, agonizing emotional pain and many near-death experiences, I arrived at peace. And it was love that brought me there. At my lowest points where I didn't want to live anymore, I thought always of my children and how deeply I love them. Then I would think of God, Jesus and Ammachi, and how they have been there for me in dark times, and shown me divine love. And as the Holy Mother Ammachi told me, *"Love always wins in the end darling daughter."* That love would always bring me back home.

> *He who recovers his primitive purity shall die with his transgressions forgiven and have the right to contemplate the majesty of God.*
> ~ Jesus as St. Issa
> Carved in ancient India

As I came out of the illusion of separateness, I saw what was happening everywhere. We're all awakening right now. We are entering the new paradigm where corruption no longer rules the day, where we all have enough and are enlivened by the Holy Spirit. Everyone will soon turn from material pursuits, business, pleasure and material-based sciences to the unquenchable thirst for Oneness with our

Creator. All energies on Earth will finally be devoted to healing, love and restoration of all systems, peoples, cultures and resources of the planet. Science and theology will finally meet in the middle of the cosmos and shake hands, creating a new branch of science/theology minus all the ego wars. Furthermore, it is this new branch of science that will become the most urgent and vital, and will make the most progress on Earth in the near future. Einstein led the way in the world of science while the monks, sages, mystics and yogis prepared the path for him. He insisted we lived in a Universal spiritual field and tried to find it before he died. His work continues on. One day it will be discovered that God is all around, within and part of us and it's quite scientific after all. We will see it and know it. Just as Galileo once explained the Earth's revolution around the Sun, we will come to understand and not fear the Oneness of ourselves with the entire Universe.

And in this new era, everyone is welcome. Even those formerly in the dark. No matter how bad you've been, once you've surrendered your darkness, a vast panorama of love and awakening awaits you. When I was running my **Reiki Recovery Project** on the streets of Santa Barbara, I met many confused souls. They came from all walks of life but had lost their way and fallen into crime, prostitution, drugs and the like. Some of them wanted to leave the darkness behind and entered my program. Even the darkest of the dark can be awakened to the light of God's love. This man was one of them.

Here is a beautiful story of transformation.

> ### *Roger's Soul Transformation* - *Roger was referred to me by the Santa Barbara Court System as a part of my **Reiki Recovery Project** for addicts and alcoholics. Like most cities at night, the streets are filled with addicts and alcoholics roaming the alleys and ghettos searching for drugs and booze. Later, you*

find them passed out somewhere in a corner by a trash bin. The police were frustrated by having to arrest the same people over and over and put them in jail to sober up, only to find them out drunk again the next night. The jails became a merry-go-round of the same drunks sobering up on a cold, cement jail floor and returning night after night to do it again. I had started my **Reiki Recovery Project** *which was a holistic, spiritually-based program for sobriety and recovery and was having great success. The Courts began referring the homeless addicts and alcoholics to me for treatment. I applied my holistic program to them, which included daily Reiki treatments and becoming attuned to First Degree Reiki to great success.*

One day, Roger was sent over to my office by a judge who gave him a choice. Roger had been arrested for robbery to support his heroin habit. It wasn't his first arrest. This time he was facing hard prison time. The judge told him he could either go to San Quentin for 10 years or come see me. Without having a clue about what I did, Roger chose me. I guess I was more appealing than San Quentin. Roger showed up at my office door looking terrified. I was a bit intimidated myself as he was a good 220 lbs., solid muscle, tattooed all over, and very tough-looking. But I was used to how addicts look so it was ok. I welcomed him in.

Love is the basis of the Universe and sustains everything. If there were no love, no creation could take place. The real source of that love is God.
~ Holy Mother Ammachi

As it turned out, Roger was pretty timid. He was scared. I introduced myself and asked him what brought him to me. He told me his story. "I've been a heroin addict for twenty years, ten of those years on the streets here in town. I steal to support my habit. I got caught this time. It's a ten-year stretch at Quentin if I don't get sober and stay straight." He told me. "Is it worth it to you to keep going back to jail, then the streets again, always looking over your shoulder, Roger?" I asked him. "No, I can't do it anymore. I'm tired of being strung out." Roger sighed. "Then you will have to do exactly what I tell you to do without question and never veer from my program. If you do, you're out on the streets again. And you must never lie to me but always be honest as we move through your recovery. Do we have a deal?" Roger agreed and we began his healing.

In addition to learning Reiki, Roger was required to attend 90 Alcoholics Anonymous meetings in 90 days along with a number of other requirements. I gave him a Reiki treatment every single day for 30 days. At the end of the thirty days, when he had more than a month sobriety, I taught him First Degree Reiki. From that moment on, he never craved heroin again. I had many heroin addicts in my Reiki Recovery Project. They all told me the same thing, that Reiki was better than heroin. Pretty strong statement coming from heroin addicts. But it's true; Reiki provides the missing spiritual connection that the addict craves through heroin. All cravings disappeared for Roger fairly soon after starting with me. But just before he learned First Degree Reiki, he had a slip. I didn't see him for a few days. One day I received a phone call from a friend of his. She told me he had been arrested and was in jail. He was requesting I come to see him at the jail. I went over to see Roger there.

*I was able to visit Roger through a glass-barred screen. I asked him what happened. He began giving me a long-drawn out story about someone who had promised him something and didn't come through. I interrupted him, "I'm not interested in the details. Did you use heroin again or not? That's all I want to know. Tell me the truth. We had a deal." Roger's face fell and he looked ashamed. "Yes, I used, just once though. And I got arrested immediately." He told me. "Roger, I warned you that once you undertake recovery and begin your process of healing, you are held to higher spiritual standards. You made a spiritual promise to be accountable to your soul and to God, as part of your healing. You are now going to be subjected to instant karma. This is a blessing in disguise. If you understand that this will be the only outcome of using drugs, death or jail, and are truly ready to recover, we can go from here. But this is the only mistake you get with me. If you use again, you are out of the program. The choice is yours. Do you want to continue in the **Reiki Recovery Project** and work with me? If so, promise me you won't use again and let's pray together right now that all cravings are lifted from this point on." I said sternly to him. Roger started to cry. He nodded his head, "Yes. I promise. This world isn't what I want anymore. You've shown me something else. Love, healing, purpose, God, all of it has come to me since working with you. I don't ever want to go back." I smiled at him, "Good choice. Now let's pray together." Roger and I prayed for his* *release from the demons of addiction and his continued commitment to his recovery. Soon, he was out and back in my office. He never slipped again.*

Roger and I worked together on his recovery for several years. He took First Degree Reiki, then months later when he was strong enough, he took Second Degree Reiki. Roger was a natural. It turned out he was an amazing healer who was never-endingly creative in the ways he would devise to use Reiki to heal himself and others. After his recovery was solid enough, Roger began to work on other addicts and alcoholics with Reiki. Soon, Roger was combing the streets of Santa Barbara looking for lives to save. He brought many of them to me. I gave them the same program and the same stern lecture I had given Roger. Some of them made it and some of them didn't. But Roger helped me work on many of them. Many of them had acquired demonic spirit attachments from years of drug use, alcoholism and living on the streets. They had been in so many dark and dangerous situations where violence, rape and death occurred that they had taken on the darkness themselves. I was called in to perform many exorcisms on these men. Roger was often there to hold them down while I did.

Roger's life transformed completely. He gave himself Reiki every single day and prayed continuously for deliverance from his former dark life. Over the course of his healing, Roger shared some of the crimes he had committed. He certainly wasn't a boy scout in his younger years. One day, Roger came to me in a very solemn manner with tears in his eyes. With a terrified look on his face he asked me, "Do you think

I'm evil? Is there any hope for me?" His face showed his fear and anticipation at my answer. I knew that Roger had committed evil acts before. I also knew he was an abused child without a father. And I saw that he now had two years of sobriety and had worked very hard at his recovery, showing great progress. He was now the one saving lives in those dark alleys. He could go in at night and bring them out when I could not. God was now using him for a Divine Purpose. The answer to his question was simple. "No, you aren't evil." I told him. "You were lost and now you are found. You were sick and now you are recovering. You have allowed God's healing into your life and it's taken hold. Congratulations." Roger burst into tears and cried a long time that night. He had reached the point in his recovery where he saw clearly how bad he was before and felt deep remorse. I never judge the addicts who come to because they've all committed crimes. What they needed was something else, my healing and support and God's divine love. And judgment was not what Roger needed then. He had chosen life, surrender and God. And his new life showed just how promising that was going to be for him.

Roger went on to become a ReikiMaster. He, too, has saved lives since then. He moved away to a new city and a new life, a sober life filled with hope, promise and joy. One day years later, I received a phone call. It was Roger. He wanted me to know that he was working, sober, happy and engaged to be married. He wanted me to talk to his fiancée. She came on the phone. "I just want to thank you for saving Roger's life." She told me. "He told me all about you, and how close he was to *death and prison. He told me you healed him, taught him Reiki and gave his life new purpose. If it wasn't for you, I would never have met him. If it wasn't for you, we would never be getting married. Thank you for giving me the love of my life." Now it was my turn to cry. "Don't thank me, thank God for giving me the gift of healing others. God is the healer; I am just the vessel for healing. I am so happy for both of you. Best wishes for your marriage."*

*Roger made the complete **Soul Transformation** from homeless heroin addict, thug and criminal to a healed, humble servant of the Holy Spirit. If Roger can do it after 10 years on the streets and 20 years as a heroin addict, anyone can. The power of God is limitless to heal you and bring you to your soul's true purpose. Let it happen.*

Reiki is capable of bringing a person out of darkness and connecting them to their inner light. Once you are reconnected to God's presence within, miracles can occur, and they often do.

Roger needed a lot of love, support and guidance to overcome his traumatic childhood and drug addiction. But he had his ***great awakening***. And it has been lifelong for him now.

The simplest and most obvious way to rise out of this mindset is to pray to God for help. God never fails to answer someone who prays sincerely. But the inner homework must still be done. If you wish to recover outside of the 12 step programs, you can follow my Stepping Stones to Soul Transformation. But be sure to get the help you need. It can't be done alone. The right teacher is needed with someone like Roger, who had lost hope and lost his way. He needed a spiritual guide to break through his confusion. Many people do today because as a nation and as a planet we have lost our way. We must return to our spiritual roots, in whatever faith we have chosen, to climb out of the moral breakdown we now find ourselves in. We must bring in God's power to break through the veil of darkness that has fallen over the world. Only a spiritual revolution at the soul level will save us. We must reclaim our soul force in its entirety, return to compassion, and step forward as a group to face down this evil that has gripped our lands.

Homelessness is the inheritance of the raped and abandoned citizen of the world, pain our daily bread. Reclaim your people America. Reclaim your heart...
~ Salini

In quantum physics there is something called the **Heisenberg Uncertainty Principle***. Remember when I spoke of the space between thoughts that have no gravitational field? There is no gravitational field there because the spaces between synapses are less than 1/1000th of an inch. That means sub-atomic particles and photons within this field can move without the limits of gravity. That would include energy, light and thought. However, the Uncertainty Principle tells us that when attention is focused upon these tiny particles, they are affected by our attention. The very act of observing alters the reality being observed. Our attention is made up of thought and energy which we can direct towards something. In other words, if you focus your attention on something, just focusing on it can change the nature and movement of that something. There is power in your attention. You may think that this only applies to tiny particles. But in reality, once you understand that all matter in the Universe is made up of particles that are simply moving slowly, you can direct your attention at anything because it's all connected. This is the basic principle of meditation and how it changes you alchemically. If you direct your attention at the spaces between thoughts, you enter the realm of all possibilities within the Unified Field of Einstein's vision. If we, as a global people, begin collectively focusing on changing the energy field of unified particles from war to peace, from hate to love, from violence to nurturance, we can make the leap from devastation and decline to resurrection and healing. After all, as Einstein said, it's all just one matrix of energy moving quickly or slowly.

When we have been compartmentalized in some way, it's impossible to heal, self-actualize and bond with other humans. We lose connection to our own souls. *Yet there is no separation between us, only particles in space suspended in love. It's an illusion, a spell, a trance that has been placed upon us.* It's time to remember this truth so we can restore ourselves. As I told you in earlier chapters on alchemy and healing, it's the calling upon the invisible love within the field everywhere in the Universe that brings in the healing force. We can do this within the field of humankind as a collective whole. And that is precisely what we must do. I'll take it a step further. If we allow ourselves to dwell inbetween the spaces between thoughts long enough, we arrive in the quantum field of the Universe where all knowledge resides and become one with the truth. It's the main principle of cloud computing, where all information is connected. Computer scientists call this metadata. It's what they search for when they surveil us. They want to know us. They are looking for the point of contact where all personal data resides. But unbeknownst to them, their higher selves are guiding them towards awakening. Towards the point of unity within us all. What they don't realize is that point is also the point within the soul where all truth resides and where all love resides. *We are all in a race to arrive at the same place, the place where truth, love and the Holy Spirit all reside!*

There is no need for competition for this information. *There is enough to go around!* It's freely available to us all. All we need to do is walk there together in peace, without malice, and meet in the middle. It will bring an end to the madness. Those of us who can approach this point in meditation must do so and include the entire unified field of this planet in our meditation when we do so. We must attempt to bring the world with us by focusing our attention on their participation in the unified field and assist them with our love to bring them into the field. When we all do this, the world heals.

The way things are now, we are programmed to be ill. The secrets they keep from us are their poisons that we carry for them. We are brainwashed into thinking we have to go outside ourselves to achieve wellness when true healing resides within. We believe we have to be dependent on a toxic system and corrupt leaders, that we can't figure it out on our own. We've been hijacked and injected with a virus of unbelief, doubt, fear, despair, depression, uncertainty and confusion. These are the tools of the dark side.

We must neutralize these weapons with faith, love, healing, community, selfless service, surrender to God, and build a new world. Let yourself feel your true feelings, they are the language of your soul. When you feel, light comes to you, your frequency rises. And frequency plus feelings equals manifestation. We can then manifest the new world we imagine.

We've lived a long time in a half-world, an imbalanced patriarchal realm devoid of heart, intuition, mystery and soul. The symbol of the patriarchy is the sword – it takes life. The time has come to return to the matriarchy whose symbol is the chalice – she gives life. We must visualize and create a society without war, hatred, domination or fear, where everyone is free to self-actualize. A place of cooperation, equality, love and peace. We do this through prayer, gratitude, faith, sacredness, surrender and community. It takes an act of great faith to overcome the barriers set before us, but it absolutely can be done. It requires an extraordinary belief in the positive forces that make up the Universe to accomplish it. All true mystics and healers have this faith and ability. Seek them out to save our world. Yes, it is possible. Someone else was once a dreamer, and I am too.

*You cannot hold back a global awakening when
the energy for it is on the move or you will spark
a revolution instead. Let no one fear this process.
It's for all of us. Let's go there together in peace.*

~ Salini

Wake up and recognize the Matrix we live in for what it really is…just an illusion. It's nothing more than a code that was written for your brief time in a 3D world. A code to imprison you…or to free you, your choice. This is but a way station on your path to divinity. The codes have now been cracked, the spell broken. The mind and body trauma codes are now exposed and have no power over you. You can be resurrected from this wound by the ancient wisdom and truth now revealed. A timeless, indestructible power that is your birthright, kept secret from you by the machinations of small minds and com-promised souls is now available to you. Walk beyond them now. We passed them when we created the world-wide web; we just haven't yet realized that this internet code extends to the entire Universe, an inter-connected, indestructible matrix of life…a force of love, light and energy….and that you are the Creator of this Matrix. You can snap your fingers and step out of this reality into the Oneness of the energy field of all of Creation. Because *you* are the Creator. They have no power over you. They can only create division, confusion and fear. But you are already love… claim it. And when you do, your power rushes into your awareness and short-circuits their game, ends their network, and diffuses the program. Maybe even opening their hearts in the process. Game over. Monster defeated. Then we all join in love, take off our masks and have a beer together. And poof, the planet awakens.

I believe there is yet a spirit of resistance in this great country which will not submit to be oppressed, and a fund of good sense which cannot be deceived.

~ Anonymous, July 1769 at the start of the Revolutionary War

A Prayer of Liberation
Breaking the Trance/Spell of Trauma, Fear and Illusion

Our liberation is upon us! In the name of the Creator of all life, we call down God's divine love to break open, dissolve and dispel all spells and trances of fear, trauma, illusion, separation, despair, doubt, hopelessness, faithlessness and defeat. We call for all truth to be revealed and its power to heal activated. Our long millenniums in bondage are now over, we claim our freedom. We ask and activate you now God, to energize, vitalize and restore all aspects of our energy field, our energy bodies, our minds, emotions, hearts and spirit and the Earth itself. We ask you to create a field of divine light of your unconditional love around everyone on Earth, and Earth herself, that is impenetrable by any form of darkness. We ask that you empower this divine field to cleanse away any ancient spells, trances, bondages, oaths, contracts, slavery, unconsciousness, denial, frozenness, fear and violence that have bonded humanity and Earth for millennia in darkness and enslavement. We call and open to you God in faith that this is the moment in world history when darkness is cleansed off Earth forever. All ancient societies, groups, clubs, and other organizations that have enslaved humanity are now disempowered. All their members will now submit to healing or leave Earth's sacred space. We know in faith God that you will vitalize every cell of every person and every living creature including Earth herself with vibrant unconditional love for their liberation, healing and restoration. We ask that you unify us in the Oneness of the Universe where we all reside and that all illusions of separation and division be permanently dissolved and that we stand free within the space of Wholeness. We ask that we are bathed eternally in the divine unconditional love that the Universe is made up of. We ask this in gratitude, respect, sacredness and humility. By the power vested in me by the Holy Spirit, as I say it so it is done.

So what are you waiting for?

~~~~~~~~~~

Om Namah Shivaya to all

Your spirit is free. Let nothing enslave you...
~ *Salini*

Chapter 16

Glossary of Terms

*The English language is an amalgam of all previous
cultures conquered, destroyed and absorbed over time
which have morphed into a new language, the language
of patriarchal oppression and denied sacred feminine.
Yet buried within it still lives the vibrant sacred
mysteries of old, waiting to be rediscovered and relived.*

~ Salini

Some of the terminology used in this book may be unfamiliar to
the reader and the general public. This is because much of this
information has been suppressed or denied for thousands of years,
or has come to be misunderstood over time through misuse or under usage of English terms. I created this glossary of terms for the
purpose of helping the reader understand the concepts presented
and to create a vocabulary in English of terms that are understood
spiritually, intuitively and mentally to awakened people, especially
mystics, healers, spiritual teachers and those who have integrated the
Sacred Feminine. Also I wish to decode and expose the terminology
of oppression and enslavement to make it visible so we can liberate
ourselves through understanding and wisdom.

It's impossible to do justice or be precisely accurate in defining
these terms in the English language. This is because the English

language itself is a patriarchal language. Its etymology has its roots in the global suppression of other root languages, conquered nations and the Sacred Feminine. Words like *history* bespeak only of the man's version of life – *his-story,* rather than *herstory* or *ourstory.* Or words like *mankind* instead of *humankind* erase the female from the equation. Even biblical terminology like *Father, Son and Holy Ghost* make no room in God's world for *Mother, Daughter and Sacred Heart* which are equally important concepts in the universe. The language revolves around the exclusive patriarchal point of view which instantaneously disempowers billions of people the world over just in daily conversation. This has the effect of imprinting thought forms of unworthiness and invisibility to women, indigenous peoples, minorities, lower classes and conquered peoples. Our language needs to evolve to become inclusive, respectful of everyone, and sacred.

Modern English is the byproduct of centuries of overcoming the cultures of other nations and tribes and absorbing their language and developing a new language, thus emerging as the conqueror tongue. This inserts inherent meaning to some words where such meaning is not intended or wanted. It also hides control and power from the masses **intentionally**. These elements of control were purposely inserted within our language as a kind of code to exclude the lower classes and inform those in the know. In contrast, ancient languages were more inclusive and sacred such as Jesus' mother tongue, Aramaic, the original language of the Bible. Sanskrit is the oldest and most sacred living language today, and its words carry much greater and purer energetic impact. The energy of chanting Sanskrit words out loud are enough to break through thought forms and energy blocks. They are sacred sounds intended by our Creator to heal, uplift, love and empower. But unfortunately, few of us speak Sanskrit.

Language is intended to be sacred because it has power. This is why we are often asked not to take the Lord's name in vain, or are told "As you speak it, so it is". Patanjali, the great Indian linguist and philosopher, would tell us that when defining the philosophy of language, there is a distinction between the sound, or *dhvani*, of a word, and the *sphota*, or meaning of a word, which together create a *shabda*, spoken word. It is a shabda that carries the most energetic power because the power and sound of the word spoken is what heals or destroys according to its meaning.

The power of speaking a word out loud cannot be underestimated. Words can kill or words can uplift. It is for this reason that Masters teach their students to pray or chant daily. I don't claim that kind of power for these terms, but I do endeavor to bring deeper meaning to commonly used terms and combinations. Many of these terms I coined for the purpose of awakening people to the truth hidden around them every day. I believe we can transform the English language as we are transforming ourselves to represent everyone with love and sacredness.

~~~~~~

The Glossary

Abuse Imprinting – The act of trauma-based abuse being imprinted on someone.

Adepts - A member of a secret occult group who holds a certain rank and powers within the group.

Akashic Memory – Stored and usually forgotten memories of past lives or the current life.

Akashic Record – The impression of all that has transpired in the physical Universe recorded in the etheric substance and dimension known by the Sanskrit term Akasha. Individually, it's the entire record of a soul's sojourn through the Universe. All memories and experiences are stored there and can be accessed by advanced intuitives for a soul reading. Your Akashic Record determines your next life according to karma you must repay.

Akashic Recovery – The moment when you recover forgotten or lost portions of your Akashic Record.

Alchemy – A purifying process of transmuting energies and substances from a lower, denser form into a higher, lighter form. The process is at once both chemical and spiritual. In the chemical version, lead is transformed into gold. In the spiritual version, impure inner energies (lead) are purified into higher, faster energies (gold) and then rise up to the crown chakra and induce spiritual awakening. (See **Sacred Alchemy**)

All-Seeing Eye – The Egyptian symbol for the pineal gland.

Allopathic – The mainstream medical system of Western medicine that treats or suppresses symptoms through drugs, surgery and other interventionist techniques rather than allowing the body to heal itself naturally.

Alpha programming – The trauma-based mind control program for training the entitled chosen, usually white male boys, for their special enslaved roles in society as judges, doctors, lawyers, leaders, teachers, etc. as part of one or more of the secret societies in allegiance to darkness.

Ammachi – The Holy Mother Mata Amritanandayi of India, known as the hugging saint, a living incarnation of the Divine Mother of astronomical spiritual power and Divine Unconditional Love. She has her main ashram in Amritapuri, Kerala State, India and travels the world giving Darshan (hugs of love and power) and doing charitable works in every country on Earth. She has hugged over 40 million people worldwide, saved untold thousands of lives, including the displaced widows and farmers of India and rebuilt all of Southern India after the tsunami building over 10,000 homes for the homeless.

Amnesiac barrier - A chemically-based neuro-synaptic brain barrier that causes amnesia created during a traumatic event. The barrier will hold the energy of the incident in amnesia, suppressed, until the soul is strong enough to deal with it. Portions of the brain are compartmentalized behind this barrier away from the conscious part of the brain.

Amygdala – An almond-shaped mass of gray matter in the front part of the temporal lobe of the cerebrum that is part of the brain's limbic system. It is involved in the processing and expression of emotions, especially anger, aggression, terror and fear and is targeted during mind-control.

Apocrypha – The missing books of the Bible.

At-One-Ment – The moment of arrival at the soul's integration and Oneness.

Awakened Unified Mind of God - When the human mind has unified its consciousness, ended duality and can see the face of God.

Axons - The part of a nerve cell or neuron that transfers a nerve impulse from the nerve cell body to a synapse with another cell.

Ayurvedic physician – A medical doctor, often of Hindu of Indian descent, who is trained in Ayurvedic techniques, which are holistic, and include Vedic astrology readings for diagnosis, and herbs for treatment. It's a very comprehensive and successful approach to healing.

Basic Soul Transformation Blueprint – A program of holistic healing designed and created by Salini for the purpose of breaking through trauma, the wounds, the ego and the masks we wear to heal into your true divine self. The goal is healing, awakening and discovering your true life purpose.

Beta programming – The trauma-based mind control program for training as a sexual slave to one or more of the secret societies.

Betrayal Bond – A state of being bonded, like a traumatic bond, to the person or persons who betrayed you.

Black Moon Lilith – a moon and alignment position in the sky and in one's astrological chart that expresses the energy of the angry, violated, denied and oppressed female. She is returning in today's paradigm to step into her power.

Black Widow Praetorians - Wives, sisters, daughters and mothers who protect and/or participate in covering for Praetorians who are protecting and participating with dark forces. They sometimes actively participate in dark activities. But sometimes they are completely unconscious to their complicity. They may have been brainwashed or mind-controlled, abused or compromised in some way like through their children. See **Praetorians**.

Body-Part Cancer – The area of the body where cancer develops is often a marker for the site and type of the wound/trauma. Breast, ovary and uterine cancer are related to feminine trauma such as rape, abuse, misogyny and other sexual trauma. Testicular cancer in men is often related to male self-image or trauma in the area of their masculinity. And so on.

Boundaried Forgiveness – A method of forgiving whereby you offer forgiveness to the perpetrator either within yourself or to them, but they must honor specific boundaries that you set.

Brow Chakra – The sixth chakra of the human energy field located in the forehead between the eyebrows. It functions to empower spiritual sight and open lower brain functions to higher consciousness and awareness. It controls the Third Eye of spiritual sight and enhances spiritual awakening. Its color is indigo. It is also known as the Ajna Chakra.

Buddhist Heart Sutra – The Buddhist chant for healing and empowering the heart – The chant goes like this - Gate Gate Parasamgate Bodhi Svaha. It means, Going, going, going on beyond, always going on beyond, always becoming Buddha.

Bulimarexic – Having an eating disorder that combines bulimia and anorexia in a binge/purge/starvation cycle of eating to control your food intake and weight. It is a neurotic disorder related to sexual abuse or other types of abuse.

Bulimia – An eating disorder where you throw up after eating every time so as not to gain weight. It is part of body dysmorphic dysfunction.

Cellular Memory – The memories of your life, especially trauma, stored within your individual and collective cell structure. They remain there until you become conscious of them and move them out.

Celtics - Indo-European peoples now represented chiefly by the Irish, Gaels, Welsh, and Bretons.

Chakra – A circular spinning energy wheel in your auric field, or the subtle body that receives and processes divine energy into your body for use as fuel for life. They are part of the subtle body, not the physical body, and are the meeting points of the subtle (non-physical) energy channels, called nadis. There are 7 major chakras in the human body, and thousands of smaller chakras.

Chemtrails - Chemtrails are plumes of toxic neurotoxins and chemicals intentionally sprayed from airplanes into the air, onto our topsoil and onto our homes for the purpose of damaging your immune system. Two metals have been found consistently worldwide during analysis of chemtrail residue - barium and aluminum, both highly toxic to humans.

Chinese physician – A physician from China who practices the Chinese version of a medical practice. Chinese physicians typically include herbal concoctions, acupuncture, Qi Gong energy techniques, standard allopathic techniques, ancient potions technique and chiropractic in their practice. In China they have been known to perform heart surgery on a patient without medication by using acupuncture for anesthetic.

CODA – Acronym for Codependency Anonymous.

Codependency Anonymous – One of the 12-Step programs based on the original Alcoholics Anonymous model created by Bill W. that has saved millions of lives. Codependents are people who obsessively care for addicts, alcoholics and abusers instead of themselves. It's as much an addiction as alcoholism and requires treatment.

Codependency Anonymous focuses on a 12-step approach to recovery from codependency.

Collateral Business Murder - A form of murder that is caused by immoral, unconscious, selfish and malicious business practices. It can be one person or whole groups of people who are murdered by the actions of a business person or corporation conducting a profit-driven, unethical business, or by weaponized corporations.

Collective Denial – When entire groups, families, cultures, nations, governments or institutions deny the existence of the suffering, deprivation or stolen power of another, or of groups so they may have it all for themselves.

Collective Traumatic Trance – The collective mindset of a nation that has been traumatized to the point of being entranced and numb to the daily images and experiences of violence and trauma. This is accomplished through false flag events, constant violence on TV, fear-mongering, war hype, trigger words, mind-control and so on. Today we are all living in a national collective traumatic trance induced by the global elite.

Compartmentalized Memory – Different and separate sections of memory created through ritual and systemic abuse. Each compartment is totally self-contained, with its own set of memories and personality. They are created separately to deal with sustained and long-term abuse and are not consciously connected.

Conspiracy Theorist – A false, meaningless term created by the CIA during the post-Kennedy assassination years to destroy the credibility of investigators, witnesses and reporters seeking to find the truth behind Kennedy's assassination. Whenever an authentic witness or investigator stepped forward with real evidence of the facts underlying the President's death, this bogus term is dragged out to silence them. The term has entered the lexicon but let it be known that it is part of the disinformation structure of this society fostered by Praetorians.

Core Self – The pure, healthy personality and self of someone; the essence of who you are.

Covenant of Shame – A group of individuals who are bonded into a cult of shame through vows, rituals, trauma and initiations that feature shame and separation from God, e.g. – Satanism, secret societies.

Cranial-Sacral Therapy - A gentle, hands-on method of healing the functioning of a physiological body system called the craniosacral system, which is comprised of the membranes and cerebrospinal fluid that surround and protect the brain and spinal cord. The goal is to release restrictions in the craniosacral system to improve the functioning of the central nervous system.

Critical Mass Consciousness – When a certain ratio/proportion of consciousness is reached where a required minimum of individual molecules of consciousness think and behave in unison that cause a molecular response whereby the rest of the consciousness joins those molecules in unison and they function as one unit, a whole.

Crown Chakra – The seventh chakra of the human energy system which also functions as the top magnetic pole stabilizing our energy field. The crown chakra is where the Divine Energy flows in from above, where visions are seen, where spiritual awakening occurs and where our Spirit leaves our body at death. It controls higher brain function, the pineal gland and many mental processes. It is the entry point for God's light and its color is violet.

Cultural Trance – The group trance-state induced by repeated trauma, brainwashing or enculturing upon a culture of people by their government or other individuals that forces certain beliefs and practices upon them that are suppressive and change their ability to think freely and consciously.

Dark Field – A place of exile with unknown powers, truths and magnetism yet to be fully explored or understood. The 85% of the Universe made up of dark field matter thought to be magnetism, or yin energy, still denied, misunderstood and exiled.

Dark Illusionists – Those individuals who dwell in the Shadow Self primarily and act out through fragmented portions of their denied selves. Their primary mode of expression is through lies, illusions, manipulations, abuse of power, theft, cunning, diversions, disinformation and sometimes violence, rape and murder. There are many varying degrees of these personas from mildly deluded to totally immersed in darkness. They are either completely unconscious of their deluded state, partially conscious of it, or totally aware and choosing this state. Their souls have been compromised and trapped.

Darshan – The beholding of a sacred person, deity or object. And it also means the receiving of a spiritual blessing from an advanced spiritual teacher, or guru. Refers to a blessing of love and awakening.

Dead Sea Scrolls - The Dead Sea Scrolls were discovered between 1946 and 1956 at Khirbet Qumran in the West Bank and are the greatest archaeological find in history. They comprise 900+ documents. They date from around 250 B.C. to 68 A.D. and were written in Hebrew, Aramaic and Greek. They contain Biblical and apocryphal works, prayers and legal texts and sectarian documents that create a more holistic and authentic view of Jesus' time on Earth.

Delta programming – The trauma-based mind control program for training as a warrior slave to one or more of the secret societies.

Dendrite - Any of the various branched protoplasmic extensions of a nerve cell that conduct impulses from adjacent cells inward toward the cell body.

Denial – The act of denying painful conditions around or within you to the detriment of yourself and others.

Denied Self – The unloved, unacknowledged, unutilized, rejected energetic fragments of the self not yet integrated into the Whole Being/Divine Self. These fragments exist without sufficient love to draw them into the whole consciousness of the Divine Self. They are partitioned or compartmentalized off in consciousness only, but not in reality.

Devil's Tone – The one dissonant tone on the musical scale, F#, which brings chaos into consciousness. The frequency associated with this tone is 440 kHz. This tone suppresses the heart chakra and keeps consciousness stuck at low levels. All music was standardized to this tone worldwide in 1939 just before the outbreak of World War II.

Dismemberment – The breaking apart and reintegration of your soul into that which is your True Self.

Divine Blueprint of Global Awakening – Our Creator's Divine Plan for the universal awakening and healing of Mother Earth and all of Her inhabitants.

Divine Law – The universal laws that rule actions and structure of the Universe and everything in it, including Earth. They are unchangeable and absolute and override all other man-made laws. They work in concert with Natural Law.

DMT - A natural neurochemical responsible for modulating consciousness found in the pineal gland.

Dr. Mikao Usui – The founder and original GrandMaster of the Reiki lineage known as the Usui System of Natural Healing, or Reiki Usui Ryoho. His lineage is the Authentic Original Reiki lineage.

Druids - An ancient order of priests in Gaul, Britain, and Ireland in the pre-Christian era.

$E = mc^2$ – Mileva and Albert Einstein's famous Theory of Relativity equation which means that energy is equal to mass multiplied by the speed of light squared. While seemingly simple, this equation has many profound implications, chief among them being that matter and energy are actually the same stuff. Basically it means that when the vibration of mass is sped up, it becomes energy. In other words, energy cannot be created or destroyed; it can only be changed in form. It was co-written by his first wife, Mileva Maric Einstein although she was not credited because she was a woman. It is believed by the Nikola Tesla Society that she was the one who developed the main theories of relativity.

Earth Soul Transformation – The current global transformation now underway that is healing, integrating and awakening the Divine Energies, especially the long dormant Divine Feminine energies that heal and empower us. The Earth is healing and will awaken and ascend to higher consciousness.

Encultured – To be taught, conditioned and initiated into the myths, legends and beliefs of a tribal system, a family system, a political system, a business system or any other system where membership hinges upon you accepting the myths and beliefs of that system.

Energy Vampires – Those individuals who drain and live off of the vital life force of others through various surreptitious, and frequently unconscious, means and behaviors.

Energy Vampiring – The act of living off of the vital life force of others, either individually or groups.

Eve – Adam's second wife made from his rib, as told in the story of the beginning of humans on Earth according to Genesis 2-3 in the Bible.

Fallen – The state of being where your lower self overtakes your higher self and you act out in harmful, duplicitous ways towards others. Your soul is more bonded to darkness than to its spiritual light. It is a state that always leads to death and destruction of the self and others.

Fascia - A sheet or band of fibrous connective tissue enveloping, separating, or binding together muscles, organs, and other soft structures of the body.

Fear Initiations – Initiations of power that revolve around instilling fear into the initiate for purposes of control.

First Degree Reiki – The first level of Reiki in the Usui system of original, authentic Reiki instruction in the healing path of divine energy. Dr. Mikao Usui re-discovered Reiki in the 1800's, creating a spiritual path of healing using divine energy, or Reiki, in Japanese. Reiki has since expanded all over the world and healed millions.

Forgetfulness Spell – A spell placed on someone by black magicians to create amnesia.

Four Directions of Trauma – The four directions a traumatized person seeks in life to escape the pain of their buried trauma. They are: seeking safety, seeking numbness, seeking release and seeking transcendence.

Freemasons – A semi-secret society of primarily white males with a multi-level hierarchy of power. There are degrees of the Masonic Order that rank from low to high. Lower level Masons have no knowledge of the real activities of higher level Masons, but are taught to believe they do know as a cover for the clandestine, illegal, and dark activities of higher level Masons. Higher level Masons carry out their secret activities behind the cover of the good Masons, much like the Mafia launders money through legitimate businesses.

Frozen Emotions or Frozen Memory – These are emotions and event memories that are frozen within the body's tissue at the moment of a traumatic event. They can be separate or together but usually happen at the same moment, the genesis of a traumatic event. They become locked in place by the fear and remain there, blocking the free-flow of energy within a healthy energy body until something unlocks and liberates them. They can be there for long periods of time, even throughout someone's lifetime. They are nearly always unconscious and inaccessible and make up a large portion of the energy within a Traumatic Trance. They are the host of numerous diseases within the human body.

Gaslighted – When those around you purposely construct a false scenario for malicious purposes to hide the truth of something you intuitively know is happening to you. You are lied to and denied repeatedly until you doubt yourself. It's done for the purpose of attempting to drive you crazy and to cover up the truth of what they are really doing. It can be a group or singular effort.

Gnostics – People who believe the Sacred Feminine, or yin principle, is equal to the male yang principle in the makeup of the Universe. Gnostics know that the forces and matter that make up the entirety of the Universe include both female and male energy, or yin and yang, and that the yin energy is necessary and vital to the process of creation. Therefore any description of God, who contains the entire Universe, must include terminology that is also feminine in etymology. They are also people who believe in the Gnostic version of Jesus Christ's history.

Gnostic Gospels - A collection of about fifty-two ancient texts based upon the teachings of several spiritual leaders that more accurately portray Jesus' life and teachings, written from the 2nd to the 4th century AD. They are a combination of his life in the Mediterranean and traditional teachings and his Eastern teachings. They represent the truth about the power and sacredness of the Sacred Feminine on Earth that has been suppressed for thousands of years, including the church's suppression of women.

Great Wound of Compassion – The heart wound during a Soul Transformation that opens you to the unconditionally loving heart.

Grey Sheet Abstinence – A required eating plan for food addicts created in the early days of Overeater's Anonymous that restricted eating unhealthy foods and binge foods, especially carbohydrates, sugars and desserts. It consisted primarily of vegetables, meats and fruit. The member was required to phone in their food every day to their sponsor.

Heart Chakra – The fourth chakra of the primary chakras in the human energy system that receives, transmutes, houses, and distributes the energy of love throughout the body.

Heisenberg Uncertainly Principle – The scientific principle that explains how the act of observing alters the reality being observed.

Heliocentrism – The belief that the Earth revolves around the Sun. It was introduced by Copernicus and supported by Galileo. It was rejected by the Pope, the Catholic Church and the Monarchies of old in favor of the belief that the Universe revolved around the Earth.

Heresy - Opinion or doctrine at variance with the orthodox or accepted doctrine, especially of a church or religious system.

Hippocampus - A seahorse-shaped structure in the cerebral cortex of the temporal lobe of the brain, composed of two gyri with white matter above gray matter. It forms part of the limbic system and is involved in the processing of emotions and memory.

Holistic physician or technique – A method of holistic health practices, or the person who utilizes them, that honors the body as a whole entity. All healing practices of this kind treat the body, mind, emotions and spirit as a whole unit and are more successful in healing people.

Holy Grail – The Womb Chakra where all creation, healing and resurrection takes place. It is infused with love from the Heart Chakra.

Homeostasis – The condition in the human body and all its systems of being balanced in all processes, organs, mental and emotional states, and actions. When the body is in homeostasis, we are not ill, diseased, upset, blocked or imbalanced in any way. This is the ideal state to aspire towards in human health.

Ida – The primary energy channel that rises up alongside the spine on the right side within the human energy system. It is also known as a primary nadi. It is part of the 3 main channels that carry the Kundalini up the inner channels to the crown chakra during a Kundalini rising and awakening experience.

Imagine – John Lennon's masterpiece of love and peace written in the key of love, 528 kHz. Imagine was the first major song by a major star written in this key, against the forced imposition by the global elite of the frequency 440 kHz, the Devil's Tone. 440 kHz creates fear, chaos and disharmony and was imposed on the world's musicians by the global elite and Josef Goebbels in 1939.

Karma – Life experiences you have had that create consequences that reverberate back to you in either a positive or negative fashion. All karmic actions and experiences are stored in the Akashic Record to be resolved in future lives. The karma will be either be repaid by you or received by you according to the nature of that experience. Example – If you saved many lives in another life, you will receive a special blessing in the next life. Or, if you've stolen something from someone in a past life, it will be taken from you in a future life and a pattern established that must be broken or overcome.

Kilohertz - The kilohertz, abbreviated kHz or KHz, is a unit of alternating current (AC) or electromagnetic (EM) wave frequency equal to one thousand hertz (1,000 Hz). The unit is also used in measurements or statements of signal bandwidth. It is used in this book as a measurement of the minimum required electromagnetic frequency of the human body required to maintain optimal health.

Khumba Mela – A sacred Hindu spiritual gathering held every 12 years at one of four places in India. It is the world's largest peaceful gathering with 120 million people in 2013 present to worship and bathe in the River Ganges. The Khumba Mela lasts nearly two months and is considered to be an especially auspicious time to bathe in the holy river for purification from sin and end reincarnation.

Kundalini – The coiled, life force energy at the base of the Root Chakra that provides each human with the potential for spiritual awakening if properly nurtured along. It is often considered the Mother energy as well as since it provides the life force for the human body. Much yogic wisdom goes into the understanding of how to bring up the Kundalini to the Crown Chakra for self-realization. A branch of yoga, Kundalini Yoga, is devoted to coaxing the Kundalini up the spine to achieve higher consciousness.

Kundalini Psychosis – A psychotic state induced by a too rapid ascent up the spinal column into the brain of divine Kundalini energy. Energies in lower chakras that have yet to be purified and transmuted, when forced too soon up the chakras and into the brain, can pollute the brain and create a form of insanity known as Kundalini psychosis.

Kundalini Rising – The process whereby the body's life force, or Kundalini, is awakened and begins to rise up the Ida, Pingala and Sushumna to the crown chakra. If this process occurs completely and the life force reaches the crown and shoots out into the outer aura, a spiritual awakening can occur.

Lilith – Adam's first wife created from the dust in the Garden of Eden and rejected by him when she refused to submit to his authority. She was sent into exile and her energy persists to this day as the wronged, denied, exiled, oppressed woman.

The Lilly Wave – A waveform invented by Dr. John Lilly for healing humanity but was co-opted and used for mind-controlling the population.

Long Distance Reiki – This is a Reiki healing treatment given to someone who is not present with the healer. It is a process learned at the Second Level of Reiki. Symbols are used to contact the soul of the affected individual wherever they are, and send them Reiki through the web of interconnected energy that unites the Universe, or the Unified Field, and a healing is initiated.

Luciferian Initiation – A trauma-based sexual initiation used in secret society initiations that damages the root chakra, spinal cord, neural pathways and brain stem for the purpose of compartmentalizing the minds of members of their society, or others used in their rituals. It also serves to insert satanic energies into the person's chakra system and to vampire off the person's energy. It also blocks access to the quantum field of spiritual awakening.

Malleus Maleficarum – A book written during the Dark Ages by Catholic Inquisitor priests that describes how to capture and kill women suspected of witchcraft. It was used to single out and murder 9 million women during the Inquisitions.

Magnetic Deficiency Syndrome – An imbalance in the levels of energy in a person's electro-magnetic field, the yin and yang energy field, that creates a disease of energy depletion and exhaustion. Those people with immune-related illnesses such as Fibromyalgia, Lupus, Chronic Fatigue, etc. are experiencing this syndrome as part of their complex of symptoms.

Manchurian Candidate – A mind-controlled person who has been subjected to trauma-based mind control to the point where they can be remotely controlled by another person and directed to carry out certain functions without remembering them.

Medical Intuitive – An intuitive person who can see inside the human body and map illness or health and body conditions much like an X-ray.

Merchants of Death – Business organizations or corporations whose charters and aims are focused on creating a death stream for profit.

Military-Industrial Complex – A term that describes the informal business and financial partnership of military, business and financial industry corporations and institutions that form a powerful triumvirate of military force combined with financial banking that threatens to dominate world affairs.

MK-Ultra Program – A program of trauma-based mind control which includes sexual abuse that segments and compartmentalizes the mind originally developed by Dr. Josef Mengele. It was adopted by the CIA to be used on genius children and other subjects for the purpose of mind-controlling them and using them in secret government programs.

MK Ultra trauma-based mind-control program – See above.

Mother-Blame – The unconscious, buried, universal cultural myth that Mothers are to blame for everything wrong with their children and their families. These myths of scapegoating were born out of the patriarchy.

Mouth of God – The soft skin-covered, indented opening at the base of the skull where the spinal cord enters into the skull and brain stem. Also the entry point to higher consciousness for Kundalini energy rising from the root chakra to the crown chakra.

Myo-Fascial Release Work – A form of body work that utilizes a hands-on technique that involves applying gentle sustained pressure into the myofascial connective tissue restrictions to eliminate pain and restore motion. It works by slowly elongating the connective tissue thereby releasing the pain stored within it.

Nadis – Thousands of tiny energy points along the body's energy meridians that act as conduits and stations of energy transfer for the body's entire energy system.

Nag Hammadi Scriptures - A collection of thirteen ancient codices containing over fifty texts discovered in Egypt in 1945. This important discovery includes a large number of primary Gnostic Gospels texts once thought to have been entirely destroyed during the early Christian struggle to define orthodoxy – these scriptures include such texts as the Gospel of Thomas, the Gospel of Philip, and the Gospel of Truth.

Narcissistic Mask – The exaggerated false persona of the ego we wear until our True Self emerges.

Natural Law - A universal system of law that is determined by nature. They work in concert with Divine Law, but not man-made law.

Negatively Charged Intimacy, or Negative Intimacy – Intimacy that is characterized by energy draining, negative and abusive behavior. Negative intimacy exists when an individual cannot sustain unconditionally loving behavior and resorts to conditional and un-loving forms of intimacy, including abuse. This type of intimacy is always energy vampiring and results in the loss and drainage of the targeted person's life force. This type of intimacy is learned and conditioned into the person.

Neurotransmitters - A chemical substance that is secreted by a neuron and then diffuses across a synapse to cause excitation or inhibition of another neuron. Acetylcholine, norepinephrine, dopamine, and serotonin are examples of neurotransmitters.

Nirvana – The arrival at full awakening by the release from the cycle of reincarnation attained by extinction of all desires and individual existence, culminating in absorption into the One Mind, or I AM presence, or merging with God.

Obliviate – The spell in the Harry Potter book series that wipes the memories clean of anyone on the receiving end of it.

OM – The Hindu symbol of the Absolute Omnipotent God.

One Mind – The Universal inter-connected consciousness of the Universe of which we are all a part.

Operant Conditioning – B. F. Skinner's psychological process by which humans and animals learn to behave in such a way as to obtain rewards and avoid punishments. It is used currently in our educational system to brainwash and mind control children.

Ouroboros – The symbolic representation of the snake eating its tail or everything in life coming full circle.

Paganism - A vast number of indigenous and polytheistic religious beliefs that primarily include the worship of nature, multiple Gods and Goddesses, magic, witchcraft, etc. and can or cannot include ritual sacrificial practices. Many different belief systems are lumped inaccurately under paganism. Not all are dark and sacrificial.

Parthenogenesis – From the Greek, partheno - of virgin origin. Women's ability to self-conceive without the presence of male sperm.

Passing the Energy Baton – the act of passing on either negative or positive energy you have generated and accumulated to someone or to a group to carry, utilize and process for you.

Patriarchal Eugenics – A form of global life and death control and decision-making over whole groups, classes, genders, races, creeds, communities, countries, economics and resources of people to serve the special beliefs, finances and interests of a small, egocentric, myopic, sexist male contingent of despotic, tyrannical leaders and decision-makers. It includes their belief they have the right to make God-like decisions over the life or death of individuals of their choosing they feel no longer serve their hegemonic, economic or scientific goals.

Pattern of Trauma – The matrix laid down upon a person holistically to systematically traumatize them into subservience. Or the unique pattern of trauma an individual has experienced.

Pineal Gland – A tiny endocrine gland deep in the base of the brain that acts as a conduit for light and higher consciousness, often called the Third Eye. It is thought to be the gateway to higher consciousness but also functions as a gland to secrete serotonin, melatonin, DMT and other brain regulatory hormones.

Pingala - The primary energy channel that rises up alongside the spine on the left side within the human energy system. It is also known as a primary nadi. It is part of the 3 main channels that carry the Kundalini up the inner channels to the crown chakra during a Kundalini rising and awakening experience.

Post-Synaptic Neuron – Part of the synaptic process pathway of neurotransmission. It is the neuron tip or axon head that receives the neurotransmitter from the pre-synaptic neuron.

Post-Traumatic Stress Disorder - An anxiety disorder that affects people who have experienced profound emotional, mental or physical trauma, such as torture, rape, military combat, or a natural disaster, characterized by recurrent flashbacks of the traumatic event, night-mares, eating disorders, anxiety, fatigue, forgetfulness, and social withdrawal.

Praetorians – Those individuals who have chosen or been com-promised or mind-controlled into serving and protecting the dark forces. They have been trained to protect those in power. They are often abused and mind-controlled, and born into the families who continue the tradition. They serve their masters, not their country, their jobs, their families or God. They often are not conscious of their misplaced allegiances due to soul deception and other forms of brainwashing. There are varying levels of praetorians from malicious to conscious to unconscious. **Black Widow Praetorians** are wives, sisters, daughters and mothers who protect and/or participate in covering for Praetorians who are protecting dark forces.

Pre-Synaptic Neuron – Part of the synaptic process pathway of neu-rotransmission. It is the neuron tip or axon head that stores the neurotransmitter prior to release into the synaptic cleft and on into the post-synaptic neuron.

Predators – Individuals, differentiated from simple energy vampires and praetorians, by the degree of severity of their predation upon the life force of others. Predators are usually conscious of their actions, praetorians are not always conscious of their actions and allegiance. One can be both a predator and a praetorian.

Programmed Survival – The conditioned pattern of very minimal survival created by profound abuse and deprivation that persists long after the original conditioning occurred.

Projection – After abuse imprinting takes place and unconscious abusive behaviors take over, the former victim will begin unconsciously projecting his pain upon anyone around him willing to take it on.

Qi Gong – An ancient Chinese energy practice that includes movement, breath and healing techniques.

Quantum Field – The field of all possibilities where there is no limit upon the ability of the consciousness to expand and awaken.

Quantum Field Theory – A division of science and physics that studies the properties, functions, realities and potentialities of the quantum field. Quantum field theory is held in place by a theoretical framework for constructing quantum mechanical models of subatomic particles, particle physics and quasiparticles interacting within condensed matter physics. Too complex to explain here, but it studies the interaction between the gravitational and electro-magnetic fields and the particles contained therein.

Re- Membering – The act of bringing back together your broken or lost soul parts and reorganizing them into a new and empowered structure/form.

Reclaimed Fragments – The split off portions of suppressed consciousness that are reclaimed when you pass through a full soul transformation and awakening.

Reiki – Reiki means Universal Life Energy in Japanese and is a system of energy healing that originated in Japan with Dr. Mikao Usui as the first Grandmaster. He discovered this system during a spiritual revelation. It utilizes the body's own energy system to activate and self-heal oneself or others through the balancing of the energy centers, clearing stagnant, diseased energy and purifying the energy field.

Reiki GrandMaster Hawayo Takata – The 3rd Reiki GrandMaster after Chujiro Hayashi in the original Reiki lineage and the first woman and first Westerner to carry the title. GrandMaster Takata was the bearer of the Authentic Original Reiki lineage and teacher of the accurate and authentic Reiki teachings. Mrs. Takata was the sole ReikiMaster to bring the teachings out of Japan and into the West, traveling the world teaching and imparting the teachings, energy and attunements of Reiki to the entire world. Her lineage is the only authentic and recognized lineage in the world.

ReikiMaster – A person who has achieved the third and final level of Reiki in the school of healing known as Reiki Usui Ryoho, or The Usui System of Natural Healing, which is the only Authentic Reiki lineage.

Reiki Soul Treatments – Deep healing treatments with Reiki and shamanism that access the soul and the Akashic records for the purpose of holistically healing and restoring someone to wholeness.

Root Chakra – The first energetic opening at the base of the spine which serves as an entry point for Earth's magnetic energy into the human body. It is also one of two magnetic poles stabilizing the energy field for the human body. It rules the adrenals and gonads and its primary energy is survival and its color is red.

Sacral Chakra – The second chakra in the human body that collects and transfers energy throughout the body. It's located below the naval in front of the reproductive organs, which it brings energy to, and serves to channel energy for procreation and creativity. Its color is orange.

Sacred Alchemy - A purifying process of transmuting energies and substances from a lower, denser form into a higher, lighter form. This version of the process is purely spiritual. The impure inner energies (lead) are purified into higher, faster energies (gold) and then rise up to the crown chakra and induce spiritual awakening. This is also how healing is accomplished. The purification of the human energy field will lead both to renewed health and spiritual awakening and make one more immune to illness. (See **Alchemy**)

Sacred Dialogue – A dialogue you, or another, has with your Higher Self to awaken and heal your dormant soul and bring it out into full actualization.

Sacred Groves – Sacred woods or any grove of trees of special religious importance to a particular culture. Part of the mythological landscape and cult practice of Celtic, Baltic, Germanic, ancient Greek, Near Eastern, Roman, and Slavic polytheism.

Salini Foundation – Salini's charitable foundation for assisting with sexual trafficking, addiction recovery, homeless teenagers, child sex slavery, counseling, domestic violence and more.

Satanic or Sadistic Ritual Abuse (SRA) – This is a form of physical, psychological, spiritual and sexual abuse that involves violence, rape, torture and often satanic spells and rituals committed often against children, but also against adults. Victims experience lifetime negative effects and often die of illnesses whose genesis began during the abuse. Sophisticated mind controllers often participate to strip individuals of their personal power and life force. Currently, there is a widespread effort online to create the false idea that this does not occur, never occurred and has been discredited. In reality, there are millions of SRA survivors and current victims the world over as this practice continues unabated today. In fact, the numbers of SRA victims is higher today than at any other previous time in world history.

Scapegoating – the person or group within an imbalanced, patriarchal system that has the least power and is scapegoated for all the wrongs the abuser is committing. In politics, it's always the rich scapegoating the poor.

Second Degree Reiki – The second level in the Usui Reiki system of natural healing. It is an energy healing path for healing and spiritual awakening. At this level, one learns how to do mental and emotional treatments and heal people at a distance.

Secret Codes – Codes connected to initiations and mind-control methodology used to control members or mind-controlled individuals, pass messages or activate missions.

Secret Holocaust – The secret agenda of the global elite to destroy consciousness, liberty, families, love, our spiritual connection to God, our lives and brainwash and enslave humanity.

Selfless Seva – The giving of service to humanity without expectation of anything in return.

Separation Consciousness – The illusion of believing yourself separate from God or from others. This belief originates during the evolution of the consciousness of the human species through limited periods of knowledge prior to its awareness of itself and subsequent rise in consciousness. It can also be created within the deliberate framework of mind control, which seeks to create separation and self-hatred, and can persist for many lifetimes.

Sexual Initiations - Initiations of power that revolve around sexual abuse that activate the sexual chakra and steal divine energy for purposes of control. Initiations for the purpose of arousing magical powers through sex and trauma.

Shadow Self – The denied portion of one's split off self that is not loved or acknowledged and acts out.

Shame Core – The wrapping of shame around the core of your being that prevents you from reaching your full power and potential. Often done intentionally during sexual initiations by secret societies.

Shame Initiations - Initiations of power that revolve around instilling shame into the initiate for purposes of control.

Shattering of the Auric Field – The moment the energy field surrounding, protecting and supplying someone's life force is penetrated and destroyed, leaking vital energy towards the source of the shattering.

Shattering the Traumatic Trance – The experience of release from the Traumatic Trance which holds one in bondage. Usually precipitated by an equivalent experience to the original wounding event that is combined with an epiphany and unconditional love, but not always a loving event. The beginning of the end of the traumatic bond that saps your life force.

Solar Plexus Chakra – The third chakra in the human body located at the stomach area. It functions to bring energy into the stomach, abdomen and intestines and controls emotional energy. Its color is yellow.

Somatization – When the body takes in emotional and/or mental energy and transforms it into illness.

Soul Fragments – Portions of the soul that have split off due to trauma, karma or other life events. These fragments are like puzzle pieces of the whole soul, and linger in the universal energy field waiting to rejoin with the soul to create wholeness.

Soul Harvesting – The harvesting of souls into either dark or light realms. The term is most often used when discussing the efforts of the dark side to steal souls for their manipulation and consumption and connotes being forced or tricked. But it can be used to describe a spiritual awakening and journey towards God when someone chooses to wake up rather than be enslaved to illusion and darkness.

Soul Murder – The experience of profound abuse that makes you lose your spiritual connection to your soul.

Soul Transformation – The commencement of a journey into healing that usually begins with a traumatic or dramatic life event and creates massive inner change resulting in healing and spiritual awakening.

Soul Transformation Therapy – Therapy that addresses all four quadrants of the soul, mind, body and emotions and heals holistically in a balanced fashion created by Salini.

Soul Trauma – Trauma to an individual soul that initiates a traumatic trance or a massive soul transformation and/or healing.

Spirit-eaters – Those beings or persons who devour your life-force or body or resources as part of an attempt to take over your soul or as part of the last stages of your Soul Transformation.

Spiritually Immune – To raise one's spiritual or energetic vibration to the point where you repel disease, attack, hatred, untruth and injury. You create a whole and perfect aura around you.

Spiritual Isolation – What happens to you when you've experienced severe abuse that separates you from God.

Spiritual Warfare – The fight for the souls of humanity between dark and light forces.

Statement of Intention – A personal statement of power and intent you create after your Soul Transformation that claims out loud your power, truth, purpose and sovereignty in the world.

Stockholm Syndrome – A form of mind-control where you are trancebonded to your abuser.

Subliminazis – Doctors, scientists and other specialists trained to mind-control and influence society and individuals for the purpose of implementing full spectrum dominance over a demoralized society.

Surrogate parent – the child in an abusive family system that acts as the parent, usually programmed to continue the family system, often protects younger siblings from abuse, or takes the opposite role of abusive parent to the other siblings.

Sushumna – The central energy channel, or primary nadi, that travels up the body's internal energy system and carries the Kundalini up towards the crown chakra during a Kundalini rising episode. This can result in a full spiritual awakening.

Synaptic Cleft – the small gap between an axon terminal and any of the cell membranes heads nearby. The gap measures $1/1000^{th}$ of an inch across to the next neuronal head.

Synaptic Pathways – These are pathways in the brain, sometimes called neural pathways, where chemical reactions and functions are performed to deliver messages to and from different parts of the brain. These functions are performed by different neural microcircuits and depend on the anatomical and physiological properties of the various synaptic pathways connecting neurons.

Synaptic Vesicles - Synaptic vesicles are part of the synaptic pathway process of neurotransmitter delivery. They are tiny storage sacs in the neuronal heads of axons that store neurotransmitters prior to release into the synaptic cleft or gap.

The Denied – Those people denied access to basic rights, power and privileges of their culture and whose voice is silenced. Usually scapegoated and/or carrying special gifts, powers and messages. Also, the poor, the children, the women, the minorities of society.

The Exiled - Those people exiled from their culture for some imagined infraction but whose voice is truthful and powerful. They are usually silenced so the truth will not be known and power remains with the corrupt.

The Force – A description of the divine spiritual energy that empowers the Universe and all living creatures within it according to George Lucas' Star Wars trilogy. Yoda was the GrandMaster of The Force and taught his Jedi Warriors how to be powerful with their inner light and light sabers of energetic power that carried *The Force*.

The Fourth Reich – The continuation of an expanded version of the policies of death and destruction of the Nazi Fascist Third Reich in today's global society by agents of the global elite in a more secretive, invisible and underhanded fashion. The efforts are now globalized and corporatized in a way that has created worldwide weaponized corporations, banks and government structures threatening all life and its ecological balance on Earth.

The Program – A term I created to describe the programmed mentality and lifestyle we are conditioned to believe in and live under that diminishes, suppresses and denies your True Self and your personal gifts and power.

The Reiki Recovery Project – A successful, comprehensive Holistic Addiction Recovery Program designed by Salini Teri Apodaca that takes chronic alcoholics and addicts off the streets and into recovery through a holistic program of Reiki, self-care, spiritual connection and counseling.

The Sacral Chalice – A seemingly void area inside the sacrum bone at the base of the spine that acts as an energetic chalice. The sacral chalice acts as a sacred storage well where divine chi energy is stored as it is processed in from the chakras and endocrine glands before it moves up the spinal column.

The Shadow Self – That part of everyone which is conscious or unconscious that participates in destructive, dishonest, denied, divisive, delusional and dark behavior. When this portion of human consciousness is acknowledged, embraced, integrated, loved and healed, all life on Earth will be healed and we will all awaken as One.

The Split (see The Unconscious Split) – The state of human consciousness when your awareness is split into portions. Sometimes it's split into halves, sometimes even more portions with only a fragment of the truth and the light of God present. This then shadows the rest of your consciousness and personal power and ability to love.

The Target Child – The child selected within every sick and/or abusive family system that is targeted to carry the family's pain, blame and scapegoating so the rest of the family can remain unaccountable for their actions, pain-free and in denial. This child is often targeted and abused to death so the secret dies with them.

The Unconscious Split (see The Split) – Separated parts of oneself broken off by repeated trauma or lifetimes lived in unconsciousness unaware of the whole Divine Self.

Third Degree Reiki – The third and final level of Reiki in the Usui system of natural healing, a spiritual path of energy healing and awakening. At this level, you learn to teach Reiki and perform advanced soul healing. Only a properly attuned ReikiMaster in the Usui

System of Natural Healing can teach you this level of Reiki. It is not possible to attain any levels of Reiki over the internet. There are no additional levels of Reiki beyond the third level.

Third Eye – The spiritual eye that resides in the sixth chakra, known as the brow chakra, in the forehead and is the manifestation of the awakened pineal gland within the brain. The awakening of the third eye is the gaining of spiritual sight that all spiritual masters teach their students.

Thought Forms – Thoughts that have become solidified in one's mind through constant repetition. A groove is formed in the brain if a thought is repetitive enough and is believed. The thought then has power to shape your life. These thoughts can be either toxic or positive but they are contributory to either health or illness.

Thousand Yard Stare - The thousand-yard stare describes the profoundly shocking affects to the psyche of prolonged trauma such as close-up battle, rape, violence and other forms of trauma. It is characteristically shown as the blank, unfocused far-ahead gaze of a battle-weary soldier. The sorrowful stare represents dissociation from trauma.

Throat Chakra – The chakra at the front of the Adam's apple where energy flows in from your energy matrix to empower that part of your body and energy system. It is primarily involved in speech, creativity, truth, empowerment and the organs connected to those functions. It's color is blue.

Trail of Tears – The century long forced removal of Native Americans from their ancestral lands to reservations by order of President Andrew Jackson. So many of them died by genocide as they were moved to isolated, unknown places that it became known as "The Trail of Tears".

Trauma Codes – The brain codes that are traumatically imprinted onto brain function patterns that control your reactions and behaviors. Codes that traumatize and paralyze the divine energy of an individual or system.

Traumatic Bond – The toxic connection that commences between two or more people, or sometimes with an experience, during the peak of a traumatic event. It is the moment of the loss of power by the person experiencing the trauma and the beginning of the vampiring of that power by the person/s orchestrating the trauma.

Traumatic Bonding – The toxic bond that exists between one person and another person, or a group of persons, or a traumatic event that remains in place *unconsciously* and dictates the actions, reactions, and feelings of that person for life, or until it becomes conscious, and the person chooses to relinquish the bond.

Traumatic Event – The moment a person experiences something so painful, fearful and traumatic that they enter an altered state, known as the traumatic trance, to survive the episode. This event is also the genesis of the traumatic bond.

Traumatic Shock – An experience that either begins a trance or shocks you out of the traumatic trance.

Traumatic Trance – The unconscious state of living in the trance created by the traumatic bond. Creation of the traumatic trance is necessitated to endure the pain of the original traumatic event and persists long after the event took place. The traumatic trance is characterized by extreme denial of the traumatic bond/ event, and related abusive behaviors. It is frequently accompanied by one or more addictions. Any attempt to break a traumatic trance will result in fiercely defensive behaviors by the entranced individual who is protecting against the possibility of having to re-experience the original trauma.

Traumatic TranceBond – A traumatic trance coupled with a bonding with the abuser or person who causes the original trauma.

True Self - Your Divine, Authentic Self.

Truth Denial – The conscious or unconscious act of denying the truth of one's Divinity and the True Divine Nature of life on Earth in favor of a divided, lower state of existence on Earth. It is also the denial of those persons who step forward with truth, divinity and healing and are cast out by a diseased, toxic culture addicted to death and trauma.

Truthspeakers – Those individuals who were given the gift of seeing through the illusion of separation and are tasked with delivering the truth of how to break through the illusion to personal and societal liberation. They are often outcasts and exiles but carry deep wisdom, courage and knowledge for restoring a society teetering on the brink of annihilation. They are often called conspiracy theorists because their wisdom is suppressed and unknown to the largest percentile of human consciousness and threatens the prevailing power structure. For this reason, attempts to discredit them are made. They are healers come to save the world.

Unified Field Theory - A uniform field theory that allows all that is usually thought of as fundamental forces and elementary particles to be written in terms of a single field. Einstein pursued this theory until the end of his life and believed it to be real and the divine state of the Universe.

Universal Life Force – The divine energy we are born with that empowers every cell in our body, mind and spirit. It can be called up to heal, awaken and transform us into divine, awakened beings.

Victim-Hostage – The personality that develops when the soul is captured and kept hostage, sometimes unconsciously, by predators and energy vampires, to drain off its life force and be scapegoated.

Weaponizing of Corporations – The creation of corporations of death that parasite off of and destroy resources, nature, animals, economies, people, towns, cities, villages, cultures, freedoms, health, energy, wages, jobs, careers, hopes & dreams, souls and happiness of people and places throughout the world for profit. It also covers the patriarchal laws created to justify the weaponization of corporations and the collateral business murders they commit.

Wetiko – A spell of denial whereby a person or group denies the existence of darkness both within themselves and in the world thereby splitting their consciousness in half and allowing that shadow part to take your power. It then means that shadow self can run rampant over you and our world. It's also the act of projecting your shadow self onto another in the form of scapegoating and forcing a weaker group to carry your shadow for you thus unbalancing the world at large.

Womb Chakra – A deep, internal chakra within the body and soul of the Divine Feminine. It is the Holy Grail of healing, where all the wounds are ultimately healed and you emerge whole.

Working Class Hero – John Lennon's masterpiece written in the key of love, 528 kHz, in defiance of the global elite who had imposed the chaotic, dissonant tone 440 kHz, the Devil's Tone.

Yellow Submarine – The Beatles movie that tells the story in cartoon fantasy-style of the enforced imposition of the musical frequency 440 kHz, known as the Devil's Tone, by the global elite. This tone, which is F# on the musical scale, when played continuously, stimulates chaos, stress, fear and disharmony. This frequency also suppresses the heart chakra and higher consciousness. The Beatles were trying to warn the world that this was happening in their masterpiece, Yellow Submarine.

Yin and Yang Energy - The balance of female and male polar energies inherent in all of Nature and the Universe.

Yoda – A small-in-stature mysterious creature with great power known for his legendary wisdom, Yoda was one of the most renowned and powerful Jedi Masters in galactic history. Yoda is considered the greatest of all Grand Masters of The Force as well as holding the title of Master of the Order. He taught his Jedi Warriors how to be powerful with their inner light and light sabers of energetic power that carried *The Force*. Grand Master Yoda trained most of the Jedi in the Order, including Obi-Wan Kenobi and Luke Skywalker. In the cosmos hierarchy of Masters, Yoda is considered a Master of Light.

Bibliographic References

Since most of this book was part of my own personal experiences and divine inspiration, there are few books to reference. There were a few books of note worth mentioning that helped me along the way. Otherwise, the list below were books that helped to awaken me in my healing journey and/or are powerful books that I recommend.

Amritanandamayi, Mata. *Awaken Children! All Volumes*, San Ramon, Mata Amritanandayi Mission Trust, 1994-2004.

Amritaswarupananda, Swami. *Ammachi, A Biography of Mata Amritanandamayi*, San Ramon, Mata Amritanandayi Mission Trust, 1994.

Beck, Sanderson. *Wisdom Bible*, Ojai, California, World Peace Communications, 2002.

Bess, Savitri L. *The Path of the Mother*, New York, Ballantine Publishing Group, 2000.

Conway, Timothy, Ph.D. *Women of Power and Grace*, Santa Barbara, California, Wake Up Press, 1994.

Eisler, Riane. *The Chalice and The Blade*, Harper & Row, San Francisco, 1987.

Estes, Clarissa Pinkola, Ph.D. *Women Who Run With The Wolves*, New York, Harper-Collins 1984.

Gandhi, Mohandes K. *The Bhagavad Gita According to Gandhi*, Berkeley, California, Berkeley Hills Books, 2000.

Hay, Louise, *You Can Heal Your Life*, Carlsbad, California, Hay House Inc., 1984.

Holy Bible.

http://www.druglibrary.org/schaffer/history/e1950/mkultra/hearing05.htm

http://edgewoodtestvets.org/articles/pdfs/MKULTRA_the_Stain_of_Dishonor_and_the_Prerequisites_for_Redemption.pdf

http://www.intelligence.senate.gov/pdfs/95mkultra.pdf

http://en.metapedia.org/wiki/Project_MKUltra

https://ritualabuse.us/mindcontrol/articles-books/the-law-and-mind-control-a-look-at-the-law-and-goverment-mind-control-through-five-cases/

Kenyon, Tom & Sion, Judy. *The Magdalen Manuscript*, Orcas, WA, Orb Communications, 2000.

Meyer, Marvin. *The Nag Hammadi Scriptures*, San Francisco, HarperSanFrancisco, 2007.

Meyer, Marvin. Abegg Jr., Martin. Cook, Edward. *The Dead Sea Scrolls*, San Francisco, HarperSanFrancisco, 1996.

Pagels, Elaine. *The Gnostic Gospels, Adam, Eve, and the Serpent*, New York, Random House, 2005

Poitras, Den. *PARTHENOGENESIS: Women's Long-lost Ability to Self-Conceive*, Lennox Ave. Publishing, 2014.

Ravenscroft, Trevor. *The Spear of Destiny*, London, Sphere Book, 1973.

Rector-Page, Linda, N.D., *Healthy Healing 9th Edition*, Healthy Healing Publications, 1992.

Spalding, Baird T., *The Life & Teachings of the Masters of the Far East - All Volumes*, Marina Del Rey, California, De Vorss & Co. Publishers, 1927

The Missing Books of the Bible, Baltimore, Maryland, Halo Press, 1996.

Washington, James. *A Testament of Hope: The Essential Writings and Speeches of Martin Luther King, Jr.*, New York, Harper-Collins, 1986.

Yogananda, Paramahansa. *Autobiography of a Yogi*, Los Angeles, Self-Realization Fellowship, 2003.

Notes on Sessions, Workshops and Trainings

This book is just the beginning of the work that must be done to heal humanity from soul intrusion, trauma-based mind control, DNA destruction, personal enslavement, abuse, spells, viral infections of the mind and soul and so on. I initiate a new field of study and healing here in this book – Soul Transformation Therapy. This is the first in a series of publications I plan to create on this topic. Much more to come to help you all heal.

For those individuals who are interested in learning more about healing trauma, sexual abuse, ritual abuse and mind control and how to restore your body, mind, emotions and spirit, I will be offering courses, workshops, and individual sessions. They will soon be available to the reader wishing to further their understanding of this field of study or to heal themselves.

You may contact me through this publisher or at this website address for further information or to book me for speaking engagements, workshops or sessions – www.emergingfromthematrix.com.

Made in United States
Orlando, FL
18 December 2021